Ideology
&Congress

Ideology &Congress

Second, revised edition of *Congress:
A Political-Economic History of Roll Call Voting*

Keith T. Poole
and Howard Rosenthal

Transaction Publishers
New Brunswick (U.S.A.) and London (U.K.)

Library of Congress Catalog Number: 2006044654
ISBN: 978-1-4128-0608-4
Printed in the United States of America

Library of Congress Cataloging-in-Publication Data

Poole, Keith T.
   Ideology and Congress / Keith T. Poole & Howard Rosenthal.
      p. cm.
   2nd, rev. ed.
   Rev. ed. of: Congress. 1997.
   Includes bibliographical references and index.
   ISBN 1-4128-0608-9 (pbk. : alk. paper)
   1. United States. Congress—Voting—History. 2. Ideology—United States—History. 3. Pressure groups—United States—History. I. Rosenthal, Howard, 1939- II. Poole, Keith T. Congress. III. Title.

JK1051.P66   2007
328.73—dc22   2006044654

for WILLIAM H. RIKER
teacher, friend, and colleague,
in memoriam

Contents

Preface to *Ideology and Congress*

Although *Congress: A Political-Economic History of Roll Call Voting* was published in 1997, the volume covered only the first 100 Congresses, 1789–1988, in its dynamic analysis of roll call voting. This new edition's major additional accomplishment is to update that work and make it current, carrying the analysis forward through 2004.

In the earlier edition, the last paragraph emphasized how Congress had evolved since the late '60s and early '70s. Members of Congress in the 1950s had distinct preferences on civil rights as well as liberal-conservative preferences on economic issues. There were plenty of moderates on both dimensions. By the 1980s, as the national debate was reframed from equality of opportunity to equality of results, the two dimensions had merged. We found a polarized, unidimensional Congress with roll call voting falling almost exclusively along liberal-conservative ideological lines. The last sentence read, "Intense conflict between these two 'new' parties will continue." We were right. This makes us feel good as scientists but lousy as citizens. Indeed, in the '90s and the '00s, Congress has become, as reported here, even more polarized and unidimensional.

Congressional roll call data is unique in that it provides a very long time series, now spanning four centuries, of data that can be applied to the quantitative study of politics. The widespread availability of voter surveys since the end of World War II, Federal Election Commission publication of campaign contribution data since the 1970s, and much other data have allowed us to explore how congressional polarization is entwined with electoral politics, income distribution, immigration, and public policy. The results, found in collaboration with Nolan McCarty, are reported in *Polarized America: The Dance of Ideology and Unequal Riches* (MIT Press, 2006). That book can be read as a companion to the longer run and more detailed analysis of congressional voting in *Ideology and Congress*.

The past decade has seen many important methodological developments in the analysis of roll call voting. These include the Bayesian MCMC (Markov Chain Monte Carlo) approach of Clinton, Jackman, and Rivers (2004), the Lagrange multiplier method of Clinton and Meirowitz (2003, 2004) for linking votes in a common agenda, and the optimal classification method (OC) of

Poole (2000). These and other developments are covered in Poole's *Spatial Models of Parliamentary Voting* (Cambridge University Press, 2005).

These developments hold substantial promise for the future but currently only one set of methods is fast enough to handle the 2,844,164 individual roll call decisions in the history of the Senate through 2004 and the even greater 11,493,013 in the history of the House. These methods are represented by D-NOMINATE, which we used in *Congress, 1997*, and DW-NOMINATE, a minor improvement, which we use now.

Because DW-NOMINATE is fully reported in *Spatial Models*, we now omit the appendices from *Congress, 1997*. (Throughout this volume, we refer to the earlier edition, *Congress: A Political-Economic History of Roll Call Voting*, as *Congress, 1997*.) Most of the tables and figures in this book have been updated using the DW-NOMINATE results. In addition to extending our analysis to include data from 1986 through 2004 and to making the DW-NOMINATE improvements in our scaling procedure, we have improved data quality in two ways. First, we have corrected more errors in the original ICPSR identification codes assigned to members of Congress for data prior to 1986. Second, we have allowed party switchers, such as Strom Thurmond (D-SC), to change their ideological positions when they change party affiliation. In *Congress, 1997*, we allowed ideological position to undergo linear change during a member's period of service. We now have concluded that most of those linear effects really reflect incorrect identification codes of members and some party-switching. The changes to method and data have resulted in our being able to report substantially better fits of the spatial model than appeared in *Congress, 1997*. In a nutshell, our previous work understated the extent to which congressional roll call voting conforms to a unidimensional model.

For Congress to have become more unidimensional, all sorts of issues, including those that are so-called moral or religious issues, as well as economic issues, must divide legislators along a single liberal/conservative dimension. A particularly salient "moral" issue is, of course, abortion. In chapter 3, we show how, in the years since the research reported in *Congress, 1997*, abortion has become increasingly defined as an issue that separates liberals from conservatives in Congress.

The results in this book differ most, albeit still not very much, from those reported in *Congress, 1997* for years in proximity to the ending point, 1985, for the D-NOMINATE analysis. Ending in 1985 did not allow D-NOMINATE to capture fully the collapse of the second, civil rights dimension and the development of a unidimensional political system. (For 1986–1995, *Congress, 1997* used results spliced from static analyses. This book, therefore, represents a complete dynamic analysis that extends *Congress, 1997* from 1985 through

2004.) The DW-NOMINATE scores used in this book, the computer programs used to generate the scores, and the original roll call vote data can all be downloaded from voteview.ucsd.edu or voteview.com. Animations of the scores can be seen at voteworld.berkeley.edu. (We have not reproduced the now outdated "Data and Methods" section of our original preface.)

We next, before concluding, present a chapter-by-chapter outline of how this volume departs from *Congress, 1997*.

Revisions to chapter 1, the introduction, and chapter 2, a non-technical explanation of roll call scaling, are minimal. We first drafted chapter 2 in 1990 and used an example of actual 1989 roll call votes of five senators. We have kept this example because three of the five senators went on to become presidential nominees. In contrast, almost all the results in chapter 3, on the accuracy and dimensionality of scaling, have been updated to reflect data through 2004. We have simplified, by dropping all results for three or more dimensions and non-linear polynomial dynamics. *Congress, 1997* established that there was no payoff from these more complex estimations. Chapter 4, the punch line on polarization, echoes chapter 3 in incorporating new data. We present additional results to emphasize the emergence of the Republican Party in the South. Chapter 5, on realignment, and chapter 7, on sophisticated voting, are also redone using DW-NOMINATE and the additional data. In contrast, chapter 6, which compares "constituency interest" models of roll call voting to our ideological approach, is largely intact. The chapter does fix the only computational error we found in checking our earlier work. Otherwise, older results using D-, rather than DW-, NOMINATE are simply reproduced. One exception is that we summarize work on bankruptcy legislation by Rosenthal and coauthors Erik Berglöf and Stephen Nunez. Similarly, chapters 8, 9, and 10 have only very minor revisions.

The development of NOMINATE scaling has led to a large number of publications that deal with Congress and American political history. Most of this literature has appeared since *Congress*. We review it in an entirely new chapter, chapter 11. Chapter 12 of this book is, like the old chapter 11, an epilogue.

Since the publication of *Congress*, we have had substantial collegial and financial support. The development of our work on scaling has benefited greatly from our collaborations with Gary Cox, Jeffrey Lewis, Nolan McCarty, and Erik Voeten. We also thank Craig Goodman, Jeff Jenkins, Tim Nokken, and Brian Sala for corrections to the identities of members of Congress. The National Science Foundation provided additional support. Both authors spent a year as fellows of the Center for Advanced Study in the Behavioral Sciences. Rosenthal was a fellow of the John Simon Guggenheim Memorial Foundation; he also spent two years as a visiting scholar at the Russell Sage Foundation. There he received able assistance from Orly Cerge in the preparation of this manuscript. His research was further supported by Russell Sage through funding of the working group on inequality at Princeton University.

Finally, we thank David Rothman for suggesting that Transaction Publishers would be appropriate for version 2.0 of *Congress* and Irving Louis Horowitz and the staff at Transaction for seeing the project to completion.

This book was dedicated to the memory of Bill Riker. In the years since publication of the first edition, we have, with deep regret and sorrow, also lost Dick McKelvey and Otto (Toby) Davis. They, like Bill, made seminal contributions to the rise of formal theory that transformed political science in the last half of the twentieth century and that motivated and informed the work reported in this book.

Preface to *Congress: A Political-Economic History of Roll Call Voting* (1997)

This book is dedicated to the memory of William H. Riker. Without Bill, "political science" would not have become a science in the late twentieth century, and, in particular, the research project summarized in these pages would never have been initiated. As our work developed, we benefited from several discussions with Bill; indeed, the material on political realignment, covered in chapter 5, received an earlier, somewhat different treatment, in *Agenda Formation*, the last volume Bill was to edit.

Bill's vision led to the best doctoral program in political science in the world. Twice, in the mid '60s, he offered Rosenthal the opportunity to join the faculty at Rochester, but living in the Arctic was not to be endured, even for the best of intellectual opportunities. Bill's influence was nonetheless transmitted, through his magnificent 1962 book, *The Theory of Political Coalitions*. This work directed the early part of Rosenthal's career, sparking a series of papers on coalitions in Fourth Republic France. Coalitions are also important in this volume, both through our concern with the relationship between party loyalty and the spatial voting model and through our discussion of the realignment of the voting space brought about — in line with Riker's Size Principle — by the overlarge Roosevelt Coalition of the Second New Deal.

In addition to writing *The Theory of Political Coalitions*, the seminal modern work on coalition behavior, Bill, jointly with Peter Ordeshook, a Rochester Ph.D. and our former colleague, wrote the seminal formal-theory essay on political participation. This work led directly to Rosenthal's life-long interest in abstention, including his work with Subrata Sen on the "FY" vote in France, his theoretical work with Thomas Palfrey — and to this volume's chapter 10, which deals with abstention on congressional roll calls.

Poole did brave the Rochester winters, as a graduate student in the mid '70s. His thesis supervisor, Richard McKelvey, also a Rochester Ph.D., is perhaps the most outstanding scientist produced by Bill's program. Dick initiated Poole's interest in scaling methods. Dick, following Ordeshook, was lured to tropical Pittsburgh. Dick, Peter, and two other Carnegie Mellon colleagues,

Otto Davis and Melvin Hinich, stimulated our quest for scaling methods that were derived from the behavioral implications of the spatial model of choice. Of particular importance was an after-dinner conversation with Dick and Peter at Dick's house in Pittsburgh in the spring of 1977. Peter described his theory of the "basic space," which Poole realized was the key to linking Converse's theory of constraint with the low-dimensional results that, even then, were coming out of early scaling studies of a variety of forms of voting data. One of these studies was by Lawrence Cahoon — a student of Mel's and Peter's — and his work was what stimulated both Peter and Mel to separately develop the theory that is the foundation of this volume.

Dick was also, after his departure for Caltech, responsible for Poole's coming to Carnegie as a postdoctoral fellow in political economy and then joining the faculty.

Dick's work on the global intransitivity of majority rule, along with earlier work by Kenneth Arrow and Charles Plott, formed part of Bill's deep concern with the instability of political processes. He referred to politics as the "dismal science" because unlike market institutions, which he saw as always tending to equilibrium, strategic behavior in political institutions always led to disequilibrium. Bill's pessimistic view on politics versus economics developed not only before markets — via the new interest in speculative bubbles — looked less stable but also before important work by scholars such as Peter Coughlin and Shmuel Nitzan, John Ledyard, Craig Tovey, and McKelvey and Ordeshook themselves, restored stability to majority voting models by putting realistic frictions in voting behavior or candidate actions. One such friction, probabilistic voting, is the basis for our empirical model.

This book only partially accords with Bill's pessimistic view. True, on two occasions — both before the Civil War — stable voting patterns break down entirely, and "chaos" results. But, for well over a century, the American political system, at least as seen in congressional roll call voting, has followed a relatively smooth path, smooth enough for the vast bulk of individual voting decisions to be captured via a very simple spatial model. In contrast, in his concern with instability, Bill sought examples of voting cycles in congressional roll calls. His examples and those also discovered by yet another Rochester student, James Enelow, led to chapter 7 of this book. Our analysis of these examples in terms of the spatial model supports Bill's conclusions about the examples. On the other hand, we, on the basis of other evidence presented in chapter 7, view the examples as the rare exceptions that prove the rule of stable spatial voting. We are sure that, were Bill still with us, he would challenge our results in a way that would lead to new findings.

Acknowledgments

We have many other intellectual debts, particularly to former and present faculty members at Carnegie Mellon, including not only Davis, Hinich, McKelvey, and Ordeshook but also Alberto Alesina, Timothy Groseclose, Dennis Epple, John Londregan, Alan Meltzer, Thomas Palfrey, Thomas Romer, Fallaw Sowell, and Stephen Spear. They were joined, for briefer periods, by visitors and post-doctoral fellows, including David Austen-Smith, Randy Calvert, Peter Coughlin, Alex Cukierman, Lawrence Rothenberg, James Snyder, and Guido Tabellini. All provided valuable discussion, as did our student and collaborator, Nolan McCarty. Epple has suggested several additional experiments we could perform; someday we will get to them. Romer has written four essays with us, applying the results of the spatial analysis to the study of campaign contributions, regulation, economic-interest voting, and shirking. He also was directly responsible for our work on computer animation of our results. In addition, he reads the literature. Ordeshook and Rothenberg read drafts of the book and provided valuable comments. Meltzer, through his Center for the Study of Political Economy, provided financial support for the project.

We would also like to thank the two deans, Richard Cyert and Robert Kaplan, who hired us at Carnegie. Both were strong supporters of our careers. Both sought to make a business school an important center for basic social science as well as an MBA mill.

We also received very useful comments on parts of the work from our West Coast colleagues Rod Kiewiet, John Ferejohn, Morgan Kousser, Mathew McCubbins, Gary Cox, Gary Jacobson, Tom Gilligan, John Petrocik, Keith Khrebiel, and Barry Weingast and our European colleagues Erik Berglöf, Mathias Dewatripont, and Gerard Roland. Lance Davis, Claudia Goldin, and Gary Libecap pushed us to make our work relevant to economic historians. Gil Rosenthal, Jean-Laurent Rosenthal, Margherita Rosenthal, and Paula Scott also contributed comments. Kathleen Much of the Center for Advanced Study in the Behavioral Sciences did an outstanding job of editing the manuscript.

The work of Kenneth Martis of the Department of Geology and Geography of the University of West Virginia has been extremely important to us. In his atlases, Martis has painstakingly assembled the data on congressional-district boundaries for all of American history. This work has led to the maps in our VOTEVIEW program, which allows one to see the geographic distribution of the vote on any roll call. Of equal importance, he has also definitively researched the political party affiliation of members of Congress. His work is far superior to the codings done in a WPA project in the 1930s that are contained in the data distributed by the Interuniversity Consortium for Political Research. The Martis codings are used throughout the book and in VOTE-VIEW.

We also need to thank those who helped us get the job done. Dave Seaman and Bill Whitson of the Purdue University Computing Center were invaluable in bringing this work to supercomputing. Seaman tutored us in Cyber FOR-TRAN and provided the basic programming insights that led to an efficient program. Carol Goldburg helped us track down errors in the ICPSR data. Ezra Angrist did much of the coding of the congressional district maps. We are especially grateful to two very talented undergraduate assistants. Douglas Skiba at Carnegie produced the basic PC animation program, ANIMATE, which he then used to provide the initial developments of VOTEVIEW, and Boris Shor at Princeton produced VOTEVIEW for Windows.

Many administrators and secretaries were of assistance. We would just like to thank a few especially competent individuals. Joy Lee, a secretary like none before or after, worked at Carnegie in the mid-1980s. Larry Yuter and Tom Bielak of the Graduate School of Industrial Administration (GSIA) computing group kept our software and hardware humming. Diane Price and Sandy Schmidt at Princeton had much to do with facilitating our collaboration.

In 1989–90, Rosenthal was a visiting professor of economics at MIT with a very reduced teaching load. It was then that we began writing this book. James Alt, Morris Fiorina, Paul Joskow, Jean Tirole, and other participants in the Harvard-MIT political economy program were supportive colleagues during that year. Over the period 1991–1993, five months in residence as a fellow at the International Centre for Economic Research in Turin, Italy, provided additional valuable time for research. Two leaves of absence, in 1991–92 and 1995 were spent as a fellow of the Center for Advanced Study in the Behavioral Science and as a Brussels region fellow at the European Center for Applied Research in Economics at the Free University of Brussels, respectively. We thank these organizations, as well as Carnegie Mellon University and Princeton University, for support.

In 1992 and again in 1995, Poole spent two quarters at Caltech where much work on this book was accomplished in a very intellectually stimulating and enjoyable environment. Deans David Grether and John Ledyard and the amateur radio club of Caltech, W6UE, are thanked for their support.

Organization of the Book

In what we believe to be a Rikerian approach, this book is not a "history" in a conventional sense. Chapters 1 and 2 provide an overview and a basic model. They are must reading for what follows. Chapters 3, 4, and 5 are closest to conventional history in that they provide a summary of the structure of congressional voting and discuss political realignment in American history; they are important background for subsequent chapters. The remaining chapters may all be read independently. That is because, with one exception, they use historical data to investigate distinct theoretical questions. Chapter 6 compares ideological models of roll call voting to those based on constituencies' economic interests. Chapter 7 analyzes strategic voting, chapter 9 deals with how congressional committees affect the policy process, and chapter 10 with the rational-choice theory of turnout. Chapter 8, which deals with interest groups and political polarization, is the only chapter in the book not to use data from the entire history of roll call voting. But it does develop a methodology that will allow many historical sources, such as newspaper editorials, to be incorporated in the framework we have used to analyze congressional behavior.

We should note that chapters 1 and 2 are entirely new. Chapter 2 attempts to explain scaling to a wide audience. Chapters 3, 4, and 5 draw heavily on Poole and Rosenthal (1991a, 1991c, 1993a, and 1994b) but contain substantial new material including unpublished results in Poole and Rosenthal (1987b). Appendix B draws on Poole (1988); Poole, Sowell, and Spear (1992); and unpublished work in Poole and Spear (1992). Chapter 6 is a synthesis of our work on economic models of voting, contained in Poole and Rosenthal (1985a, 1991b, 1993b, and 1994a), Poole and Romer (1993), and Romer and Rosenthal (1985); substantial new material is added. Chapters 7, 8, 9, and 10 are new work.

In addition to our work on Congress, other scholars have begun to apply our methods to other voting bodies (DeBrock and Hendricks, 1996; Myagkov and Kiewiet, 1996; Rothenberg, 1994). Our scaled legislator positions have already been used in published work by Macdonald and Rabinowitz (1987); Cox and McCubbins (1993); Kiewiet and McCubbins (1991); Romer and Weingast (1991); and Rothenberg (1994). Readers stimulated by this volume may wish to pursue those works as further reading.

We hope this book will have an audience among readers with general interests in the social sciences, including economics, history, and political science. Consequently, we have written this book for readers without technical training. We have included help boxes for most of the mathematical and statistical concepts we use in the main text. The hard technical work is reserved for the appendices. The book should certainly be accessible to anyone having completed even an introductory course in statistics.

1

Introduction:
The Liberal/Conservative Structure

Roll Call Voting and the Liberal/Conservative Continuum

"All politics are local," said Tip O'Neill, Speaker of the House from 1977 to 1987. If only because the Congress of the United States must amalgamate the diverse preferences of constituencies,[1] the task of finding a simple structure to explain how members of Congress vote when the roll is called might well be a hopeless one. Perhaps only detailed accounts of action on particular bills can fully capture the legislative process. But any science of politics must, on the contrary, seek to find simple structures that organize this apparent complexity. We have developed a parsimonious model that accounts for the vast majority of millions of individual roll call decisions during the 217 years of roll call voting in the House of Representatives and the Senate. The spatial model of voting, outlined in chapter 2, is the technical foundation of our model. For short, we refer to it as the ideological model.

Aggregating the local loyalties of members of Congress into legislation is a matter of solving an institutional labyrinth replete with committees, subcommittees, and conference committees.[2] The outcomes reflect not only the preferences of the legislators themselves, but the pressures and appeals of countless staff, lobbyists, and constituents. Moreover, activity in Congress will be responsive to the veto power of the president. One might expect chaotic rather than orderly behavior.[3]

When, on the other hand, local concerns give way to a disciplined two-party system, day-to-day roll call voting is devoid of interest. A stylized description of Great Britain, for example, would indicate that national elections create a parliamentary majority.[4] Until the next elections, the winning party proposes legislation. The legislation is routinely approved by all members of the majority and opposed by all members of the minority.[5]

Such a model obviously doesn't work on our shores. President Reagan was able to enact his economic program in 1981, including a large tax cut and cuts in domestic spending, in spite of a divided government, with the Democrats being in the majority in the House of Representatives. Defections of "Boll Weevil" Democrats from the South eroded the majority. Even in the disciplined world of Tom "The Hammer" DeLay, the McCain-Feingold campaign reform act passed the House of Representatives when forty-one Republicans defected to join the Democrats.[6]

It was once tempting to resuscitate a model of pure party conflict by arguing that the United States really had a three-party system, with the Democrats split into northern and southern factions. In the three-party model, majorities would be formed by shifting alliances between two of the three parties. But this model doesn't work cleanly either. When the 1964 Civil Rights Act was passed, northern and southern Democrats took opposite sides. But, the Republican Party also split, its more conservative members joining the southern Democrats. Similarly, throughout the 1830s and 1840s, slavery roll calls cut across parties, dividing North from South rather than Whigs from Democrats.

More generally, roll calls typically split one or both of the parties. Why are there splits? Perhaps it is because American legislators are parochial — "all politics are local" — and they are overwhelmingly responsive to the needs of their constituents and not responsive to national interests.[7] If so, for many issues, we would need an issue-specific economic model that specifies and measures the constituency interests. When a roll call involves a strong element of *geographic* distribution of resources, our simple structure may in fact fail to account for voting behavior. More typically, as we shall show in chapter 6, roll call voting is accounted for by the structure and little is gained by attempting to enrich this accounting by introducing measures of economic interests of constituencies.

Searching for the impact of specific economic interests may be, more fundamentally, fruitless because the legislative process is dynamic, with a vast set of issues considered as time progresses. In a dynamic setting, rational actors may find it in their interest to coalesce and log roll (trade votes).

The linkage of commercial issues was nicely captured by Representative Hewitt (D-NY) during the debate on the Interstate Commerce Act in 1884:

> Men of business in New York despair of wise legislation upon these great commercial questions from this House. They have seen this House resist the resumption of specie payments. They have seen this House thrust the silver bill down the reluctant throats of an unwilling community; and now they behold this House and this side of it forcing reactionary measures upon the commerce of the country which will paralyze the business of the port which is the throat of the commerce of this country.[8]

In other words, Hewitt saw railroad freight regulation as linked to previous votes on the gold standard and on a direct subsidy to the silver interests in Nevada. Each vote can thus reflect coalition behavior as well as the apparent substance of the vote. "Anticommercial" interests are likely to stick together on a large set of bills. When such coalitions are stable, a parsimonious model of simple structure may encapsulate the coalitions and account better for voting patterns than attempts to deal with the substance of the roll call in isolation. We in fact find that a model of flexible coalitions typically is far superior to models in the literature that use economic interests.

What simple structure permits flexible coalitions? Briefly, one in which legislators can be described by a continuum of positions. Although the continuum is an abstraction, it is convenient to use the word *ideology* as a shorthand code for these positions. Henceforth in this book, we use *ideology* as a shorthand in the sense intended by Converse (1964) in his seminal paper on belief systems. That is, voting is ideological when positions are predictable across a wide set of issues. Someone who favors higher minimum wages is also likely to favor lower defense spending, affirmative action programs, higher capital gains taxes, and so on. We can think of the continuum of ideological positions as ranging from Left to Right or from very liberal to moderate to very conservative.

In contemporary America, this continuum is a perceived reality, a part of the common knowledge of not only the players on K Street and the Beltway but also many ordinary citizens. Consider these six senators: Edward Kennedy (D-MA), Robert Byrd (D-WV), Sam Nunn (D-GA), Alphonse D'Amato (R-NY), Strom Thurmond (R-SC), and Jesse Helms (R-NC). There would be widespread agreement among American politics buffs that the order given above is the appropriate liberal/conservative ordering. Our method of estimating the continuum allows us to provide interval level measurements of position, not only for the contemporary period but also for all Congresses, beginning with the first, which convened in 1789.[9] Moreover, we show that this structure is a predominant feature of nearly all roll call voting.

We can represent most roll calls as splits along the continuum — everyone to one side of a critical point will vote one way and everyone to the other side will vote the opposite way. Which side wins depends on where the critical point is located. If it is to the left of the median of legislator locations, the conservatives get a majority. Conversely, if it is to the right, the liberals win. As the critical point shifts, coalitions shift. Coalitions are therefore flexible, but they must conform to splits along the continuum.

The fact that most roll calls are splits implies that we can represent most votes as mappings from the issues onto the continuum — examples would be the level of the minimum wage; the extent to which assault weapons should be banned; and whether prayer, silent or vocal, should be permitted in schools. Consequently, nearly everything becomes a straight liberal/conservative issue.

Nonetheless, several caveats should be noted.

1. *The simple ideological structure does not lead to a predictive model for specific issues.* True, in the short term one can predict with accuracy. For example, in Poole and Rosenthal (1991a), we show how the final vote on confirmation of Robert Bork as a Supreme Court justice could have been forecast from the early announcements of members of the Senate Judiciary Committee. Indeed, divisive voting on Supreme Court nominations, when it occurs, fits very nicely into the structure. But to obtain medium- and long-term forecasts, one would need to model how issues *map* onto the structure. This book will not help one to understand why, sometime before Bork was rejected, a perhaps equally conservative nominee, Antonin Scalia, was confirmed by a 99–0 vote. The book's basic message is more limited: If issues do come to a vote, a mapping will tend to occur and make votes consistent with the structure.

2. *Just one continuum of positions may not be enough.* We may need two or more sets of positions to describe roll call voting behavior. Each underlying continuum is termed a dimension. For most of American history, the structure is indeed one-dimensional; at times a second dimension is an essential part of the picture. A second continuum was most important during two periods when the race issue was central to American politics. The first time was during the debate over slavery in the 1830s and '40s. (By the 1850s the slavery issue had become so intense that at first roll call voting patterns were chaotic rather than structured; later, patterns were restructured with the slavery issue becoming the primary dimension.) The second occasion was the civil rights controversy of the 1940s, '50s, and '60s. From the late 1970s onward, roll call voting again became largely a matter of positioning on a single, liberal/conservative dimension.

   In addition to the substantive issue of race, party loyalty — ranging from strong loyalty to one party in the two-party system to strong loyalty to the other — could provide a basis for a second continuum of positions. Indeed, legislators might be viewed, on every vote, as trading off the implementation of their liberal/conservative preferences against the need to be loyal to their party coalition. In 1989, for example, Senate majority leader George Mitchell (D-ME) was able to defeat President George H. W. Bush's proposed capital gains tax cut by transforming a vote on an economic issue into a crucial test of party loyalty.

Undoubtedly, party loyalty is involved in our finding that there is a slightly better accounting of roll call votes from using two dimensions, even in periods when the race issue is largely inactive. One's loyalty to the party, however, is hardly totally independent of one's liberal/conservative position. Indeed, for most of American history, parties define clusters on the first dimension, which, at some risk of oversimplification, basically represents conflict over economic redistribution. Nonetheless, the clusters are just clusters rather than permanently jelled voting blocs. Some degree of intra-party diversity has always been tolerated in Congress. In the contemporary Congress, there will be some issues, such as the 1981 tax bill, where moderate Democrats vote with Republicans and others, such as the 1991 Civil Rights bill, where moderate Republicans vote with Democrats. On those occasions when whips and leaders enforce party discipline, the roll call split will occur at the point on the first dimension that most clearly divides Democrats from Republicans.

3. *Our method for finding the dimensions is blind both to the party affiliation of the legislator and the substance of the roll call vote.* The simple structure we find is an abstraction. The fact that a simple abstraction accounts for the data suggests that, although there is some flexibility in forming coalitions, coalition formation is constrained. Parties are obviously an important constraining influence.[10] We observe not only clustering of legislators by party but also clustering of roll calls by substance. Although these clusters enable us to interpret the results, the basic finding is that a simple abstract model accounts for the data.

4. *Voting may appear as splits along a continuum even on bills that represent packages dealing with a multitude of policy areas.* On these bills, substantial vote trading or vote buying may have taken place. For example, President Reagan obtained the defection of the "Boll Weevils" in exchange for subsidies to Louisiana sugar producers that ought to have been anathema to the free-market credo of his administration. Yet when all the deals are done, roll call voting respects the continuum. If votes are in fact bought on an issue, the buyers will seek legislators with a low price. These should be legislators who are indifferent or nearly indifferent on the issue, that is, legislators who would be close to the point that would separate Yea from Nay voters if there was no vote buying.[11] So vote buying is likely to move the separating point rather than to create a chaotic pattern of voting.[12] Similarly, even on issues where a specific constituency interest could cause a legislator to deviate from his usual

voting patterns, the legislator must be sure that the deviation is correctly perceived by constituents. Otherwise, the legislator's reputation may be better served by voting with people that the legislator usually votes with.

5. *Voting may not appear as splits along the continuum if legislators are behaving strategically with respect to the agenda represented by a sequence of amendments to a bill.* For example, conservatives might strategically vote with the liberals and against the moderates. Suppose, for example, that a bill looked too liberal to be likely to win passage and an attempt was made to moderate the bill in introducing a "saving" amendment. If the amendment were passed, it, rather than the original bill, would be voted on against the status quo. Conservatives who would like to see the status quo preserved might strategically vote *against* the amendment even though they would prefer a more moderate bill to a very liberal one. But, as we explain in the next chapter, as long as legislators know each other's preferences and the agenda, "both ends against the middle" and other deviant voting patterns should not occur. In our example, the reason is that the liberals will not be fooled by the tactics of the conservatives. They, too, will be strategic and vote *for* the "saving" amendment even though they truly prefer the original bill. Thus, even when legislators are strategic, the roll call will still engender a split along the continuum.

6. *The structure will not be perfect.* As in almost any social science endeavor, allowances must be made for errors. We allow for error via a probabilistic model of voting. Legislators who are very close to the critical point on a roll call are almost as likely to vote Yea as they are to vote Nay whereas legislators who are very far from the critical point are highly predictable. Thus, on a roll call that was close to a 50–50 vote in the Senate, we would be very surprised if Kennedy voted on the conservative side or Rick Santorum (R-PA) on the liberal side. Overall, the structure will be useful only if we can find critical points on each roll call that yield very few errors.

There are, to be sure, occasional mavericks in Congress. Senator William Proxmire (D-WI) had a "folk" reputation for being a maverick. He had the poorest fit to our model during his period of service. Similarly, John McCain (R-AZ), normally one of the very most conservative members of the Senate, has been the worst fitting member of the Senate in each of his eight Senates, most notably the 103rd (2001–02), where he frequently voted with the Democrats, perhaps in pique over losing the race for the presidential nomination in

2000. Fortunately, these exceptions are rare enough that critical points can be pinned down with accuracy.

When we seek the critical point on each roll call, however, we do not aim to minimize the number of legislators incorrectly classified — those on the liberal side of the point who vote conservative and vice-versa. Rather, roughly speaking, we pick the point to minimize errors weighted by distance from the point. This seems natural; Ernest Hollings (D-SC) supporting the Bork nomination was a less serious error than a vote to confirm by Ted Kennedy. When we estimate positions of the legislators and the critical points (or cutting lines if there are two dimensions), we in fact find that voting errors are overwhelmingly concentrated among legislators whose positions are close to the point. This pattern of errors would not hold if, in contrast, both ends frequently voted against the middle, because extremists were either voting together for strategic reasons or simply expressing their distaste for the winning motion. This pattern of errors is an important element of support for our model of simple structure.

The Dynamics of the Structure of Roll Call Voting

Finding a liberal-conservative structure at any moment in time would be interesting but our effort is more ambitious. We study the dynamics of the structure. Exploring dynamics will allow us to examine many interesting questions, including:

- Is the voting continuum stable? In the professional jargon of political science, do major "realignments" occur at key points in American history — the collapse of Federalism and the advent of Jacksonian democracy, the Civil War, the 1890s, the Great Depression? In contrast to some earlier literature, we find remarkable stability since the Civil War, the only perturbation being the emergence of the civil rights continuum in the 1940s.

- Are individual senators and representatives stable in their positions on the continuum? Again, we find remarkable, increasing stability. At least since the turn of the twentieth century, the relative order on the continuum barely changes. Members of Congress come to Washington with a staked-out position on the continuum and then largely "die with their ideological boots on." In particular, they do not alter their behavior and "shirk" just before they retire.

- Is the range of political conflict, the length of the continuum, changing? We find a gradual shrinkage of the continuum for the first seven decades of the twentieth century, a diminishing of conflict. During this same period, the amount of intraparty diversity has remained roughly constant.

The shortening of the continuum is due almost entirely to a reduction in the separation of the two parties. For the last thirty years, this long-term trend has reversed. The parties have polarized. Their differences have widened dramatically and are approaching the record highs reached around 1900.

A Look at the Rest of the Book

The second chapter of this book presents the details of our dynamic model of the structure of roll call voting and discusses how we estimated the model. The rest of the volume is concerned with substantive insights drawn from the estimation results.

In chapter 3, we first discuss the overall fit of the model — we find that a two-dimensional model with a simple linear time trend in legislator positions is the best fit to the roll call record. We then turn to a discussion of the issue content of the two dimensions over time. We end the chapter with a discussion of a variety of different sets of supporting evidence for our finding of low dimensionality.

Our finding of low dimensionality initially generated widespread disbelief. In 1985, our working paper "The Unidimensional Congress"[13] had provoked both our colleagues in political science, many of whom have studied the intricate inner workings of the Hill, and in economics, many of whom have been struck by the complex web of economic interests that seek to influence legislation. Indeed, Van Doren (1990) has argued that roll call voting is only a small part of the congressional process and that most issues are screened out without reaching the floor. Snyder (1992) has formalized this argument in terms of committee gatekeeping. Koford (1989, 1990, 1994) presented a series of methodological arguments against the finding of low dimensionality. Our discussion of low dimensionality in chapter 3 replies to these arguments.[14]

In chapter 4 we discuss the stability of our estimated coordinates. We find that after the Civil War legislators are very stable in their estimated coordinates. Spatial movement in our dynamic model was never large relative to the span of the space and declined steadily after the Civil War except for some slight upturns during the realignment of the 1890s and during the late 1930s. We find that changes in congressional voting patterns occur almost entirely through the process of replacement of retiring or defeated legislators. During the New Deal, these replacements among the northern Democrats had the effect of moving the Democratic Party sharply to the left. In effect, legislators elected during the early stages of the New Deal were willing to have the federal government become much more active in managing in the economy. This was true, to some extent, also of Republicans who became more liberal roughly from the onset of the Depression until the middle of the Nixon presidency. The liberal trend among Republicans was countered, beginning with the Second New Deal, by a conservative trend among southern Democrats. The result was a reduction in the polarization of the two parties. In the past three decades, however, new Republican cohorts have been increasingly conservative, southern Democrats increasingly liberal, leading to an increase in polarization.

In chapter 5 we discuss realignment by examining two episodes, both in the antebellum era, when the model breaks down entirely; and two other episodes, both involving race, when a second continuum must be brought into play. These episodes all center about major changes in the party system: the collapse of the Federalists; the collapse of the Whigs; and the split, in the mid-twentieth century, between northern and southern Democrats. We also indicate why we do not regard 1896 and 1932, two dates that are commonly thought of as denoting realignments, as dates that correspond to realignments in the structure of roll call voting.

Our discussion of issues continues in chapter 6. We argue that the presence of spatial voting is not inconsistent with voting on the basis of economic interests. Economic interests, while difficult to measure, arguably have an important impact. However, we show through several case studies that members of Congress oftentimes express these interests strategically by "logrolling"; that is, trading votes across issues. This logrolling can be implicit or explicit but the essential point is that various interests are packaged. This packaging tends to take place along a single dimension. We examine five issues in detail: the interstate commerce legislation of the 1870s and '80s; the minimum wage since 1937; food stamps in the 1960s; strip mining in the 1970s; and bankruptcy for much of American history.

We also show in chapter 6 that economic interests cannot be viewed as those of a representative or pivotal voter in each constituency. We do this by a very simple analysis that demonstrates that, even if economic interests were perfectly measured, pivotal voter type models would fail as models of congressional voting.

Although chapter 6 argues that simple models of voting on economic interests are poor alternatives to the spatial model of voting, the chapter indicates that economic interests have a role to play in the process that maps issues into a low-dimensional spatial model. As a result, the mapping between quantitative issues and the space can shift in time. We illustrate this point by examining minimum wage legislation and legislation on inspection of firms by the Occupational Safety and Health Administration (OSHA).

In chapter 7 we study amendment voting and agendas. There we examine the rare episodes of strategic voting that have been noted in the literature and study the performance of our model in those cases.

Chapter 8 ties our analysis of roll call voting to the ratings of members of Congress published by interest groups such as the Americans for Democratic Action (ADA), the Chamber of Commerce of the United States (CCUS), and the National Farm Organization (NFO). We treat the interest groups as voters and use their "votes" to place the House and Senate in a common framework. The results confirm our earlier analysis. In addition, the analysis also reveals a substantive message: The interest groups turn out to be more polarized than the legislators. Liberal and conservative groups are pulling at both ends, contributing to the polarization of politicians.[15]

In chapter 9, we explore the representativeness of congressional committees. Our major finding is that, particularly before 1947, committees are representative of the full chamber. Few committees are dominated by extreme conservatives or extreme liberals. But the evidence also shows that committees are likely to be information specialists in their oversight areas and to have common interests in these areas. Committee members vote together more often than would be expected from their party positions and liberal/conservative positions.

Chapter 10 looks at turnout. In recent years, abstention, particularly after paired and announced votes are considered, is not an important aspect of voting in Congress. (For this reason, we did not update this chapter with data more recent than the 100th Congress.) Historically, however, participation rates were far lower. The global increase in turnout rates reflects better transportation and better health. At all times, abstention has also reflected preferences and strategy. Indifferent voters near the critical dividing points on roll calls tend to abstain; voters on the majority side of a roll call tend to be more silent than those on the minority side.

Finding a simple structure that accounts for roll call voting is, from a scientific viewpoint, merely a beginning. There is now (2006) a large literature where the results from this finding have been applied to the study of the inner workings of Congress, to the interaction of Congress with the other branches of government, and to the policy outputs of Congress. In chapter 11, we provide an overview of this literature and of the application of NOMINATE to other voting bodies. Future research will need to ask what produces a stable structure and how specific issues map into the structure. We conclude, therefore, in chapter 12, with a summary directed at focusing future research on roll call voting and tying the analysis of roll call voting to the study of the larger legislative process. The final chapter also contains an epilogue that places our analysis in the context of the polarized politics of the twenty-first century.

Notes

1. The viewpoint that, due to the reelection motive, local constituency interests are the dominant influence in the choices made by members of Congress is so widespread

that a complete set of references would be a very lengthy one. Among the more prominent works are Mayhew (1974); Fiorina (1974, 1989); and Cain, Ferejohn, and Fiorina (1987).

2. Among the numerous case studies of the legislative process, Bailey (1950) and Redman (1973) are two excellent examples.

3. The "chaos" school is represented by Riker (1980).

4. But see Schonhardt-Bailey (2003, 2004), who applied NOMINATE to the analysis of the House of Commons in the Victorian era.

5. For evidence that diversity has increased in the House of Commons, see Gaines and Garrett (1992).

6. See http://clerk.house.gov/evs/2002/roll034.xml, downloaded Jan. 26, 2002.

7. A discussion of responsiveness is found in Ansolebhere et al. (1992) and Fiorina (1989). That nonresponsiveness to national interests is the norm is suggested by John F. Kennedy's characterizing those voting in the national interest as *Profiles in Courage* (Kennedy, 1955).

8. *Congressional Record*, December 19, 1884, p. 368.

9. To be precise, our analysis centers on a dynamic analysis that covers all roll call voting between 1789 and 2004. This analysis considerably extends our earlier work for 1789–1985 conducted at the Purdue University Supercomputer Center and the John Von Neumann National Supercomputing Center at Princeton University. The current work was carried out on a personal computer.

10. See Cox and McCubbins (1993), for example, on how the House Democratic caucus constrained the behavior of conservative Democrats. Whether parties discipline votes on specific roll calls has led to a lively debate in political science, with one of us appearing on both sides! See Snyder and Groseclose (2000, 2001), McCarty, Poole, and Rosenthal (2001), and Cox and Poole (2002).

11. See Groseclose (1994a).

12. This displacement of the cutting line occurs in the model of Groseclose and Snyder (1996). In their model, the largest payments can go to legislators who are otherwise far from indifferent. The reason is that these legislators must receive large bribes to keep them from being bought back by opponents of the buyer. To deter opponents, the buyer needs to purchase a supermajority. The roll call, nonetheless, still appears as a liberal/conservative split.

13. This paper can be found on our website at http://pooleandrosenthal.com/The_Uni dimensional_Congress.htm.

14. More detailed rejoinders can be found in Poole and Rosenthal (1991c, 1994b) and Rosenthal (1992).

15. For similar results with respect to individuals who contribute to congressional campaigns, see McCarty, Poole, and Rosenthal (2006), chapter 5.

2

The Spatial Model and Congressional Voting

The Constraint Hypothesis

Congress both considers a wide variety of different substantive issues and represents the diverse constituencies of 435 congressional districts and fifty states. If we succeed in accounting for individual roll call decisions with a parsimonious model, it follows that considerable constraint operates across issues.[1]

The presence of constraint is evident in the everyday language used to discuss politics. Expressions such as liberal, moderate, and conservative are part of the common language used to denote the political orientation of a member of Congress; such labels are useful because they quickly furnish a rough guide to the positions a politician is likely to take on a wide variety of issues. A contemporary liberal, for example, is likely to support increasing the minimum wage, oppose a reduction in the capital gains tax, oppose the use of military force abroad, oppose further funds for Star Wars, support mandatory affirmative action programs, and support federal funding of healthcare and daycare programs. Indeed, just knowing that a politician favors increasing the minimum wage is enough information to predict, with a fair degree of reliability, the politician's views on many seemingly unrelated issues.

To illustrate how constraint relates to roll call voting, consider some well-known members of the 101st Senate. Practitioners and observers of American politics will readily agree that John Kerry (D-MA) is an extreme liberal, Al Gore (D-TN) is a liberal near the center of his party, Sam Nunn (D-GA) is a moderate, Robert Dole (R-KS) is a conservative near the center of his party, and Jesse Helms (R-NC) is an extreme conservative. In other words, we can line up these gentlemen, from left to right, as below:

Liberal Kerry Gore Nunn Dole Helms **Conservative**

If roll call voting is constrained to satisfy a single liberal/conservative dimension, we ought to observe only the following voting patterns:

Unanimous Agreement

Kerry against everyone else

Kerry and Gore against Nunn, Dole, and Helms

Kerry, Gore, and Nunn against Dole and Helms

Helms against everyone else

Other possible patterns are ruled out. For example, Kerry and Helms cannot combine against the middle. No one in Washington would think this could happen, except in very unusual circumstances. The cartoon reproduced in Figure 2.1 is amusing because it depicts a rare agreement. To see if roll call voting fits the expected pattern, we can look at every roll call to see if one of the allowable voting patterns holds. For example, of the five senators cited above, only Kerry supported the Leahy amendment on September 26, 1989, that would have cut funding for the B-2 bomber; only Kerry and Gore opposed the Robb amendment on July 20, 1989 giving the president authority to pursue funding for non-Communist forces in Cambodia; only Dole and Helms voted to confirm John Tower as secretary of defense on March 9, 1989, and everyone else rejected Helms' May 2, 1989 amendment to remove funding for the commission for Martin Luther King, Jr. day. Of course, all five vote together on non-controversial measures, such as confirming James Baker as secretary of state. Omitting the uninteresting unanimous vote, we can then simultaneously order these roll calls and the senators as follows:

Kerry *B-2 bomber* Gore *Cambodia* Nunn *Tower* Dole *MLK, Jr.* Helms

The basic implication of the constraint hypothesis is that all issues tend to be mapped onto a fixed ordering or placement of legislators.[2] This fixed ordering can be thought of as the underlying, "basic" or "predictive," dimension.[3]

In this book, we represent the positions of legislators not just by a simple ordering but by an interval scale, like the Fahrenheit temperature scale. Thus each legislator has a position that can be described by a number. The number represents the legislator's ideal point — his preferred level of conservatism that

Figure 2.1. An extreme liberal, John Kerry (D-MA), and an extreme conservative, Jesse Helms (R-NC) have a rare agreement. Copyright 1989, Boston Globe; distributed by Los Angeles Times Syndicate. Reprinted by permission.

he would like to see in any issue that is voted upon. Moreover, the legislator's preferences along the dimension are assumed to be single-peaked and symmetric, as illustrated by Figure 2.2. *Single-peaked* means that as the policy moves further away from the ideal point in either direction — either more liberal or more conservative — the legislator is worse off. *Symmetric* means that the legislator is indifferent between two policies that are equidistant from the ideal point.[4]

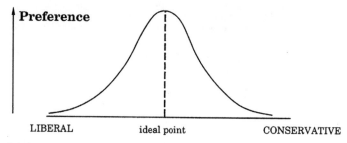

Figure 2.2. Single-peaked preference on the underlying dimension. The ideal point represents the point of highest preference. Positions more liberal than the ideal point or more conservative than the ideal point are less preferred.

To order an issue along the underlying dimension as well, we need a mapping between policy outcomes and the underlying dimension. To take an example drawn from actual roll call votes we analyze in chapter 6, consider legislation specifying which firms will be subject to inspection by the Occupational Safety and Health Administration (OSHA). Firms with more than a legislated number of employees will be subject to inspection; smaller firms will be exempt. Presumably, the liberal pole (here defined as the maximum government intervention in the market, with all firms being inspected) of the mapping is anchored by zero employees and the conservative pole is anchored by an unlimited number of employees (no inspections). Figure 2.3 shows an illustrative mapping and the hypothetical preferences of our five senators.

We have created Figure 2.3 so that the legislators are evenly placed on the underlying dimension. Kerry, the most liberal, is at −1; Gore is at -0.5; Nunn at 0; Dole at +0.5; and Helms at +1. The hypothetical mapping used for illustration in the figure shows that the most preferred levels of inspection for our five senators are Kerry two employees; Gore, four; Nunn, six; Dole, fifty; and Helms no inspections. For inspection levels higher than his ideal point, each senator is worse off as the inspection level is increased. Similarly, a senator is worse off as an inspection level is decreased below his ideal point. Note that the mapping need not be linear. In our hypothetical mapping, the difference between two and four employees is just as important as the difference between six and fifty.

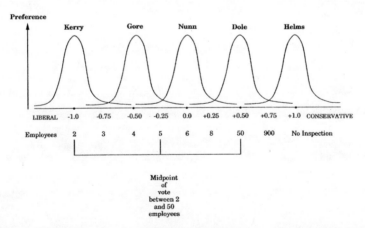

Figure 2.3. Five senators and the mapping of the OSHA inspection issue. All five senators have single-peaked preferences. More conservative senators desire higher firm-size limits on inspection. The midpoint between the mapped positions of two policies determines voting behavior. Senators with ideal points to the left of the midpoint vote for the lower inspection levels; those to the right vote for the higher level.

In this book, we assume that for every roll call vote, legislators vote as if they were voting *sincerely* on a mapping of the Yea and Nay outcomes. That is, a legislator votes for whichever alternative is closer to his ideal point.[5] There is a simple rule for deciding which is closer. Just average the mapped positions of the Yea and Nay outcomes. The average is the roll call midpoint. The midpoint represents the critical point discussed previously. If the Yea outcome is to the left of the midpoint, the Yea voters are all the legislators with ideal points to the left of the midpoint. The other legislators vote Nay.

To illustrate, suppose a committee reported a bill permitting inspection of firms with at least fifty employees, Dole's ideal point, and Kerry proposed his ideal point, two employees, as an amendment. The mapped position of the bill is 0.5; of the amendment -1. The midpoint is $(0.5 + (-1))/2 = -0.25$, so only Kerry and Gore support the amendment. (See Figure 2.3.)

If the status quo were no inspection, Helms would be expected to oppose any departure from the status quo, but all the other senators might support some form of an inspection program. If the inspection bill were voted on with an open rule where all amendments are freely entertained, the outcome would be expected to be Nunn's ideal point of 6. The reader can quickly verify that 6 will beat any other level in a pairwise vote.[6]

If, on the other hand, someone could force a take it-or-leave it "closed" vote of a proposal against the status quo, an inspection level lower than a firm size of six could be passed.[7] From Figure 2.3, we see that, since Nunn prefers Gore's ideal point of four employees to no inspection, if Gore could force a take it-or-leave it vote, an inspection level of four employees would win by a 3–2 vote, with Kerry, Gore, and Nunn prevailing over Dole and Helms. The mapping midpoint of 4 versus no inspection is +0.25.

For the constraint hypothesis to hold, one must be able to map most issues onto the underlying dimension. Thus, if we consider the minimum wage rate and the capital gains tax rate and OSHA as issues, the mapped ideal points might be similar to the following diagram:

	Issue	Kerry	Gore	Nunn	Dole	Helms
	OSHA	2	4	6	50	No inspection
Mapped	Minimum	$8	$6	$5	$4	$0
Ideal	Wage					
Points	Capital-	60%	33%	20%	10%	0%
	Gains Tax					

Of course, not all issues are as readily quantified as OSHA inspections, the minimum wage, and the capital gains tax. For example, the Cambodia funding issue from 1989 might involve a combination of policies. Which of the contending factions should receive support? Should they receive just humanitarian aid or military aid as well? What types of weapons should be delivered? Indeed, our quantitative examples must be similarly qualified. Minimum wage bills, for example, also specify which occupations are covered, whether teenagers are covered, and so on. Even for issues with complex alternatives, however, we maintain the constraint hypothesis: The roll call alternatives map onto the underlying dimension.

Why Constraint May Operate in the Presence of Strategic Behavior

It would be naive, however, to expect that members of Congress will always vote sincerely. One possibility is that they logroll or trade votes. Even if preferences all mapped onto a single dimension, vote trading might result in voting patterns that contradicted a unidimensional model.

If we voted on the minimum wage and a capital gains tax, for example, sincere voting with an open agenda would lead in both cases to Nunn's ideal point for a $5 minimum wage and a 20 percent tax rate. But what if Helms cared a great deal about the capital gains tax and very little about minimum wage, whereas Kerry cared a great deal about minimum wage and little about taxes? Then Helms might agree to support a $6 minimum wage in return for Kerry's supporting a 10 percent capital gains tax. The minimum wage bill would be passed with the votes of Kerry, Gore, and Helms, and the tax bill would pass with the votes of Kerry, Dole, and Helms.[8] Although a Kerry-Helms trade is possible, such a trade would be highly unexpected and therefore highly publicized. Even if the trade were beneficial to constituents, the constituents might not process the relatively complex information correctly. If constituents are mainly sensitive to consistent voting patterns along the predictive dimension, Kerry and Helms may find such trades ill-advised.

More likely trades simply involve changing the mapping. What if the Democratic leadership promised Nunn that a committee would act favorably on another matter of interest to Nunn, if he would oppose any lowering of the capital gains tax from a status quo rate of 28 percent? Then Nunn would vote with Kerry and Gore on the issue (rather than Dole and Helms), but this strategic vote would still be consistent with a unidimensional voting pattern.

Moreover, if legislators, perhaps as a result of a concern to establish a reputation for consistency, seek to sustain a pattern of unidimensional voting, vote trading may allow observations of roll call votes to appear as if preferences mapped onto an underlying dimension even when true preferences have a far more complex pattern. Consider the following hypothetical scrambling of the original preferences:

	Issue	Kerry	Gore	Nunn	Dole	Helms
	OSHA	6	4	2	50	No inspection
Mapped	Minimum	$4	$6	$8	$0	$5
Ideal	Wage					
Points	Capital-	0%	33%	20%	10%	60%
	Gains Tax					

Say the status quo on OSHA was firms with fifty employees. Then with an open agenda, six employees would prevail. Kerry, Gore, and Nunn would prevail over Helms and Dole under sincere voting. If $3.35 were the status quo on minimum wage, $5 would prevail, with only Dole and Kerry being opposed. If the capital gains tax were 28 percent, 20 percent would prevail with Gore and Helms in the minority.

Say, too, that Helms cared nearly exclusively about capital gains, Nunn about the minimum wage, and Dole about OSHA inspections. The three senators make a trade; they agree to enact, for each issue, the ideal point of the senator who cares. Kerry and Gore continue to vote sincerely. So the outcome is fifty employees on OSHA, an $8 minimum wage, and a 60 percent capital gains tax. The parties to the deal, Nunn, Dole, and Helms, would oppose any attempts by Kerry or Gore to have tighter OSHA enforcement. Only Kerry would vote against a proposal to move the minimum-wage to $8 from $3.35, and only Kerry and Gore would oppose the attempt to raise the capital gains tax. So any votes would still be consistent with a mapping onto an underlying dimension where the ordering of legislators was Kerry-Gore-Nunn-Dole-Helms. In sum, logrolling does not necessarily render the notion of constraint inoperative and may in fact contribute to strengthening the operation of constraint.

Logrolling is one form of *strategic* voting. In seeking to further their own interests or those of their constituents, strategic voters may not vote for the closer of two alternatives on a roll call. Strategic voting may also occur when voting on a bill is preceded by voting on one or more amendments. Strategic voting on amendments, however, does not necessarily invalidate the model's hypothesis that all votes can be treated as sincere votes. We illustrate this point with House action on the Common Situs Picketing Bill in 1977.[9]

Common Situs would have allowed a single union to shut down an entire construction site or other business operation. As it appeared likely that the strongly pro-labor bill reported out of committee would fail, Representative Ronald Sarasin introduced a "saving" amendment. The Sarasin amendment was designed to temper provisions of the bill, making it more appealing to moderates. That is, denoting the mapped location of the bill as B, the amendment as A, and the status quo as Q, the true liberal/conservative ordering of the outcomes was B-A-Q. Since A is closer than B to Q, A might succeed even if B were to fail.

House rules forced, first, a vote between the committee bill and the amendment. The winner of that vote would face the status quo in a final vote. *Suppose sincere voting were to result in the amendment being passed in the initial vote.* Then liberal voters to the left of (B+A)/2, the A-versus-B midpoint, would have voted first against the amendment and then for the amended bill, those more moderate voters between (B+A)/2 and (A+Q)/2 would have voted for the amendment and for the amended bill, and the most conservative voters, those to the right of (A+Q)/2 would have voted for the amendment but against the amended bill.

With such an agenda, however, sincere voting clearly doesn't make sense. Suppose on the final vote A would defeat Q but B would lose to Q; then, if A wins the initial vote, the final outcome is A, whereas if B wins, the final outcome is Q. Consequently, strategic (sophisticated) voters view the initial vote as one between A and Q. Conservative voters, then, should vote against the amendment, because the status quo would be more likely to prevail if the final vote pitted it against the more extreme committee bill. So they should vote Nay on the initial vote and Nay on the final vote. Similarly, liberals should support the amendment if they believe the committee bill is doomed to failure, so they should vote Yea on both votes. Moderates can be of two types. The more liberal type likes the amended bill best, the committee bill second best, and the status quo least. People of this bent clearly should be Yea on both votes. The less liberal type also likes the amended bill best but places the status quo second. This type should vote Yea on the initial vote on the amendment (A) versus the committee bill (B) and Yea on a final vote between the amended bill and the status quo. On the vote between the bill and the amendment, then, we should expect to see liberals and all moderates, that is, all legislators to the left of (A+Q)/2 voting Yea and all legislators to their right voting Nay. On the final vote, between the amended bill and the status quo, we should also expect to see sincere voting with a midpoint of (A+Q)/2.

Whether voters are sincere or sophisticated, we thus expect to see both votes split perfectly on the underlying dimension. The difference is that on the initial vote, with sincere voting, the bill appears in its true location as the liberal outcome (B) whereas with strategic voting the bill appears as its sophisticated equivalent, the conservative outcome (Q). (The amendment [A] exhibits, under either sincere or strategic voting, its true location on both votes; the status quo [Q] exhibits its true location on the final vote.)

The actual roll call voting patterns on the Common Situs picketing bill will, even when voting is strategic, provide useful information about the legislator locations because we will observe liberal/conservative splits. A strategic vote means only that we have to do a little reinterpretation of alternatives. On the initial vote, the legislators, instead of voting sincerely on A versus B, are voting strategically. But being strategic means acting as if one is voting sincerely on A versus Q. This insight allows us to learn the true location of A.[10] If the amendment passes, both the initial and the final vote would be votes between A and Q, so we would expect an identical vote in support of A on both votes.

Consequently, neither logrolling nor strategic voting on agendas necessarily invalidates our use of the simple spatial model. We consider logrolling in chapter 6 and amendment voting, including the Common Situs votes, in chapter 7.

Multidimensionality

Our examples of roll call voting, whether sincere, logrolled, or strategic votes over agendas, have all been phrased in terms of a single underlying dimension. Political discourse often distinguishes between economic and social conservatives. An economic conservative is generally thought of as believing that government should not intervene in private economic transactions with redistributive taxation; in kind transfer programs; and regulation of wages, working conditions, and externalities such as air and water pollution. On the other hand, social conservatives believe that government should intervene to regulate personal behavior in matters of freedom of speech and association; sexual and reproductive behavior; gambling; consumption of drugs and alcohol; and (in earlier times) enslavement or segregation of non-whites.

Of course, economic and social conservatism might be highly correlated. True libertarians, those who want to minimize government regulation of all forms, may be hard to find outside the economics department of the University of Chicago. On the other hand, economic liberals who are social conservatives, such as some blue-collar Roman Catholics, may be more numerous. Thus, more than one underlying dimension may be required to describe voting behavior.

When there are two dimensions, we still model individual legislator preferences as declining with distance from an ideal point. Because preferences in the model are a function of (Euclidean) distance, political scientists refer to our analysis as a *spatial model*. The unidimensional concept of symmetric preference is generalized to the concept of circular indifference contours. For any circle centered on his ideal point, the legislator is indifferent concerning policies whose mappings are points on the circle. The larger the circle, the greater the distance from the ideal point, and so the less desirable any policy that is mapped onto the circle.

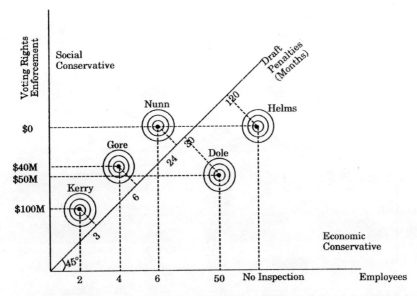

Figure 2.4. Two-dimensional indifference contours and the mapping of three issues in the basic space. Lines from each senator show ideal points on the issues. The circular indifference contours indicate that preference is decreasing in distance from the ideal point.

A set of indifference contours is illustrated for our hypothetical five-person Senate in Figure 2.4. Abstractly, the space can be thought of as having a horizontal dimension and a vertical dimension. In the figure, the OSHA inspection level is assumed to be a horizontal dimension issue. Its earlier mapping is preserved. Appropriating funds for enforcement of the Voting Rights Act is mapped as an issue on the vertical dimension.[11] Other issues may be neither strictly horizontal nor strictly vertical. We illustrate this in the figure by having penalties for non-registrants for the military draft mapped as an issue at an angle of 45° to the horizontal axis.

The concept of the midpoint in one dimension generalizes to a cutting line in two dimensions. The cutting line is the perpendicular bisector of the line joining the two alternatives, and separates the Yea and Nay voters. Figure 2.5 shows a cutting line for a vote between punishments of six months and ten years. The three-dimensional analogs of circular indifference contours and cutting lines are spherical indifference surfaces and separating planes.

Just how many dimensions are needed to describe the structure of roll call voting is an empirical question. The analysis we present shows a structure that is largely unidimensional, with a second dimension having a more

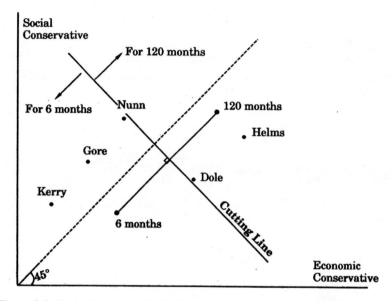

Figure 2.5. Cutting line on a roll call for punishment for draft evasion. The outcomes are on a line parallel to the 45° line. The cutting line is the perpendicular bisector of the line joining the outcomes. Positions on the draft issue combine aspects of economic conservatism and social conservatism.

minor although sometimes important influence. As shown in *Congress, 1997*, p. 28, virtually no substantive concern is served by going beyond two dimensions.

As with one dimension, a pattern of voting constrained to a low-dimensional mapping can be consistent with strategic behavior. To see this, we can recall the Common Situs picketing example. In this scenario, a moderate saving amendment (A) defeats a more liberal committee bill (B) on an initial vote and then is matched against the status quo (Q). With a single dimension, only four possible strict preference orderings are possible: B>A>Q (B preferred to A preferred to Q); A>B>Q; A>Q>B; and Q>A>B. But, unless the three options are on a line in two dimensions, two dimensions will produce the other two possibilities, B>Q>A, and Q>B>A. This is shown in Figure 2.6. Although the saving amendment is closer to Q than B is, it is off the line joining B and Q. The three cutting lines mark off six regions of the space that correspond to the six types of legislator preferences. Below each type we give (assuming A wins the initial vote) first its sincere and then its sophisticated voting pattern. If in a final vote Q loses to A but beats B, under sophisticated voting, the initial B-versus-A vote once again is really an A-versus-Q vote. Even in strategic voting, voters

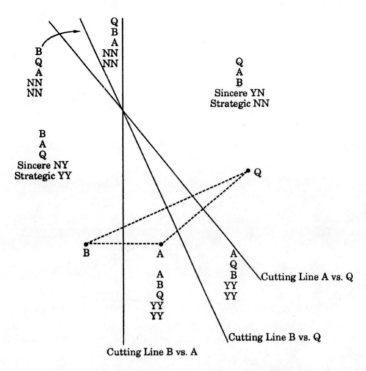

Figure 2.6. Sincere and sophisticated voting in two dimensions. With three alternatives, there are six types of strict preferences in two dimensions. The three cutting lines between the three pairs of alternatives determine six wedges or pie-slices. Each slice corresponds to one of the preference types. If the status quo (Q) defeats the bill (B) in the final vote but loses to the amended bill, legislators who have preferences QAB and BAQ vote differently on the initial vote between A and B if they are strategic than if they are sincere.

are split by a cutting line. This split provides information about the true locations of the A and Q outcomes.

Even with two dimensions, however, about 15 percent of the individual votes fail to fit a simple spatial structure. This is illustrated in Figure 2.7, which shows votes on the Panama Canal treaty and the National Science Foundation (NSF) budget. The ideal points of northern Democrats are marked by D tokens; of southern Democrats, by S; and of Republicans, by R. Some locations are so close that there is overlapping, but a particular letter always overlaps the same letter. The left panels show all the senators and cutting lines for the votes. The right panels show that there are some errors — Yea voters on the Nay side of the cutting line and vice versa. Nevertheless, the errors tend to be close to the cutting line.

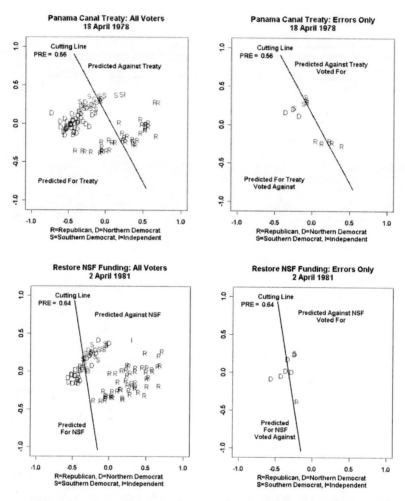

Figure 2.7. Ideal points, cutting lines, and errors on two roll calls. Each token corresponds to a senator's ideal point. Errors are concentrated near the cutting lines. The ideal points and cutting lines are the estimates of the DW-NOMINATE model, with a linear trend in legislator positions. (The "Independent" is Harry Byrd, Jr. [VA].)

A probabilistic model accounts for this pattern. The closer a legislator is to an alternative, the more likely he is to vote for it. At one extreme, if one alternative is at the legislator's ideal point and the other alternative is very far from it, he has a probability close to one of voting for the closer alternative. At the other extreme, if the alternatives are equidistant from him, the legislator acts as if he based his decision on a coin toss. Since legislators close to the cutting line are close to equidistant from the two alternatives, their actual votes are more likely to be errors than are the votes of legislators with ideal points far from the cutting line.

Estimation

Our discussion has concerned a set of examples in which all the spatial locations were known. But our task is to recover the locations of over 11,000 legislators and nearly 100,000 roll calls from the more than 14,000,000 recorded individual decisions in congressional history stretching from 1789 through 2004. How do we do this?

Minimizing Classification Error in One Dimension

If we had but a single dimension with errorless voting, we could recover the true order of the legislators and the roll call midpoints very simply. Poole (2005, chapter 2) has proven a theorem that shows a simple solution for this problem. However, if there is some voting error, a simple iterative procedure works quite well and, in practice, needs only a few steps to converge. This technique resembles arranging a deck of cards by first sorting the cards by suit and then sorting by order within the suit.[12]

To illustrate, let us return to our original example. Say we started out with the following highly erroneous ordering of the senators,

Nunn   Helms   Gore   Kerry   Dole

and we observed only that the splits were Kerry against the others on the B-2; Kerry and Gore against the other three on Cambodia; Dole and Helms against the other three on Tower; and Helms against the others on MLK, Jr. The (nonunique) placement of roll call midpoints below minimizes classification errors:

Cambodia

Nunn   Helms   *Tower*   Gore   *B-2*   Kerry   Dole

MLK, Jr.

Note that this placement of the roll call midpoints minimizes classification errors only if the substantively liberal outcome on each issue is supported by senators placed at the right end of the order. Thus, Kerry and Dole are both predicted to oppose further funds for the B-2 bomber. The placements of the roll calls lead to five classification errors. Dole is incorrectly classified on B-2, Cambodia, and Tower, and Nunn is incorrect on Tower and MLK, Jr.

After this first step, the next step is to see if, holding the midpoints fixed, we can move the senators, one by one, and reduce the classification errors. The following rearrangement eliminates all but two errors, Dole on MLK, Jr. and Nunn on Cambodia:

Cambodia

Helms   Dole   *Tower*   Nunn   Gore   *B-2*   Kerry

MLK, Jr.

But after this step, we can hold the legislators constant and rearrange the midpoints and eliminate all the errors:

Helms *MLK, Jr.* Dole *Tower* Nunn *Cambodia* Gore *B-2* Kerry

The order is correct; it is just the mirror image of the common sense order assumed in the example given earlier. Our recovery example was deliberately chosen to emphasize that what is left and right is just a convention. An ordering and its mirror image both contain the same information.

When voting is errorless, as in our example, we can use Poole's (2005, chapter 2) solution to find the true ordering in one step. We would not need the iterative procedure used in our example to obtain an ordering. However, if the actual data contains error, our iterative procedure is a simple and highly reliable method of obtaining an ordering of legislators and cutpoints. The sorting process is, in statisticians' lingo, a robust way of finding out where the senators and cutpoints are located. Thus, the recovery based on optimal classification isn't likely to be sensitive to the process generating the errors; that is, to whatever causes roll call voting to be less than a perfect fit to the spatial model.[13]

Unfortunately, optimal classification has an important disadvantage — it gives us no information about the locations of the alternatives. Only the midpoint is relevant to classification. Any pair of outcomes that have the same midpoint make the same classification predictions. So we can't work back from classifications to identify roll call outcomes.[14]

NOMINATE

Because of this disadvantage, we developed an alternative procedure, which we have named NOMINATE, for *NOMINAl Three-step Estimation*. This procedure can be used with relative ease in multidimensional settings. It involves a specific probabilistic model, which allows us to use the pattern of errors to recover the outcome coordinates. Think first of Yea and Nay outcomes that are very close to each other. In this case, most legislators will be nearly indifferent and will be voting with probabilities close to 0.5. Then consider a second roll call with the same cutting line but with Yea and Nay outcomes that are very far apart. In this case, preferences will be sharper and more probabilities will be close to 1 or 0. Fewer errors should occur.

It is evident, paradoxically, that we need error to recover the roll call outcomes. We oversimplified earlier when we said we could recover the true locations in the case of errorless strategic voting. In fact, we could only recover the cutting lines.[15] Without error, the midpoint in one dimension or cutting line in two dimensions or separating hyperplane in higher dimensions is nicely tied down and identified by the basic liberal/conservative split on a roll call in one dimension, or, more generally, the split of the Euclidean space into Yea and Nay camps. In contrast, the Yea and Nay locations are revealed only by the pattern of error.

The use of errors to identify outcome locations has two potentially severe problems. First, our model includes a signal-to-noise ratio. This parameter measures how strong the spatial component of the voting decision is relation to whatever generates errors. We assume the signal-to-noise ratio is constant across all of American history. (Attempts at relaxing that assumption did not make important improvements in our ability to account for the data.) Although some roll calls are almost certainly noisier than others, the data do not provide enough information to identify both the noise level and how far the outcomes are from the cutting line. Thus, our outcome estimates will be much "noisier" than our estimates of legislator positions or cutting lines. We do have simulation evidence (*Congress, 1997*, pp. 248–49) that shows that our recovery of legislator positions and cutting lines is quite robust to the mix of signal-to-noise ratios across roll calls. (Variations in noise across legislators are a smaller problem. A legislator is analogous to a roll call midpoint. Unless the legislator's voting pattern is extremely noisy, his position will be pinned down by his overall pattern of voting, even when there is little or no error.)[16]

Second, to recover the outcome coordinates, we need to assume a specific form to preferences, not just the ordinal assumption that preference is decreasing in distance. Basically, how preference decreases is shown in Figures 2.2 and 2.3. (The mathematical specification appears in Poole [2005].) Not all specifications that decrease in distance will do the trick. When preferences are quadratic in distance — a form that often facilitates theoretical modeling — the outcomes cannot be recovered, even when error is present. The form assumed in NOMINATE is exponential or bell-shaped utility. (See Figure 2.2.) This form is perhaps a politically realistic one in that voter preferences are not very sensitive to small departures from the ideal point, shift sharply for intermediate changes in outcome locations, but then show little distinction between outcomes that are very far from the ideal point.

The procedure we use to recover the space works in an alternating fashion, directly analogous to our illustration of ordinal sorting. We start with an initial configuration of legislators and a signal-to-noise ratio. We then sequentially process the roll calls, estimating the outcome coordinates. We then reestimate the signal-to-noise ratio, holding all spatial coordinates fixed. And then we sequentially process the legislators, keeping the roll call coordinates and the signal-to-noise ratio fixed. As we move the parameters of the model, we don't try to minimize classification errors. Instead we try to maximize the probabilities the model assigns to the observed votes. That is, if a senator voted Yea on a roll call, we would like the corresponding ideal point to be as close as possible to the Yea outcome and as far as possible from the Nay outcome. Of course, we have to trade off the senator's probabilities on this particular roll call against her probabilities on all the other roll calls. We continue the described iterations until we find that the locations have stabilized. A global iteration of the model is a pass through the roll calls, signal-to-noise ratio, and legislator steps. Stability occurs after three or four of the global iterations.

The results of the estimation are likely to be quite accurate with respect to legislator ideal points and roll call cutpoints or cutting lines. A typical legislator in American history cast 900 votes during her career (and many more in the modern period) — 900 is a rough but reliable indication of the effective number of observations used to estimate the legislators. The roll call cutpoints and cutting lines are also pinned down sharply, particularly in the modern House where the effective number of observations is close to 435 on most roll calls. Less accurate estimates pertain to earlier periods, particularly to the first several Senates where there were as few as twenty-six senators.

As mentioned above, our estimates of roll call outcomes are much less reliable than the estimates of legislator locations or roll call cuts. Consequently, this book contains no discussion of the outcomes for individual roll calls. However, the average location of sets of outcomes, such as all winning outcomes in a House, will, by appeal to the law of large numbers, be quite accurately estimated.[17] A discussion of winning outcomes is contained in section 4.5.

Legislators' Positions over Time

With respect to legislators, we need to ask not only what a legislator's position is at any point in time but how his position changes over time. A strong hypothesis is that the legislator has a constant position over time. Rather than adapt to changing constituent preferences, legislators enter a house of Congress and stay put until they die with their ideological boots on. If this hypothesis is maintained, we can then, using the fact that periods of service overlap, place all the legislators in a house of Congress in a common space for all of American history. In fact, we can estimate a common space as long as there is sufficient constraint on how legislators are allowed to move. We impose such a constraint by limiting movement to polynomial functions of time. The simplest function assumes that legislators maintain constant positions throughout their congressional careers. The next simplest is linear trend, which allows a legislator to become, in one dimension, either more conservative or more liberal during his career. With linear trends, legislators can thus never do ideological flip-flops; switching back and forth is possible only with quadratic and higher polynomials. Empirically, however, we find that essentially all movement is captured by simple linear movement as illustrated in Figure 2.8. Our dynamic procedure is named DW-NOMINATE.

Estimating the dynamic model is very similar to estimation with a static model. The only real difference is that, when a legislator's position is estimated, the coefficients of the time polynomial, as well as the constant, must be estimated.

It is natural to think that the largest changes in a member's position will occur when a legislator shifts the party with which he or she affiliates in Congress. To capture this, we estimate a new set of legislator parameters for legislators whenever they switch parties. We have found, as we report in chapter 3,

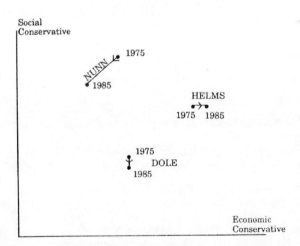

Figure 2.8. Linear movement of senators. In the linear-trend model, senators' ideal points move on lines throughout their careers. Some senators, such as Nunn, move more than others, such as Dole. Typically, they move very little, relative to the space, as illustrated by the figure.

that accounting for party switching accounts for almost all changes in the spatial positions of legislators. Unless they change party, legislators do indeed stay put and die with their ideological boots on.

Summary of the Model and Estimation Methods

To summarize: First, we have adopted a simple spatial model with probabilistic voting. Second, assuming this model is a correct model of actual behavior, we have developed a method for recovering the positions of legislator and roll call outcomes solely from observed individual roll call decisions. That is, the method is blind to any external information, such as political parties, about the legislators and the roll calls. The direct linkage of the recovery method to the spatial model is our innovation to the modern methods of roll call analysis introduced by MacRae (1958, 1970). Third, the recovery of legislator positions and roll call cutting lines is likely to be very accurate even if the technical assumptions of our procedure are violated. And fourth, the recovery of roll call outcomes may be very sensitive to the technical assumptions.

In the remainder of this book, we employ DW-NOMINATE to estimate dynamic models of roll call voting. To estimate static models for a single Congress, we use W-NOMINATE (Poole, 2005; Lewis and Poole, 2004). Having established the methodological basis for the remainder of the book, we can now proceed to a discussion of the results of the analysis.

Notes

1. See Converse (1964).
2. Indeed, on 520 of 638 roll calls (81.3 percent) cast in the 101st Senate (1998–90), the voting of Kerry, Gore, Nunn, Dole, and Helms was consistent with their left-right ordering.
3. Ordeshook (1976); Hinich and Pollard (1981); Enelow and Hinich (1984).
4. See Poole (2005) for the technical reasons for these assumptions.
5. Indifference is an empirical knife edge and need not be discussed.
6. Nunn's ideal point is the median of the five ideal points. Our example illustrates the median voter theorem (Black, 1958).
7. The theoretical implications of "open"-versus-"closed" rule are analyzed in Denzau and Mackay (1983). The importance of the status quo is analyzed by Romer and Rosenthal (1978; 1979).
8. We do not consider here whether such a trade could survive as a stable outcome in a world of vote trading. For further discussion of vote trading, see Ordeshook (1986, pp. 89–94).
9. This example is one of those discussed by Enelow and Koehler (1980) and is discussed at length by Ordeshook (1986, pp. 289–90). The votes discussed occurred on March 23 and are numbers 22 and 23 in VOTEVIEW.

10. More generally, if legislators have complete information about each other's preferences, any strategic pairwise vote in a binary amendment tree can be represented as a sincere vote between two of the true alternatives (Ordeshook, 1986, pp. 271–274). Therefore, methods of roll call analysis developed for the analysis of sincere voting can be directly applied to this form of strategic voting.
11. The Voting Rights Act was passed in 1965 and was primarily aimed at ensuring that blacks could vote in the southern states.
12. We show a simple example of this using actual playing cards on our website at http://pooleandrosenthal.com/edith.htm.
13. When error is present, there is no guarantee that the alternating procedure we have described will find the globally best ordering or that the same ordering will be produced from different starting configurations. But extensive use of actual roll call data leads us to conclude that, although there may be slight differences, final configurations are very robust to the choice of starts (Poole, 2000).
14. Subsequent to *Congress, 1997*, Poole (2000) produced an efficient algorithm for multidimensional classification. At this writing, however, the algorithm cannot be applied to the dynamic models used in this book.
15. If there is strategic voting with some error, we can recover the correct roll call outcomes.
16. See *Congress, 1997*, pp. 246–47, for further discussion and qualification of this point.
17. There is some bias to the estimate of roll call outcome coordinates. As the bias decreases rapidly with sample size, bias should not be a major problem for any House or Senate with more than fifty members. See Poole and Rosenthal (1985b) for a more detailed discussion of bias.

3

The Spatial Model: Accuracy and Dimensionality

In this chapter, we investigate the performance of low-dimensional spatial models and discuss the substantive meaning of the dimensions. With respect to performance, we show that a simple spatial model adequately accounts for the roll call data. Our preferred model has only two dimensions; it limits temporal change in the positions of individual legislators to simple linear functions of time. In fact, this very simple model improves only marginally, albeit significantly, on a still simpler model which is one-dimensional with legislators constrained to a fixed position throughout their congressional careers. These basic results are presented in the first section of this chapter, which gives the overall fit of the various spatial models that we estimated.

In the next section, we address the issue content of the first and second dimensions; the first dimension almost always picks up the fundamental economic issues that separate the two major political parties of the time, while the second dimension divides the parties internally over regional issues (usually race).

In the third section, we offer supporting evidence for our basic finding of low dimensionality. This section also confronts the controversy this finding has raised in the professional literature.

Overall Fit of the Spatial Models

We applied the DW-NOMINATE algorithm to all roll call votes cast in the House and Senate from 1789 through 2004 (the first 108 Congresses). All roll calls with at least 2.5 percent minority voting were included (97–3 and closer votes if 100 senators voted). For a given Congress, every legislator casting at

32

least twenty-five votes was included.[1] Applying these criteria, 10,378 members of the House and 1,818 senators were included in the analysis. For the House, 45,994 roll calls were analyzed with the total number of individual decisions being 11,493,013. For the Senate, there are 46,135 roll calls and 2,844,164 decisions. One-, two-, and three-dimensional spatial models were estimated, and time polynomials up to degree 3 (cubic) were estimated for the legislators. A two-dimensional model with a linear time trend (like the one shown in Figure 2.8) for the legislators accounts for about 85 percent of the individual decisions. Adding dimensions and/or time trend terms did not appreciably increase the fit of the model.[2]

A straightforward method to measure the fit of the model is simply to count, across all roll calls, the percentage of correct classifications. The classification results for the two-century history of both houses of Congress are shown in Table 3.1. The table reports classifications both for all roll calls in the estimation and for close roll calls where the minority got over 40 percent of the vote cast. With a two-dimensional model, classification is better than 84 per cent for close votes, as well as all votes.

A reasonable fit is obtained from a one-dimensional model in which each legislator's position is constant throughout his or her career. On the other hand, there is considerable improvement — between two and three percentage points — from adding a second dimension. Allowing for a linear trend in legislator positions adds less than a pecentage point. The gains from a linear trend are substantially less than those reported in *Congress, 1997*. The reasons for this are fourfold. First, as we report in chapter 4, there is very little linear trend for members for the past fifty years. By adding the data from Congresses 100 to 108, we get less of an overall boost from a linear trend. Second, we estimated a trend only for members serving in at least five Congresses rather than just three or more. We believe that many of the shorter-term estimates were not real trends but just "random walks." Third, we corrected several data errors where the original, pre-1985 data from the Inter-University Consortium for Political and Social Research had assigned the same identification number to two different members. Fourth, we now always reestimate the positions for those members who have switched parties and served in at least five Congresses in each party. A part of the linear movement that we were previously estimating is now captured by allowing for party-switching in the "Constant" model of Table 3.1. There were, however, only twenty-six such members in the House and five in the Senate (including Wayne Morse [R to D-OR] and Strom Thurmond [D to R-SC]).[3] That we get less of a boost in the percentages from the time trend than the dimensions is, moreover, expected for statistical reasons (see the box on adding parameters to the model).

Table 3.1
Classification Percentages, Proportional Reduction in Errors, and Geometric Mean Probabilities (1789–2004)

Degree of Polynomial	HOUSE NUMBER OF DIMENSIONS		SENATE NUMBER OF DIMENSIONS	
	1	2	1	2
Classification Percentage: All Scaled Votes				
Constant	84.5[a]	86.5	82.3	85.2
Linear	84.7	86.7	82.6	85.5
Quadratic	84.8	86.7	82.7	85.7
Cubic	84.8	86.8	82.7	85.7
Classification Percentage: Votes with at Least 40 Percent Minority				
Constant	83.6[b]	86.1	81.4	84.7
Linear	83.8	86.3	81.7	85.1
Quadratic	83.8	86.3	81.8	85.2
Cubic	83.9	86.3	81.9	85.2
Aggregate Proportional Reduction in Error (*APRE*): All Scaled Votes				
Constant	.534	.593	.476	.563
Linear	.540	.598	.485	.573
Quadratic	.541	.600	.488	.577
Cubic	.542	.601	.489	.578
Geometric Mean Probability: All Scaled Votes				
Constant	.713	.740	.688	.728
Linear	.715	.743	.692	.733
Quadratic	.716	.744	.693	.735
Cubic	.716	.745	.694	.736

[a] The percentage of correct classifications is for all roll calls that were included in the scalings — i.e., those with at lest 2.5 percent or better on the minority side.
[b] The percentage of correct classifications for all roll calls with at least 40 percent on the minority side.

Adding Parameters to the Model

When legislator positions are allowed to have a time trend, we add parameters to the model. We add only one parameter per legislator for each dimension. If, for example, we add a time trend to the one-dimensional, constant-position model for the House, we would add 10,378 parameters if we had a time trend for every representative. But since we have time trends only for representatives voting at least twenty-five times in at least five Congresses, we in fact add only 2,184 parameters. When a dimension is added to a model, the number of roll call parameters added equals twice the number of roll calls, since each roll call is represented by Yea and Nay points in the space. In addition, legislator parameters are added. (The number of parameters added for a legislator equals the degree of the time polynomial for the legislator. See Appendix A to *Congress, 1997.*) For example, adding a second dimension to the one-dimensional, constant position model for the House, adds 2*45,994 + 10,378 = 102,366 parameters.

More generally, since roll calls outnumber legislators by over 5-to-1, we add about 10 times as many parameters in adding a dimension as in adding another polynomial term in legislator position. It is thus not surprising that classification shows more improvement when we increase the dimensionality of the space than when we increase the order of the time polynomial.

Introducing more parameters in a dynamic spatial model — through extra dimensions or higher order polynomials — does not appreciably add to our understanding of the political process. That is, the additional dimensions have no obvious interpretation, nor does the complexity inherent in higher order polynomials. Moreover, adding extra parameters results in only a very marginal increase in our ability to account for voting decisions. For example, consider adding parameters to the one-dimensional linear model in the Senate. Allowing for a quadratic term in the time polynomial improves classification only by 0.1 percent at a cost of 584 additional parameters (584 senators serving in six or more Congresses). Allowing for a second dimension improves classification by 2.9 percent at a cost of 93,785 more parameters (two additional parameters per roll call and one or two more per legislator). Allowing for both generates an improvement of only 3.1 percent.

Gains from time polynomials higher than quadratic are trivial, as reported in Table 3.1. Gains from a third dimension for D-NOMINATE, as reported in *Congress, 1997*, p. 28, were also quite small. Because Congress is now highly unidimensional, on the one hand, and because higher dimension estimations are very lengthy in terms of computer time, on the other, we did not run DW-NOMINATE beyond two dimensions.

Another way to evaluate the fit of the models is to focus on the proportional reduction in error or *PRE* of the models.[4] A *PRE* measure allows us to see how much the DW-NOMINATE model improves on a suitable benchmark model. In other words, does DW-NOMINATE make substantially fewer classification errors than the benchmark? Our benchmark number of errors is the minority vote — that is, the minimum of the Yea vote and the Nay vote. In technical lingo, the majority-minority split on a roll call is known as the "marginals."

Why is the minority vote an attractive benchmark? Suppose the actual vote was sixty-five Yeas to thirty-five Nays. Without any information from the spatial model, one could always predict on the basis of the marginals. In the example, one would correctly classify sixty-five of the votes by predicting that everyone would vote Yea. There would be thirty-five classification errors from this prediction. Clearly, if there is useful information in the legislator positions and roll call outcomes estimated by DW-NOMINATE, classification should result in fewer than these thirty-five benchmark errors. When the minority vote is the benchmark, *PRE* is equal to the minority vote minus the number of DW-NOMINATE classification errors with the difference being divided by the minority vote. That is:

$$PRE = \frac{\text{Minority Vote} - \text{DW-NOMINATE Classification Errors}}{\text{Minority Vote}}$$

This measure is 1 if there are no classification errors and zero if the number of spatial model errors equals the minority vote. In the example, if DW-NOMINATE also leads to thirty-five errors, *PRE* is 0. Suppose, alternatively, that the first dimension classifies seventy-five legislators correctly and adding the second dimension results in eighty-eight legislators being correctly classified — that is, the first dimension has reduced the thirty-five benchmark errors to twenty-five, and adding the second dimension has reduced the errors to twelve. The *PRE* would equal (35–25)/35 or .286 for one dimension and (35–12)/35 or .657 for two dimensions. In this book, we will frequently use the *PRE* measure to analyze individual roll call votes because it controls for the margin of the roll call and facilitates comparisons between votes. (Note that the *PRE* can be negative if the spatial model makes more errors than the marginals.) We denote the *PRE* for the one-dimensional linear model as *PRE*1, and we use *PRE*2 for the two-dimensional linear model.

Groups of roll calls may be evaluated with the aggregate proportional reduction in error (*APRE*). Specifically, we sum over all roll calls, indexed by j, $j=1$, 2, ..., n, with n being the number of roll calls in the group being aggregated.

$$APRE = \frac{\sum_{j=1}^{n}\{\text{Minority Vote - DW - NOMINATE Classification Errors}\}_j}{\sum_{j=1}^{n}\text{MinorityVote}_j}$$

$APRE1$ and $APRE2$ are defined analogously to $PRE1$ and $PRE2$. Table 3.1 shows the $APRE$s for the various spatial models.[5]

In addition to computing classification percentages, the model may be evaluated by an alternative method that gives more weight to errors that are far from the cutting line than to errors close to the cutting line — for example, a vote by Edward Kennedy (D-MA) to confirm Judge Robert Bork to the Supreme Court would be a more serious error than a similar decision by Sam Nunn (D-GA). Such a measure is the geometric mean probability (GMP) of the actual choices (see the box on GMPs).

Summary GMPs for the various estimations are presented in Table 3.1. The pattern matches that found for the classification percentages — little is gained by going beyond two dimensions or a linear trend.[6]

Figure 3.1 plots the percent correctly classified for the one and two dimensional dynamic models for every Congress. The striking thing about Figure 3.1 is how closely the Senate and House track each other over time. The correlations between the Senate and House classifications are 0.75 for the one-dimensional dynamic model and 0.71 for the two-dimensional dynamic model. The spatial model breaks down during two periods. The first, from 1815 to 1825 (the period of the 14th through the 19th Congresses) is marked by the collapse of the Federalist Party and the "Era of Good Feelings" when the United States had, in effect, a one-party government. The era perhaps reached its peak with the elections of 1820, when only a single electoral college vote was cast against President Monroe's reelection and when the Jeffersonian Republicans won over 85 percent of the seats in the House of Representatives. The second period was in the early 1850s (during the 32nd and 33rd Congresses) when the conflict over slavery led to the collapse of the Whig Party. Later in this chapter, we offer evidence that allowing for more dimensions in these breakdown periods does not improve the model—that is, either the spatial model fits with one or two dimensions, or there is "chaos" in voting.

Another way of measuring how well our dynamic spatial models fit the roll call data is to look at the residuals — that is, the distribution of the errors (involving those legislators whose roll call votes are not predicted correctly). As discussed in chapter 2, the errors should be close to the cutting line. In our model, the probability of voting either Yea or Nay is ½ for a legislator located

---

Geometric Mean Probability

The *likelihood* of an observed choice is simply the probability the model assigns to that choice. Thus, if a legislator who actually voted Yea was "predicted" to vote Yea with a probability 0.9 by the DW-NOMINATE two-dimensional linear model, the likelihood of the choice for that model would be 0.9. Since all choices are assumed to be independent, the likelihood of all the choices for all the legislators is just the product of all the likelihoods.

The log-likelihood is the natural logarithm of the likelihood. As examples, the natural logarithm of 0.9 is –0.105, of 0.5, –0.693, and of 0.1, –2.303. The log-likelihood for all the choices for all the legislators is just the sum of all the log-likelihoods for the choices.

The *geometric mean probability is the exponential (or anti-log) of the average log-likelihood* — that is:

$$GMP = \exp[\text{log-likelihood of all observed choices}/N]$$

where N is the total number of choices.

Since the GMP is a probability, its maximum value is 1.0. This would occur if the model assigned a probability of 1.0 to every observed choice. The minimum value is 0.0, which occurs if the model assigned a probability of 0.0 to every observed choice.

As a measure of fit, the GMP penalizes models that assign very low probabilities to observed choices. For example, compare a model that assigned a probability of 0.5 to every observed choice to one that assigned a probability of 0.9 to half the choices and 0.1 to the other half. The average probability assigned by both models is 0.5. But the geometric mean probability for the latter model is 0.3 [$\exp(((\ln(0.9)+\ln(0.1))/2) = \exp((-0.105-2.303)/2) = 0.3$].

---

on the cutting line. Legislators far from the cutting line will have very high or very low probabilities (see the box on the GMP). Consequently, if our model is correct, the errors should drop off sharply with distance from the cutting line. Figure 3.2 shows the distribution of error for our preferred two-dimensional dynamic model along with the theoretical distribution of error.[7] To reduce clutter in the figure, we only show the House of Representatives. The graphs for the Senate are very similar to those shown for the House.

Figure 3.2 shows the percentage of the total choices that were errors as a function of the legislator's distance from the cutting line. (Recall that, as the cutting line is distinct for each roll call, each legislator's distance from the cutting line

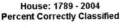

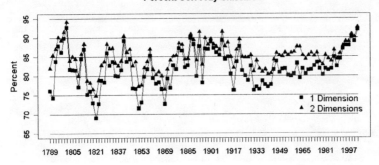

Figure 3.1. Classification in the dynamic spatial model. The graphs show the percentage correctly classified for all roll call voting decisions in each Congress. Each symbol corresponds to a Congress. The one-dimensional model usually classifies almost as well as the two-dimensional model. The patterns for the House and Senate are very similar. The model shown is the dynamic model with linear trend in legislator positions. (In all time-series graphs in this book, each plotted point refers to a Congress or a two-year period. The year that corresponds to each Congress is the year following congressional elections. Many early Congresses had their first votes only in December of that year and their last votes in March of the year we use to designate the next Congress.)

will vary with the roll call.) The distances are grouped in intervals of 0.1 unit of the space. While the career-average ideal point for a legislator must fall within a space 2 units in diameter, most of the distances between a legislator and a cutting line are less than .5 units. For example, the "All" graph in Figure 3.2 is based on the individual roll call vote choices included in our dynamic two-dimensional model for the first 108 Houses.[8] The estimated legislator ideal point was within .1 units of the roll call cutting line for 1,727,590 actual choices. But for a more

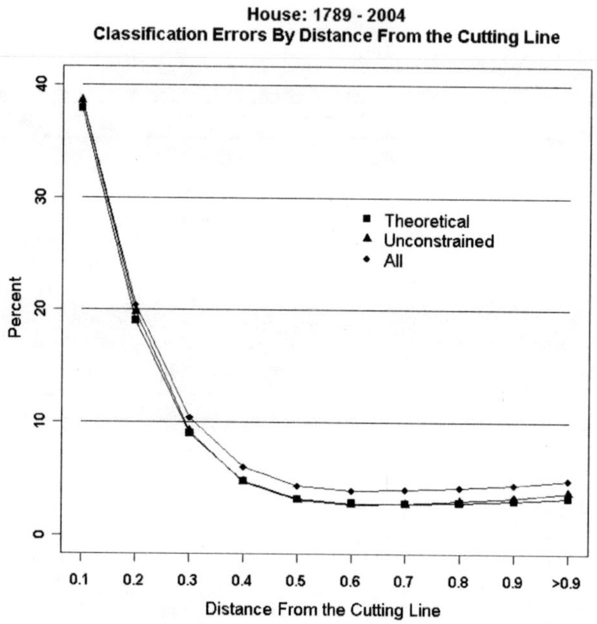

House: 1789 - 2004
Classification Errors By Distance From the Cutting Line

Figure 3.2. Classification error by distance from the cutting line in the House of Representatives, (1789–2004). The error rate falls sharply as legislators become more distant from the cutting line. The "0.1" refers to all instances where a legislator ideal point was 0.1 units or less from the cutting line on a roll call. The "All" line includes all roll call votes; the "Unconstrained" line has all roll call votes where the DW-NOMINATE cutting-line estimate was unconstrained.

distant interval of 0.1, that where the legislator ideal point was 0.5 to 0.6 units from the cutting line (corresponding to ".6" in the figure), there were only 981,876 actual choices. Note that the error rate decreases sharply with distance to the cutting line. The error rate for the 0 to 0.1 interval is 38.6 percent. In contrast, the error rate for the 0.5 to 0.6 interval is a mere 4.0 percent.

Figure 3.2 shows the theoretical error distribution along with the actual error distributions both for all roll calls and for just those roll calls that were "unconstrained." The estimated policy locations for very lopsided roll calls—for example, 95–5—often had to be constrained. That is, if the estimated cutting line fell outside the legislators' locations so that a unanimous vote was predicted, we constrained the cutting line to be at the edge of the space.[9] Voting behavior on lopsided, constrained roll calls is somewhat more erratic; there is a certain amount of non-spatial, protest voting. On lopsided votes, protesters know that their protest (e.g., voting against funding for the State Department) will have no effect on the outcome. Consequently, the error rate for unconstrained roll calls is systematically less than that for all roll calls. The difference in the error rates understandably increases as distance increases.

The figure also shows a perhaps surprising upward bend in the error rates, even the theoretical rate, when distances exceed 0.6. The reason for this comes from the bell-shaped utility function illustrated in Figure 2.2. As a legislator gets far from both the Yea and Nay outcomes, both outcomes fall on the flat part of the legislator's utility function, causing the probabilities of the choices to approach a 50–50 coin toss. As the legislator gets far from the outcomes, the legislator also, obviously, gets far from the cutting line. For the larger distances, there is both a theoretical and actual uptick in error rates.

As we pointed out above, either the spatial model fits with one or two dimensions, or there is "chaos" in voting. Chaos is rare, as the information in Table 3.1 and Figures 3.1 and 3.2 has disclosed. Quite the contrary: The important regularity we have found is that over 85 percent of all individual decisions can be accounted for by a two-dimensional model where individual legislators have ideal points that are fixed throughout their tenures in office. Put differently, the *PRE* measure shows that the spatial model "explains" over half the decisions not explained by the minority-vote benchmark. This regularity is an important pattern, but the pattern does not arise from a well-specified theoretical model that would fix the dimensionality of the space.

It is clear that what is not explained by a low-dimensional model with stable individual positions is not explained by a higher-dimensional, more dynamically flexible model. We can allow for substantial readjustment in legislator positions by estimating each Congress separately. Later in this chapter, we show that separate estimates for various Congresses disclose little improvement over the two-dimensional linear fit, even with as many as fifteen dimensions. The unexplained votes thus reflect either responses to specific constituency interests on particular issues, special interest lobbying, and logrolls or other forms of strategic behavior.

The Issue Content of the First and the Second Dimensions: An Overview

What is the substantive content of the space? To begin with, consider what the space would look like in a classical British two-party system with a very high degree of party discipline in roll call voting. The space would be largely one-dimensional, with the ideal points of the members of the Left party forming one tight cluster, and the ideal points of the Right party forming another tight cluster. The roll call cutting lines would all be vertical or nearly vertical and tightly clustered, equidistant from the two party clusters. The tight clusters would in fact be single points or lines except for the fact that occasionally discipline breaks down or free votes are allowed.

In many figures in this book, the American political parties also present distinct clusters, even though the parties are not as disciplined as they are in Great Britain. Indeed, throughout most of American history, we found that numerous roll calls in nearly every Congress had cutting lines through the space that perfectly, or nearly perfectly, divided the two parties. These would be the cutting lines for party-line votes. We show below that these cutting lines typically define votes that fall on the first dimension.

The political parties, either through the discipline of powerful leaders, such as Tom "The Hammer" DeLay (R-TX), or through successful trades, function as effective logrollers. Parties thus help to map complex issues (to bundle diverse economic interests) into a low-dimensional space. The first dimension represents conflicts over the role of government in the economy. The historical exceptions to this statement are 1817–25, during the Era of Good Feelings, and 1853–76, before and after the Civil War. When party is coterminous with the first dimension, the second dimension allows party members to be differentiated with respect to a second set of issues. For example, in the 1840s, the first dimension was largely concerned with internal infrastructure improvements and the second with slavery (which was a sectional economic issue [Fogel and Engerman, 1974], as well as a moral issue [Fogel, 1990]).

To indicate the issue content of the two dimensions more systematically, we discuss, in the next section, the history of the spatial positions of legislators, grouped by the major political parties. We then discuss the issue content of the first and second dimensions.

Spatial Maps of the Party Systems

The United States has had three periods with distinct two-party systems. The first, the Jeffersonian Republican/Federalist system, ended with the Era of Good Feelings. The second, the Democratic/Whig system, was organized after the Era of Good Feelings and lasted until the early 1850s. The third, the Democratic/Republican system, was organized by the late 1850s and continues today, although we will frequently refer to this system as having been perturbed into a three-party system (northern Democrats, southern Democrats, Republicans) by civil rights issues that arose in the mid-twentieth century. Figures 3.3 and 3.4 show two-dimensional spatial maps for representative Senates and Houses in each of the three two-party systems and in the three-party perturbation. As we note below, the first dimension almost always divides the two major political parties while the second dimension picks up divisions within the parties.

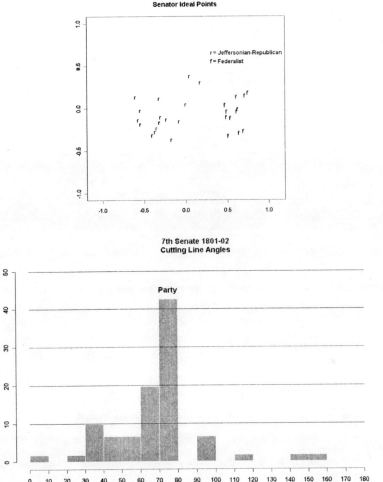

Figure 3.3. Ideal-point and cutting-line angle estimates for selected Senates. In the top panel for each Senate, each lowercase letter represents a legislator. The bottom panel shows the distribution of cutting-line angles. The values shown by the bars sum to 100 percent. The label "Party" shows where the party-line votes were concentrated. Where relevant, the labels "N vs. S" and "Conservative Coalition" show, respectively, the concentrations of votes that were regional North-South splits and votes that pitted Republicans and southern Democrats against northern Democrats. Votes in the 80 bar are those with cutting lines between 80° and 90°. These and those in the 90 bar represent vertical cutting lines or first-dimension votes. Those in the 0 and 170 bars represent second-dimension votes. The graphs show that pure second-dimension votes are very rare.

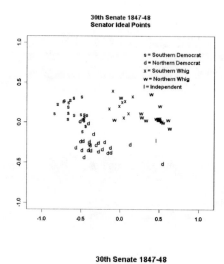

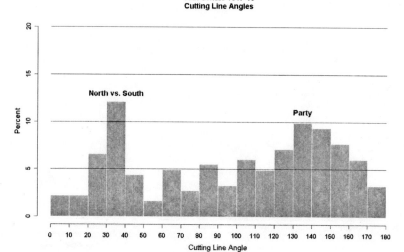

Figure 3.3. (*continued*)

We noted in chapter 2 that votes that involve only the first dimension will have vertical cutting lines — that is, cutting lines at an angle of 90° to the horizontal axis of the space. In contrast, purely second-dimension votes will have angles of 0° (or, equivalently, 180°). Votes that mix the two dimensions, such as our draft-evasion punishment example in Figure 2.5, will have angles that vary from 0° to 180°. Consequently, just as we can summarize the informa-

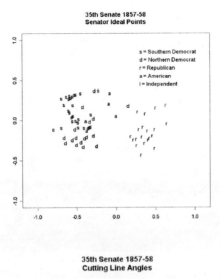

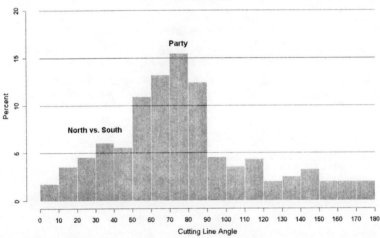

Figure 3.3. (*continued*)

tion about the distribution of legislators' ideal points in a scatter plot (the top plot, of Figures 3.3 and 3.4, for each of the Senates and Houses covered), we can summarize the information about the distribution of roll calls in a bar graph (a histogram) of cutting line angles (the bottom plot of Figures 3.3 and 3.4).

On the bar graphs we have indicated where the party-line votes fell. For these plots, we defined a party-line vote as one where at least 65 percent of

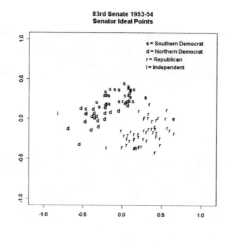

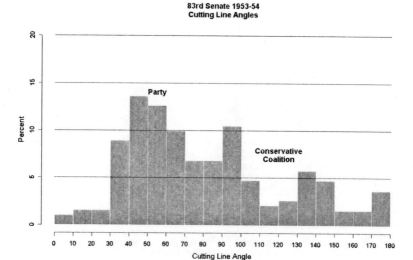

Figure 3.3. (*continued*)

one party opposed at least 65 percent of the second party.[10] Since the first dimension always divides the political parties during stable periods, the cutting-line angle of a party-line vote will be close to 90°. We exclude constrained roll calls because they almost always are constrained at the far left or right edge of the first dimension and therefore have an angle of 90°. Including them would exaggerate the number of party-line cutting angles.

108th Senate 2003-04
Senator Ideal Points

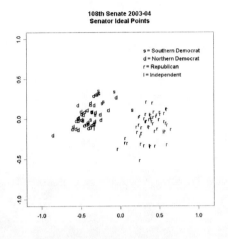

108th Senate 2003-04
Cutting Line Angles

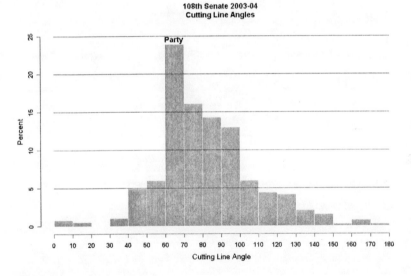

Figure 3.3. (*continued*)

The Federalist period. By the 3rd Congress, the factions associated with Jefferson and Hamilton began to solidify into the Jeffersonian-Republican and Federalist parties respectively. This division initially occurred because of sharp disagreements over foreign policy regarding the French Revolution and its aftermath and Hamilton's economic program of excise taxes, tariffs, a national bank, and the payment of the Revolutionary War debt of the states and the Con-

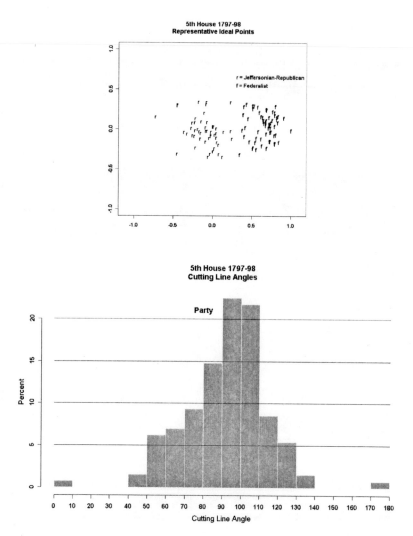

Figure 3.4. Ideal point and cutting-line angle estimates for selected Houses. See the caption to Figure 3.3 for details.

tinental Congress. Figure 3.4 covers the 5th House (1797–98) during which the infamous Alien and Sedition Acts were passed; and Figure 3.3 shows the 7th Senate (1801–02) during which Jefferson served his first term. The gap between the Republicans and Federalists, and the grouping of the cutting line angles around 90°, are typical of a well organized political party system.

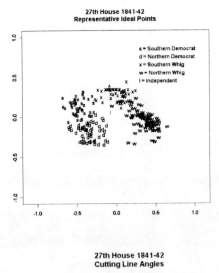

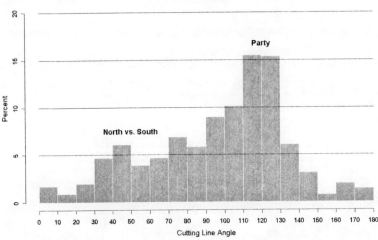

Figure 3.4. (*continued*)

The Era of Good Feelings. The War of 1812 produced a deep regional split in the United States. New England and the coastal areas of the middle states opposed declaring war on Britain. The South and West largely supported the war.[11] Opposition in New England was so pronounced that the British did not blockade the coast above New London, Connecticut. The War of 1812

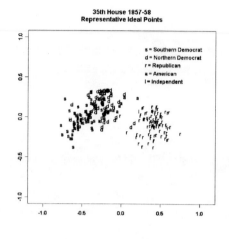

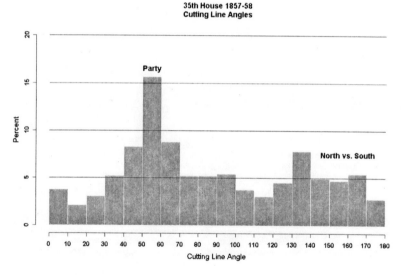

Figure 3.4. (*continued*)

destroyed the Federalist Party and led to a period of one-party rule from 1815 to 1824. This became known as the Era of Good Feelings after President Monroe in 1817 toured New England in large part to bring about greater national harmony.

The effect of this period on congressional voting was dramatic. Figure 3.1 shows that roll call voting through the period fit the spatial model very poorly.

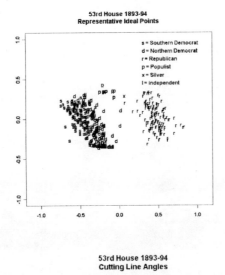

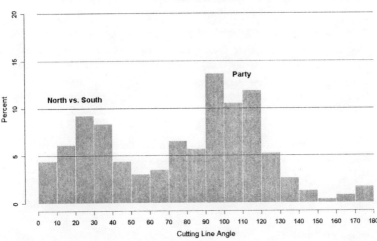

Figure 3.4. (*continued*)

With the collapse of the Federalist Party, the first dimension becomes a regional dimension pitting the northeastern Jeffersonians of various hues against the southern and western Jeffersonians. As we discuss in chapter 5, the first dimension largely accounts for the sectional splits in voting on the Missouri Compromise of 1820. The poor fit would have been even worse were it not for such sectional votes.

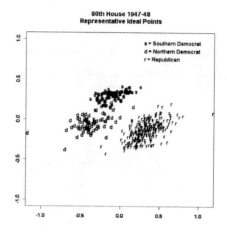

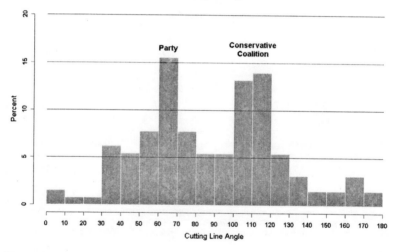

Figure 3.4. (*continued*)

The Whig/Democrat period. During the 1830s and 1840s the first dimension reverts to a party dimension and the second dimension picks up the conflict between the North and the South over slavery. This can be seen clearly in the spatial maps of the 30th Senate (1847–48) and 27th House (1841–42). The s token denotes the southern Democrats and x denotes southern Whigs.[12] The

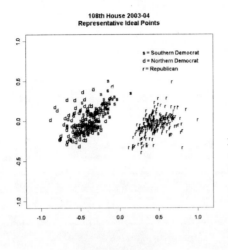

108th House 2003-04
Representative Ideal Points

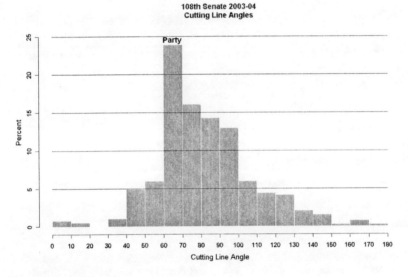

108th Senate 2003-04
Cutting Line Angles

Figure 3.4. (*continued*)

clear separation of the southern and northern Democrats and the southern and
northern Whigs is evident. On the cutting-line angle plots, we have indicated
the cutting-line angle of the North-versus-South votes (shown as "N vs. S" in
Figures 3.3 and 3.4).[13] Note that the cutting-line angle for political party is now
tilted towards approximately 120°. As is evident from an examination of the

legislator configurations, the first dimension is primarily party, but it also has a small regional component because the southern and northern Whigs are slightly separated along it.

The Civil War era. The realignment of the 1850s wiped out the Whig Party. It was replaced by the Republican Party in the North. The Democratic Party was predominant in the South. Consequently, the first dimension, until roughly the 1870s, is concerned mainly with issues related to slavery, the Civil War, and reconstruction. For the 35th Congress (1857–58), the southern Democrats are to the left of the northern Democrats on this new first dimension. There is still some North-versus-South component in the new second dimension, but it is very weak. Indeed, as is evident from the legislator configurations, a 90° cutting line separates the bulk of the southern Democrats from their northern colleagues. However, since there were no southern Republicans, all the North-versus-South votes split the Democratic Party.[14]

From Reconstruction to the New Deal. In the late nineteenth century the second dimension weakly separates the western and southern states from the northeastern states. This effect was stronger in the House than in the Senate. For example, Figure 3.4 shows the 53rd House (1893–94) just before the mass voting realignment of the 1890s.[15] The d tokens in the southeast quadrant are from the northeastern states. The North-versus-South votes during this period were really a case of the South plus the West against the Northeast — the regional lineup on bimetalism that we discuss in chapter 5. The second dimension in this period thus involved an agrarian-industrial, or urban-rural, contrast. Representatives from the largest cities were at the bottom of the plot on the second dimension.[16]

The three-party system of the mid-twentieth century. The period from the late New Deal until the mid-1970s saw the development of the only genuine three-political-party system in American history. The southern and northern Democrats may have joined together to organize the House and Senate, but as the plots of the 83rd Senate (1953–54) and 80th House (1947–48) show, they were widely separated on the second dimension. This dimension picked up conflict over civil rights. The approximate inclination of 45° for the two parties reflects the strong presence of conservative coalition voting (Republicans and southern Democrats versus northern Democrats) that occurred throughout this period on a wide variety on non-race-related matters.

In the three-party system period, it is useful to think of a major-party loyalty dimension as defined by the axis through the space that captures party-line votes. This dimension can be thought of as ranging from strong loyalty to the Democrats to weak loyalty to either party and to strong loyalty to the Republicans. (In other periods, when party cutting lines are vertical, the horizontal dimension can be thought of as both a party-loyalty dimension and an economic dimension.) An axis perpendicular to the party-loyalty dimension would then express a liberal/conservative dimension that is independent of party loyalty. Votes with cutting lines that are on neither the party-loyalty axis nor the independent liberal/conservative axis represent votes in which legislators make a tradeoff — instead of voting on their liberal/conservative preferences they maintain some loyalty to their parties. Almost all votes reflect, to some degree, this type of tradeoff.

The contemporary Congress: a return to unidimensional politics. Finally, Figures 3.3 and 3.4 show the spatial maps for the 108th Congress. Note that the separation between northern and southern Democrats has decreased from what it was in the 80th House and 83rd Senate. A two-dimensional scatterplot is now just a useful device for displaying the legislators' ideal points. The second dimension has withered away and all but disappeared. The bar graphs show that there are almost no votes with horizontal or near-horizontal cutting lines. The modern Congress is truly unidimensional.

In sum, one way of interpreting the dynamics of the space is that the horizontal axis usually picks up the conflict between, roughly speaking, rich and poor (or, more accurately, rich and less rich). Other issues (slavery, civil rights, currency inflation) crosscut this basic conflict. If (to anticipate chapter 5) one of these other issues becomes too intense, dimensional alignments break down and a reorganization of the party system results.

The First Dimension Captures Political Party

Except for very brief periods, the first dimension divides the two major political parties (as noted previously). This dimension can be thought of as ranging from strong loyalty to one party (Jeffersonian Republicans or Democrat) to weak loyalty to either party to strong loyalty to the second, opposing party (Federalist, Whig, or Republican). The second dimension differentiates the members by region within each party.

In Figure 3.5 we show *APRE* for party-line votes in the House and Senate for the first 108 Congresses. We use a more stringent definition of party-line voting than we used in Figures 3.3 and 3.4 in order to isolate the effect of party as much as possible. We define a party-line vote as one where 90 percent of the majority party votes against 90 percent of the minority party. We graph *APRE*1 and the gain in *APRE* from adding the second dimension (*APRE*2-*APRE*1). We show only those Houses and Senates where there were at least five party-line roll calls.[17]

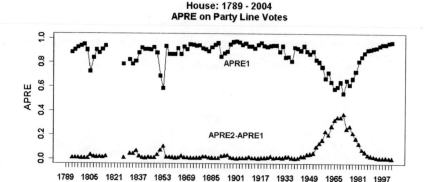

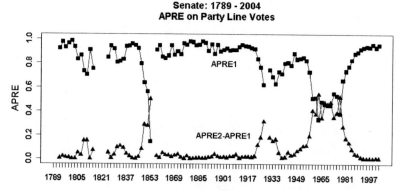

Figure 3.5. Aggregate Proportionate Reduction in Error (*APRE*) on party-line votes, (1789–2004). Party-line votes are ones for which at least 90 percent of the majority party opposes 90 percent of the minority party. *APRE1* refers to the first dimension, and *APRE2-APRE1* to the additional reduction in errors brought about by the second dimension. The *APRE1* graph shows that party-line votes always fit the spatial model very well except for three periods: the time of the collapse, around 1852, of the Democrat/Whig system; the period of the three-party post-World War II system; and, only in the Senate, the Progressive Republican era in the 1920s. In contrast to the "chaos" around 1852, party-line voting in the three-party period is still fit by the spatial model, but two dimensions are required. The Senate during the Progressive era is an intermediate case.

In the House the patterns are very clear. The second dimension plays no role in party-line voting until after the 80th Congress. As we will discuss at length in chapter 5, the striking pattern in the *APRE* plots of the House is due to the emergence of a three party system in the late 1930s — northern Democrats, southern Democrats, Republicans — brought about by race. Almost by definition, to get 90 percent of Democrats voting the same way on a roll call meant that southerners and northerners were in agreement. Since the second dimension of the space throughout this period separated northerners from southerners, a party-line vote fell along both dimensions. After passage of the civil rights laws in the 1960s, this division in the Democratic party slowly faded in the mid-to-late 1970s so that party-line voting returned to a more normal pattern.

The pattern of party-line voting in the Senate is essentially the same as the House (and for the same reasons). The exception is the period from the 69th through the 74th Senates (1925–1936), when the second dimension also plays an important role. During this period a small group of midwestern, farm state Republican senators voted with the Democrats to such an extent that they were located among the Democrats along the first dimension but above the Democrats on the second dimension. These included the two prominent Progressives, George Norris of Nebraska and Robert M. Lafollette Jr. of Wisconsin (Lafollette Sr. had bolted the Democratic Party and run for president as a third party candidate in 1924).[18] Consequently, a party line vote fell along both dimensions with a cutting line angle of about –45°. By the middle of the New Deal, most of these Republicans were replaced by Democrats and party-line voting returned to a more normal pattern of being along the first dimension.[19]

The Content of the Second Dimension[20]

Relatively few issues have consistently sparked a second dimension in spatial terms. We coded all the roll calls for the first 100 Houses and Senates on a wide variety of issues ranging from slavery, presidential impeachment, the national bank, voting rights, disputed elections, price controls, and so on.[21] (The appendix, below, shows the specific issue codes schemes we used to categorize the roll calls.)[22] To isolate strongly second-dimensional votes, we listed all issue areas in which there were at least ten roll calls with a gain in $APRE$ (in D-NOMINATE) of at least 0.2 from adding the second dimension ($APRE2–APRE1$). These are shown, for the House, in Table 3.2 and, for the Senate, in Table 3.3. (Issue areas for which $APRE1$ is less than 0.2 are indicated by italics.)

Before the formation of the Democrat-Whig party system in the mid 1830s,[23] the public-works issue is the one most often picked up by the second dimension. After 1837 (the first year of the 25th Congress), slavery and the disposition of public lands dominate until the fateful 32nd Congress and the Compromise of 1850 after which slavery becomes a first-dimension issue (see chapter 5). From the Civil War until the realignment of the 1890s (see chapter 5), the predominant second-dimension issue is bimetalism (U.S. currency; banking and finance). After the turn of the century, there is no consistent pattern on the second dimension in either the House or Senate until after World War II, when

Table 3.2
Second Dimension Issues in the House

Congress	No. of Votes	APREI	APRE2	APRE2 - APREI	Issue
2	17	.394	.643	.249	Ratio of representatives to population
9	13	-.006	.260	.266	Slavery
14	18	.130	.349	.219	Tariffs
16	10	.430	.647	.217	Tariffs
17	15	.063	.395	.332	Public works
18	10	.167	.691	.524	Public works
19	13	.326	.578	.252	Public works
20	39	.363	.588	.225	Public works
22	18	.237	.511	.273	Military pensions/veterans benefits
23	41	.213	.579	.367	Public works
24	23	.072	.587	.515	Public works
25	39	.495	.731	.237	Slavery
	30	.309	.595	.286	Public works
26	27	.490	.695	.205	Slavery
27	20	.022	.335	.313	Election of House officers
28	44	.433	.719	.286	Slavery
30	29	.324	.793	.469	Slavery
31	26	.357	.678	.320	Slavery
32	111	.215	.439	.225	Public lands
	14	.279	.495	.216	Slavery
33	65	.164	.370	.206	Public lands
	75	.238	.524	.286	Public works
39	20	.156	.368	.211	Banking and finance
41	49	.225	.445	.220	Public lands
43	14	.026	.248	.222	Congressional pay and benefits
	30	.156	.376	.220	U.S. currency
44	18	.440	.682	.242	U.S. currency
45	15	.368	.672	.304	U.S. currency
52	29	.375	.638	.262	U.S. currency
53	41	.372	.742	.370	U.S. currency
62	10	-.016	.365	.381	Immigration/naturalization
66	18	-.024	.437	.461	Temperance and liquor
69	11	.222	.480	.259	Agriculture
81	10	.484	.692	.208	Union regulation/ Davis-Bacon
82	11	.429	.633	.204	Price controls

Table 3.2   (*continued*)

Congress	No. of Votes	APRE1	APRE2	APRE2 - APRE1	Issue
89	22	.527	.757	.230	Civil rights/ desegregation/busing
91	12	.171	.409	.238	*Agriculture*
92	16	.314	.557	.244	*Agriculture*
93	32	.136	.459	.322	*Agriculture*
96	20	.141	.359	.218	*Public works*
97	14	.109	.380	.271	Public works

Note: This table shows only those Congresses with an issue area in which there were at least ten roll calls with a gain in *APRE* of at least 0.2 from adding the second dimension. Issue areas for which *APRE1* is less than 0.2 are indicated in italics.

civil rights issues split the Democratic Party and created the three-party system we discussed above in connection with Figure 3.5.

There are more second-dimension issues in the Senate than in the House, which is consistent with the finding (in Table 3.1) that the second dimension is, overall, more important in the Senate than in the House. For example, in the linear model, classifications are improved by 2.9 percent in moving from a one-dimensional to a two-dimensional model for the Senate but only 2.0 percent in the House. The increase in the second-dimension issues in the Senate dates from the late nineteenth century. For the period prior to the 52nd Congress (1891–93), the number of entries in the Senate table and in the House table are exactly equal. Some of the increase for the Senate may reflect the absence of closed rules and an agenda that is correspondingly more open than in the House. On the other hand, a very large number of entries for the Senate concerns civil rights and voting rights during the time of the three-party system, with eleven entries in these categories, as against only one for the House. This almost certainly reflects the fact that the Senate was the body in which southern legislators, using the filibuster, sought to block legislation that occasioned much less debate in the House, where it enjoyed broad majority support. Thus, on the whole, race-related matters — slavery in the nineteenth century and civil rights in the twentieth — predominate among the issues where the second dimension results in a big gain in the *APRE*. This observation supports our view that a one-dimensional model typically provides a good fit to the data, with a second dimension needed in periods when race issues are distinct from economic ones.[24]

Table 3.3
Second Dimension Issues in the Senate

Congress	No. of Votes	APREI	APRE2	APRE2 - APREI	Issue
1	27	.286	.641	.355	Banking and finance
2	20	.313	.656	.344	Ratio of representatives to population
14	12	.397	.675	.278	Military pensions/ veterans' benefits
17	*18*	*.045*	*.270*	*.225*	*Public lands*
18	57	.375	.580	.205	Tariffs
18	*13*	*.097*	*.531*	*.434*	*Public works*
19	18	.394	.643	.249	Public works
20	16	.235	.562	.327	Public lands
	20	.410	.686	.276	Public works
23	14	.222	.676	.454	Public works
24	*42*	*.119*	*.415*	*.296*	*Public works*
30	14	.265	.475	.210	Impeachments and investigations
	12	.331	.799	.468	Slavery
31	*49*	*.181*	*.437*	*.256*	*Public lands*
	77	.379	.774	.395	Slavery
	12	*−.068*	*.233*	*.301*	*Treaties*
32	29	.235	.454	.219	Public lands
33	73	.220	.432	.213	Public lands
40	*11*	*.073*	*.318*	*.245*	*Public lands*
	11	*.055*	*.411*	*.356*	*Public works*
41	*12*	*.163*	*.378*	*.215*	*Supreme court*
	19	*.056*	*.375*	*.319*	*U.S. currency*
43	*20*	*.083*	*.576*	*.493*	*Banking and finance*
	30	*.190*	*.453*	*.263*	*Public works*
	46	*.055*	*.712*	*.657*	*U.S. currency*
45	11	.256	.604	.348	Banking and finance
	37	*.180*	*.639*	*.459*	*U.S. currency*
47	10	.251	.536	.285	Public lands
52	17	.290	.804	.515	Banking and finance
	16	.328	.856	.527	U.S. currency
	10	*.078*	*.278*	*.200*	*Judiciary*
53	*49*	*.157*	*.765*	*.609*	*Banking and finance*
	52	*.180*	*.758*	*.578*	*U.S. currency*
62	14	.218	.491	.273	Agriculture
	21	.205	.522	.317	Tariffs

Table 3.3   (*continued*)

Congress	No. of Votes	APRE1	APRE2	APRE2 - APRE1	Issue
63	18	.228	.526	.298	Judiciary
	27	.280	.549	.269	Interstate commerce/antitrust
65	*41*	*.128*	*.569*	*.441*	*Tax rates*
	16	.301	.533	.232	Banking and finance
	27	*.028*	*.274*	*.246*	*Temperance and liquor*
	116	*.172*	*.445*	*.273*	*World War I*
66	*11*	*.133*	*.464*	*.330*	*Interstate commerce/antitrust*
71	*10*	*.120*	*.536*	*.416*	*Tax rates*
	33	.297	.501	.204	Agriculture
73	12	.215	.508	.293	Tax rates
	17	.365	.619	.254	Banking and finance
	14	.504	.711	.206	Tariffs
	10	*.152*	*.388*	*.236*	*Public works*
74	*11*	*.126*	*.378*	*.252*	*Military pensions/ veterans' benefits*
74	*11*	*.126*	*.378*	*.252*	*Military pensions/ veterans' benefits*
77	*14*	*.152*	*.421*	*.269*	*Agriculture*
81	*10*	*.128*	*.583*	*.455*	*Civil rights/ desegregation/busing*
86	16	.306	.579	.273	Civil rights/ desegregation/busing
87	10	.221	.687	.466	Civil rights/ desegregation/busing
	24	.381	.614	.233	Education
88	13	.282	.520	.239	Tax rates
	59	*.158*	*.779*	*.621*	*Civil rights/ desegregation/busing*
	10	.429	.717	.289	Impeachments and investigations
	25	.255	.661	.407	Education
	13	.340	.616	.275	Campaign contributions/ ethics/lobbying
	16	.226	.776	.551	Workplace conditions/ 8-hour day
	13	*.066*	*.789*	*.723*	*Judiciary*
90	23	.380	.682	.303	Civil rights/ desegregation/busing

Table 3.3   (*continued*)

Congress	No. of Votes	*APRE1*	*APRE2*	*APRE2 - APRE1*	Issue
	10	.369	.578	.208	Campaign contributions/ ethics/lobbying
	13	.314	.514	.200	Interstate commerce/ antitrust
	17	.305	.617	.312	Housing/housing programs/ rent control
91	16	.485	.770	.285	Civil rights/ desegregation/busing
	18	.392	.627	.235	Education
92	44	.395	.612	.217	Tax rates
	47	.402	.713	.311	Civil rights/ desegregation/busing
	38	.376	.657	.280	Education
	27	.460	.764	.304	Campaign contributions/ ethics/lobbying
	20	.562	.785	.223	Judiciary
94	21	.555	.771	.216	Civil rights/ desegregation/busing
	28	.543	.861	.318	Disputed elections to congress
	22	.521	.740	.219	Voting rights
96	15	.473	.692	.219	Civil rights/ desegregation/busing
97	19	.399	.675	.276	Civil rights/ desegregation/busing
98	12	.219	.475	.256	Debt ceilings

Note: This table shows only Congresses with an issue area in which there were at least ten roll calls with a gain in *APRE* of at least 0.2 from adding the second dimension. Issue areas for which *APRE1* is less than 0.2 are indicated in italics.

The Dimensionality of Congressional Voting

Since low dimensionality is an important and, to many, unexpected, empirical result, we will discuss a variety of different sets of supporting evidence for it, including two sets of quite technical evidence. Can the "true" dimensionality of roll-call voting be determined? The answer is a qualified yes. In Appendix B of *Congress, 1997,* we offered evidence that it is extremely unlikely that there are more than three — and, in most Congresses, no more than two — dimensions of voting. Also in that appendix, we compared our ability to classify with a one-dimensional model with what might be expected if legislators and roll calls were distributed within a multidimensional sphere and there was perfect voting in this higher-dimensional space. We show that our empirical results are very unlikely to have been generated by "perfect" voting in a high-dimensional (that is, more than two) voting space.

In this section we discuss four sets of less technical evidence. First, restricting ourselves to three Houses, we show the increments to the percent classified correctly when W-NOMINATE is used to estimate as many as fifteen dimensions. Second, we evaluate the classification ability of the second dimension from the dynamic, two dimensions with linear-trend estimation, and compare this to the first dimension. Third, we show that the results of W-NOMINATE are reasonably stable when the algorithm is applied to subsets of roll calls that have been defined in terms of substantive content. Fourth, since dimensionality may depend on the agenda, we compare the model's performance with measures of the diversity of the agenda.

What Happens When a High Dimensional Model is Estimated?

To check the dimensionality of our dynamic models, we selected three Houses and estimated the constant or *static* (to distinguish it from our dynamic estimations on multiple Congresses) model up to fifteen dimensions. We chose the 32nd House (1851–52), the 85th House (1957–58), and the 97th House (1981–82) for our high-dimensional analyses. The 32nd is one of the worst-fitting Houses in two dimensions and thus a good candidate to exhibit high dimensionality. The 85th House represents the post-World War II civil rights era when the two dimensional linear model clearly dominates the one dimensional linear model.[25] The 97th House is included because it appears that roll call voting became nearly unidimensional by the 1980s.

Figure 3.6 displays the classification gains for the second through the fifteenth dimensions for each of the three Houses. The classification percentage for the first dimension was 70.3 for the 32nd House, 79.0 for the 85th, and 84.6 for the 97th. The lines in the figure indicate how much the corresponding dimension adds to the total of correctly classified. Note that the lines do not drop off smoothly because, as explained in chapter 2, W-NOMINATE is maximizing log-likelihood, not classification.

The 97th House is, at most, two-dimensional, with the second dimension being very weak. After two dimensions the added classifications are minuscule, for there is a clear pattern of noise fitting beyond two dimensions. Even though, in contrast to the 97th, the 85th House is strongly two-dimensional, there is

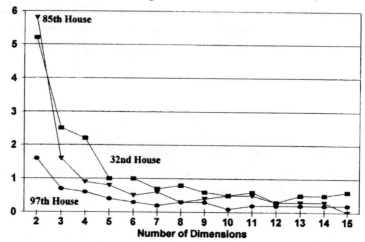

Increase in Classification Percentage

Figure 3.6. Classification gains from adding dimensions for three Houses. The lines plot the increase in classification percentage as dimensions are added. The 97th House (1981–82) shows a strong one-dimensional result, to which additional dimensions add very little. The 85th House (1957–58) was elected during the three-party system and shows a substantial gain from adding a second dimension. The "chaotic" 32nd House (1851–52) shows gains but the overall level of classification remains low. Additional dimensions are largely fitting "noise" in the data. The results are from W-NOMINATE.

little evidence for additional dimensions. The 32nd does show evidence for up to four dimensions, but even four dimensions account for only 80 percent of the decisions, and ten, for 85 percent.

The results for the 32nd House carry over to our other period of "spatial collapse" during the Era of Good Feelings. Classification on the first dimension is 70 percent for the 17th House and reaches only 80 percent in four dimensions, and 88 in ten. These results show that either voting is accounted for by a low-dimensional spatial model or it is, in effect, spatially chaotic. There appears to be no middle ground. In other words, there is never a period in American history in which, if we do not obtain a good fit with a one- or two-dimensional model, we can obtain a good fit with a three- or four-dimensional model.

The Relative Importance of the Second Dimension

Although the evidence presented above suggests a marginal role for (at most) a second dimension — and a weak one at that — it is important to evaluate the second dimension by other than its marginal impact. Specifically, Koford (1989, 1991) argues that a one-dimensional model will provide a good fit even when spaces have higher dimensionality. For example, in a truly two-dimensional space, one dimension will have some success at classifying any vote that is not strictly orthogonal to the dimension. As a result, the marginal increases in fit, on the order of two or three percent, may understate the importance of the second dimension.

The natural question, then, is, How well does the second dimension do in classifying by itself? To study this, we took the second-dimension legislator coordinates from our preferred model — two dimensions with linear trend — and, for each roll call, found a cutpoint that minimized classification errors. We used the minimum errors to compute classification percentages. We made the same computation for the first dimension.

The results of these computations for the House and Senate are shown in Figure 3.7. The average percent classification for the first 108 Houses using the

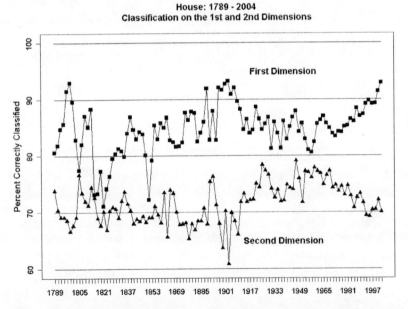

House: 1789 - 2004
Classification on the 1st and 2nd Dimensions

Figure 3.7. Classification on the first and second dimension. The graphs shows the results when roll calls are placed to minimize classification errors holding the DW-NOMINATE legislator coordinates fixed. The first dimension coordinates almost always classify at a rate of 80 percent or better. The second dimension barely betters the benchmark model of the percentage voting on the winning side.

first dimension is 86.0 percent but the second dimension accounts for only 71.9 percent. The 71.9 percent is particularly unimpressive given that predicting by the marginals would lead to 66.8 percent. If the two dimensions were indeed of equal importance, then in some Congresses dimension two might do better than dimension one. But in all 108 Houses, the first dimension did best (although the difference between the two was slim in the 17th House). The Senate results are a tad weaker — 85.0 percent for one dimension versus 74.0 for two. The marginals here led to a 66.2 percent classification. In addition, dimension two does better in Senates 2 and 17. But the second dimension is clearly a second fiddle.

Our overwhelming results that show that the first dimension dwarfs the second and higher estimations convinced even Koford (1994), who admitted that his first critique was incorrect. At the same time, however, he claimed that we would find higher dimensionality if we, unparsimoniously, allowed variation in the salience the legislators place on the dimensions. That is, legislators, in addition to being characterized by ideal points would be characterized by weights on each dimension.[26] Their squared distances to roll call alternatives would then be computed as a weighted sum over the dimensions. But we were also able to show (Poole and Rosenthal, 1994b) that allowing for variable salience would not result in a high-dimensional model with important gains in classification over a low-dimensional, constant-salience model.

Do Different Issues Give Different Scales?[27]

In contrast to our emphasis on low dimensionality, Clausen (1973) has argued that there are five "dimensions" to congressional voting represented by the issue areas of government management, social welfare, agriculture, civil liberties, and foreign and defense policy. We have coded every House and Senate roll call from 1789 to 2004 in terms of these five categories, and, for completeness, a sixth category termed "miscellaneous" (see appendix, below). If the issues are really distinct dimensions, we ought to get sharp differences in legislator coordinates when the issues are scaled separately.

To conduct this experiment of separate scalings, we chose the 95th House because it had the largest number of roll call votes (1,540). There were 714 government-management votes; 286 social-welfare votes; 311 foreign-and-defense votes; and, to have enough votes for scaling, 229 in a residual set that combined agriculture, civil liberties, and miscellaneous issues. We then ran one- and two-dimensional (static) W-NOMINATE on each of these four clusters of votes. Because it is difficult to directly compare coordinates from two-dimensional scalings, we based our comparisons on correlations between all unique pairwise distances among legislators. (If there are N legislators, there are $N(N-1)/2$ unique pairs of legislators.)

Correlations between the management, welfare, and residual categories for one dimensional scalings are, as shown in Table 3.4, all high, around 0.9. Correlations between the foreign-and-defense policy category and the other three were somewhat lower, in the 0.7 to 0.8 range.[28] As a whole, the results hardly suggest that each of these clusterings of substantive issues generates a separate spatial dimension.

When the same subsets of votes are scaled separately in two dimensions, the correlations are somewhat lower than they are in one dimension (see Table 3.4). This result is not surprising: The 95th House had nearly unidimensional voting. From the D-NOMINATE unidimensional scaling with linear trend that was applied to the whole dataset, we find one-dimensional correct classifications for 83 percent of the votes in each of the four categories. With two dimensions the percentages increase only to 84 percent for social welfare and for foreign and defense policy and to 85 percent for the other two categories.

Moving from one to two dimensions doubles the number of estimated parameters with only slight increases in classification ability. In breaking down the roll calls into four categories and estimating separately, the number of legislator parameters is effectively quadrupled. With a further doubling of all parameters, by moving from one to two dimensions, one is likely to be fitting idiosyncratic noise in the data. The fit to the noise weakens the underlying strong correlations between legislator positions. We also note that the spirit of Clausen's work suggests that each category should be scaled in only one dimension. In summary, our breakdown of the 95th House by use of Clausen categories indicates that the categories represent highly related, not distinct, dimensions.

Table 3.4
Interpoint Distance Correlations,
the Clausen Category Scalings, 95th House

| | CORRELATION | | | |
Clausen Category	(1)	(2)	(3)	(4)
(1) Government management	1.0	.914[a]	.796	.908
(2) Social welfare	.883[b]	1.0	.765	.881
(3) Foreign and defense policy	.770	.654	1.0	.724
(4) Miscellaneous policy, civil liberties, and agriculture	.832	.746	.613	1.0

[a] Numbers above diagonal are correlations from one-dimensional scalings.
[b] Numbers below diagonal are correlations from two-dimensional scalings.

The Agenda and Dimensionality

Macdonald and Rabinowitz (1987) argue that American political conflict is basically one-dimensional within the time span of any one Congress but that the dimension of conflict evolves slowly. One basis for the Macdonald-Rabinowitz argument would be that short-term coalition arrangements enforce a logroll across issues that generates voting patterns consistent with a unidimensional spatial model. Another potential consideration is that short-run unidimensionality may reflect the fact that, in any two-year period, Congress must place some restriction on the issues that can be given time for consideration.

An explanation related to that of Macdonald and Rabinowitz is a selection-bias argument originally made by Van Doren (1990) and developed in the context of a simple formal model by Snyder (1992b). Van Doren's basic idea is that only a small fraction of the potential issues ever get voted on, either because they are supported by only a small fraction of the membership or because, even if there is widespread support, the issue is screened from roll call voting by committees. Snyder formalized the role of committees in a simple model where committees had gatekeeping power.[29] If there was more voting, the story goes, there would be more dimensions uncovered by scaling techniques.

The selection-bias story is logically correct but empirically irrelevant. One important observation is that our low-dimensionality result applies not only to the House, but also to the Senate, where gatekeeping is less prevalent. Another is that certain legislation, particularly in regard to appropriations, must be considered annually and cannot be screened. Indeed, a very diverse set of issues gets voted on, even in a relatively small portion of the time that Congress is in session. Consider the three-month period between January 10, 1967 and April 10, 1967, during the 90th Congress, one of the textbook Congresses that inspired the new institutionalism's emphasis on committee jurisdictions and rules (Shepsle and Weingast, 1994), including gatekeeping powers. How winnowed were the issues? During this period, contested votes (over 2.5 percent on the minority side) in the House of Representatives were taken on the following issues:

1. The seating of Adam Clayton Powell, Jr.
2. The debt ceiling
3. Foreign travel by members of the Agriculture Committee
4. The Vietnam War
5. Emergency food assistance to India
6. The interest-equalization tax

7. The establishment of a National Holiday Commission

8. Appropriation for the Trust Territory of the Pacific Islands

9. Appropriations for various cabinet-level departments

10. The Alliance for Progress

11. The size of the staff for the Committee on Science and Astronautics

12. Funds for the House Un-American Activities Committee

13. Copyright law

Winnowing may have occurred but the range of substantive issues voted on remains vast. If one were to consider the entire length of the 90th House, a much wider variety of issues would appear. Clearly, the breadth of issues is large enough to manifest high dimensionality.

To make our observation for the 90th House more systematic, at least in a crude way, we computed, for each of the first 100 Houses and Senates, the Herfindahl concentration index[30] for the six Clausen categories. The lower the degree of concentration, the more diverse the agenda. The observation that the index is related to trend (the correlation [R] is $-.046$ for the House and -0.53 for the Senate) suggests that the congressional agenda has become more diverse as government has expanded. The index is significantly correlated with the geometric mean probabilities from the two-dimensional, linear-trend model, but in a counterhypothesis direction for the House ($R= -0.31$), with the results for the Senate being quite low ($R= 0.15$) but in the "correct" direction. For the House, as the roll call set becomes more diverse, the model fits better. The House result is undoubtedly spurious. The worst fitting years occur early in the time series while the agenda has become more diverse over time. Indeed, diversity of the agenda, at least as measured by this index, is not significantly related to the ability (difference in geometric mean probabilities) of the two-dimensional model to improve over the one-dimensional linear model ($R=-0.06$ for the House and -0.05 for the Senate, respectively).

One reason for these generally negative results for the diversity hypothesis is that the index has exhibited little variation. For Congresses 40 to 100, the index averaged 0.347 with a standard deviation of 0.061 in the House and averaged 0.361 with a standard deviation of 0.166 in the Senate. At least since the end of the Civil War period, Congress has had a full and wide-ranging agenda, so low-dimensional voting has not occurred simply because votes are restricted to a narrow topical area.

In a nutshell, the roll call voting agenda of Congress is always a cornucopia of diverse issues, even if many issues are screened from the agenda. This diversity notwithstanding, to the extent that spatial models are useful in describing the roll call voting data, only low-dimensional models are needed.

Summary

Congressional roll call voting, throughout most of American history, has had a simple structure. A two-dimensional spatial model that allows for a linear time trend accounts for most of roll call voting. The primary dimension is concerned with political party and economic redistribution while the second dimension picks up issues that split the two major parties. Race has been the most important issue dividing the political parties internally.

We now turn to an examination of the temporal stability of individual legislator positions; the changes in position that are brought about by the replacement of legislators; and the polarization of the parties within each of the political-party systems.

Appendix: Roll Call Coding Categories

Coding Schemes

Below, we detail the three coding schemes we used to classify all the roll call votes in the first 100 Houses and Senates. For the Clausen and Peltzman schemes, we list some illustrative issue areas that fall within each category; our own specific issue codes comprise the third scheme.

Each roll call received at most one specific issue code, exactly one Clausen code, and one or two Peltzman codes.

Our specific issue codes are not exhaustive. Some historical topics were not covered. Researchers interested in other topics can find them quickly by using the keyword search structure in VOTEVIEW. VOTEVIEW is freeware that can be downloaded from either voteview.ucsd.edu or voteworld. berkeley.edu.

Clausen Categories

1. Government management: environmental control; government regulation of business; natural-resource management; government ownership of business; government control of the economy; budget balancing; tax policy; interest rates; management of the bureaucracy.

2. Social welfare: social security; public housing; urban renewal; labor regulation; education; urban affairs; employment opportunities and rewards; welfare; Medicare; unemployment; minimum wage; legal services.

3. Agriculture: price supports and subsidies; commodity control; acreage limitations.

4. Civil liberties: civil rights; equality; criminal procedure; privacy; guarantees of the Bill of Rights; slavery; Hatch Act.

5. Foreign and defense policy: international policy; foreign aid; aid to international organizations; armament policy; defense procurement; international trade; military pensions.

6. Miscellaneous policy: unclassifiable or unidentifiable votes; all votes concerned with internal organization of Congress; procedural motions.

Peltzman Categories

1. Budget — general interest: debt limit; budget targets; revenue sharing; unemployment insurance; tax rates; continuing appropriations.
2. Budget — special interest: authorization/appropriations for agencies, departments; public works; subsidized housing; NSF; parks; food stamps.
3. Regulation — general interest: general tariffs; minimum wage; gasoline rationing; auto emissions; water pollution.
4. Regulation — special interest: union regulations; coal mine regulations; export/import controls; fish and wildlife.
5. Domestic social policy: abortion; school prayer; busing; criminal code and federal courts; immigration; gun control; Hatch Act; veterans' preferences; Legal Services Corporation; voting rights; slavery.
61. Defense policy-budget: authorization/appropriations for the military; military pensions.
71. Defense policy — resolutions: number of Army divisions; duties of officers.
62. Foreign policy — budget: authorization/appropriations for State Department and international organizations.
72. Foreign policy — resolutions: condemn/thank foreign nations; U.S.-Taiwanese relations; disapproval of apartheid.
8. Government organization: setting up new agencies/bureaus/commissions; civil service regulations; government reorganization; Federal Election Commission; constitutional amendments; admission of states; census.
9. Internal organization: election of House Speaker; party ratios on committees; creating committees; procedural rules; disputed elections; congressional pay.
10. Indian affairs: Indian treaties; appropriations for Indian Department; Indian lands and reservations.
11. D.C.: all votes dealing with the District of Columbia.

Specific Issue Codes

1. Abortion/care of deformed newborns
2. Agriculture
3. Airlines/airports/airline industry
4. Alien and Sedition Acts
5. Amnesty (all wars)

6. Arms control
7. B-1 Bomber
8. Banking and finance
9. Breeder reactor
10. Budget resolution
11. CIA/spying/intelligence
12. Campaign contributions/house ethics/lobbying/campaign laws
13. Central America
14. Children (aid, infant mortality, etc.)
15. Civil rights/desegregation/busing/affirmative action
16. Civil service and patronage
17. Coal mining regulation/strip mining/black lung
18. Communists/Communism/un-American activities
19. Congressional pay and benefits
20. Constitutional amendments
21. Consumer Protection Agency/consumer protection
22. Debt ceilings
23. Disputed elections to Congress
24. Education
25. Election of House officers
26. Election of the Speaker of the House
27. Electoral votes
28. Emergency fuel assistance
29. Energy
30. Exchange rates
31. Firearms
32. Fish & wildlife
33. Food stamps/food programs
34. Gasoline rationing/allocation
35. Handicapped
36. Homosexuality
37. Housing/housing programs/rent control
38. Human rights
39. Humanitarian assistance (foreign)
40. Immigration/naturalization
41. Impeachment of the president
42. Impeachments and investigations
43. Interstate commerce/anti-trust/restraint of commerce
44. Iran
45. Judiciary
46. Korean war

47. MX missile
48. Mediterranean pirates
49. Military pensions/veterans benefits
50. Minimum wage
51. Minorities (nonblack)
52. Narcotics
53. National bank
54. Neutron bomb
55. Nuclear power
56. Nuclear weapons
57. Nullification/secession/reconstruction
58. OSHA
59. Panama Canal
60. Parks and conservation
61. Peace movements/pacifism/anti-military
62. Pollution and environmental protection
63. Impeachment of officials other than the president
64. Price controls
65. Public health
66. Public lands
67. Public safety
68. Public works
69. Radio/television/motion pictures/telecommunications
70. Railroads
71. Ratio of representatives to population
72. Religion
73. Supersonic transport
74. School prayer
75. Science and technology
76. Selective service (the draft)
77. Shipping/maritime
78. Slavery
79. Social Security
80. South Africa/Rhodesia
81. Space exploration/NASA
82. States' rights versus federal government
83. Supreme Court
84. Taiwan (1979–80)
85. Tariffs
86. Tax rates
87. Temperance and liquor

88. Treaties
89. United Nations
90. U.S. Currency
91. Unemployment/jobs
92. Union regulation/Davis-Bacon/Common Situs Picketing Bill
93. Vietnam War
94. Voting rights
95. World War I
96. Welfare
97. Whiskey Rebellion
98. Women's equality
99. Workplace conditions/eight-hour day

Notes

1. Pairs and announced votes were treated as actual votes.
2. A correct classification is, as in chapter 2, one for which the legislator's ideal point is on the "correct" side of the estimated roll call cutting point or cutting line — that is, the DW-NOMINATE model assigns a probability greater than $\frac{1}{2}$ to the actual choice (Yea or Nay).
3. These were changes from major party to major party or major party to independent. For a complete list of all party changes see Nokken and Poole (2004).
4. See Costner (1965) and Hildebrand et al. (1977) for discussion of the use of PRE measures in evaluating the fit of models.
5. Since the denominator in the expression above is constant for all entries for a house of Congress in Table 3.1, the entries in the *APRE* part of the table are simply linear transformations of the corresponding classification entries.
6. In this book, we rely mainly on substantive relevance and less often on tests of statistical significance (or on standard errors). Previously (Poole and Rosenthal, 1991a) we have presented various tests of significance. The standard tests presented there typically supported our substantive statements at truly infinitesimal p-value levels (see chapter 9 for discussion of p-values). The luxury of over 14,000,000 observations allows us to focus on the big picture and not to be preoccupied with whether a tree belongs in the forest. For example, given our sample size, adding dimensions or time-polynomial terms always makes statistically significant increments to the log-likelihood without really adding to our ability to understand roll call voting behavior. For a discussion of standard errors, see Appendix A to *Congress, 1997* and Lewis and Poole (2004).
7. To derive the theoretical distribution of error we computed the probabilities for each legislator on every roll call using the estimated model parameters (see Appendix A in *Congress, 1997* for details). The smaller of the Yea probability and the Nay probability is the probability of an error. The "theoretical" line shown in Figure 3.2 is the average of these error probabilities broken down by distance from the cutting line.
8. Recall that our dynamic estimation included all nonunanimous roll calls from 1789 through 2004.

9. About 15 percent of all roll calls are constrained, but constraints are most often invoked for lopsided roll calls. Constraints are invoked for less than 1 percent of the roll calls that are closer than 55–45. Almost all roll calls of interest to scholars are unconstrained. In contrast, constraints are needed on more than half of the most lopsided votes — those with a minority percentage of less than 10 percent. See Poole and Rosenthal (1991a) and Appendix A to *Congress, 1997* for more detail.

10. We used Kenneth Martis's (1989) *Historical Atlas of Political Parties in the United States Congress: 1789–1989* to determine the majority and minority parties for each of the first 100 Houses and Senates.

11. Indeed, in the presidential election of 1812 Madison and the Jeffersonians became identified as the "war party" and Madison won reelection with the solid backing of the South and the West. De Witt Clinton, the Federalist candidate, carried every northern state except Pennsylvania and Vermont. For a good summary account of the War of 1812, see Hofstadter, Miller, and Aaron (1959, vol. 1, pp. 332–347). For its effect on the Federalist party see Hofstadter (1969, chapter 5).

12. Throughout this volume, the South is defined as the eleven states of the Confederacy plus Oklahoma and Kentucky.

13. We defined a North-versus-South vote as one where at least one political party was divided along regional lines, with a majority of southern members opposing a majority of northern members on the roll call. We then examined a histogram for just these roll calls; the "N vs. S" in Figures 3.3 and 3.4 indicates where the bulk of these roll call cutting lines fell.

14. Note that the North vs. South roll call cutting line angles for the 35th Congress were concentrated between about 10 degrees and 35 degrees in the Senate and about 150 to 170 degrees in the House. These differences are not as great as they appear because the angles wrap around. Furthermore, not only were there no Republicans in the South but also southern Democrats tended to be to the left of northern Democrats. These two facts imply that the cutting lines separating the North and the South are not as pinned down as in other eras.

15. We argue in chapter 5 that a realignment, in congressional voting, must be a structural change in the basic dimensions of voting. No such change occurred in the 1890s or 1930s. These realignments of the mass electorate were marked by a wholesale replacement of members of Congress. However, the replacement did not affect the basic structure of congressional voting, as it did in the 1850s.

16. See Poole and Rosenthal (1994a) for details.

17. Because of our stringent definition of a party-line roll call, the number of roll calls meeting the definition was quite small in some Houses and Senates. In fifteen Senates and eight Houses, the number of party-line votes dropped below five. Not surprisingly, these were concentrated in the Era of Good Feelings (Congresses 15-18, [1817–1824]), when there was, as a practical matter, no minority party.

18. The other main culprits were John Blaine of Wisconsin; Robert Howell of Nebraska; William McMaster of South Dakota; Lynn Frazier of North Dakota; and Smith Brookhart of Iowa. In addition, William Borah of Idaho, Peter Norbeck of South Dakota, and Gerald Nye of North Dakota were located at the right edge of the Democrats on the first dimension and above most of the Democrats on the second dimension.

19. The midwestern Republicans in the House during this same period were more moderate than their northeastern counterparts. They were located on the left edge of

the party cloud and somewhat above the northeasterners on the second dimension. Unlike their senatorial counterparts, however, they were much closer to their fellow Republicans than to the Democrats.

20. This section on the second dimension is incorporated from *Congress, 1997* and is based on the D-NOMINATE scaling.

21. Not every roll call received a specific issue code. Our ninety-nine-issue categories were designed to pick up the most important policy issues, not all issues.

22. The accuracy of our coding depends on the accuracy of the descriptions of the roll call votes in the ICPSR codebooks. The codebook descriptions sometimes do not reflect the true character of the roll calls. For example, a critical vote on the Wilmot Proviso (August 8, 1846) concerning slavery was, formally speaking, a vote on foreign-affairs appropriations—the codebook description does not mention the Wilmot Proviso. Whenever, from other sources, we know of such instances we have coded the roll calls and corrected the codebooks appropriately. (We are thankful to Barry Weingast for alerting us to this example.)

23. The first presidential candidates to identify themselves as Whigs were William H. Harrison, Hugh L. White, and Daniel Webster, all of whom received electoral votes in 1836. For the Jacksonian period (1823-1837), Martis (1989) codes members of Congress as being either "Jacksons" or varieties of "Anti-Jacksons." We use Martis's codings throughout this book and follow his classifications.

24. We recognize that slavery, before the Civil War, was an economic issue as well as a race issue. Indeed, as Fogel (1989) argues, the abolitionists were not very successful in their fight against slavery until they were able to cast it as an economic issue ("Free soil, free speech, free labor, and free men"). We maintain the distinction for clarity.

25. We also chose the 85th House because it was studied with other methods by Weisberg (1968). Weisberg analyzed roll calls for sets of issue areas, such as foreign policy, within this House. He finds very high dimensionality. Our results indicate that his methods were inappropriate.

26. Weighting the dimensions causes the indifference curves shown in Figure 2.4 to become ellipses. Some legislators could have ellipses elongated on the vertical dimension; others, on the horizontal. An even more general, and still less parsimonious, model would allow for variation in the angle of rotation with respect to the basic space, of the axes of the ellipses. See Enelow and Hinich (1984) for technical details.

27. Dynamic model results in this section are based on the D-NOMINATE scaling and incorporated directly from *Congress, 1997*.

28. It is difficult to pin these lower correlations on a specific item. In the 95th Congress, foreign- and defense-policy votes included 14 on the CIA, spying, or intelligence; 11 on South Africa or Rhodesia; 7 on the Panama Canal; 7 on the B-1 Bomber; 5 on arms control; and 5 on the United Nations.

29. The original gatekeeping model was presented by Denzau and Mackay (1983), who adapted the agenda-control model in Romer and Rosenthal (1978, 1979) to a legislative setting.

30. If ρ_a is the proportion of roll calls in category a, the index H is given by $H = \Sigma_a \rho_a^2$. H equals 1.0 if all the votes are in one category. For the Clausen categories, H would reach a minimum of 1/6 if the roll calls split evenly among the six categories.

4

The Spatial Model: Stability, Replacement, and Polarization

Introduction

This chapter takes a broad look at policy change in American history, with policy measured by both the location of groups of legislators and the locations of winning roll call outcomes in the voting space. Policy change can occur either because legislators' preferences change or because there is a change in the institutional structure that aggregates the preferences to produce policies. In this chapter, we concentrate on changes in preferences and on how changes in majority control of either house translates preferences into policy outcomes.

In the first section of the chapter, we look at changes in the mean positions of the major political parties in the three major party systems: the Federalist/Republican system; the Whig/Democratic; and the Republican/Democratic. We find that there were some important changes in the positions of the parties, but much more modest changes in the mean positions of either house. Nonetheless, as a result of the "tyranny of the majority," slight changes in mean position, when accompanied by a shift in majority control, can lead to substantial changes in policy. The policy changes are discussed in the second section. We find that the swings in policy during the nineteenth and early twentieth centuries were much greater than those of the later twentieth century. Although the New Deal initiated a large policy shift comparable to those of the nineteenth century, after the end of World War II policy swings dampened considerably. After the Republicans took control of Congress in the 1994 elections, policy has swung sharply to the right, resembling the abrupt shifts found a century earlier. This chapter seeks to identify the origin of these changes.

Indeed, the preferences expressed in a legislature can change because individual legislators change their own preferences, as measured by their spatial position. We show in the third section that our estimates of legislator coordinates are very stable from Congress to Congress, with the correlations almost always exceeding 0.95. Given this stability in legislator coordinates, changes in preferences must occur almost entirely through the process of replacing retiring or defeated legislators. Therefore, in the fourth section, we consider replacement in Congress, including a detailed analysis of replacement since Reconstruction. In particular, we note that, beginning in 1936, successive waves of northern and southern Democratic replacements in Congress had the effect of shifting the northern Democrat delegation to the Left on the first dimension and shifting southern Democrats to the center on the first dimension and sharply upward on the second dimension. The Republican Party remained fairly stable, although, through the 1960s, it drifted to the Left in the House and Senate and subsequently has moved back to the right again. In the early years of the twenty-first century, the Republicans in Congress are as conservative as they were at the beginning of the twentieth century.

Finally, we investigate the polarization of preferences. We develop measures of the dispersion of political parties around their respective party mean positions, and of the degree of separation of the two major parties within each stable period. These measures allow us to compare various party systems over time. We find that the most polarized period in Congressional voting was from post-Reconstruction through the end of World War I. In contrast, the post-World War II period was the least polarized of the major party systems largely due to the north-south split within the Democratic Party. In contrast, the last thirty years have been one of increasing polarization, reaching levels that match those a century earlier.

The History of Party Positions in the Basic Space

The overall first dimension mean positions since Reconstruction for the House and the Senate are one of the two series shown in Figure 4.1. The same information for the Federalist/Jeffersonian Republican period and the Whig-Democrat period is shown for the House in Figure 4.2.

There is little variation in these overall means. The shifts are largely due to shifts in the party balance in a house. For example, the mean has a general liberal tendency in the upper panel of Figure 4.2, reflecting the Jeffersonians' gradual rise to dominance. In the lower panel, the two instances of Whig control are marked by a conservative movement. Similarly, Figure 4.1 shows Congress becoming more conservative during the realignment to the Republicans

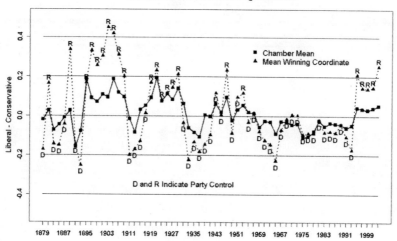

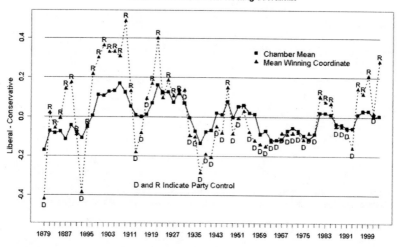

Figure 4.1. Chamber means for legislators and winning outcomes on roll calls, post-Reconstruction (1879–2004). The legislator series is quite stable, reflecting a competitive two-party system. The winning outcomes are more volatile, largely reflecting changes in control within a chamber. Outcomes in both houses become very liberal after the Great Depression, but only the Senate swings to the right after 1980, when the Republicans take the Senate but the Democrats retain the House. The results are for the first dimension, DW-NOMINATE model with linear trend. The tokens "D" and R" indicate which party controlled each house.

of the mass electorate in the 1890s. The change is especially evident in the Senate, which had been stacked (Stewart and Weingast, 1992) with senators from pro-Republican Western states. This is followed by a liberal shift during the Progressive Era; a conservative shift during the period of Republican dominance that followed World War I; a liberal shift begun by the Great Depression; and a conservative swing of the pendulum again in the 1940s. The House shows a long period of stability during the years of Democratic control beginning in 1954; the stability is ended by the rightward movement produced by the 1994 elections. The same stability is broken earlier for the Senate by the Republicans making unexpected gains in the 1980 elections.

We can discuss changes in the mean for both houses in the same breath because these changes reflect more fundamental issues that politicians had to confront (such as the Great Depression), than the differences in the institutional structure of the two houses. That the power of the Speaker has varied in the history of the House (Cooper and Brady, 1981), or that the use of closed rules has varied, or that cloture rules were changed in the Senate seem not to count for very much. During the post-Reconstruction period (after 1879), the first-dimension chamber means correlate at 0.77; and they correlate at 0.87 after 1900. Much of the differences in the series have to do with differences in the party ratios in the two chambers, due, in turn, either to differences in apportionment and mode of election; to staggered, six-year terms in the Senate; or to random shifts in votes, such as the election in which the Republicans won control of the Senate in 1980 by capturing several states with very small margins. Indeed, a simple regression, with the Senate first-dimension mean as the dependent variable and the House first dimension-mean and the difference between the Republican chamber proportions as independent variables, produces an R^2 of 0.87 for the post-Reconstruction period. For the period from 1901 through 2004, the R^2 is 0.95.

In contrast, the second dimension exhibits little overall variation. The second dimension is important, only sporadically, when it captures the conflicts involving race in the mid-nineteenth and mid-twentieth centuries. In the post-Reconstruction period, the second dimension is only modestly correlated across houses (0.45). This is because the second dimension has generally served only to differentiate parties internally on secondary issues that are rarely central to national politics.[1]

Figures 4.3 and 4.4 show that, in contrast to the chamber means, party means exhibit more variation during the post-Reconstruction period. The most striking features on the first dimension are the seventy-year rightward drift of the southern Democrats in both chambers and the narrowing of the gap between the Democrats and Republicans by the 1950s. These changes are largely common to the party delegations in both chambers. The cross-chamber

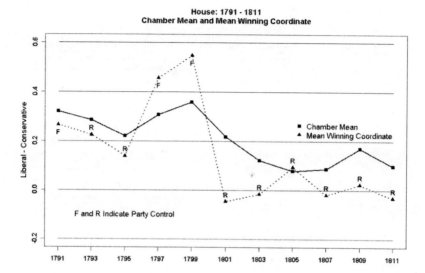

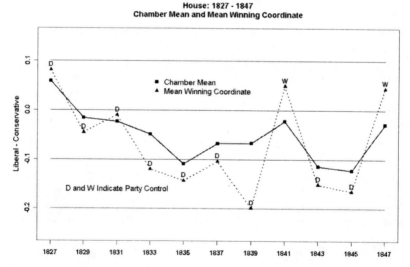

Figure 4.2. Chamber means for legislators and winning outcomes on House of Representatives roll calls in the first two-party systems. The legislator series is quite stable, reflecting a competitive two-party system. The winning outcomes are more volatile, largely reflecting changes in control within a chamber. Outcomes become more liberal with the ascendancy of the Jeffersonians in 1801. There is less volatility in the Whig-Democrat period but the most conservative outcomes do occur in the two Houses controlled by the Whigs (1841 and 1847). The results are for the first dimension, DW-NOMINATE model with linear trend. The tokens indicate which party controlled the House.

correlations are 0.93 for Republicans and 0.84 for Democrats. Both of these correlations are higher than the entire chamber correlation (0.77), which is consistent with our claim that cross-chamber differences are largely matters of differences in party ratios.

In the nineteenth century, the southern Democrats were to the Left of their northern counterparts on the first dimension. Beginning at the turn of the twentieth century, both northern and southern Democrats drifted towards the center, until the 1920s, when the northern Democrats began moving back to the Left. The northern Democrats generally move leftward through the New Deal, with the effect being more pronounced in the Senate. The southern Democrats cross over the northern Democrats by the early 1940s and continue to move steadily to the Right until the mid-to-late 1960s. After the passage of the Civil Rights Act of 1964 and the Voting Rights Act of 1965, the southern Democrats began to slowly move back to the Left again but were still considerably to the right of their northern counterparts at the end of our time series in 2004.

The House Republicans drift slowly to the Left until the early 1970s, dramatically narrowing the gap between themselves and the Democrats. Beginning in the 1970s they begin to move back to the Right. The pattern for the Senate Republicans is basically the same as their House counterparts but the leftward movement is not as smooth as in the House. That the House Republicans are now somewhat more conservative than Senate Republicans is consistent with House Republicans, led by Newt Gingrich and defined by the "Contract with America," being the more radical advocates of conservative policies in the mid 1990s.

The two chambers differ somewhat in their patterns of change on the second dimension. The Democrat cross-chamber correlation is 0.69. Similarly, the correlation for northern Democrats is only 0.60 while the correlation for southern Democrats is 0.67. The pattern here is somewhat different than what we reported in *Congress, 1997*. The two chambers became more similar in the 1990s, so adding data since 1989 made a difference. At the same time, adding the more recent data weakened the correlation for the southern Democrats, probably because Democratic representatives from southern minority-majority districts in the House were distinct from southern Democratic senators. The senators, of course, all represented constituencies where no minority was a majority. At the same time, earlier events leave this correlation higher than that for northern Democrats. In the civil rights era, in both houses, the southern Democrats separated from northern Democrats and moved upward in a "socially" conservative direction. The Republicans responded to the same issues by moving downward in a "northern" or "socially liberal" direction. The biggest separation of the parties on the second dimension occurs in the mid-1960s during the voting on the civil rights bills. After the New Deal, the second dimension captures the race or civil rights issue.

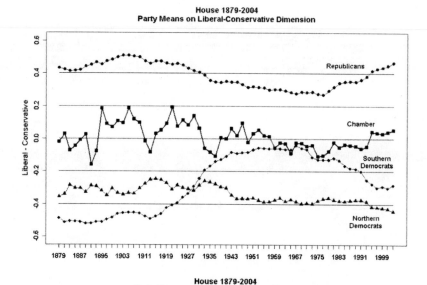

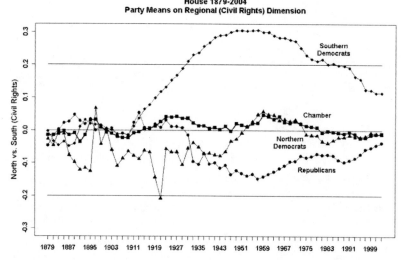

Figure 4.3. Mean legislator coordinates, by party, House of Representatives, post-Reconstruction (1879–2004).

Before the second New Deal, there is an important difference between the chambers that relates to the Republican cross-chamber correlation being only 0.59. In 1925, the second dimension mean in the House was higher for the Republicans than for the Democrats. The reverse was true in the Senate. Recall our discussion of party-line voting in chapter 3 — specifically, the results dis-

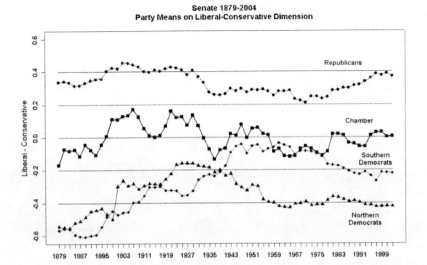

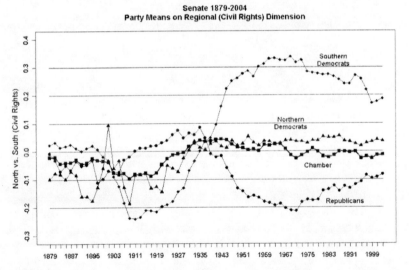

Figure 4.4. Mean legislator coordinates, by party, Senate, post-Reconstruction (1879–2004).

played in Figure 3.5. The second dimension was needed from the 69th Senate through the 74th (1925–1936) to fully account for party line voting because a small group of midwestern Republican senators voted with the Democrats to such an extent that they were located just above the Democratic Party — among them on the first dimension but above them on the second. The midwestern

Republicans cause the Republicans' mean on the second dimension to be greater than the mean of the Democrats in the 1925 Senate. The Republican mean crosses over the Democrats only in 1940.[2] Thereafter, the Republicans' second-dimension mean is less than the mean of the Democrats.

The pattern of sharp differences in overall party means, including important regional differences within parties, holds also for the two earlier party systems, which are shown in Figures 4.5 and 4.6. In both cases, we have broken the parties down into northern and southern wings to aid in the interpretation of the dimensions.

Figure 4.5 shows the development of the Federalist/Jeffersonian Republican system for the 1789–1811 period (Congresses 1–12) for the House of Representatives. Although the authors of the Constitution opposed political parties (Hofstadter, 1969, pp. 40–73), by the second Congress two voting blocs emerged — one being identified with the policies of Alexander Hamilton and the other with Thomas Jefferson's policies. These became the Federalist and Jeffersonian Republican parties.[3]

Figure 4.5 clearly shows the evolution of a political party system. By the 5th House (which was elected in 1796), the Federalists and Jeffersonian Republicans are distinctly separated on the first dimension with no meaningful North-South effects occurring. The emergence of party polarization on the first dimension does not affect the stability of the chamber mean, as shown in Figure 4.2. A coherent two-party pattern on the second dimension does not emerge until the 7th Congress (which was elected in 1800). After 1800, the second dimension, though minor in importance, is clearly a North-South dimension, which arises as slavery takes a more important place on the agenda (see chapter 5).

Figure 4.6 shows the Whig-Democrat party system for the 1827–1848 period.[4] We begin with the elections of 1826 because the presidential election of 1824 split the Jeffersonian Republicans into blocs that aligned themselves with the presidential candidates, Jackson, Clay, and Crawford.[5] It ends with the elections of 1846, because the Congress elected in 1848 wrote the Compromise of 1850, which destabilized the Whig/Democrat party system (see chapter 5).

Once again we see the emergence of a coherent two-party system. Before the election of Andrew Jackson in 1828, the two wings of the Democratic party are quite distinct on the first dimension, with no coherent structure at all on the second dimension. By 1833 the two wings of the Democratic party are indistinguishable on the first dimension; the southern Whigs are the more moderate wing of the Whig party. The second dimension clearly evolves into a North-South dimension, with the separation occurring as early as 1829.

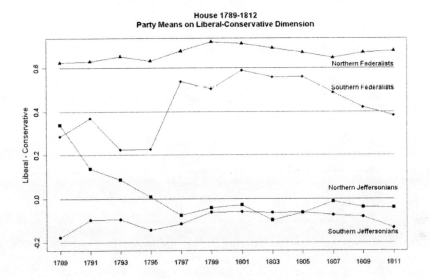

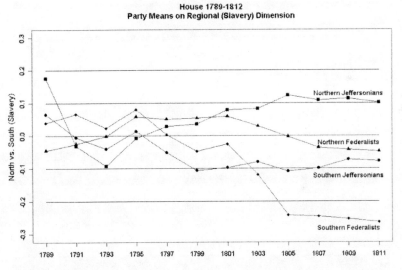

Figure 4.5. Mean legislator coordinates, by party and region, House of Representatives, Federalist-Jeffersonian party system (1789–1812). As the party system becomes organized, party differentiates on the first dimension and region on the second.

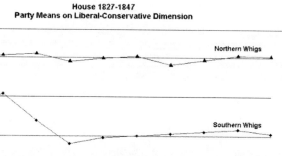

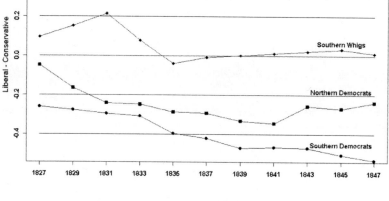

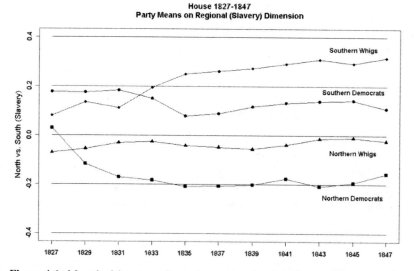

Figure 4.6. Mean legislator coordinates by party and region, House of Representatives, Whig-Democrat system (1827–1848). Party differentiates on the first dimension. As the conflict over slavery builds, regions become differentiated on the second dimension.

Party Polarization and Policy Swings

We have observed that during the periods of the three two-party systems in American history, the parties have been polarized on at least the first of the two dimensions of the basic space. At the same time, the means of the two dimensions are quite stable. In contrast to our finding of stability, shifts in the means could have occurred in the following way. Moderates, when elected, would have long tenures in office and be a fixed point in our dynamic estimation. Electoral swings would put large numbers of extreme liberals in office in one year and replace them with extreme conservatives two years later. But, the data tell us that very large swings of this form rarely happen in American politics. If extreme liberals enter Congress, they are typically offset by the entry of extreme conservatives.

The result is not surprising. Because the parties need to win office to enjoy the spoils and to make policy, competitive forces should lead them to be reasonably balanced. At the same time, they could represent polarized rather than convergent positions, both out of a need to appeal to partisan bases or to satisfy their own ideology[6] and out of incentives to polarize inherent in the American system of checks and balances.[7]

Suppose the two parties were very disciplined and at loggerheads on every issue. In this case, every roll call vote would be along party lines and every member within each party would vote identically. Then every member within each party would have the same coordinate so just two points would represent all the legislators — all the members of one party at one point; all the members of the second party at another point. Such a system would be a perfectly polarized one.

In this perfectly polarized system, the majority party would win every vote and every vote would be a "perfect" one in that a simple spatial model, with two locations for the corresponding members of the two parties, would fit the voting perfectly. One party would vote Yea, the other Nay, and there would be no voting errors. Moreover, the disciplined, majority party would exercise agenda control and propose its ideal point on every roll call. The outcome would always be the majority party's ideal point. Thus, any shift in party control would lead to a large swing in policy. In the Senate, shifting from a 51R–49D ratio to a 49R–51D would change the mean coordinate only slightly, but policy would shift dramatically.

In such a system, a graphic plot of policy outcome means in time would look like a perfect square wave with the swings corresponding to whichever party had majority control. Unfortunately, measuring these swings accurately is very difficult. As we explained in chapter 2, even though the cutting line (or point in one dimension) is always identified, we need some error to be present to identify the Yea and Nay outcome locations. If a roll call vote fits our model perfectly — that is, everyone on the Yea side of the cutting line votes Yea and everyone on the Nay side of the cutting line votes Nay — then any pair of points equidistant and on opposite sides of the cutting line is consistent with the perfect vote. Unfortunately (or fortunately) for us, as we have documented in this chapter and in chapter 3, our model fits the roll call data so well that, on many roll calls, there is not enough error to clearly identify the Yea/Nay outcome locations.

Nevertheless, we can at least get a rough idea of the extent of policy swings by selecting the subset of roll calls with at least one outcome inside the space spanned by the legislators and by using the mean of the winning coordinate of this subset as a measure of policy swings over time.[8] This will not be a perfect measure, but it will at least identify the periods of dramatic change.[9] Of course, our measure is an imperfect measure of policy since many roll calls are directed at position-taking by legislators rather than at actual legislation and because many provisions passed by one house are not passed by the other house, deleted by a conference committee, or subjected to a sustained veto by the president.

Figure 4.1 shows the policy swings on the first dimension for the House and Senate for the post-Reconstruction, Democratic/Republican party system and Figure 4.2 shows the House for the other two periods we analyzed above. In both figures, policy swings are much more volatile than changes in the chamber medians.

With the end of Reconstruction and the revival of the Democratic Party, policy swings become quite large through World War II. There is a large, prolonged conservative swing during the period of Republican dominance from the election of 1896 to that of 1912. There is also a conservative swing in the House in the 1920s. It is dampened in the Senate because of the group of midwestern Republicans (discussed earlier) who were voting with the Democrats on many issues. The Great Depression induced a liberal swing. It occurred earlier in the House, since the Democrats first gained control of the House in the 1930 elections and took the Senate only in 1932.

After World War II, the splitting of the Democratic Party into northern and southern wings had the effect of considerably dampening swings in both chambers. There is some volatility induced by Republican control in the 80th (1947–48) and the 83rd (1953–54) Congresses. Policies between 1954 and 1980 were generally liberal, especially during the Great Society and the Watergate period of the Nixon presidency. Policies were less liberal when Democratic congressional majorities were offset by a weak Democratic president (Johnson in his last two years and Carter) or a strong Republican president (Nixon in his first term and Reagan in his first two years). The sharp swing in the Senate due to the Republicans gaining control of that body in 1981 foreshadowed the swing in both chambers after the Republican victory in the 1994 midterm elections.

As the southern Democratic Party faded and the two parties became more homogeneous, polarization increased. Policy swings like those seen in the nineteenth and early twentieth centuries are likely to return.

Figure 4.2 shows that the victory of the Jeffersonians in the elections of 1800 had a dramatic impact on policy. This comports well with historical accounts of the bitterness of the landmark 1800 elections (Hofstadter, 1969). Subsequent to the 1800 elections, policy moderated dramatically.

Recall that Figure 4.6 shows that in its early period, the Whig/Democrat party system was not well structured and we see the same lack of structure in Figure 4.2. The two wings of the Democratic Party did not coalesce until 1833, and it was only then that policy swings to the left of the chamber mean. The two large peaks in 1841 and 1847 correspond to the only Whig majorities during this period.

Our observations about the sources of policy swings are summarized in the regressions reported in Table 4.1. In the first column for either chamber, we regressed the mean winning policy coordinate on the indicator variables for party control of the House, the Senate, and the presidency and for the Republican Party's seat share in both houses. In the second column, we eliminated party control of the opposite house and control of the presidency since these variables were not statistically significant in the first column. (Because the policy process can be expected to exhibit persistence over time, we corrected for first-order autocorrelation.) The observations are given for the sixty-three Congresses that served from 1879 through 2004. Note that every variable (except for the intercept) has the theoretically expected positive sign, although the Senate share variable is not significant in the House regression.

Each chamber is quite responsive to internal partisan balance. A shift in partisan control in the House shifts the mean winning coordinate a little over 0.2 units or about one-tenth the span of the space. The shift in the Senate is only about one-half as much as in the House, consistent with the well known lesser degree of majority control in the Senate. A one percent increase in the Republicans' seat share moves policy rightwards more than 0.05 units. In Table 4.1, all internal chamber effects are highly statistically significant.

In contrast, neither chamber seems very responsive to the presidency. Although we pointed to shifts under Johnson, Nixon, Carter, and Reagan, there is no systematic evidence that, after controlling for seat shares, Congress responds to the partisan identity of the president. Similarly, there is no evidence that one house accommodates to partisan control of the other. There is evidence that the Senate responds to seat share in the House but not vice-versa. The Senate's response to the House Republican share is somewhat smaller than its response to its own Republican share.[10]

We have obtained a strong positive result: Winning outcomes are highly responsive to the balance of partisan forces within each house of Congress.[11]

Table 4.1
Shifts in the House (1879–2004): Regressions with the Mean Winning Policy Coordinate First Dimension, as the Dependent Variable

| | COEFFICIENT | | | | |
| | HOUSE | | SENATE | | |
Variable	(1)	(2)	(1)	(2)	
C	−0.422***	−0.409***	−0.539***	−0.572***	Intercept Term
	(0.074)[a]	(0.073)	(0.089)	(0.083)	
HDUM	0.218***	0.192***	0.018		Party Controlling House
	(0.035)	(0.030)	(0.042)		(0=Democratic, 1=Republican)
SDUM	−0.048		0.096**	0.105***	Party Controlling Senate
	(0.031)		(0.037)	(0.031)	(0=Democratic, 1=Republican)
PRESDUM	0.031		0.038		Party Controlling presidency
	(0.023)		(0.027)		(0=Democratic, 1=Republican)
HREP	0.565***	0.579***	0.494**	0.513***	Republican Party's share of House Seats
	(0.146)	(0.146)	(0.174)	(0.147)	
SREP	0.253	0.220	0.577**	0.675**	Republican Party's share of Senate Seats
	(0.187)	(0.161)	(0.224)	(0.210)	
ρ	0.405	0.415	0.422	0.416	First-order autocorrelation
Adjusted R^2	0.792	0.780	0.682	0.682	
Standard error of regression	0.068	0.070	0.081	0.082	
Durban-Watson	1.157	1.146	1.100	0.960	
F-statistic	47.38	74.23	27.14	44.59	
Mean dependent variable	0.024	0.024	0.018	0.018	
Number of observations	63	63	63	63	

[a] Standard errors in parentheses.
* Statistically significant with one-tail p-value < 0.05.
** Statistically significant with one-tail p-value < 0.01.
*** Statistically significant with one-tail p-value < 0.001.

On the other hand, a negative result is that each house of Congress adopts its winning outcomes in a way that ignores the institutional structure of the legislative process. The overall absence of significant accommodation, particularly in the House, may indicate that most accommodation takes place in conference. Since conference reports are typically approved by overwhelming majorities, they tend to be constrained roll calls that are excluded from our analysis of winning coordinates. This finding would be consistent with the view that the bulk of roll call voting is concerned with position-taking rather than policy-making. Future research should investigate whether these results would hold when the computation of mean winning policy coordinates is restricted to policy-relevant votes.

Spatial Stability

We have seen that, to whatever extent roll call voting can be captured by a spatial model, a low-dimensional model — say, a one-and-a-half-dimensional one — suffices. Our estimates of the model have disclosed that, while the overall chamber means are relatively stable, there is considerable internal change within parties. Moreover, changes in party control induce dramatic changes in policy, as measured by mean winning coordinates.

Of course, it is meaningful to speak of changes in policy only if the dimension itself is stable in time. In this section, therefore, we address two issues: Is the major, first dimension stable in time, and are individual positions stable? If the answers to these two questions are both positive, we have to conclude that changes in the preferences expressed in the legislature occur through the replacement of legislators, a topic investigated in the next section. Replacement, particularly through its effect on party control, then induces the changes in policy we saw in the previous section.

The Stability of the Major Dimension

Given the pace of events, it would be possible for the major dimension to show rapid legislator shifts. In our dynamic model, very rapid shifts are foreclosed by our imposition of the restriction that individual movement can be only linear in time. This restriction fails to capture a few cases. For example, John McCain (R-AZ) started as a conservative, became a moderate after losing the Republican nomination to George Bush in 2000, and recently reemerged as very conservative. McCain is an exception. Though the absence of substantial gains in fit from using higher-order polynomial models (see Table 3.1) constitutes evidence that legislators do not shift back and forth in the space, we thought it important to evaluate stability in a manner that allows for the maximum possible adjustment.[12]

To perform this evaluation, we separately estimated coordinates for each House and Senate (W-NOMINATE coordinates) of Congresses 1 to 108. This procedure finds the best one-dimensional fit for each Congress and allows for the maximum Congress-to-Congress adjustment of individual positions. Because there is no constraint that ties the estimates together, we cannot compare individual coordinates directly, but we can compute the correlations between the coordinates for members common to two Houses or two Senates. Rather than deal with a sparse 108 by 108 correlation matrix, we focus on the correlations of the first 104 Congresses with each of the succeeding four Congresses.[13] This choice allows us to look at stability as far forward as one decade.

We averaged these correlations across the first 104 Congresses and for five periods of history. For both Houses of Congress, the separate scalings are remarkably similar, especially since the end of the Civil War, as seen in the upper portion of Table 4.2.[14] After 1861, a senator could count on a stable alignment, relative to his colleagues, over an entire six-year term. (A $t+1$ correlation refers to the correlation of coordinates of common members in one Congress and the succeeding Congress.) Since the election of Ronald Reagan in 1980, the stability has been especially striking.

In the lower portion of Table 4.2, we display the individual pairwise correlations only for situations where either the correlation of $t+1$ was less than 0.8 or a later correlation was less than 0.5 — that is, we show periods of instability. Consistent with the preceding discussion and the discussion of overall fit in chapter 3, the low correlations are overwhelmingly concentrated in pairs where at least one Congress preceded the end of the Civil War. No low correlation was found for any Congress after the 87th Congress through the last Congress we estimated, the 108th.

It is also noteworthy that a preponderance of the low correlations falls, for both Houses, in the Era of Good Feelings (pairs where at least one Congress falls in Congresses 14 to 18), and, for the Senate, in the period around 1850. These cases are not spatial flip-flops, where two solid major dimensions bear little relation to one another, but simply cases of a bad fit, where there is not a strong first dimension in a Congress. (The only geometric mean probabilities below 0.6 for the House W-NOMINATE scalings occur in Congresses 14, 15, 17, and 32; for the Senate W-NOMINATE scalings, Congresses 32 and 33 were the only ones below 0.6.)

Subsequent to the Civil War, there are no $t+1$ correlations below 0.8 for the House. In the Senate, there are some low correlations for the early 1930s (Senates 72–74 [1931–37]), during the party realignment in mass voting that was due to the Great Depression. But these are minor effects. The party realignments in mass voting in the 1890s and 1930s were reflected in congressional

Table 4.2
Correlations of Legislator Coordinates
from Static, Biennial Scalings

Averages For Years	SENATE t+1[a]	t+2	t+3	t+4	HOUSE t+1	t+2	t+3	t+4	Number of Congresses
1789–1860	.77	.77	.69	.55	.87	.81	.75	.70	36
1861–1900	.94	.91	.91	.91	.96	.95	.93	.95	20
1901–1944	.90	.85	.81	.78	.94	.93	.92	.91	22
1945–1980	.94	.92	.90	.87	.96	.94	.93	.91	18
1981–1996	.98	.97	.97	.97	.99	.98	.97	.96	8
1789–1996	.88	.86	.81	.75	.93	.90	.87	.85	104

Individual Congress[b]									
1 (1789)	.62	.72	.59	—[c]					
2 (1791)	.27	.35	—	—	.88	.84	.68	.38	
3 (1793)	.84	.75	.50	.01					
8 (1803)					.75	.78	.86	.79	
9 (1805)	.77	.93	.86	.83					
11 (1809)	.76	.73	.85	—					
13 (1813)	.93	.94	.64	.15	.93	.45	.30	.18	
14 (1815)	.70	.34	.13	.73	.18	.02	.07	.49	
15 (1817)	.30	.51	.46	.44	.88	.46	.55	.46	
16 (1819)	.10	.26	.57	.42	.60	.73	.78	.88	
17 (1821)	.22	.30	.05	.40	.59	.62	.74	.78	
18 (1823)	.26	.56	.51	.63	.62	.72	.79	.64	
20 (1827)					.94	.90	.55	.39	
21 (1829)					.94	.64	.46	.66	
22 (1831)	.77	.77	.85	.59	.73	.60	.78	.83	
27 (1841)	.95	.98	.93	.39					
30 (1847)	.62	.90	.69	.51					
31 (1849)	.26	.71	.89	.82					
32 (1851)	.65	.60	.62	.63	.76	.69	.63	.63	
36 (1859)					.90	.90	.59	.49	
37 (1861)					.96	.93	.42	.80	
72 (1931)	.90	.89	.60	.41					
73 (1933)	.90	.81	.70	.42					
74 (1935)	.78	.63	.40	.55					
77 (1941)	.74	.70	.79	.82					
84 (1955)	.97	.88	.89	.50					
87 (1961)	.78	.92	.85	.87					

[a] The notation $t+k$, $k = 1,2,3,4$ refers to the correlation of legislator coordinates for legislators serving in Congress t, given in the left-hand column, with their coordinates in Congress $t+k$. Correlation computed only for those legislators serving in both Congresses.

[b] Results shown only for those cases where either the $t+1$ correlation was less than 0.8, or where any $t+k$ correlation, $k = 2,3,4$, was less than 0.5, and there were at least 4 legislators in a pair of Congresses.

[c] A blank entry indicates that there were less than four legislators in common for a pair of Congresses.

voting as changes in the center of gravity along an existing dimension and not in any structural change of the voting dimensions. (See chapter 5.) The first dimension is remarkably stable; the stability persists except for two Senates between 1955 and 1962, when a second dimension was also important.

Stability of Individuals

It is possible to obtain high correlations when individuals are moving in the space. If members serving at time, t, all had nearly equal trend coefficients, their coordinates would remain highly correlated even if they were moving relative to individuals elected later than that time.

To assess the stability of individual positions in the space, we computed for each legislator the annual movement implied by the estimated trend coefficients in our two-dimensional, linear estimation. Given that the space we estimate is identified only up to translations and rotations, one has to interpret the movements in relative terms. The trend coefficient tells us whether an individual is moving relative to legislators whose careers have overlapped this member's.

Average trends for each Congress are shown in Figure 4.7. The figure shows only legislators serving in at least five Congresses — roughly a decade or more.[15] There is, at the most, only a slight decrease of trend with length of service. Senators serving in five or six Congresses (and thus reelected only once) showed an average trend of 0.08, compared to a slightly smaller trend of 0.07 for those serving in seven or more. But in the House there was no difference.[16]

In addition, spatial position is not related to length of career. The correlation between length of service and the absolute value of the first dimension position is only –0.03 in the House and –0.10 in the Senate.[17]

Another result — one we see as more important than the finding that spatial movement is limited for legislators with long careers — is shown in Figure 4.7. For the period before the Civil War, there is a choppy pattern in the figure, most likely, in part, a consequence of the smaller number of legislators who served in this period. Not only was Congress smaller, but a smaller proportion of its members served long terms. Our central result is for Congresses after the Civil War. Spatial movement, which was never very large relative to the span of the space, has been in secular decline, except for small upturns in the 1890s and the period following the Depression. Since roughly the mid-1950s, biennial movement has amounted to no more than 0.02 units. Since the 100th Congress, movement has increased in the House of Representatives. This increase appears to be largely an adaptation by Republicans to increased conservatism in new members of the Republican delegation. We emphasize, however, that this additional movement remains very small, no more than one percent of the span of the space.[18]

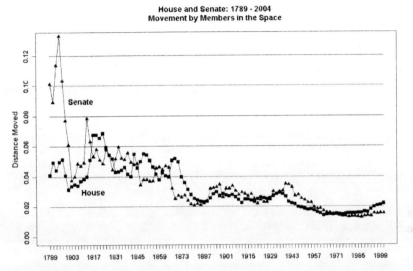

Figure 4.7. Movement of representatives and senators in the space. This figure shows the average distance moved by a member over a two-year period for those members serving at least five Congresses. The distance moved is computed from the linear trend coefficients for the two dimensions. Although the House and Senate are scaled independently, their patterns of movement have been highly similar since 1880. Movement has declined dramatically in both houses. The last points plotted represent the change from the 107th Congress (2001–02) to the 108th.

What is more striking than small differences between the House and Senate is the long-run similarity between the two houses. The patterns for the House and Senate are very similar over the post-Reconstruction period. The correlation between the House and Senate for Congresses 46 through 108 is 0.81.[19] Whatever forces are working to produce spatial stability have been operating on both chambers with equal intensity. Contemporary members of Congress do not adapt their positions during their careers but simply enter and maintain a fixed position until they die, retire, or are defeated in their ideological boots.

Indeed, this stability is so great that, even in their last Congress, members do not alter their liberal/conservative positions much. Similarly, they don't alter their positions if they are redistricted. The major change in behavior is that exiting members vote less often. This is shown in a study by Poole and Romer (1993). They used the absolute value of a representative's change in position from House t-1 to House t, in NOMINATE single House scalings, as their dependent variable.[20] Their principal independent variables measured the type of exit from the House of Representatives from 1947 through 1984.[21] Poole and Romer's regression analysis shows that, controlling for absenteeism, the type of exit — including voluntary retirement — has no effect on a member's position in the last Congress. Table 4.3 shows a portion of the Poole and Romer analysis.

None of the exit (dummy) variables is statistically significant.[22] (A representative who remained in Congress and was not redistricted has a 0 score on all exit variables.) Although there may in fact be shirking, it appears to be in the form of not working so hard (not showing up for roll calls) rather than indulging one's personal ideology or preferences at the expense of those of

Table 4.3

Change in Liberal/Conservative Position of House Members (1947–84): Regressions with Absolute Value of the Coordinate Change on First Dimension, from Congress t-1 to Congress t, as Dependent Variable

Variable[a]	COEFFICIENT		Variable Definition
	(1)	(2)	
APPOINT	0.018		Appointed to higher office
	(0.009)[b]		(1=appointed, 0=otherwise)
DIED	0.008		Died in office
	(0.006)		(1=died, 0=otherwise)
HIRUN	0.003		Ran for higher office
	(0.004)		(1=ran, 0=otherwise)
LOST	0.004		Lost primary or general
	(0.003)		election (1=lost, 0=otherwise)
RETIRE	0.0009		Voluntary retirement
	(0.003)		(1=retired, 0=otherwise)
NOTVOTE	0.029*	0.034*	Fraction not voting
	(0.008)	(0.007)	in House t
REDIST	0.0004		Redistricted
	(0.002)		(1=redistricted, 0=otherwise)
VOTESHR	−5.17E-06		Share of two-party vote in
	(4.31E-05)		previous election

Fixed-effect variables only	(1)	(2)	
0.107	0.110	0.110	Adjusted R^2
0.055	0.055	0.055	Standard error of regression
45.221	31.988	43.999	F-statistic
	0.061		Mean Dependent Variable
	6,288		Number of Observations

[a] Not shown: 18 fixed-effect indicator variables for each pair of Congresses from 80–81 through 97–98 (all statistically significant with two-tail p-values <0.001 in all equations).

[b] Standard errors are in parentheses.

* Statistically significant with two-tail p-value <0.001.

the constituency. Similarly, changing the composition of the representative's district has no significant effect on the representative's liberal/conservative position.[23] The representative does not shirk by indulging a personal ideology only in the last period of service but, on the contrary, maintains a well-defined ideology — even if the district's boundaries are changed — throughout his career.

Indeed, further evidence on this score is shown in Table 4.4. Using the fraction of roll calls in which the representative did not vote — NOTVOTE[24] — as a dependent variable and regressing the other seven variables on it yields very interesting results. All coefficients on the five exit variables are positive and highly significant with two-tail p-values of less than 0.001. (The largest coefficient is on the variable DIED, which makes sense in this context.)[25] When a member knows he is going to exit, he votes less but, as Table 4.3 shows, his

Table 4.4
Abstention of House Members (1947–84): Regression with NOTVOTE, the Fraction of Roll Calls in which the Representative Did Not Vote n House t, as the Dependent Variable

Variable	Coefficient	Variable Definition
C	0.056[a] (0.005)[b]	Intercept term
APPOINT	0.080 (0.014)	Appointed to higher office (1=appointed, 0=otherwise)
DIED	0.096 (0.009)	Died in office (1=died, 0=otherwise)
HIRUN	0.152 (0.006)	Ran for higher office (1=ran, 0=otherwise)
LOST	0.054 (0.005)	Lost primary or general election (1=lost, 0=otherwise)
RETIRE	0.105 (0.005)	Voluntary retirement (1=retired, 0=otherwise)
REDIST	0.004 (0.003)	Redistricted (1=redistricted, 0=otherwise)
VOTESHR	0.0006 (0.00007)	Share of two-party vote in previous election
	0.160	Adjusted R^2
	0.089	Standard error of regression
	172.028	F-statistic
	0.117	Mean Dependent Variable
	6,288	Number of Observations

[a] All variables except REDIST are statistically significant with two-tailed p-values <0.001. Two-tailed p-value for REDIST is 0.097.

[b] Standard errors are in parentheses.

voting pattern, when he votes, remains the same. In other words, shirking is not ideological; it simply is voting less.[26] In any event, shirking, interpreted as indulging one's own preferences rather than representing the district's preferences, is, at best, a second order phenomenon.

The redistricting variable, REDIST, is positive, and has a two-tailed p-value of 0.058 quite close to the traditional 0.05 level of statistical significance. This means that changing the geographic boundaries of a representative's district produces a slight increase in his abstention record. This increase could be due to the representative spending more time in the new district than he normally would and, therefore, voting less often than he normally would.

Finally, the VOTESHR coefficient is positive and statistically significant. This implies that the higher the previous election margin, the freer the representative feels to vote less. The effect, however, is very small. (We treat not-voting in detail in chapter 10).

Further evidence for the stability of member positions comes from examining the 216 members who, after passage of the Seventeenth Amendment for the popular election of senators, first served in the House and then were elected to the Senate. Given the stability of position detailed above, we used the constant (static) coordinates estimated simultaneously for all 108 Congresses (see Table 3.1). In this model, each legislator was constrained to a constant spatial position throughout his or her career.

The correlation between a legislator's position in the House and his or her later position in the Senate is 0.92 on the first dimension. This high correlation indicates that representatives not only die in their ideological boots, but they do not change them when they run for the Senate. In contrast, the correlation for the second dimension is only 0.76.[27] The lower correlation for the second dimension is not surprising given the structural differences between the two chambers on the second dimension.[28]

Replacement and Stability

A reasonable inference from the above discussion is that replacement and stability might be related. The potential sources of any statistical relationship are both real and artifactual. A true relationship might result because high rates of replacement would indicate periods of political instability, when legislators have strong incentives to adjust their positions in order to win reelection. The potential artifactual relationship comes from the fact that, when turnover is high, there are few legislators to tie adjacent Congresses together in the DW-NOMINATE estimation. The instability of the legislature might be accompanied by unstable, biased estimates with overly large time trends.

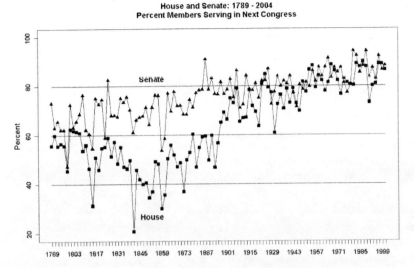

Figure 4.8. Percentage of the current House and Senate members that served in previous House and Senate. The Senate historically had less turnover than the House as a result of six-year terms; in both houses, turnover began to decrease in the 1870s and '80s. The last points plotted represent the turnover from the 107th Congress (2001–02) to the 108th.

Figure 4.8 shows the proportion of each current House and Senate that served in the previous Congress. The proportions for the Senate are higher in the nineteenth century simply because of the six-year term. But a sudden change takes place in the House after the 54th (1895–96) Congress. The average proportion continuing to the next House jumps from about 55 percent to around 70 percent in the period through World War I. The Republicans controlled the 54th through the 61st Houses (1895–1910) with 200 seats or more in all but the 56th House. At the same time, except for a handful of seats, the Democrats controlled all the seats for the eleven states of the Confederacy. Consequently, the conditions were ripe for longevity. Finally, this period is the one immediately following what many scholars have identified as the beginnings of the "professionalization" of the House (Polsby, 1968).[29]

A comparison of Figure 4.8 with Table 4.2 suggests that turnover and stability (in terms of the correlations between adjacent Congresses) may be related. That is, the proportion that continues to serve from a particular Congress to the next should be positively correlated with the correlations (some of which are shown in Table 4.2) in positions of members who continue to serve from that same Congress to the next. The correlations of these two series are indeed positive, but only very weakly so — the correlation is only 0.27 for the Senate and 0.21 for the House. The correlations for 1901–2004 (57th Congress on) are only 0.24 and 0.31, respectively. This finding leads us to conclude that the decline in movement shown in Figure 4.7 is genuine and not simply a consequence of low turnover in Congress. We speculate that the decline in movement is more likely to result from how changes in mass communications have affected representative's incentives to establish roll call voting reputations with their constituents.

An immediate implication of this spatial stability from the post-Reconstruction period of the nineteenth century until the present (and especially after World War II), is that changes in Congressional voting patterns must occur almost entirely through the process of *replacement* of retiring or defeated legislators with new blood. Politically, selection should be far more important than adaptation. One way of approaching this problem is to compare the coordinates of new (or entering) members with those of exiting members. We do this for the post-Reconstruction (1879–2004) period for the House in Figure 4.9.

The figure shows the effects on the first dimension of entering and exiting members of the House for northern Democrats, southern Democrats, and Republicans. By *exiting*, we mean those members who were in the previous House but are not in the current House. For the northern Democrats, there is no clear-cut pattern until 1897 (after the 1896 elections). Between 1897 and 1909 entering northern Democrats were generally to the left of those who entered from 1879 to 1895. Beginning with the 1908 elections, entering northern Democrats were at least as conservative as exiting northern Democrats for twelve consecutive elections ending in the 1928 elections. Interestingly, the northern Democrats elected in 1930, 1932, and 1934 were indistinguishable from those elected between 1914 and 1928. However, beginning with the 1936 elections, entering northern Democrats are to the left of exiting northern Democrats for ten of the next eleven elections ending with the 1956 elections. Members elected in the 1970s tended to be more conservative while those in the 1980s tended to be more liberal.

For the southern Democrats the effects of entering and exiting members are quite dramatic. In twenty of twenty-eight elections from 1914 through 1968, entering southern Democrats were to the right of exiting southern Democrats. The effects of the civil rights laws passed in the mid 1960s can be seen in the last sixteen elections in our series — 1970 through 2004. In these sixteen elections entering southern Democrats were to the left of exiting southern Democrats in ten elections.

The pattern for the Republicans is very interesting. The Republican entrants after the turn of the twentieth century are to the left of their exiting counterparts all the way through the Progressive era (1901–1916) and World War I. The few

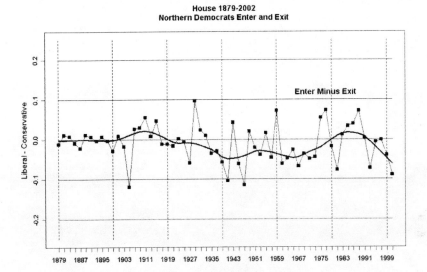

Figure 4.9. Difference between mean first-dimension positions of entering and exiting members, House of Representatives, 1879–2002. Entering northern Democrats were consistently more liberal and southern Democrats more conservative than representatives from the same region leaving Congress during the New Deal era. In recent times, entering Republicans have been more conservative than those leaving, reversing the pattern at the turn of the last century and immediately after World War II; and, the graph for southern Democrats is volatile because few new southern Democrats have entered Congress. The last point plotted is for 2001–02. Information was unavailable for members exiting the 108th Congress (2003–04).

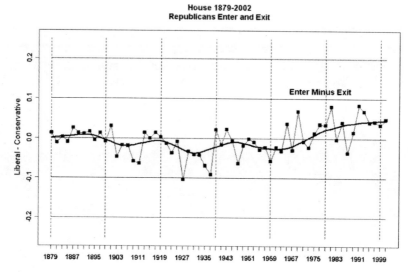

Figure 4.9. (*continued*)

entering Republicans during the New Deal tended to be more liberal but the pattern is not very dramatic. However, beginning with the 1944 elections, entering Republicans are either to the left of or equal to exiting Republicans all the way through the 1972 elections with the exception of the 1964 and 1968 elections. With the exception of the 1986 election, in every election since 1974 the entering Republicans have been more conservative.

The patterns we have described for replacements largely parallel those we described for the party means. The party means change mostly because the composition of the party delegation changes, not because individual members change. Of course, given party polarization, far greater changes in position and in policy occur when constituencies replace a representative with a member of the opposite party. We now take a more detailed look at the evolution of party polarization.

Party Polarization and Dispersion

Figures 4.3–4.6 show that the distances between the mean positions of the two major parties can vary considerably during the three periods of relative stability we analyzed above. The distance between the major party means is one aspect of party polarization. Polarization is accentuated when party members are concentrated around the party mean.

Polarization thus has two highly related, but quite distinct, aspects. For parties to be polarized, they must be far apart on policy issues, and the party members must be tightly clustered around the party mean. Clearly, if the two parties have a high degree of overlap — with the Left wing of the "conservative" party overlapping the Right wing of the "liberal" party — then they are less polarized than if they have no overlap whatsoever.

Figure 4.10 shows our first measure of party polarization, which is a measure of overlap. This is the proportion of legislators of each major party who are closer to the opposing party's centroid (for example, a Democrat who is closer to the centroid of the Republicans). The periods of high overlap in the 1820s (the Era of Good Feelings) and the early 1850s correspond exactly to periods we discussed earlier, in which the spatial structure of voting broke down because of the disintegration of one or both of the major political parties (the Federalists and the Jeffersonian Republicans in the first instance; the Whigs in the second). We truncate the graph at 20 percent so that the other periods can be seen more clearly.[30]

The period from the Civil War until about 1920 was one of almost complete polarization of the Democratic and Republican parties in terms of over-

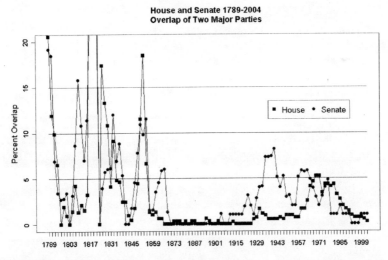

Figure 4.10. Overlap of the two major parties: percentage of party's members closer to the centroid of the opposing party than to the centroid of own party, 1789–2004. Overlap was almost totally absent at the turn of the twentieth century. Overlap increased during the Kennedy, Johnson, and Nixon presidencies, but has fallen sharply since then. The missing values for the three Congresses serving from 1817 to 1823 are, in order, 0.32, 0.44, and 0.44 for the House, and 0.23, 0.22, and 0.36 for the Senate.

lap. In the House, where agendas are more controlled and leadership stronger, polarization was almost perfect up until the 1960s. In contrast, overlap begins to increase in the Senate in the 1920s due to the small group of midwestern Republicans we discussed earlier. Again, we see the effect of issues related to civil rights for African Americans in the increase of overlap in the early to late 1960s: Some moderate Republicans are closer to the Democratic Party mean, and some southern Democrats are closer to the Republican Party mean. Note that, after 1979, overlap once again begins to fall as liberal Republicans became rarer and southern Democrats moved closer to northern members of the party.[31] The House and Senate patterns are highly similar. The correlation between the two over the 108 Congresses is a substantial 0.82. In both houses, overlap in the early twenty-first century is now at the extremely low level found a century earlier.

For our next two measures of party polarization, we look at how far apart the members of the two major parties are, and how tightly dispersed the members of the two major parties are around their respective party means. To measure how far apart the members of the parties are, we compute the distance (in two dimensions) between the party centroids. To measure the dispersion of the parties, we compute the average distance between all pairs of members of the same party.[32] Figure 4.11 shows these measures for the post-Reconstruction Democrat-Republican party system for the House and Senate.

The patterns for the House and Senate are very similar. The period of greatest polarization ran from the start of the modern two-party system after Reconstruction to early in the twentieth century. Polarization then fell dramatically in both houses until the onset of World War II. After the war, polarization plateaued at a low level. It started up in the Senate in the 1950s only to fall in the 1960s. By the 1970s, polarization took off in both houses. Polarization has now increased to where it is near levels of a century ago. The correlation between the House and Senate measures of between-party polarization is 0.92, indicating once again that the same political-economic macro forces are at work in both chambers.[33]

The two chambers present, nonetheless, two interesting differences. First, the Republican-controlled Senate was more highly polarized throughout the post-Reconstruction period of the nineteenth century. This was largely due to the fact that the eleven former Confederate states almost always sent two Democrats each to the Senate. In addition, the five border states that had also been slave states (Missouri, Kentucky, West Virginia, Maryland, and Delaware) also sent mostly Democrats to the Senate through this period. Consequently, the Democratic Party in the Senate was dominated by southerners. In contrast to the Senate, the more balanced, but typically Democratic-

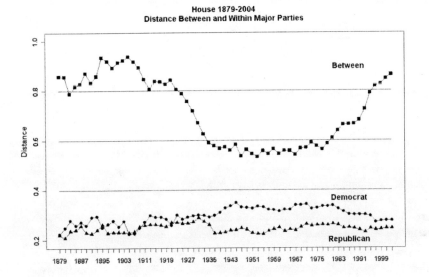

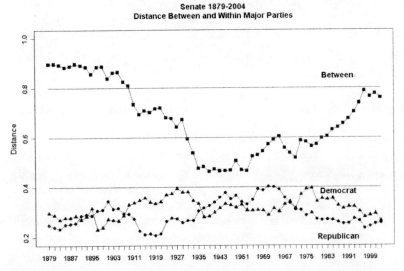

Figure 4.11. Party centroid differences and between-party distances, 1879–2004. Computations use the two-dimensional, linear-trend model. The within-party differences have always been much smaller than the distances between the parties. Party differences declined sharply after 1900 but have recently returned to levels indicating a high degree of polarization.

controlled House of Representatives only reached its highest level of polarization after it fell to the Republicans in the "realignment" at the end of the nineteenth century.

Second, the process of moderation in the twentieth century was somewhat accelerated and earlier in the Senate because of the progressive Republicans in the farm states. Because the farm states had much greater relative representation in the Senate than in the House, the effects of Progressive Republicanism were more pronounced there.

In contrast to the between-party polarization measure, our measure of dispersion shows that the Republican Party had not only a higher level of dispersion in the Senate than in the House but a distinctly different pattern. In the House, Republican within-party distances were always quite low, just above 0.2. In contrast, the dispersion of the Republican Party in the Senate increased greatly through the Progressive Era and this dispersion persisted until the early 1970s. This pattern in part is due to the group of midwestern Republican senators that we discussed above. No such pattern occurred in the House. The correlation for the Republican Party dispersion measures in the two chambers is only 0.48.

The Democrats are quite a different story. Here the correlation between the two chambers is 0.73. The increase in dispersion because of the split of the party into northern and southern camps in the 1930s and beyond is clearly evident in both chambers.

We show in Figure 4.12 our polarization measures for the House of Representatives for the Federalist-Jeffersonian Republican period and the Whig/Democrat period we analyzed in Figures 4.5 and 4.6. Not surprisingly, as the Federalist and Republican parties coalesced, polarization increased steadily, peaking in Jefferson's first term. The Whig-Democrat system polarized, in terms of the two-dimensional distance measure, through time as conflict over slavery increased. Polarization in the first two party systems was, in terms of within-party distances, much more similar to that in the post-Depression Congresses than in the highly polarized systems that followed Reconstruction and developed in contemporary times. The dispersion within parties, from Jefferson's presidency onwards, was similar to that within the Democratic Party in the House post-World War II, reflecting the important role of the second dimension in separating the northern and southern wings of each party.

Finally, Figures 4.10 and 4.11 taken together indicate that the current Democrat/Republican party system is highly polarized. As the southern Democrats were largely replaced by Republicans with the remaining southern Democrats representing urban and minority-majority southern areas, the two parties have gravitated towards a system more polarized than at any time since the early 1900s.

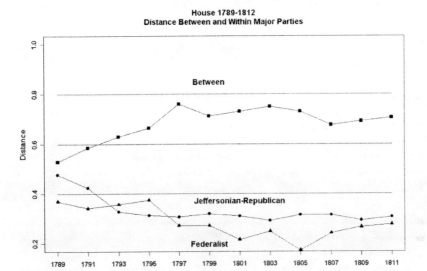

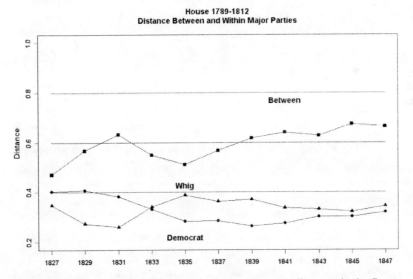

Figure 4.12. Party centroid differences and between=party distances in the first two-party systems, House of Representatives. The results are quite similar to those in the previous figure.

Summary

The high degree of stability in legislator positions since the end of World War II may in part be due to the role of reputation in American politics.[34] On the one hand politicians might choose to adapt to changes in issues, demographics, incomes, and other considerations that are relevant to their constituency; on the other the process of adaptation may result in voters believing the politician is less predictable. In turn, risk-averse voters will value predictability (Bernhardt and Ingberman, 1985). Therefore, a politician faces a tradeoff between maintaining an established reputation and taking a position that is closer to the current demands of the constituency. Politicians also may find a reputation useful in cultivating campaign contributors. Some mixture of reduced change in constituency demands, increased incentives to maintain a reputation, and, perhaps, other factors are manifest in the stability of legislator positions.

Although legislator positions, particularly in recent times, are stable in the basic space, political change occurs through replacement. Because party positions have been polarized in each of the three major-party systems in American history, very substantial swings in policy, in terms of the position of roll call outcomes, can take place when majority control changes, even though the center of gravity of the space is relatively stable. Replacement, which can result in large differences in spatial positions for successive representatives from the same district (see chapter 6), causes changes in the positions of the parties and the dispersion of these parties. These changes cause fluctuations in polarization. But the major changes in the space correspond much more to important events in American history, such as the conflicts over slavery and civil rights and the Great Depression.

The greatest changes in the space are not represented by the periods of stability captured in the party systems but by the periods of spatial collapse that separate the party systems. We now turn to an examination of these periods and a comparison of them with other major events where, even though the mass electorate may have realigned, the party system and the structure of the basic space were not.

Notes

1. The R^2 values for the regressions described above using the chamber means on the second dimension are .019 for the post-Reconstruction period and 0.22 for the twentieth century.
2. Note that during this period, the dispersion of the Senate on the second dimension was very low. Consequently, even though the bulk of the Republican senators were located at the center of the second dimension only a few Republicans with sub-

stantial second-dimension coordinates were necessary to get the mean above the Democrats.

3. There is an extensive literature on the emergence of the first political-party system. See Martis (1989, pp. 27–28) and the literature cited therein. We follow Martis's party designations so that for Houses 1–3, we use *proadministration* and *antiadministration* for the two "parties." Subsequent to the 3rd House, these groups become the Federalists and Jeffersonian Republicans, respectively. (For Houses 1–3 in Figure 4.6, we use *Federalist* and *Jeffersonian Republican* to identify these earlier blocs.)

4. Ibid., pp. 30–31 codes the two parties as "Adams" and "Jackson" during the administration of John Quincy Adams (1825–1829). He then changes these codes to "Anti-Jackson and "Jackson" respectively for the period of Andrew Jackson's presidency (1829–1837). Thereafter, he codes them as "Whig" and "Democrat."

5. The Martis codes for the 18th Congress (1823–1825) include factions for Adams, Jackson, William H. Crawford, and Henry Clay.

6. See Alesina and Rosenthal (1995, chapter 2) for a review of the literature on the theory of political polarization.

7. See ibid., pp. 127–136.

8. If only one outcome is inside the space, it is almost always the winning outcome.

9. Poole and Rosenthal (1987b) discuss results with similar substantive implications when the data are not filtered. Similar results also obtain when one considers only close votes. The measure we use underestimates the change, because the excluded roll calls have extreme outcomes.

10. The significance of Republican House share in the Senate equation is a change from the results presented in *Congress, 1997*. We have checked that the change was not produced by adding data from 1986–2004. The change therefore reflects how DW-NOMINATE, in distinction to D-NOMINATE, treats roll calls that require constraints.

11. The fact that the response is to both seat share and control supports the checks-and-balances model of Alesina and Rosenthal (1995, chapter 3).

12. Both in the research reported below and in DW-NOMINATE, where time is kept constant for each Congress, we do not deal with shifts in preferences within a given Congress. This is an important topic for future research.

13. There are obviously no members common to the 1st and 108th Congresses and many other pairs.

14. This table differs somewhat from Table 5 of Poole and Rosenthal (1991a) because we used W-NOMINATE rather than the original NOMINATE to estimate the legislator coordinates in the static scalings for this book. The differences are not very great, however.

15. This figure shows even more stability than the corresponding one in *Congress, 1997*. Both figures were computed for legislators serving in five or more Congresses; the linear trends in the original D-NOMINATE were estimated for legislators serving in three or more Congresses. Eliminating the linear terms for members serving in only three or four Congresses should have little effect on the estimates for legislators serving in five or more. Legislators who both switched parties and served in five or more Congresses in both parties had separate estimations under DW-NOMINATE. Since there were only two such switchers, this effect on the average distance moved will be small. Another small effect in reducing aver-

age movement involves correction to the identification numbers of legislators. These corrections reduce average movement, particularly in early Congresses. Finally, changes in the estimation algorithm, particularly with respect to "constrained" legislators, will change the average distances. The trends in both the present and the earlier figure are, however, highly similar.

16. In *Congress, 1997*, we reported larger trends for legislators serving only in three or four Congresses. Two hypotheses are consistent with this observation. On the one hand, legislators with abbreviated periods of service tend to be unsuccessful legislators; their movement may reflect attempts to match up better with the interests of constituents. On the other hand, short-run changes in the central issues before Congress — such as the Vietnam War or free trade — may result in the spatial position resembling an autoregressive random walk. In this case, the estimate of the magnitude of the true trend will be biased upward, with greater bias for shorter service periods. We are now inclined toward the second hypothesis. Trends based on only three or four Congresses will tend to over-fit the data.

17. We calculated these correlations between the absolute value of a member's coordinate for each Congress and the length of service, including the current Congress. The number of observations for the House was 35,300 and for the Senate 8,542 (Congresses $(1-108)$. The correlation between the absolute value of a member's *last coordinate* in his or her career and his or her total length of service was 0.00 for the House and -0.10 for the Senate (10,378 and 1,818 observations respectively). For 1902–2004, the correlations corresponding to the two definitions given above were -0.06 and -0.06 for the House (22,537 and 5,231 observations), and -0.12 and -0.11 for the Senate (4,805 and 963 observations).

18. Recall that the space has a diameter of 2 units.

19. The correlation for all 108 Congresses is 0.66.

20. Poole and Romer (1993) regressed the one-dimensional NOMINATE coordinates for each House on the corresponding one-dimensional D-NOMINATE coordinates. That is, they estimated: $x_i^{(d)} = \beta_0 + \beta_1 x_i^{(s)} + e$, where $x_i^{(d)}$ and $x_i^{(s)}$ are the dynamic and static coordinates, in one dimension for the i-th representative. The estimated coefficients were used to transform the static coordinates; that is: $\tilde{x}_i^{(s)} = \hat{\beta}_0 + \hat{\beta}_1 \tilde{x}_i^{(s)}$, where $\tilde{x}_i^{(s)}$ is simply a linear transformation of the original static coordinates. This has the effect of putting each pair of Houses in the same metric. See Loomis (1995) and Poole and Romer (1993) for further detail. Results here differ slightly from Poole and Romer (1993) because we redid their analysis using W-NOMINATE rather than the original NOMINATE.

21. The exit coding was performed by Loomis (1995).

22. An F test on the 18 fixed-effect variables indicates that they are jointly significant ($F = 36.82$). An F test on the 8 other variables indicates that they, too, are also jointly significant ($F = 4.16$).

23. This conclusion might be modified were the Poole and Romer analysis carried forward into the twenty-first century. McCarty, Poole, and Rosenthal (2006, chapter 3) show that, in more recent Congresses, DW-NOMINATE scores are more closely linked to constituency characteristics than before. This suggests that redistricting might have more impact now than in the past.

24. If a representative died in office, *NOTVOTE* is the fraction of roll calls the representative was eligible for but did not vote in (that is, roll calls taken after the representative died are not used in the computation).

25. That is, illness may have prevented a member from voting for some period before his death.
26. Lott and Bronars (1993), using interest group ratings, show that there is little change in the voting behavior of members of Congress in their last Congress.
27. The correlations for the entire post-Reconstruction period (N = 322) are 0.92 for the first dimension and 0.63 for the second.
28. More elaborate specifications failed to find any further meaningful structure. For example, we tried to incorporate measures of moderation by using the number of congressional districts in the state, which we interacted (in various combinations) with a representative's party and how extreme the representative was in the House (on the theory that the representative, if extreme, must become more moderate to represent a large state in the Senate). Some coefficients in some of the various multivariate specifications were statistically significant, but never was the magnitude of the effect substantively meaningful. Hence we opt for reporting simple Pearson (R) correlations.
29. Also, see Hibbing (1993) for a discussion of, and references to, this sizable literature.
30. See the caption to Figure 4.10 for the missing values.
31. For more details on the adjustment of southern Democrats, see Poole and Rosenthal (1991a, pp. 258–264).
32. Technically, this is

$$\sqrt{\left[\frac{\sum\limits_{i-1}^{m-1}\sum\limits_{j=i+1}^{n}\sum\limits_{k=1}^{s}\left(x_{ik}-x_{jk}\right)^2}{m(m-1)/2}\right]}$$

   where m is the number of members of the political party, and s is the number of dimensions, with $s = 2$.
33. The results are similar when the analysis is conducted solely in terms of the first dimension. See http://pooleandrosenthal.com/polarized_america.htm.
34. Numerous studies by political scientists, using a variety of techniques, have shown that members of Congress vote consistently over time on issues and are very sensitive to their voting history (Clausen, 1973; Fiorina, 1974; Clausen and Van Horn, 1977; Asher and Weisberg, 1978; Stone, 1980; Bullock, 1981; Smith, 1981).

5

Party Realignment in Congress

A realignment represents a fundamental change in the way substantive issues map onto the spatial model we described in chapter 2. Our findings differ from those found in the realignment literature in political science, which has largely drawn its evidence from the voting behavior of the *mass electorate* rather than from the roll call record of the *congressional elite*. In contrast to the usual finding that there have been three major realignments since Jackson's presidency, we claim that there has been only a single *legislative* realignment. This realignment was produced by the conflict over slavery, and the critical years are 1851–52, well before the Civil War.

There was no realignment in either the 1890s or the early 1930s. Nevertheless, the Democratic landslides of the 1930s initiated a minirealignment, or perturbation, of the space. Like the conflict over slavery, this minirealignment arose over matters related to the rights of African Americans. In contrast to these race-related issues, most issues in American politics are simply absorbed into the major dimension of political conflict. Indeed, the politics of race has, for much of American history (including the contemporary period), also been encompassed by the major dimension.

In this chapter, we present a simple model of realignment that is based on the spatial model in chapter 2. We then seek evidence in the roll call voting behavior of realignments in Congress that would be concurrent with changes in the mass electorate that occurred during the 1850s, 1890s, and 1930s. We find that only in the early 1850s does a major change in the structure of congressional voting occur; the realignments of the 1890s and 1930s occurred along the line of cleavage that solidified after the Civil War. The late 1930s witnessed the birth of a second realignment focused on the issue of civil rights for

African-Americans. But as this second realignment proved to be less intense than the first (and only a temporary one), we describe it more appropriately as a perturbation.

We also examine the nature of issue change more generally. We investigate how new issues are accommodated within an existing spatial structure. In the galaxy of policy issues that confronts Congress, no other issue was as intense or enduring as the question of race, which led to the realignment of the 1850s and the perturbation of the 1940s to the 1970s. If an issue is to result in sustained public policy, we hypothesize that the policy must eventually be supported by a coalition that can be represented as a split on the first, major dimension. Policy developed by coalitions that are non-spatial or built along the second dimension is likely to be transient and unstable. We analyze several issue areas including abortion and prohibition, and find considerable support for our hypothesis.

The Realignment Literature

E. E. Schattschneider, in his classic *Party Government* (1942, p. 1), wrote that the "political parties created democracy" and "modern democracy is unthinkable save in terms of the parties." Schattschneider argued that freedom of association and the guarantee of regular elections with plurality winners made the development of two mass-based political parties inevitable. American political history can be written almost entirely around the conflict between and within political parties because the parties have acted as mirrors of the great social and economic conflicts that have divided the country. When the political parties failed to mirror such conflicts, they have been torn apart and swept aside by new parties that represent mass opinion.

The realignment literature in political science is concerned with such changes in the mass support for the political parties and how the leaders of the parties responded to the changes. The prevailing view in this literature is that there have been three major realignments since Jackson assumed the presidency: one in the 1850s over the issue of the extension of slavery to the territories; one in the 1890s over the issue of currency inflation (greenbacks and bimetallism); and one in the 1930s because of the collapse of the economy in the Great Depression.[1]

The most complete statement of this thesis is by Sundquist (1983, p. 4). He argues that a realignment is a durable change in patterns of political behavior. His basic model of realignment is that a new issue emerges that cuts across the existing cleavage and reorganizes the political parties around it. He notes (1983, p. 37): "The party system has a new rationale, an old conflict has been displaced by a new one for a segment of the electorate, and that segment of the electorate has formed . . . new party attachments on the basis of that rationale. If the segment is large enough . . . a new party system supplants the old one."

Sundquist marshals an impressive body of evidence for his thesis — including changes in party registration and voting at the county level in various states. There can be little debate about the fact that major changes in the mass electorate occurred during the 1850s, 1890s, and 1930s. The evidence is convincing. Less convincing is Sundquist's argument that these changes in the mass electorate "shifted" the party system on its axis. In Sundquist's model, if a new issue does not seriously divide the political parties *internally* then "the crisis will be reached and resolved relatively quickly," and the scale of the realignment "will be relatively minor" (1983, pp. 44–45). In other words, the severity of a realignment is a direct function of the internal divisions of the parties.

In Sundquist's work the mass electorate and the professional politicians are part and parcel of the same process. Sundquist's evidence comes from changes in the mass electorate. We draw our evidence from changes in congressional voting behavior as revealed by our dynamic spatial model.

We set forth a simple model of realignment based upon the spatial model of party competition and offer evidence that the realignments of the 1890s and the 1930s did not change the basic structure of congressional voting that preceded these realigning periods. Indeed, the basic structure set in place during the 1870s was not changed by either realignment. A fundamental change in the structure of congressional voting occurred in only two realignments in American history.[2] The first was the 1850s realignment due to the extension of slavery to the territories. The second realignment began in the *late* 1930s with voting on the minimum wage (see chapter 6) and then intensified with voting during World War II over the voting rights of blacks in uniform. This later realignment was only indirectly the result of the Great Depression. Indeed, the large Democratic majority created by the economic catastrophe split over the race issue. The realignment forced by the North-South conflict was (as we noted earlier) less intense than the 1850s realignment and only a temporary one; we more appropriately call this realignment a perturbation of the long-run liberal-conservative conflict.

Interpreting Realignment in Terms
of the Spatial Model of Voting

Realignment, as defined by Sundquist, is easily accommodated by the dynamic spatial model we outlined in chapter 2. For example, before a realignment is initiated, roll call voting should be stable and organized around the cleavage of the last realignment. In terms of spatial theory this means that the policy space is stable — the same dimensions structure voting over time, and legislators' ideal points should show little change from Congress to Congress. A new issue then emerges that splits the political parties internally and begins the process of polarization. This can be modeled as a new dimension — orthogonal to the stable set from the last realignment, across which both political parties become increasingly polarized. This is due in part to replacement of members — the newly elected members are more atuned to the new issue — and in part to modifications of the spatial positions of continuing members (see Figure 4.7). As the process continues more and more of the voting is concerned with the new issue so that the old stable set begins to wither away. Finally, the old spatial structure collapses entirely, and a new alignment emerges in which the major dimension is coterminous with the new issue.[3]

Figure 5.1 shows the realignment process at five stages: early, middle, and late stages of the old alignment; the period of spatial collapse; and the new

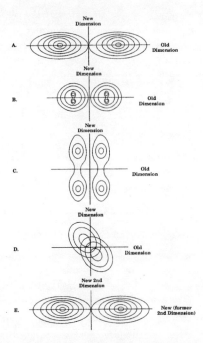

Figure 5.1. Spatial realignment. The contours in the figures show the distribution of legislators' ideal points, with legislators concentrating near the more central concentric contours. Before a realignment (part A), legislators have a largely unidimensional distribution. The major parties are clusters on the dimension. As a new issue arises, it polarizes the parties on the second dimension (parts B and C). When the new issue becomes too intense for the old alignment to survive, the party system collapses (part D). A new system forms with the new dimension as the first dimension (part E).

alignment. Two political parties are shown as contour maps over a space of two dimensions, with most members located near the center of the contours. One dimension is the original line of cleavage, and the other is the new, realignment issue. Early in the process, as shown by part A of the figure, the two parties are relatively homogeneous with some diversity. The new issue has not yet produced polarized factions within the parties. The legislators, as a whole, are centrally distributed over the original dimension, and because the new issue has only recently emerged, not all members have been forced to take positions on it. Then, as the issue heats up within the electorate and becomes more salient, the legislators begin reacting more forcefully and the polarization process begins, as shown in part B. Part C of the figure shows the process in its later stage: Both political parties are now polarized. The new dimension is now the primary focus of voting and the legislators are bimodally distributed across it. The parties are highly divided internally.

When internal party divisions become too strong, the space can collapse, as shown in part D — parties are no longer distinct clusters in the space. In addition, the fit of the model (which cannot be seen from the map of the legislators' ideal points) will be poor. (See, for example, the evidence on the 31st House, in Figure 3.6.) Voting alignments within the legislature are unstable. After the collapse, the political system is reorganized, possibly with the formation of new parties. The contours of the new party system, part E, are the same as those in the old system (part A), except that the first dimension is now represented by the realigning issue.

Below we test this model with our two dimensional DW-NOMINATE scaling. We first discuss our scaling results for the 1850s, 1890s, and 1930s. We then cover the period from the 1940s to the 1970s and show that a minor realignment, or perturbation, occurred after World War II.

Evidence of Realignments?

Our model of realignment has three potential implications: Continuing members should be more volatile in the space, making more changes in their positions; replacements should position themselves distinctly from continuing members; and the realigning issue should change its orientation in the space.

The evidence on continuing members was already presented in Figure 4.7. The situation for the 1890s and 1930s is clearest. In the figure, there is an uptick for both houses of Congress for both of these periods, but it is small. Movement never reaches the levels observed from the initiation of the Era of Good Feelings (1815) through the emergence of the Whig-Democrat system in the elections of 1836 or, particularly, for the Senate, during the realignment in the 1850s and '60s. Nevertheless, two caveats are in order. First, it is difficult to compare the upticks of the 1890s and 1930s to the antebellum realignments since there has been a secular increase in the stability of legislators' positions. Second, the antebellum picture is less systematic than that postbellum one — in large part because replacement, rather than adjustment, is the major vehicle of realignment in this period (see Figure 4.8).

In order to reanalyze realignments and issue change in more detail, we select all roll calls on the relevant issue and examine the spatial voting patterns over the issue across time. In particular, we focus on how well voting on each roll call is accounted for by the first dimension of our estimation as well as the increase in fit from adding the second dimension. In our analysis of specific roll call votes in the following sections, we will focus on the *PRE1* and the *PRE2* for that roll call. To analyze an issue area, we will compute the aggregate *PRE* (*APRE*) using all scaled roll calls in the area.

Comparing the *APRE* for one dimension (*APRE1*) with the *APRE* for two dimensions (*APRE2*) gives a good indication of the spatial character of the roll calls. If *APRE1* is high and *APRE2-APRE1* is small, then the votes are concerned primarily with the first dimension. If *APRE1* is low and *APRE2-APRE1* is large, then the votes are along the second dimension. If both *APRE1* and *APRE2* are low, the votes are poorly fit by the model (or very lopsided). In our charts below, we focus on these sorts of differences by issue areas.

Note that, for a specific roll call, it is possible for *PRE2-PRE1* to be negative for two reasons. First, our scaling maximizes a likelihood function, not classification.[4] Second, the legislator coordinates are chosen as a function of all the votes and not just the vote on one roll call; therefore, two-dimensional coordinates can improve the fit overall while decreasing the fit on some individual roll calls.

Slavery and the Realignment of the 1850s

Slavery, of course, was the issue that produced the realignment of the 1850s. By the 1850s, slavery was not a new issue but a very old one that had become more intense in both the North and the South. Indeed, slavery was already an issue in the writing of the Constitution, which reflects a compromise: the counting of each slave as three-fifths of a person, for purposes of congressional apportionment, and the ending of importation of slaves in 1808. Slavery fits nicely into our model of realignment, but not exactly, as many other issues surfaced between 1789 and the 1850s. Indeed, before the spatial collapse of the 1850s, the space also collapsed in the Era of Good Feelings. As we look at slavery, therefore, we will have to keep in mind other "shocks" to the political system.

A total of 891 roll calls concerning slavery were included in our scaling of the House and 386 in the Senate.[5] For every Congress in which there were at least five scaled roll call votes concerning slavery we computed *APRE1* and *APRE2*.

In the first fourteen Congresses, the compromise concerning slavery embodied in the Constitution basically held. During this period, we coded only twenty-seven slavery roll calls for the House. While some of these concerned two issues — fugitive slaves and slavery in the District of Columbia, which would remain active until the eve of the Civil War — the bulk of the roll calls concerned the taxation of slaves and, in particular, slave imports. In fact, thirteen of the twenty-seven roll calls were held on slave imports in 1806 and 1807. But this issue vanished when the constitutional ban on slave imports became effective in 1808. Subsequent to the end of the 9th Congress in March 1807, no slavery roll calls occurred for a decade.

Slavery roll calls were slightly more frequent in the Senate, where thirty-four roll calls were coded. A very large part of these were represented by eleven roll calls early in 1804, when the Senate was drafting legislation to organize the land acquired in the Louisiana Purchase. These roll calls can be used to illustrate part A of Figure 5.1. The closest roll calls were two 16–12 decisions on a provision to bar the bringing of slaves into the territory, except by settlers who were slaveholders. Consistent with slavery not being a salient issue in the old alignment, the *PRE2* is low for those roll calls. The highest *PRE2* occurs on a January 31, 1804 vote and is only 0.33.

The vote is illustrated in Figure 5.2. Throughout this chapter, scatterplots like Figure 5.2 have two panels. One shows the actual vote and the predictions associated with the DW-NOMINATE cutting line. The other shows the prediction errors for the model. In Figure 5.2, parallel to part A of Figure 5.1, the parties are distinctly separated on the first dimension; the second dimension shows little dispersion; and the parties are smoothly clustered around a central point. Although the cutting line on the roll call passes through the heart of the Jeffersonian Republicans, there is also one proslavery vote among the Federalists. Moreover, as the United States map panel in the figure shows, except for New England, Tennessee, and Georgia, proslavery and antislavery voters could be found on both sides of the Mason-Dixon line. (South Carolina's two senators did not vote.) Southern legislators, particularly those from the middle and border states of the South, were not yet prevented from expressing mild antislavery positions, as they would be later (Freehling, 1990).

The relative peace that preceded the 15th Congress was not to continue. Figure 5.3 displays *APRE1* and *APRE2-APRE1* for the House from the 15th Congress to the 38th (1815–1865). The corresponding graph for the Senate is similar but less smooth. We begin with a discussion of the period before 1831 — and there were only thirty-nine additional roll calls in the House and twenty in

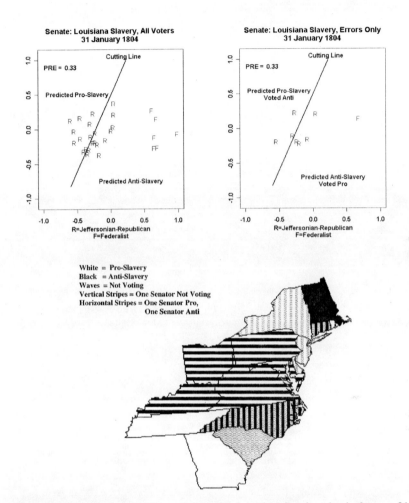

Figure 5.2. Vote on the prohibition of slavery in Louisiana Purchase lands, January 31, 1804 (VOTEVIEW number 49).

the Senate between 1817 and 1831. The remaining 823 House roll calls and 332 of the 386 Senate roll calls came after 1831.

Nearly three-fourths of the roll calls, in both the House and the Senate, in the 1817–31 period came in the 15th and 16th Congresses. The central issue at the time was slavery in Missouri. This proved far more explosive than any previous slave issue since each new state influenced the balance of power in Congress and the Electoral College (Weingast, 1991). Figure 3.1 shows that the 15th and 16th Congresses (elections of 1816 and 1818) occurred in the period

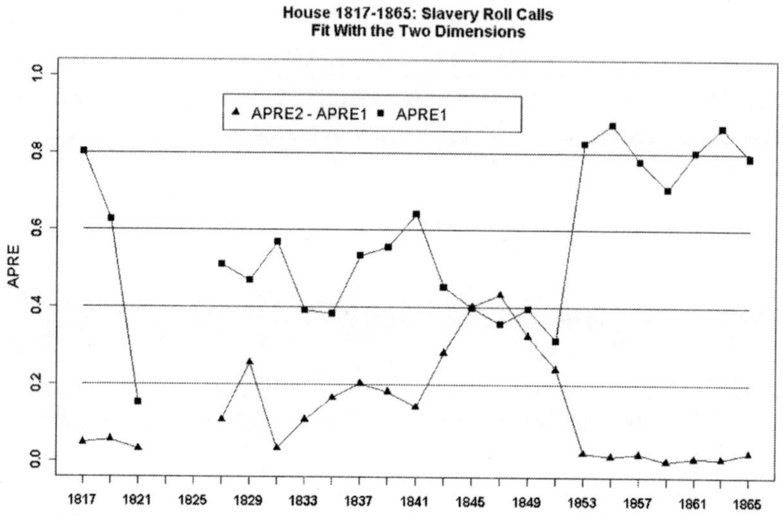

House 1817-1865: Slavery Roll Calls
Fit With the Two Dimensions

Figure 5.3. Slavery votes in the House of Representatives (1815–65). The first dimension becomes weaker (APRE1) and the second stronger (APRE2-APRE1) in accounting for slavery votes until the old alignment collapses. In the 32nd House (1851–52), the two dimensions together fail to account for the votes. By the 33rd House (1853–55), the new alignment is largely in place and slavery has become the major dimension.

of spatial collapse constituted by the Era of Good Feelings, with the 17th Congress — in both Houses — being the worst fitting Congress in American history. Yet, as illustrated by Figure 5.4, slavery votes in the 15th and 16th House fit very well in one dimension. Even in the Senate, where the fits are poorer, the 16th House has the best slavery fits in one dimension before the 33rd Congress. Indeed the level of House fits in the 16th House would have been even higher were it not for several lopsided procedural votes or votes unrelated to Missouri with very low and even negative *PRE*s. The critical votes all exhibited a high degree of spatial structure.[6]

What explains these results is that the spatial collapse of the Federalist/Republican system was unrelated to slavery but arose when the end of the Napoleonic Wars eliminated the foreign policy issue dividing the parties and when the economic issue was eliminated by partial Republican embrace of Alexander Hamilton's economic program. But slavery remained active as a divisive issue. Indeed, an examination of all roll calls for the 16th House revealed that slavery was the only issue with a high degree of fit. Without the slavery votes, the classifications in Figure 3.1 would have been even worse. Because slavery was the only strongly spatial issue at the time, it defines the first dimension when there is spatial collapse on most issues.

To illustrate this period, we use the critical vote on the Missouri Compromise in the House, which occurred on March 1, 1820. The compromise admitted Missouri as a slave state for the South and admitted Maine as a free state and banned slavery north of 36°30′ latitude in the Louisiana Purchase lands for the North. The Compromise was actually passed as two votes — one admitting Missouri and Maine, which allowed the North to take antislavery positions by voting against, and the other on the 36°30′ line, which allowed the South to take proslavery positions by voting against. The first vote was close, 90–87, and fit the model well, with only four classification errors; it is illustrated in Figure 5.4. This ideal point distribution resembles the spatial-collapse panel, part D, of Figure 5.1. The parties, in contrast to Figure 5.2's picture for 1804, are no longer well-differentiated. The vote indeed splits both parties (the Federalists: 12 Yeas and 14 Nays; the Republicans: 78 Yeas and 73 Nays). Yet there was a solid southern vote in favor and there were only a few northern defections (but strategically sufficient to guarantee passage).

The Missouri Compromise did not give the South a long-run commitment to maintain a free state/slave state balance in the Senate. (Our view here contrasts with that of Weingast [1991], who argues that such a commitment existed until 1850, when California entered as a free state and no slave state was admitted.) On the contrary, because slavery was banned in most of the territories, the Compromise placed the South at a long-run disadvantage that it sought to undo. The Compromise succeeded, in the short-run, in our view, largely because the pace of settlement slowed down after the Panic of 1819 resulted in a severe economic downturn. The next states admitted, Arkansas and Michigan, entered

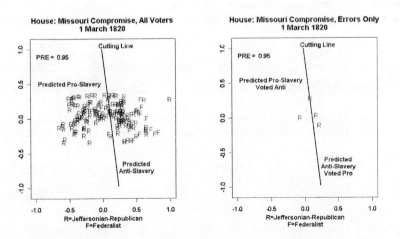

Figure 5.4. Critical vote on the Missouri Compromise in the 16th House, March 1, 1820 (VOTEVIEW number 18).

only in 1836 and 1837. There were no sufficiently populated areas outside the existing states to make slavery an intense issue for many years after the Missouri Compromise. There were fewer than five slavery roll calls in the 17th, 18th, 21st, and 22nd Houses, and none at all in the 19th.

Consequently, the collapse of a well-organized party system in the Era of Good Feelings (evident in Figure 5.4) did not occur because slavery was the new, destabilizing dimension. The Federalist/Republican system collapsed largely because the previously salient foreign policy and economic issues had waned. The movement of settlers into Missouri made slavery, for a brief period, a salient issue with strong regional divisions. Both the success of the compromise and the absence of new settlement in the 1820s and 1830s implied that the Whig/Democratic system was able to arise along an economic dimension. However, slavery never completely vanished as an issue. Voting on slavery intensified just as the Whig/Democratic system emerged.

Indeed, the great bulk of all slavery roll calls were cast after 1835, during the period of the Whig/Democratic political-party system. Voting on slavery fell increasingly along the second dimension. In line with the scenario outlined in Figure 5.1, the gap between *APRE2* and *APRE1* trends upward from 1835 until the late 1840s (Congresses 24 to 30) and then drops to nearly zero after the 33rd Congress (1851–52). In addition, *APRE1* climbs dramatically after 1852, and the gap between *APRE2* and *APRE1* disappears, indicating that the first dimension is now the slavery dimension. The picture is clear: As the conflict within the country grew, the Whig and Democratic parties split along North-South lines *along the second dimension*, and the first dimension continued to divide the Whigs from the Democrats along traditional economic issues (for example, tariffs, internal improvements, the national bank, and public lands). By 1853, this economic dimension collapsed and was replaced by the slavery dimension.

The 32nd Congress (1851–52) was pivotal. By then the conflict had become so intense that it destroyed the spatial structure of congressional voting — the spatial model simply does not fit, or fits very poorly, voting in the 32nd Congress.[7] Outside Congress, the Compromise of 1850 was unraveling. Northern resistance to the Fugitive Slave Law was at first scattered, but with the publication of Harriet Beecher Stowe's *Uncle Tom's Cabin* in 1852, northern disregard for the law increased. The number of fugitive slaves was never very large (only about 1,000 out of population of 3,000,000 in 1850 [Hofstadter et al., 1959]) but the law had great symbolic importance for southerners. Northern aid to the fugitives was seen as evidence of hostility to the South and only deepened suspicions between the regions.

The realignment was sealed by the passage of the Kansas-Nebraska Act in May 1854 by the 33rd Congress. Both parties were badly split. The Whigs were primarily against the bill, and the Democrats mostly for it. Senator Stephen Douglas, an Illinois Democrat, tried to buy southern votes for a northern (as against a southern) route for the transcontinental railway. He introduced a measure that would have allowed the Nebraska territory, which was north of the Missouri Compromise 36°30' line, to enter as two states. One, Kansas would be a slave state, and the other, Nebraska, would be free, even though slavery was almost certainly economically unworkable in Kansas. The bill passed, after being pushed by the longstanding Democratic Party alliance in which the current Middle West traded votes on slavery for votes on economic matters (Weingast, 1991).

Douglas thought that the act would settle the territorial question once and for all by repealing the Missouri Compromise of 1820 and allowing the new states that were to be formed in the territories to decide the issue for themselves (popular sovereignty). Douglas evidently thought that by repealing the Missouri Compromise and thereby removing the federal government from deciding the slavery issue, the act would mollify southerners. Since most of the territories would undoubtedly be settled by migrants from the more populous northern states, popular sovereignty would ensure free-soil victories in the new states, thereby pleasing the northerners. Unfortunately for Douglas, however, regional divisions were much more powerful than he thought.[8]

Voting on the act was along regional lines and the spatial structure of the voting is very coherent (see Figure 5.8). Slavery became the primary dimension of voting. Northern politicians unwilling to trade away the slavery issue displaced the old political class of the Whig/Democratic party system. The Republican Party, and its 1860 presidential candidate, Abraham Lincoln, came to power, sealing the spatial realignment

The realignment is illustrated by Figures 5.5 to 5.9. Because slavery was already present as a salient issue when the Whig/Democratic system arose,

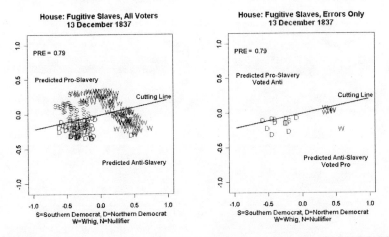

Figure 5.5. Motion for a fugitive slave resolution, December 13, 1837 (VOTEVIEW number 357).

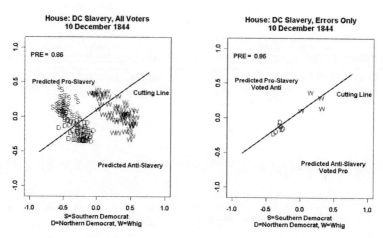

Figure 5.6. Vote on a petition about slavery in the District of Columbia, December 10, 1844 (VOTEVIEW number 433).

there is no equivalent, in these figures, to part A of Figure 5.1 or to Figure 5.2. The phases of the realignment corresponding to parts B and C (of Figure 5.1) are shown by Figures 5.5 and 5.6. Part B is illustrated by Figure 5.5, which shows the vote on a fugitive slave resolution on December 13, 1837; part C, by Figure 5.6, which shows a vote on whether to accept a petition concerning slavery in the District of Columbia, on December 10, 1844. In both figures,

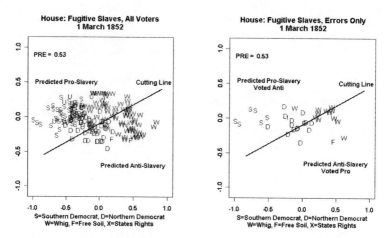

Figure 5.7. Vote to support fugitive slave provisions of the Compromise of 1850, March 1, 1852 (VOTEVIEW number 71).

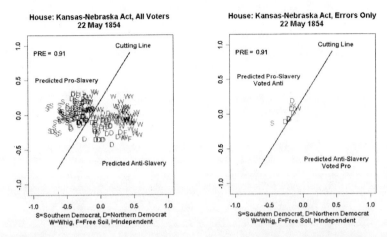

Figure 5.8. Passage of the Kansas-Nebraska Act, May 22, 1854 (VOTEVIEW number 309).

the first dimension separates the Whig and Democratic parties, and the second dimension separates the representatives into southerners (on top) and northerners (on bottom). The spatial structure shown in the figures held from approximately 1832 to 1849. The main difference in the figures — parallel to the differences between parts B and C of Figure 5.1 — is that the parties are more strongly separated into regional blocs by 1844.

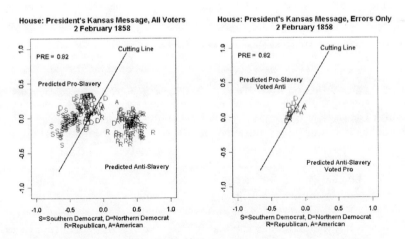

Figure 5.9. Vote to postpone consideration of president's message on Kansas, February 2, 1858 (VOTEVIEW number 45).

After the passage of the Compromise of 1850, however, a spatial collapse transpired quickly, as illustrated by a vote on March 1, 1852, calling for support of the fugitive slave portions of the compromise.[9] Although this vote had the highest turnout of any slavery roll call in the 32nd Congress, the *PRE2* was a relatively meager 0.53. Figure 5.7 shows, consonant with part D of Figure 5.1, the overlap in party positions.[10] Minor parties are prolific in Figure 5.7. The cutting line has rotated considerably from its location in the two previous figures. Strategic voting has much to do with the poor fit. Many northern Democrats, seeking to maintain their party's dominance of national politics, voted Yea. On other hand, although only seven southerners voted Nay, five of these (and two abstainers as well) came from the most strongly proslavery delegation, that of South Carolina. Note further that, consistent with an earlier discussion of Figure 5.1, the South Carolina delegation moved from the top of the plot in Figure 5.6 to the left-most position in Figure 5.7.

The collapse of the party system is illustrated again in Figure 5.8, which shows the vote that passed the Kansas-Nebraska Act on May 22, 1854.[11] Although most minor parties have vanished in Figure 5.8, the Democratic and Whig parties are mixed together in the center of the space, which is similar to part D of Figure 5.1. The cutting line has, compared to Figures 5.5 and 5.6, become more vertical, foreshadowing slavery's emergence as the main dimension of the realigned space. Indeed, unlike the fugitive slave vote and other votes in the preceding Congress, the Kansas-Nebraska Act votes have a high degree of fit — the *PRE* for the illustrated vote is 0.91.

Finally, Figure 5.9 shows the first slavery roll call in the 35th House, which took place on February 2, 1858. The vote was on a proposal by the Democratic majority to postpone consideration of the president's message on Kansas. The vote has a *PRE2* of 0.82 and is now fully on the first dimension. The move to postpone failed (105–109) because of defections of moderate Democrats, as the figure shows; these were all northerners. (The only slave-state representative to vote against the motion was an American Party member from Baltimore.) The realignment was complete by this time, and the new party — the Republicans — was tightly clustered, in line with part E of Figure 5.1. Southern representatives for the next eighty years remained on the Left on the major dimension, with views on the treatment of African Americans being highly correlated with views on economic regulation, the tariff, and monetary policy (as seen later in this chapter and in chapter 6).

Figure 5.3 and Figures 5.5 through 5.9 show that the 1850s realignment within Congress was sudden and was initiated *before* the Republican Party became a real force in American politics. This result questions some recent work by political economists and historians.

Fogel (1990) studies the realignment that produced Lincoln's electoral victory by comparing the elections of 1852 and 1860. But, at least in Congress, we see that the old Whig system had largely disintegrated by the time of the elections of 1852. To compare the old system to the new, 1848 would appear to be a better benchmark.

Weingast (1991) correctly identifies 1850 as a crucial date in the slavery conflict. The old spatial alignment collapsed in the 1851–52 House and Senate. But Weingast attributes the sudden change to a single event: the destruction of a credible commitment to slavery in the South by breaking the North-South balance in the Senate with the admission of California as a free state in 1850. What we show is that the tension over slavery had built gradually over time, as shown by the steadily rising importance of the second dimension in the 1840s. The realignment of the 1850s was more a matter of a process that gradually increases stress until a breaking point is reached than one of a single overwhelming event.

This pattern does fit Sundquist's (1983) model rather nicely. A new issue (actually a version of a very old issue), the extension of slavery into the territories, emerges, which cuts across the existing line of cleavage (conflicts over economic policy), and causes the two political parties to polarize. One party is destroyed in the process, and a new party system forms around the new issue. In spatial terms, a stable two-dimensional two-party system becomes unstable. The first dimension disappears and its place is taken by the old second dimension.[12]

Gold and Silver and the "Realignment" of the 1890s

Sundquist (1983) notes that in the aftermath of the Civil War the new dimension of conflict was concerned with Reconstruction, secession, black rights, and related issues. The groups shut out of the system were the farmers and the emerging labor movement. The 1866–1897 period saw a persistent, long-run deflation marked by falling commodity prices (Friedman and Schwartz, 1971). This was the driving force behind the inflation issue; and according to Sundquist (1983), this issue represented the new line of cleavage that culminated in the realigning election of 1896, in which the Gold Democrats deserted the Democratic Party for the Republican Party. The Silver Republicans were not able to overcome their aversion to the Democrats because of the Civil War and remained in the Republican Party. This made the Republican Party the majority party until the 1930s.

The inflation issue had its roots in the tremendous expansion of the money supply during the Civil War. The cost of the Civil War forced the Union government to borrow heavily and print "greenbacks." Although some of the colonies had experimented with fiat money (paper money with no specie backing [Weiss, 1970]), the issuance of greenbacks in 1862 marked the first time that the United States had resorted to paper money not backed by specie. The expansion of the money supply during the war caused inflation and the abandonment of the gold standard. By the war's end inflation had approximately doubled the overall price level.

The efforts of the government to deal with the inflation problem immediately after the war became an issue in the 1868 presidential election, prefiguring the splits within and between the two major parties that were to reoccur for the next twenty-five years. The effort by Secretary of the Treasury Hugh McCulloch to contract the money supply by withdrawing greenbacks from circulation contributed to postwar deflation. Heeding the protests of midwestern farmers, the Democrats proposed in their 1868 party platform that the greenbacks be reissued to redeem war bonds, which did not specifically require redemption in gold. This was the first of many inflationary, or "soft money," proposals and it became known at the time as the "Ohio Idea."[13]

A total of 481 roll calls in the House and 523 roll calls in the Senate were cast on banking and currency during the 1865–1908 period (39th to 60th Congresses). For every House and Senate for which there were at least five roll calls on banking and currency, we computed *APRE1* and *APRE2*. The results are shown in Figure 5.7, which is in the same format as Figure 5.3.

The pattern for the currency issue is quite different than that for slavery in that there is no *sustained* gap between *APRE1* and *APRE2*. Rather, the gap peaks in the 43rd to 45th Congresses (1873–1879) and in the 52nd to 53rd Congresses (1891–1895). These two peaks coincide with the financial panics of 1873 and 1893. (Once again, the pattern for the Senate is similar to that for the House.)

The financial panic of September 1873 produced a contraction in the money supply and generated demands for inflation. Prior to the panic, farmers were, in general, suspicious of paper money. After 1873, however, farmers' support for greenbackism increased (Unger, 1964, pp. 228–233). The result was the Inflation Bill of 1874 that was passed by the 43rd Congress and vetoed by President Grant. Figure 5.11 shows the final passage votes in the House and Senate in April of 1874 on the Inflation Bill.[14]

Voting on the bill split both political parties along the second dimension. Prefiguring the splits that were later to occur on the silver question, the opposition to the inflation bill was concentrated in the New England states and New York; the proponents came primarily from the South and the Midwest. During this period, however, the regional coalitions were not yet completely solid. All the representatives and senators from Nevada and Texas and all the repre-

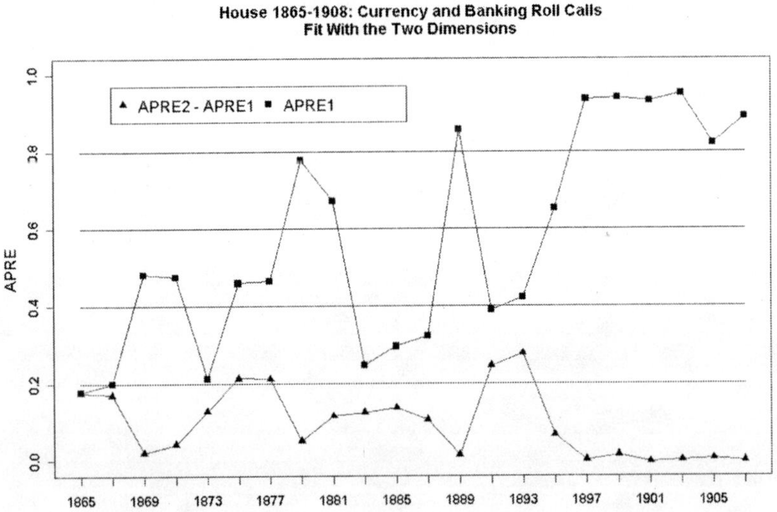

House 1865-1908: Currency and Banking Roll Calls
Fit With the Two Dimensions

Figure 5.10. Banking and currency votes in the House of Representatives (1865–1908). The first dimension gradually becomes stronger over time. The second dimension never clearly becomes the more important dimension. A realignment does not occur. (APRE2–APRE1 is sometimes slightly negative because the two-dimensional model actually resulted in worse classification than the one-dimensional model. For all roll calls in a Congress, however, the two-dimensional model always improves classification.)

sentatives from California (the senators from California did not vote) opposed the inflation bill.

After the 1876 elections, the focus of the inflationists shifted from greenbacks to remonetizing silver. The tremendous increase in silver production in the western states after the Civil War produced a decline in the price of silver in the 1870s. This produced a coalition of convenience of the western mining interests, farmers, and greenbackers. The result was the Bland-Allison Act of 1878 that passed in the 45th Congress. It required the Treasury to purchase between 2 and 4 million ounces of silver per month and to coin it into silver legal-tender dollars. Figure 5.12 shows the votes of February 18, 1878 in the House and Senate to override the veto of President Hayes.[15]

Voting on the act was primarily along the second dimension, which is now clearly a regional dimension. Only seven representatives and four senators from the western and southern states voted to sustain Hayes's veto while only ten representatives and no senators from New York and New England voted to override.

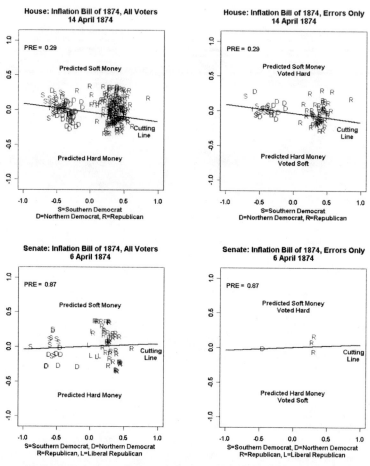

Figure 5.11. Final passage of the inflation bill of 1874. The House vote (VOTEVIEW number 126) was on April 14; the Senate vote (VOTEVIEW number 119) was on April 6.

With the triumph of the "soft money" forces, voting on banking and currency-related issues from 46th through the 51st Congresses (1879–90) reverted to a more "normal" pattern; that is, voting was more along party lines, and therefore the gap between *APRE1* and *APRE2* is small.

In the 1888 elections the Republicans gained control of both the Congress and the presidency. The blessings of unified government allowed them to admit to the union only those parts of the frontier that would be firmly in the Republican camp. While relatively heavily populated Arizona and New Mexico were denied statehood, Washington, Idaho, Montana, Wyoming, and North and

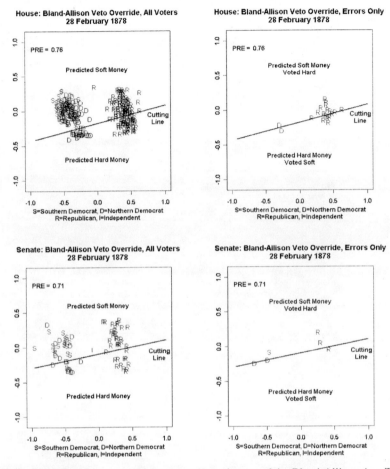

Figure 5.12. Votes to override President Hayes's veto of the Bland-Allison Act. The House (VOTEVIEW number 93) and Senate (VOTEVIEW number153) both voted on February 28, 1878.

South Dakota were admitted in 1889 and 1890 and promptly sent an additional twelve Republican senators to Washington.[16] The entry of the western states created great pressure within the Republican Party for further action on inflation. The Republicans pushed through the McKinley Tariff, the Sherman Anti-Trust Act, and the Sherman Silver Purchase Act, all in 1890.

In return for western votes in the Senate and House in favor of the McKinley Tariff, the eastern Republicans supported the Sherman Silver Purchase Act, which was passed in both Houses in July by straight party-line votes. In effect, the Sherman Silver Purchase Act obligated the government to buy nearly the entire output of the western silver mines. But even this measure did not brake the decline of the price of silver. The falling price of silver only further encouraged people to exchange silver and paper money for gold. The result was a steady drain of the Treasury's gold reserves.

The financial panic that began in May of 1893 was touched off, in part, by the drop in the nation's gold reserves. The resulting crisis led to the repeal of the Sherman Silver Purchase Act in October 1893. Figure 5.13 shows that voting on the repeal served to again split the two political parties along regional lines.[17]

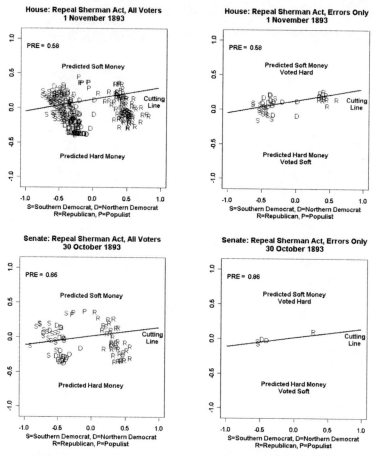

Figure 5.13. Votes to repeal the Sherman Silver Purchase Act. The House vote (VOTEVIEW number 60) was on November 1, 1893; the Senate vote (VOTEVIEW number 80) was on October 30.

In the Senate, six southern Democrats and four western Republicans along with all the senators from New England, New York, and New Jersey, voted to repeal. In the House eleven of the eighteen Republicans who voted against repeal were from the western states, whereas thirty-one southern Democrats — mostly from Kentucky, Virginia, North Carolina, and Texas — voted for repeal. New England, New York, New Jersey, and all of the representatives from the major eastern cities — New York City, Boston, Philadelphia, and Baltimore — voted for repeal.

With the repeal of the Sherman Silver Purchase Act by the 53rd Congress, the banking and currency issue once again reverted to a more normal pattern of voting along the first dimension. Indeed, after the 53rd Congress, the gap between $APRE2$ and $APRE1$ disappears and $APRE1$ climbs to above 0.8 in both chambers indicating that the banking and currency issue is absorbed into the first dimension after the 53rd Congress.

What killed the inflation issue was not the "realignment" of the 1890s, but inflation itself. Farm prices started back up in 1896, and the general price level began to increase shortly thereafter. Several major gold discoveries and the introduction of a cheap cyanide process for extracting gold from tailings dramatically increased the money supply after 1896 (Hofstadter et al., 1959; Friedman and Schwartz, 1971).

That the issue was finally drawn into the first dimension does not mean that the regional differences disappeared. Indeed, an examination of the spatial maps for Congresses throughout the post-Civil War period shows that the second dimension tended to separate westerners from easterners — and the effect was greater within the Republican Party. In addition, this separation was maintained after the 1896 election.

In sum, the evidence indicates that the status of inflation as an issue changed. That is, the basic configuration of the House and Senate was fairly stable throughout this period but the *mapping* of inflation changed — inflation slowly changed from a two-dimensional issue to a strongly one-dimensional issue over the period. Unlike the 1850s, though, the first dimension was never replaced. The realignment at the level of congressional voting did not change the basic structure of voting; rather, as an issue, inflation evolved until voting on it lined up along the first dimension.

The Great Depression and the "Realignment" of the 1930s

The collapse of the stock market in October 1929 was followed by an economic slide that turned into the Great Depression of the 1930s. By the summer of 1932 industrial production was down 50 percent, commodity prices were down 50 percent, and unemployment was around 24 percent. The consequences for the Republican Party were equally severe. The four congressional elections between 1930 and 1936 resulted in a massive replacement of Republicans by Democrats in the Congress. By 1937 the Democratic Party held a 334-to-88 margin over the Republicans in the House (thirteen congressmen belonged to minor parties), and a 76-to-16 lead in the Senate (four came from minor parties). This wholesale replacement is the result of realignment in the voting behavior of the mass electorate in the 1930s. Never before or after this time were the Democratic and Republican parties so imbalanced in Congress during peacetime.[18]

The economic catastrophe changed the agenda of Congress. Prior to the Great Depression, providing relief for the destitute was the function of private and religious organizations, not the federal government. Moreover, the New Deal altered for good the role of the federal government in regulating the economy. Sinclair argues that the New Deal agenda "increased the ideological content of American politics" and produced "a much clearer ideological distinction between the congressional parties" (1977, p. 952). Ginsberg argues that "changes in policy after 1933 are in keeping with voter choices favoring alterations in the economic system and redistributions of opportunities in favor of urban working class elements" (1976, p. 49).

There is no question that the congressional agenda radically changed during the 1930s. The real question is: Did the change in content bring with it a change in the spatial structure of voting? The answer is no. The change in agenda was accommodated within the existing framework. What *did* change was the ratio of Democrats to Republicans. This fact is shown in Figures 5.14 and 5.15, which show the estimated positions of representatives in the 71st House (1929–30) and 74th House (1935–36), respectively. In both figures, southern Democrats (denoted by a lowercase s) represent the left wing of the Democratic Party. The shape of the Republican cluster changes, but largely as a result of the elimination of a part of the cluster.

The spatial structure of Figure 5.14 is essentially repeated in Figure 5.15, indicating that the Depression did not result in an immediate realignment of congressional voting patterns. In addition, through this period, the fit of the two-dimensional dynamic model to the roll call data is quite good. That is, the results in Figure 3.1, for this period, do not show a dramatic drop in *PRE*, like the ones in the 16th and 31st Congresses. The second dimension through this period picked up a weak western-versus-eastern states effect, along with voting on the social issues of the day — prohibition and immigration.

The stable spatial structure shows that the legislation of the *first* New Deal was indeed largely accommodated within the spatial structure that had prevailed since the end of Reconstruction. The legislation either reflected new issues that mapped readily onto the old lines of conflict or old issues, latent during the period of the Democrats' prolonged minority status, that could be

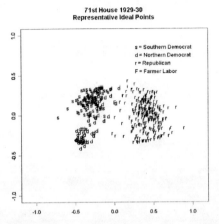

Figure 5.14. Ideal points of representatives in the 71st House (1929–30). On the first dimension, the southern Democrats are to the left of the northern Democrats.

brought to the table as new measures and passed into law with the new Democratic majorities.

A good illustration of the absence of realignment in the Depression is illustrated by roll call voting in the labor area, shown in Figure 5.16. In the House, 358 such roll calls were cast from the 59th Congress through the 106th.[19] For every House for which there were at least three roll calls on labor regulation,

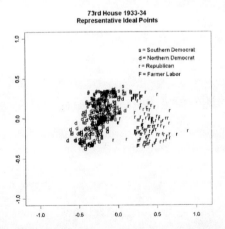

Figure 5.15. Ideal points of representatives in the 73rd House (1933–34). Although there are many more northern Democrats than in the previous figure, the relative positions of southern Democrats and northern Democrats have shown no substantial change. Indeed, the Great Depression did not produce an immediate realignment in Congress.

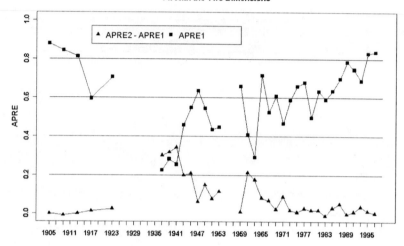

Figure 5.16. Labor-regulation votes in the House of Representatives (1905–2000). Before the second New Deal votes on labor were rare but were fit by the first dimension when they did occur. After the second New Deal perturbed the position of southern Democrats in the space, labor votes became almost entirely first-dimension votes. (APRE2–APRE1 is sometimes slightly negative because the two-dimensional model actually resulted in a lower correct-classification rate than the one-dimensional model. For all roll calls in a Congress, however, the two-dimensional model always improves classification.)

we computed *APRE1* and *APRE2*. Not until the battle over the Fair Labor Standards Act — the original minimum wage bill — in 1937–38 (75th Congress) did the second dimension play any role in legislation in the labor area. When the second dimension did come into play, it closely tracked the North-South division within the Democratic Party over the race issue. Similar results are found for the Senate.

Another illustration of the non-realignment of the Depression is roll call voting within Clausen's social welfare category, shown in Figure 5.17 for the House (results for the Senate are similar to those for the House). We removed voting on liquor regulation and immigration from the category because they were strongly two dimensional *before* the Depression. (See Figures 5.20 and 5.21; these issues will be further discussed below.) In the House, 2,638 roll calls were cast on social welfare during the 1905–2000 period (59th to 106th Congresses). For every House and Senate for which there were at least three roll calls on social welfare, we computed *APRE1* and *APRE2*. Social welfare has been largely a first-dimensional issue since 1905 with occasional minor

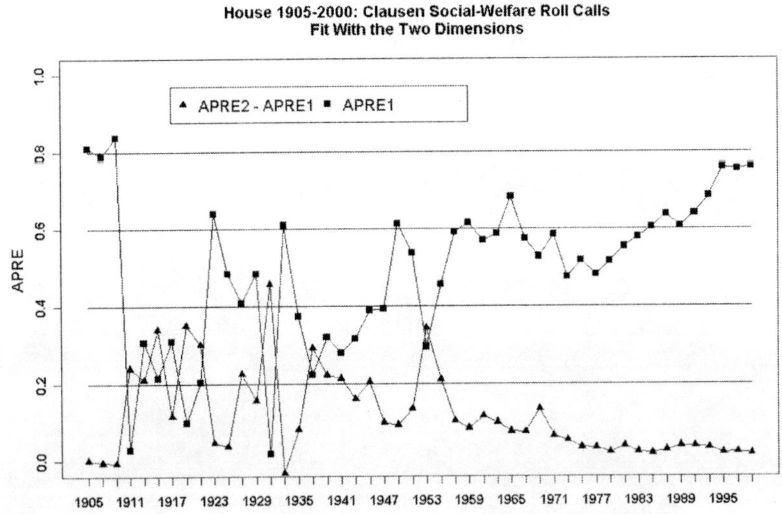

**House 1905-2000: Clausen Social-Welfare Roll Calls
Fit With the Two Dimensions**

Figure 5.17. Votes coded in Clausen's social-welfare category, House of Representatives (1905–2000). These votes have always been predominantly first-dimension votes. They have been, since the second New Deal, an increasingly good fit to the dimension.

increments arising from the second dimension. These increments occurred in the late 1930s, the 1950s, and the 1960s. There is no evidence of a realignment brought about by the Depression.

Civil Rights and the Perturbation of the Space, circa 1940–70

In perhaps a classic illustration of Riker's (1962) size principle, the extraordinarily large Democratic majority of 1937 was too good to last. Northern Democrats, who outnumbered southern Democrats 219 to 115, embarked on the second New Deal. Many of the new programs were not to the liking of the South. The conflict is most evident in the area of civil rights for blacks.

Roll calls on civil rights area are shown in Figure 5.18. Totals of 563 roll calls in the House and 792 in the Senate were taken on civil rights for blacks from the 37th through the 106th Congresses (1861–2000). In the Senate, very few votes were taken on civil rights for blacks from the 46th through the 75th Senates. Consequently we focus on the House, where we computed *APRE1* and *APRE2* for every Congress in which there were at least three roll calls on the civil rights.

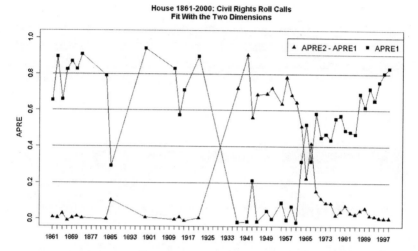

Figure 5.18. Votes on civil rights for blacks, House of Representatives (1861–2000). Having traditionally been first-dimension votes in postbellum America, civil rights votes became entirely second-dimension votes (with the *APRE1* near zero) during the era of the three-party system. After the passage of the Civil Rights Act and the Voting Rights Act in the 1960s, this issue area returned to the first dimension as the civil rights agenda shifted toward issues of economic redistribution.

During the Civil War and Reconstruction (37th House through the 44th), civil rights votes were highly structured on the first dimension. During the Civil War, there were many votes on the role of African Americans in the military. The Reconstruction period saw votes on the Bureau of Freedmen and civil rights bills. Between Reconstruction and the New Deal, votes on civil rights had somewhat lower *PRE*s, but the voting was picked up on the first dimension. This is largely because being left on economic issues meant favoring redistribution from richer whites in the Northeast to poorer whites in the South.[20] The split on economic issues happened to match, with reverse logic, the split on a host of anti-lynching roll calls in 1921 and 1922 (the 67th House).

Between 1922 and 1937 (the 68th Congress through the 74th), there were only two civil rights roll calls, with only one falling in the first Roosevelt administration. By the time votes on lynch laws recurred, in 1937 and 1940, and were joined, during World War II, by roll calls on the poll tax and voting rights in the armed forces,[21] there was a horde of northern Democrats who voted left on economic issues. A second dimension became necessary to differentiate northerners and southerners on civil rights votes.

The economic agenda itself became infused with the conflict over race. While the opposition of the South to the minimum wage legislation introduced in 1937 and passed in 1938 might be motivated by the economic interest of a low-wage area,[22] southern white congressmen also explicitly opposed minimum wages as favoring southern blacks (see chapter 6). To accommodate the South, the initial minimum wage coverage excluded the tobacco industry and other sectors of the economy concentrated in the South (and in areas where competition with the North was not an issue). Even so, southerners largely opposed the labor legislation of the second New Deal. Consequently, labor also had an important second dimension component from the late 1930s onward. (See both Figure 5.16 and the discussion of minimum wage legislation in chapter 6.)

As economic issues also turned from redistribution between whites to redistribution from whites to blacks, particularly in the South, the southern Democrat delegation in Congress gradually became more conservative on the first dimension as it began to define a pole on the second dimension. By the late 1950s, this realignment of southern Democrats meant that the first dimension alone was largely sufficient to classify roll call votes, greatly reducing $PRE2-PRE1$ on most labor issues. By 1970, first dimension PRE levels returned to those found in the twenties and thirties (see Figure 5.16).

Civil rights remained a second-dimension issue longer than labor did. Economic conservatives in the Republican Party joined northern Democrats to pass the Civil Rights Act of 1964 and the Voting Rights Act of 1965. After these two events, civil rights could increasingly be accounted for by the first dimension. In signing the legislation and "delivering the South to the Republicans for 50 years," Lyndon Johnson signaled a realignment in mass voting behavior. But this did not lead to spatial realignment in Congress. Rather it ended the perturbation of the space by the civil rights issue. As southern Democrats took on a black clientele, they became increasingly like northern Democrats. Unlike the 1920s, there is now a consistent rightwing position, personified by Jesse Helms in the 1980s, on economics and race. Not a single southern Democratic senator failed to vote to override President Bush's veto of the Civil Rights Bill of 1990. The veto was sustained by conservative Republicans, from the North and the South. Indeed, the bill involved substantial economic redistribution, and its impact would have been nationwide.

Figure 5.19 shows the override vote in the 101st Senate. What is striking about the configuration is that the southern and northern Democrats are no longer clearly separated on the second dimension. The most conservative southern Democrats are now indistinguishable along the main dimension from liberal Republican senators such as Bob Packwood of Oregon. Indeed, the second dimension adds only 2 percent to the 83 percent of the total choices classified by the first dimension. The second dimension has been gradually disappearing

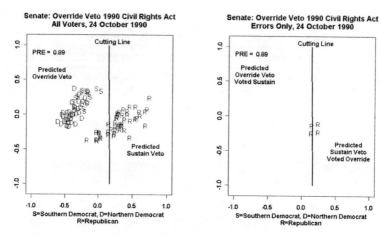

Figure 5.19. Senate vote to override President Bush's veto of the 1990 Civil Rights Bill. Southern Democrats are no longer distinctly separated from northern Democrats, as all southern Democrats voted to override. There are only four classification errors, all very close to the cutting line.

since the middle of the 1970s. The trend continued into the twenty-first century (see chapter 12).

The civil rights episode, lasting roughly from 1940 to 1966, is very instructive in regard to spatial realignment. While race and economics are substantively quite distinct, only one dimension was needed before 1940. This was just fortuitous, as conservative positions on race and economics just happened to be strongly, albeit negatively, correlated. The breakup of the overly large Roosevelt coalition and the subsequent enfranchisement of southern blacks took place in a framework of spatial perturbation. While a second dimension was needed to capture the resolution of this conflict, the conflict never managed to dominate the basic economic conflict inherent in democracy. Voting never became chaotic, as in 1851–52. The perturbation ended with legislation that induced a strong positive correlation of conservative positions on race and economic policy. Converse's (1964) view of constraint in ideology is now reflected in a basically one-dimensional political space in Congress.

Incorporation of Substantive Issues into the Basic Space

As we noted earlier, most of the galaxy of policy issues that confront Congress are neither as intense nor as enduring as the question of race that led to the realignment of the 1850s and the perturbation of the 1950s. How are these issues accommodated in the basic space?

We indicated earlier that if an issue is to result in sustained public policies, we hypothesize that the policies must eventually be supported by a coalition that can be represented as a split on the first, or major, dimension. Policy developed by coalitions that are non-spatial or built along the second dimension is likely to be transient and unstable.

To investigate this hypothesis requires us to sharpen our focus and look at issue areas that are relatively narrowly defined, permitting us to keep substance relatively constant. Our first effort of this type was a detailed study of the history of minimum wage legislation (Poole and Rosenthal, 1991b; see also chapter 6 of this book). Before World War II, the minimum wage issue was relatively poorly mapped into the space. Even using two dimensions, the classifications were much worse than after the war. After the war, minimum wage became a first-dimension issue with a high degree of classification accuracy.

Another example of an issue that ripened into a first dimension split is the abortion issue. Between 1973 and 2000 (93rd through 106th Congresses) a total of 200 roll calls in the House and 159 in the Senate were cast on abortion. Figure 5.20 shows the *APRE* values for each House and Senate for which there were at least three roll calls on abortion. As shown in Figure 5.20, when abortion first came onto the agenda shortly after the Supreme Court's *Roe v. Wade* ruling in 1973 (93rd Congress), the issue did not fit the existing spatial dimensions very well. It basically falls along the first dimension but with a low level of *APRE*. But the *APRE* has gradually increased over time.[23] Part of this increase has resulted from well known flip-flops, such as Richard Gephardt's (D-MO) conversion to a pro-choice position. It no longer seems possible that abortion policy can be decided by single-issue politics because it has been drawn into the first dimension.

The prohibition issue is a nice counterpoint to the abortion issue. The temperance movement was a classical movement of single-issue politics. Seventy-three roll calls in the House were taken on liquor regulation from the 59th Congress through the 74th (1905 to 1936). For every House for which there were at least three roll calls on liquor regulation we computed the *APRE*s. Unfortunately, there were not enough Senates with three or more roll calls to make a comparison between the House and Senate.

Figure 5.21 shows that voting on prohibition did not map at all into the first dimension and had only a moderately high level of *PRE* on the second dimension. (The exception is the first dimension votes in 1935, after repeal.) Although the special-interest coalition was strong enough to amend the Constitution, it did not produce a lasting element of public policy.

While much more work is required on how specific issues map into the basic unidimensional structure of congressional voting, the results from minimum wage, abortion, and prohibition issues (and, in an earlier period, from that of

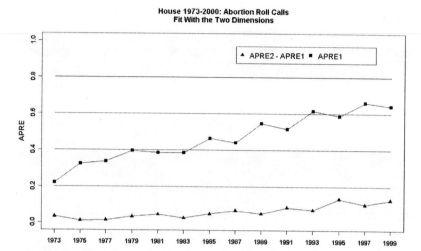

Figure 5.20. Abortion roll calls, House of Representatives (1973–2000). Abortion slowly became a liberal-conservative, first-dimension issue with a good fit to the spatial model.

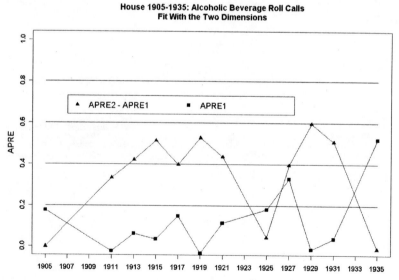

Figure 5.21. Alcoholic beverage roll calls, House of Representatives (1905–1935). Single-issue politics prevail, with APRE

monetary policy) support our hypothesis that stable policy coalitions are built on the first dimension.

Summary

Major changes in the voting behavior of the mass electorate occurred during the 1850s, 1890s, and 1930s. Only in the 1850s, however, is there evidence that these changes produced a corresponding shift in the structure of congressional roll call voting. The changes of the 1890s and 1930s were largely massive replacements of legislators of one party by new legislators from the opposing party. These replacements did not change the basic structure of congressional voting in the late 1890s and early 1930s. The great changes in the voting behavior of the mass voting public at these times produced new majorities but not a fundamental alteration of how issues mapped into the space.

Beginning in the late 1930s, however, a perturbation of the space occurred that *did* change the structure of congressional voting. The overlarge Roosevelt coalition gradually fell apart over the old issue of race. It gave rise to the three-party system with distinct clusters for northern Democrats, southern Democrats, and Republicans (see Figure 3.3). This division peaked in the 1960s and has slowly faded away. Southern Democrats are now to the left of Republicans.

Our results suggest a general model for issue change. We have found that the first dimension, throughout most of American history, has captured the main economic conflicts between the two major political parties. During normal periods, a weak second dimension is usually present, capturing the social, or regional, issues of the day. New issues that have staying power will eventually be drawn into the exiting one- or two-dimensional alignment because it is easier to build stable coalitions within the existing stable structure of voting.

Notes

1. See Burnham (1970), Ginsberg (1972, 1976), Sinclair (1977, 1981), Brady (1979, 1982), and Sundquist (1983).
2. Following most authors, we do not treat the long transition from the collapse of the Federalist Party until the emergence of the Whig and Democratic parties, in the late 1820s and early 1830s, as a realignment. Before 1824, election statistics are not reliable, and turnout was low. In 1824, the legislatures of six states were still choosing their presidential electors. By 1828, twenty of the twenty-two states were choosing electors by popular election (the holdouts were Delaware and South Carolina). Consequently, there are no reliable mass-voting data, before 1828, to analyze.
3. See also Aldrich (1983).
4. Consequently, it might be preferable to focus on changes in probabilities rather than classifications (Poole and Rosenthal, 1991a). But because the results are similar, we develop the discussion in terms of the more easily interpretable *PRE* measure.

5. These totals are for the first thirty-nine Congresses — that is, for those until the end of the Civil War.

6. See McCarty, Poole, and Rosenthal (2002) for a more detailed discussion of Missouri Compromise votes.

7. It is the second worst-fitting House in American history. (The worst occurred in the 17th Congress, when the Federalists collapsed.) Joel Silbey (1967) in his analysis of voting in the 32nd Congress in *The Shrine of Party* writes: "The most significant fact in the legislative voting in 1851 and 1852 was that large-scale cohesive forces no longer influenced Congressional behavior to the degree they once had . . . . Congressional voting had broken down . . . into a multiplicity of factional groupings, behavioral factors, and individual decision-making, with only occasional alignments of these patterns into large-scale partisan or sectional groupings" (p. 135).

8. Douglas's motives in pushing the Kansas-Nebraska Act have generated a very large literature. Douglas was a complex man and no one can be completely certain about his motives. An excellent discussion and summary of the various points of view on this debate is given in Nevins (1947, chapter 3). An interesting account of the opposition to Douglas is given in Donald (1960, pp. 249–259).

9. The vote is VOTEVIEW number 71 in the 32nd House. The division on the vote was 119 Yeas to 74 Nays. There were thirty-six classification errors.

10. The overlap is in fact understated to the extent that the linear adjustment in positions used by DW-NOMINATE prohibits rapid changes of member positions during a spatial collapse.

11. The vote is VOTEVIEW number 309 in the 33rd House. The division on the roll call was 113 Yeas to 100 Nays. DW-NOMINATE correctly classified 205 of 213 votes.

12. The destabilization of the existing political parties is precisely what many opponents of slavery wanted and set out to achieve. See the discussion by Riker (1982, chapter 9).

13. See Unger (1964, chapters 2 and 3) for a detailed discussion of the various "soft money" proposals made during the 1865–1870 period.

14. These are VOTEVIEW number 126 in the 43rd House and number 119 in the 43rd Senate, respectively. In the House, the division on the roll call was 140 Yeas to 102 Nays. With pairs, the vote was 150 Yeas to 111 Nays. DW-NOMINATE correctly classified 182 of 261 representatives (69.7 percent; 0.29 *PRE*). (*There were thus 10 paired Yea and 9 paired Nay. That the numbers don't balance reflects the original data. This is true of other imbalances throughout this book.*) In the Senate, the division on the roll call was 36 Yeas to 31 Nays. With pairs, the vote was 51 Yeas to 31 Nays. DW-NOMINATE correctly classified sixty-one of sixty-seven senators (91.0 percent; 0.81 *PRE*.)

15. These are VOTEVIEW number 93 in the 45th House and number 153 in the 45th Senate. The vote to override in the House was 196 Yeas to 73 Nays. With pairs, the vote was 203 Yeas to 78 Nays. DW-NOMINATE correctly classified 249 of 269 representatives (92.6 percent; 0.74 *PRE*). The vote to override in the Senate was 46 Yeas to 19 Nays. With pairs the vote was 51 Yeas to 21 Nays. DW-NOMINATE correctly classified sixty-six of seventy-two senators (91.7 percent; 0.71 *PRE*).

16. See Stewart and Weingast (1992) and McCarty, Poole, and Rosenthal (2002) for extensive discussions of the admission of new states during this period.

17. These are VOTEVIEW number 60 in the 53rd House and number 80 in the 53rd Senate. The vote to repeal in the House was 194 Yeas to 94 Nays. With pairs the vote was 195 to 97. DW-NOMINATE correctly classified 251 of 292 representatives correctly (86.0 percent; 0.58 *PRE*). In the Senate the vote to repeal was 43 Yeas to 32 Nays. With pairs the vote was 47 to 35. DW-NOMINATE correctly classified seventy-six of eighty-two senators correctly (92.7 percent; 0.83 *PRE*.)

18. The Civil War Congresses — 37, 38, 39, and 40 — were lopsidedly Republican, but the Democrats managed to hang onto about 20 percent of the seats, even with the eleven states of the Confederacy absent. The imbalance in favor of the Republicans peaked in the 40th Congress at 80.3 percent of the total seats, but three states (Texas, Mississippi, and Virginia) were not yet back in the Union.

19. This analysis and those in the remainder of this chapter end with the 106th Congress. At the time of writing, we had issue-coded the roll calls only through the 106th Congress, even though DW-NOMINATE was run through the 108th.

20. See chapter 6 for a more detailed discussion of civil rights voting in the 48th Congress.

21. For an account of the fights over voting rights, see Young (1956, pp. 82–89). For the origins of the conservative coalition, see Brady and Bullock (1980).

22. Sinclair (1977, p. 948) argues that "Southerners feared that a nationwide minimum wage would nullify their region's advantage in attracting industry." Sinclair also argues that the North-South split on minimum wage was also due in part to the fact that it was a permanent measure, as opposed to temporary measures such as work relief. "A positive vote on them does imply a commitment to continued government activism in the social welfare area. It is on such programs that the North-South split in the Democratic party begins to appear" (1977, p. 949).

23. Roll calls on abortion increased in frequency as the roll calls mapped onto the first dimension. In the seventeen years from 1973 through 1989, there were only 61 House votes and 67 Senate votes on abortion. In the eleven years from 1990 through 2000, there were 139 votes in the House and 92 in the Senate.

6

Issues, Constituent Interests, and the Basic Space

We have demonstrated that the great bulk of congressional roll call voting can be accounted for by the simple one- or two-dimensional spatial model. How is this so, given the complex and diverse interests that must be addressed by every session of Congress?

In this chapter, we suggest some answers to this problem and illustrate our answers with important substantive examples: (1) House voting that initiated the food stamp program in 1964 and renewed it in 1967; (2) the development of railroad regulation from 1874 to 1887, culminating in the passage of the Interstate Commerce Act; (3) minimum wage legislation from the initial passage of the Fair Labor Standards Act in 1937 through the increase in the minimum wage, in 1990; (4) strip mine legislation in 1974; (5) Senate votes on the Occupational Safety and Health Administration in 1975; and (6) America's first bankruptcy law in 1800 and voting on new bankruptcy law two centuries later, in 2000.

Most of these topics have been intensively studied by other researchers. Ferejohn (1986), in his case study of food stamps, stresses the importance of logrolling, which, we believe, is critical to the process that projects specific economic issues onto the abstract, low-dimensional space. In contrast, Gilligan et al. (1989) analyzed railroad regulation in terms of economic interests specific to the railroad issue; a similar approach was taken by several researchers studying the minimum wage.[1] With respect to strip mining, Kalt and Zupan (1984) made the seminal attempt at comparing a detailed model of economic interests with an ideological explanation of roll call voting.[2] As a measure of ideology, they constructed a pro-environment index from votes supported by the League of Conservation Voters (LCV), a single-issue environmental group.

Kalt and Zupan, controlling for ideology, find that most other variables are of minor importance. We go one step further and report that the general D-NOM-INATE[3] measure of ideology does just as well as the LCV measure that is related to the topical issue. We also find that ideology dominates economic interest measures for railroads, minimum wages, and food stamps. A similar result is obtained in comparing ideology to a set of economic and demographic variables used on a large set of roll calls in the manner of Peltzman (1984). In all the analyses presented in this chapter, NOMINATE scores are the variables that have the most influence on individual roll call votes.

One important reason that our scores are such powerful variables is their ability to incorporate party-line voting. As previously seen in Figures 3.3, 3.4, and 5.2 to 5.15, throughout nearly all of congressional history, the parties are represented as two distinct clusters of legislators in the space. Cutting lines that separate the clusters represent party-line votes. When the party whip is used to enforce the long-term logroll that is represented by party affiliation, members vote in a manner that is consistent with spatial voting even if they appear to be voting against their constituency's issue-specific economic interest.

Moreover, parties do not just impose discipline but also package logrolls. Although votes on particular roll calls may appear contrary to the constituency's economic interest, the package as a whole may be beneficial. For example, Ferejohn (1986) points out on food stamps, southern Democrats were bought off by northern Democrats' support for agricultural subsidies. When we attempt, below, to explain voting on food stamps solely in terms of constituency economic interests on food stamps alone, à la Gilligan et al. (1989) or Kalt and Zupan (1984), we find at best weak support for the proposition that members vote purely on the basis of constituent interests. But, in a larger context, members used a logroll to further constituency interests. If the constituency orientation is captured in a logroll that is spatially clustered, NOMINATE will capture the logroll.

Indeed, the spatial logrolls need not be wholly on party lines. Because the Democrats had a healthy majority in the House in 1964, they did not require unanimous support from their southern wing to pass food stamp legislation. The most conservative Democrats, nicely demarcated by D-NOMINATE, defected. Similarly, the House coalition for railroad regulation in the 1880s was built through the Democratic Party but included some agrarian Republicans from the Middle West and did not include many northeastern Democrats. The Democratic majority, in any case, was large enough to pass a regulation bill. Members of both parties were allowed to vote on the basis of sectional economic interests. In chapter 1, we quoted Representative Hewitt to illustrate that sectional economic interests on railroads were correlated with interests on many other economic issues, such as free silver and antitrust. Although such broad sets of economic interests may be difficult to measure directly,[4] they are captured in the D-NOMINATE scores.

Our analysis of House voting on railroads will illustrate that major bills are very complicated packages with a slew of provisions. This complexity is characteristic of legislation, even on bills that, unlike the food stamp measure in 1964, are not packaged as part of a larger deal. On any major piece of legislation, therefore, the bill manager's role is to keep a bill coalition together, not allowing it to break apart on amendments in which one provision is put to the test of specific economic interests. In the case of the interstate commerce bill, there were articles with respect to pooling (sharing of revenues), rebates (discounts or "kickbacks" typically given to large shippers), short-haul versus long-haul pricing (not charging a price on a short route that is higher than the price on a longer route that includes the short route), and enforcement (in courts rather than in a regulatory commission). Each of these articles had provisions with different impacts for different constituencies. For example, wheat farmers west of Chicago might have supported the pooling clause, which prevented price-fixing, but not the short-haul pricing clause, which disadvantaged long-haul shippers. Farming interests east of Chicago might have acted more favorably to short-haul pricing constraints. But the cutting lines on amendments to all the economic provisions of the bill were very similar, attesting to the manager's ability to maintain a logroll of interests on the bill.

Logrolls, of course, are not invulnerable, and attempts will be made to destabilize a logroll using killer amendments that introduce another salient issue.[5] In chapter 7, we show how the Republicans nearly killed railroad regulation in the House by introducing an amendment to end racial discrimination in passenger service. To avoid destabilization of the railroad bill, the bill manager, after forcing a party line vote that led to an adjournment at a critical juncture, regrouped and engaged in strategic behavior that allowed the South to accept a regulatory bill that contained a separate-but-equal clause on racial discrimination. (On this issue, see also chapter 7 and, especially, Poole and Rosenthal, 1994a).

Although the Interstate Commerce Act roll calls thus involved a substantial degree of strategic behavior, this behavior still resulted in votes that are captured by the spatial model. In particular, the antidiscrimination votes are accounted for by D-NOMINATE because positions on the race issue are nicely picked up the first dimension in the 1880s. The South, the economic left of the time, also staunchly supported Jim Crow policies. Much of the strategic behavior simply involved moving the cutting line by getting first-dimension moderates to vote for the separate-but-equal provision but against fully eliminating discrimination.

The House votes on railroads in the 1880s and on food stamps in the 1960s demonstrate that roll call voting behavior typically incorporates party pressures and issue-specific economic interests, both of which are correlated with more general interests and personal ideology captured by D-NOMINATE.[6] The importance of party depends, to some extent, on the closeness of the partisan division in a chamber. When the division is close, the majority party has more need to use the whip. Consequently, a substantive issue can have cutting lines with different angles in the two chambers. For example, in contrast to the House, where the Democrats had a substantial majority in the late 1880s, the Republicans controlled the Senate, but by a slimmer margin. The large Democratic majority in the House permitted substantial position-taking in terms of economic interests, with the result that the roll calls on regulation divided both parties internally. In contrast, the regulatory votes in the Senate were strictly party-line votes, with the cutting line separating the parties.

The blending of interests into a bill, either along party lines or via an interparty logroll, need not occur as soon as the issue appears on the national agenda. Indeed, the history of minimum wage and railroads will be used to illustrate the point that new issues are typically fit by the spatial model less successfully than mature ones; ones in which enduring logrolls have been constructed.

Moreover, economic interests can change the nature of the coalition behind a bill even though the roll call votes continue to be captured by D-NOMINATE. We illustrate this point with food stamps. As constituents in moderate Republican congressional districts began to receive food stamps, their representatives became "hooked" on the program. In contrast to 1964, when food stamps were opposed by nearly all Republicans, increased Republican support by 1967 removed the need for southern Democrat support. While voting on food stamps continued to fit the D-NOMINATE model, *economic interests had shifted the cutting line*. In addition, even when the cutting-line angle does not change, a change in the perception of economic interests can affect the mapping of an issue onto the D-NOMINATE space. Thus, although liberals have always been the core of support for minimum wage, a diminished general level of support facilitated a lowering of the real value of the minimum wage. To show this, we will examine the voting on minimum wage by pivotal members over several years. We will argue that their ideal points for the real value of the minimum wage have shifted downward over time. This drop in support culminated in the Clinton administration's failing to raise the minimum wage in 1993–94, when the Democrats controlled both Houses of Congress. (A very modest increase was passed in 1996.) Sometimes, as we will show for legislation on inspection levels for the Occupational Safety and Health Administration, the mapping can change in a few months.

In this chapter, then, we will argue that the presence of spatial voting is not inconsistent with voting on the basis of economic interests. Economic interests, while difficult to measure, arguably have an important impact on how issues are mapped into the space captured by NOMINATE. Moreover, members of Congress will express these interests strategically, voting in logrolls, implicit or explicit, in which various interests are packaged. Thus, we find only a few dimensions of voting, not because legislators are simple-minded with respect to the multitude of issues that arise, but because they are strategic actors, seeking to enter into coalitions that further their own, or their supporters', interests on the issues.

Although we recognize the role of economic interests, we also argue that these interests are neither the same as the interests of a median or pivotal voter in each constituency nor the same as the interests of pivotal voters in each of the major parties in each constituency. A very simple analysis demonstrates that, even were economic interests perfectly measured, pivotal voter type models would fail, dramatically, as models of congressional voting. Below, we show, using comparisons of the two senators from each state, how purely economic models based on pivotal voters can be discarded. On the other hand, once the legislator's ideology in the basic space has been taken into account, there is evidence that points to a modest degree of representative-voter influence on roll call voting behavior. We show the limits of this auxiliary role by comparing the success of economic models and NOMINATE. We then show the short-term stability of coalitions by indicating that cutting lines on diverse economic provisions of a bill maintain the same angle across a sequence of votes. In contrast, the projection of economic issues onto the space can vary as underlying preferences on economic policy change. This is shown by looking at changes in the projection for regulation by OSHA, for the minimum wage level, and for food stamps. The projection, as we show with railroads, is also affected by the tradeoff between maintaining party discipline and allowing legislators to engage in position-taking that appeals to constituents.

Purely Economic Theories of Voting: A Failed Idea

In economic approaches to roll call voting (for example, Peltzman, 1984, 1985) the legislator is the agent of a constituency. In the simplest version, the agent would look at the constituents' interests on each roll call and vote those interests. The decision on each roll call would be uninfluenced by, that is, independent of, decisions on other roll call votes.

This very simple model leads to a straightforward test for the Senate. Each state's two senators should vote the same way on all roll calls because they have the same constituency. The test starts as follows: On every roll call on which both senators from the state "vote" in the form of an actual vote, pair, or announced vote intention, if both vote "Yea" or both vote "Nay," count two successes. This scoring does not count as errors some votes that are against constituent interests, such as two "Nays" when the senators should have both voted "Yea."[7]

The case where the two senators cast opposing votes (or pairs or announced) is more complicated. If the two senators vote differently, one could count one success and one error.[8] If one were able to perfectly measure economic interests on an issue, this error rate is the minimum a purely economic model could possibly hope to achieve. This procedure would guarantee at least 50 percent successes. On the other hand, counting both of the two opposing votes as errors would be too severe a penalty. We have split the difference and counted one-half a success for the two votes. We call this the "hybrid" model.

The results of this test for the first 108 Congresses are shown in Figure 6.1 as the constituency (hybrid) model. This model is compared to the two-dimensional, linear-trend DW-NOMINATE classification and to the success of one-dimensional optimal classification (described in chapter 2). It is striking that a state's two senators disagree on over $\frac{1}{4}$ of all roll calls. The success rate of the hybrid

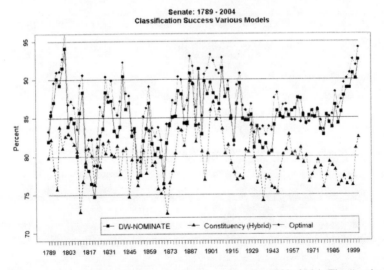

Figure 6.1. Classification success for Senate roll calls, 1789–2004. The "optimal" model is optimal one-dimensional ordinal classification for each Congress, analyzed separately. DW-NOMINATE refers to the two-dimensional linear-trend in position model. The constituency (hybrid) model refers to the prediction that two senators from the same state vote the same way. When the two senators vote the same way, there are two correct classifications. When they do not, there is one-half correct classification. The constituency model underperforms the two spatial models throughout the history of Congress, especially so since 1930.

constituency model is below that of the other models since 1860 and sharply below since 1930. Even the more generous constituency model (not reported), which counts one success for opposing votes, is below the other two models for the most recent Congresses, 98–104. Indeed, it is somewhat surprising that constituency models give their worst performance in the modern period of large economic impacts from government in the form of both spending and regulation.

The pure constituency model cannot be saved by claiming that senators could disagree because one senator sold his vote or logrolled in the state's interest. The two senators should still operate as a team and bundle the pricing of their two votes. The buyers of votes should seek out the cheapest states among the sellers. Thus, pairs of votes from the cheapest states should be bought up to the point where the buyers have enough votes to win on the roll call vote. With the possible exception of the last vote to be bought, one senator from a state should be in a trade if the other senator is in a trade. Thus, even with trading, the constituency model would be expected to be correct for ninety-nine of the 100 senators.

A way out for proponents of economic voting is to hold, as Peltzman (1984) suggests, that each senator represents a state-party constituency rather than the constituency of all the voters in the state. Thus, we would count as errors only discordant votes from two senators of the same party in the state. We refer to this as the 100-party model, since it does not claim, for example, that all Republicans vote together, just that two Republicans from the same state vote together. This model must do better than the constituency model since it can never be in error for a state with a split delegation. If the two senators are not from the same party or if the two senators are from the same party and agree, we count two successes. If they are from the same party and disagree we count one success (and one error).

The 100-party model does, as shown in Figure 6.2, better the classifications of both the two-dimensional D-NOMINATE model with linear trend and optimal classification in one dimension. In periods of substantial polarization, however, near the turn of the twentieth and twenty-first centuries, the spatial models do nearly as well as the 100-party model. This model lacks parsimony; it requires 50 (one per state) "parameters" per roll call, or, for q roll calls, 50q. In contrast, optimal classification requires one location for each of 100 senators and q midpoints. Since q+100 is much less than 50q, the 100-party model is clearly a bad starting point for the analysis of roll call voting.

If economic models must be, on their own, failures, they may play an auxiliary role once ideology is taken into account. The marginal relevance of "economic" factors is nicely shown in work by Loomis (1995). Loomis modified W-NOMINATE to be a probit model with correlated errors for same-state senators. This modification permitted him to view the errors in voting as correlated

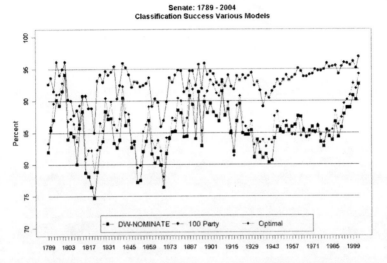

Senate: 1789 - 2004
Classification Success Various Models

Figure 6.2. Classification success for Senate roll calls, 1789–2004. The "optimal" model is optimal one-dimensional ordinal classification for each Congress, analyzed separately. DW-NOMINATE refers to the two-dimensional linear-trend in position model. The 100-party model refers to the prediction that two senators from the same party and the same state vote the same way. When a state's delegation is split, the votes of the two senators are always counted as successes. The very unparsimonious and imprecise 100-party model does have more classification success than the spatial model, but the differences have attenuated substantially in recent years.

across senators from the same state and to estimate the degree of correlation.[9] He estimated one correlation, ρ_S, which applied to all pairs of senators who belonged to the same political party and another correlation, ρ_D, which applied to all senators who belonged to different parties. If the senators are agents of "median voters," $\rho_S = \rho_D > 0$; if senators are agents of the "100 parties," $\rho_S > \rho_D = 0$; and if elements of both median and party representation are active, $\rho_S > \rho_D > 0$. The results of the estimation are shown in Figure 6.3.

The median model receives only weak support. The correlation of the errors in cases where the senators are from the same state but different parties averages only around 0.2. The 100-party model fares better, as the same party correlation, ρ_S, averages around 0.5. Monte Carlo work by Loomis (1995) shows that the ρ_D's, though small in magnitude, still are at least 3 times the level of their standard errors. Consequently, it is clear that, if one controls for ideology, the two senators from the same state do not vote independently. Still, most of what W-NOMINATE does not explain can not be explained by common interests of the two senators from the same state, even when they are from the same

Correlation

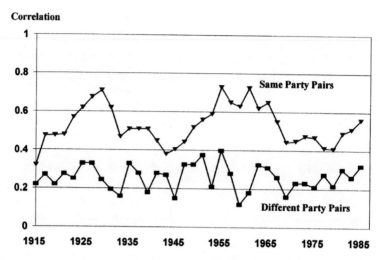

Figure 6.3. Correlations of errors in the W-NOMINATE utility function, Senate (1915–1986). "Same party pairs" refers to two senators from same party in same state. The moderately high correlations suggest that their votes reflect common interests that are independent of ideology. These common interests are much weaker for different-party pairs, when the two senators belong to different parties. Source: Loomis (1995).

party. A clear indication of the weakness of the "economic" approach can be obtained by looking directly at the influence of economic factors. This is the focus of the next section.

The Horse Race: "Economic" vs. "Ideological" Models

To compare how D-NOMINATE fared against standard models of constituency interest, we used a standard methodological technique. We evaluate the fit of each model separately and then run a combined model, within which both the economic models and D-NOMINATE are "nested." If D-NOMINATE, as a stand-alone model, outperforms the economic variables model, and if the impact of the economic variables is greatly diminished in the combined model, we can safely say that the D-NOMINATE model better accounts for the data than the economic variables.

The Interstate Commerce Act

We start with the critical vote (see Gilligan et al., 1989) in the House that preceded the passage of the Interstate Commerce Act (ICA). On July 30, 1886, the

Reagan (D-TX) bill was paired against a bill recently passed in the Senate, the Cullom (R-IL) bill. The Reagan bill, which was a stronger, more antirailroad regulatory measure than the Cullom bill, passed by a 134–104 margin.[10]

To simplify the discussion, we present linear regressions, where the dependent variable is the vote, with 1 being the value corresponding to a vote for the Reagan bill and 0 being the value corresponding to a vote for the Cullom bill. The coefficients show the impact of each independent variable on the vote. For example, in the D-NOMINATE model column, the constant of 0.502 shows that a representative with a zero score on both the first and the second dimension would have voted for Reagan with probability 0.502. In the

Table 6.1
The House Vote on the Reagan Bill
versus the Cullom Bill (1887)

Variable[a]	D-NOMINATE Model	Economic Model	Combined Model
Constant	0.502**	1.182**	0.700**
	(0.012)	(0.063)	(0.057)
1st dimension	−0.917**	—	−0.831**
	(0.035)		(0.052)
2nd dimension	0.980**	—	0.661*
	(0.141)		(0.175)
CENTER	—	−0.066	−0.124
		(0.077)	(0.053)
WEST	—	−0.696**	-0.122
		(0.122)	(0.107)
CAP	—	−1.223**	−0.384**
		(0.131)	(0.127)
ROI	—	-0.043**	−0.012**
		(0.005)	(0.004)
LAND	—	0.996**	0.316*
		(0.163)	(0.152)
R^2	0.702	0.375	0.737

Note: Estimates are from linear-probability model. White (1980) asymptotic standard errors are in parentheses. N = 238.
[a] Economic-variable definitions (see Gilligan et al. [1989] for greater detail): *CENTER:* 1 for district with a major rail center, 0 otherwise; *WEST:* 1 for district north and west of Chicago, 0 otherwise; *CAP* is a measure of railroad capitalization; *ROI* is a measure of railroad return on investment; *LAND* is a measure of the value of farmland.
* One-tail significant at the 0.05 level.
** One-tail significant at the 0.01 level.

economic-model column, a representative from a major rail center would have 0.066 less of a chance of voting for the Reagan bill than a representative whose district did not contain a rail center.[11]

Among the independent variables, we include the D-NOMINATE scores on the first and second dimensions.[12] The constituency-interest variables are the five variables used by Gilligan et al. (1989) in their study of the Interstate Commerce Act. These include *CENTER* (which equals 1 for districts in a major rail center, 0 otherwise), *WEST* (=1 for states North and West of Chicago, and 0 otherwise); *CAP*, a measure of railroad capitalization; *ROI*, a measure of railroad return on investment; and *LAND*, a measure of the value of farmland.[13]

On the railroad vote, the results of the "horse race" between the constituency interest model and D-NOMINATE are apparent from the table. By itself, D-NOMINATE does quite well. The R^2 value of 0.70 indicates that D-NOMINATE scores explain 70 percent of the variation in the vote. The two coefficients are very precisely estimated; both are over 8 times their estimated standard errors.[14] The set of five economic variables has a far more limited success, with an R^2 of only 0.38. The *CENTER* variable is not statistically significant. Moreover, the combined model shows that the constituency interest model adds little to D-NOMINATE, increasing R^2 only from 0.70 to 0.74, and the *WEST* and *CENTER* variables are not statistically significant at conventional levels. The impact of the economic variables is also noticeably less. The magnitude of the coefficients of the economic variables in the combined model drop considerably. They are only about one-third of their values when the D-NOMINATE scores are not included. In contrast, the magnitudes of the D-NOMINATE score variables drop much less. Clearly, as measured, constituency interests are less important than ideology on railroad voting.

There are several reasons to view these initial results with skepticism.

- Have we chosen a vote particularly favorable to D-NOMINATE?
- Is a bias introduced from the use of the Reagan-versus-Cullom vote and later votes in the estimation of the D-NOMINATE scores?
- Is R^2 misleading as a measure of evaluation?
- Does the use of linear regression distort the comparison?

The answer to all these questions is "No." Table 6.2 captures the essence of the answer. It shows the results for all votes on the Cullom bill, the Reagan bill, and final passage of the Interstate Commerce Act in the 49th House. Restricting the ideological model to just the first-dimension score, it compares the results from using the D-NOMINATE score to those from using a score produced by applying the W-NOMINATE algorithm to just the first 161 roll calls in the 49th Congress that preceded the first ICA vote.[15] In model evalua-

Table 6.2
Classification on the 49th House's ICA Roll Calls, by Model

	PERCENTAGE CORRECTLY CLASSIFIED BY LOGIT ESTIMATION						
	VOTEVIEW NUMBER FOR ROLL CALL[b]						
Model[a]	177	190	191	192	193	231	239
One-dimension D-NOMINATE	93	83	87	86	84	90	83
One-dimension NOMINATE 161	93	82	87	84	83	90	83
Combined (D-NOMINATE)	93	88	93	92	89	91	84
Combined (NOMINATE 161)	92	87	92	90	90	91	85

[a] D-NOMINATE is the first-dimension score from the full D-NOMINATE estimation. NOMINATE 161 is the first-dimension score from 161 roll calls preceding the ICA votes (see note 13 in this chapter, for further details).
[b] Description of roll calls (VOTEVIEW number is sequential for each House):
177—Hiscock motion, Reagan bill versus Cullom (Senate) bill, July 27, 1886.
190—Reagan: ordering of the previous question, July 30, 1886.
191—Reagan bill versus Cullom bill, July 30, 1886.
192—Recommittal of Reagan bill, July 30, 1886.
193—Passage of Reagan bill, July 30, 1886.
231—Crisp motion to consider conference-committee report, January 17, 1887.
239—Final passage: acceptance of conference-committee report, January 21, 1887.

tion, it uses the percentage of votes correctly classified rather than R^2. Finally, Table 6.2 is based on logit estimates rather than linear probability.

The results in the table are not sensitive to our earlier choice of the Reagan vs. Cullom vote. The improvement in classification brought about by adding the economic variables is typically not better for the other six votes in Table 6.2 than it was for Reagan versus Cullom. Classifications are also only slightly affected by the sample used to estimate the ideological scores. Classifications average under 1 percent less when using the sample of 161 votes than when using the D-NOMINATE scores. Using classifications as the measure of success in the logit estimates echoes the results based on R^2. Several votes, even when the D-NOMINATE model is based on just one dimension, show almost no improvement in classification in the combined model.

The comparison between D-NOMINATE and the economic variables in Gilligan et al. (1989) indicates a preference for the spatial model rather than a model based on aggregate economic indicators. One could argue that better economic horses, in the form of better measures of constituencies' economic interests, might run a better race. But we have already shown that bettors should want very good odds to back even the best possible measures of such interests.

Food Stamps

The much higher explanatory power for D-NOMINATE variables in comparison to standard "economic" variables on railroad roll calls in the nineteenth century is replicated in the analysis of three 1960s and 1970s issues: food stamps, the minimum wage, and strip mining.

Our food stamp analysis focuses on two key (Ferejohn, 1986) House votes on the food stamp program. The first was the April 8, 1964 vote on passage of the Food Stamp Act; the second, the September 19, 1967 vote on the conference report extending the program. In both cases voting Yea represented the pro-food stamp position. The dependent variable is coded 1 for Yea, 0 for Nay. The logit model is used for estimation.

As was the case for railroads, we use the two D-NOMINATE coordinates in the set of independent variables. The independent variables also include — as is typical for constituency-interest studies — all variables that we could tap that were potentially relevant to the pursuit of economic interests. These included:

- Food stamp payments per capita: Higher levels of food stamp payments should make a representative more likely to support food stamps. Recipients of food stamps clearly represent a constituency that supports the program.

- Federal farm subsidies per capita: The presence of the farm bill in the initial logroll; the administration of the program by the Department of Agriculture; and the subsidy that food stamps represent to agricultural producers — these factors suggest that agricultural interests would support the program.

- Farm income per capita: Like the previous variable, this is a measure of agricultural interests.

- AFDC (Aid to Families with Dependent Children) payments per capita: The poor, even if a food stamp program were not present in the district, would represent a constituency for the program.

- Personal income per capita: Wealthier states could be less inclined to support a redistribution program.

- Wheat-cotton states: Because the logroll was used with a farm bill in which wheat and cotton supports figured prominently, representatives from major wheat-and cotton-growing areas should be more inclined to vote for food stamps. The value of this variable equals 1 if district is in a wheat-cotton state, 0 if not.

Note that the economic variables are all measured at the state level, a problem we address below.

In addition to economic variables, political-party affiliation is often included as an independent variable in research papers that adopt a constituency-interest perspective. We not only follow the literature in this respect but also break down the Democrats into northern and southern contingents. Because food stamps represented an intraparty logroll in 1964, it is important to see if party affiliation identifies a propensity to support food stamps that is not contained in the D-NOMINATE scores. Party affiliation is measured as follows:

- Southern Democrat: The value of the variable equals 1 if the representative is a Democrat from a southern state; 0 otherwise.
- Northern Democrat: The value equals 1 if the representative is a Northern Democrat; 0 otherwise.

The data analysis based on these variables is shown in Table 6.3. The "Separate" column for each year shows the results for two logit estimations, the D-NOMINATE coordinates in roman type and the other variables, run separately as a set, in italics. Clearly, D-NOMINATE fits the data much better than do the economic/party variables.

The results of the logit estimation for the full set of variables are shown in the "Full" columns of Table 6.3. None of the economic variables are significant in 1964, and just two, food stamp payments and farm income, are significant for 1967. One of the party variables — southern Democrat — is significant. Southern Democrats, even in the presence of the 1964 logroll, were more opposed to food stamps than was expected from the D-NOMINATE coordinates. In contrast, there is no distinction between northern Democrats and the residual group of Republicans, once spatial position has been taken into account.

This is a common finding. For example, party is insignificant if added in the railroad example discussed earlier. *The effects of party are typically contained in NOMINATE measures.*[16] Party is largely just a very coarse encoding of spatial position, except for some special circumstances, such as southern Democrats' votes on food stamps.

To return to the economic variables, these may have been individually insignificant in 1964 simply because we used a large set of highly intercorrelated variables. In the "Final" column of Table 6.3, we show the estimates obtained when we drop all variables not statistically significant in either year. The dropped variables, judged by a standard likelihood-ratio test, are also not significant as a set. In the "Final" regressions, food stamp payments are significant in 1964 and 1967, farm income in 1967. The standard pseudo R^2 measure discloses that the logit regressions explain about 73 percent of the voting on food stamps.

Table 6.3
Food Stamps in 1964 and 1967—Logit Estimates

Variable	1964			1967		
	Separate[a]	Full	Final	Separate	Full	Final
Constant	0.590*	3.440	1.364*	1.466**	4.776	3.029**
	(0.228)[b]	(2.996)	(0.669)	(0.291)	(3.143)	(0.865)
1st Dimension	-12.043**	-15.533**	-13.269**	-14.372**	-26.178**	-24.953*
	(1.270)	(2.412)	(1.587)	(1.691)	(3.983)	(3.534)
2nd Dimension	4.592**	10.026**	7.989**	-0.415	6.070*	6.498*
	(0.646)	(2.517)	(1.627)	(0.688)	(3.056)	(2.150)
Southern Democrats	3.474**	-3.455*	-2.260*	1.127**	-5.872**	-5.050
	(0.677)	(1.41)	(0.991)	(0.432)	(1.798)	(1.389)
Food stamp Payments	1.057	1.301	1.959*	0.562*	1.553*	1.660*
	(1.080)	(1.291)	(0.998)	(0.261)	(0.551)	(0.473)
Farm income	0.064	0.402	-0.041	-0.045	0.398*	0.304**
	(0.319)	(0.429)	(0.156)	(0.104)	(0.106)	(0.093)
Farm subsidies	-0.022	-0.051		0.013	-0.017	
	(0.028)	(0.041)		(0.011)	(0.016)	
AFDC payments	0.132*	0.113		0.017	-0.077	
	(0.063)	(0.082)		(0.026)	(0.054)	
Income	-0.001	-0.0008		0.001	-0.0003	
	(0.001)	(0.001)		(0.001)	(0.001)	

Table 6.3 (continued)

Variable	1964 Separate[a]	1964 Full	1964 Final	1967 Separate	1967 Full	1967 Final
Wheat-cotton state	*0.022*	−0.760		*0.038*	0.944	
	(0.409)	(0.549)		*(0.359)*	(0.604)	
Northern Democrats	*6.963***	−1.488		*5.601***	−0.489	
	(0.787)	(1.430)		*(1.021)*	(2.099)	
Log likelihood	−84.021	−72.509	−77.763	−89.889	−63.211	−65.792
	−107.991			−155.453		
Pseudo R^2	0.712	0.751	0.733	0.633	0.742	0.732
	0.629			*0.366*		
Number of Observations	423	423	423	357	357	357

Note: For data sources, see note to Table 6.5.

[a] Italicized figures in "Separate" column refer to economic-variables model: roman figures, to D-NOMINATE model; constant reported is for D-NOMINATE model only.

[b] Asymptotic standard errors are given in parentheses.

* Significant at the 0.05 level.

** Significant at the 0.01 level.

163

Table 6.4
Change in Probability of a Pro-Food Stamp Vote

Variable	CHANGE IN PROBABILITY[a]	
	1964	1967
First Dimension	−0.69	−0.94
Second Dimension	0.36	0.24
Southern Democrat	−0.18	−0.41
Food Stamp Payments	0.09	0.18
Farm income	−0.01	0.10

[a] Changes are for a one-standard-deviation change in the variable, centered about the mean of the variable, with the other variables held at their mean values.

Of all the variables, the D-NOMINATE coordinates, particularly the first dimension, have the greatest effect on voting behavior. This is disclosed by Table 6.4, where we show how the estimated probability of a pro-food stamp vote is influenced by a one-standard-deviation-change in the independent variable, holding all other variables at their sample means. Clearly, ideology predominates. A change in the first dimension affects probabilities at least five times greater than a similar change in either food stamp payments or farm income.

A caveat is in order: The fact that the other variables are less important than D-NOMINATE variables does not mean that they are unimportant. For example, instead of looking at the southern Democrat variable through its standard deviation, which is only 0.43 in 1964 and 0.41 in 1967 — one can simply compare the probability of a pro-food stamp vote for southern Democrats to that for other representatives, holding all other variables at their means. In 1964, this probability was 0.36 for southern Democrats but 0.89 for others. In 1967, reflecting the breakup of the logroll and the increased attractiveness of food stamps in the North, the disparity was greater: The probability dropped to 0.05 for southern Democrats and increased to 0.96 for others. The high level for others reflects the increased mean level of food stamp payments, rising from 15 cents per capita in 1964 to 51 cents per capita in 1967. Even though the coefficient of food stamps declined slightly between the 1964 estimates and those for 1967, the total impact of food stamps increased, as representatives became "hooked" through the higher mean levels. The sample standard deviation of payments also increased, from 24 cents in 1964 to 66 cents in 1967, resulting in the change in probability shown in Table 6.4 — a doubling, from 0.09 to 1964 to 0.18 in 1967. Thus, although overall ideology is the major influence on a legislator's voting behavior on food stamps, ideology is deflected to some extent by factors captured in regional-economic measures.

We now discuss the methodological problem raised by our use of state-level variables to measure the economic variables. Since the level of income in a congressional district will, for example, differ from that in the state, we have a classic error-in-the-variables problem that will downwardly bias our estimate of the economic effects. To put the D-NOMINATE measures and the economic variables on an equal footing, we reran the "Final" analysis using the log of the odds ratio of the state's delegation voting for food stamps. That is, the dependent variable was $\ln(PRO/CON)$ where PRO is the number of pro-food stamp representatives in the state and CON is the number against.[17]

This aggregated analysis basically confirms the previous results, as we see in Table 6.5. Again, the first D-NOMINATE dimension is the most important variable. As the "Economic" column of the table indicates, there is very little stand-alone explanatory power in the three economic variables (one of which is just southern Democrat) retained in the final model of the disaggregated analysis. In the "Combined" columns, food stamp spending is again significant, with similar magnitudes in both years, and farm income is significant in 1967, but the southern Democrat variable no longer has much punch. In contrast to the disaggregated analysis, the behavior of southern Democrats, who were part of a logroll in 1964 but not in 1967, is captured by the second dimension, which is highly significant in 1964 but not in 1967. Thus, the analysis of the state averages provides further support for the claim that roll call voting is largely accounted for by the spatial model.

The Minimum Wage

The story for minimum wages parallels that for railroads and food stamps. We are able to compare our results to those of three other studies: Bloch (1980), Silberman and Durden (1976), and Krehbiel and Rivers (1988). The work of these authors has shown that measures of constituency interest, in terms of wage levels, unemployment levels, and union membership, are far less important to voting decisions than party membership. For example, Krehbiel and Rivers, in their analysis of 1977 Senate votes on minimum wage amendments, found that Democrats, ceteris paribus, would prefer a minimum wage of 17 cents to 22 cents higher than Republicans would, whereas a 10 percent increase in the percentage of the labor force belonging to unions in the state would induce a preferred increase in the minimum wage of only 4 cents to 8 cents. Similar conclusions can be drawn from Bloch's work on 1966 and 1974 Senate voting. In probits run separately for each party, Bloch found that neither the wage nor the union variable was significant at the conventional 0.05 level in 1966. To put matters simply, two senators from the same state will tend to oppose each other on minimum wage if they are from

Table 6.5
Log of the Odds Ratio of a State Delegation Voting in Support of Food Stamps

Variable	1964			1967		
	D-NOMINATE Model	Economic Model	Combined Model	D-NOMINATE Model	Economic Model	Combined Model
Constant	0.141*	0.286	-0.003	0.315***	0.363	-0.258
	(0.075)[a]	(0.204)	(0.060)	(0.112)	(0.264)	(0.067)
First dimension	-4.345***		-4.349***	-4.917***		-5.825**
	(0.555)		(0.579)	(0.737)		(0.758)
Second dimension	2.349***		2.216**	0.431		0.145
	(0.360)		(0.925)	(0.689)		(1.159)
Southern Democrats		0.682**	0.143		-1.121**	0.134
		(0.266)	(0.507)		(0.437)	(0.596)
Food stamp payments		-0.010**	0.607*		0.401*	0.428***
		(0.528)	(0.377)		(0.218)	(0.149)
Farm income		-0.132**	-0.003		-0.053	0.118***
		(0.065)	(0.052)		(0.053)	(0.042)
Adjusted R²	0.62	0.14	0.66	0.51	0.11	0.61
Number of states	50	50	50	50	50	50

Sources: Food stamp payment data were obtained from USDA, Food and Nutritional Service, in a report of bonus coupons issued for the 1960s by participating counties and cities. Government farm subsidies and farm income for each state came from USDA, Agricultural Marketing Service, Farm Income Statistics, found in the *American Statistical Index (ASI)*. AFDC payments came from the "Public Assistance" table in the *ASI*, supplied by the Department of Health, Education and Welfare. Personal income per capita came from *ASI*, using information from the U.S. Bureau of the Census, *U.S. Census of Population 1970,* vol. 1. The variable southern Democrats was created by multiplying a dummy variable for southern states (1 if South, 0 otherwise) times the proportion of state congressional delegation that is Democratic. Thus a value of 1 means a southern state with all Democratic representatives. The proportion of a state delegation that favored food stamps is calculated on the basis of delegation members who voted or were paired or announced.

[a] Asymptotic standard errors are given in parentheses.

* Significant at the 0.10 level, two-tail.

** Significant at the 0.05 level, two-tail.

*** Significant at the 0.01 level, two-tail.

different parties. The partisan effect overwhelms aggregate measures of constituency interest.

The importance of ideology, as against simple party-line voting, is apparent when we consider the D-NOMINATE analysis. In our detailed study of minimum wages (Poole and Rosenthal, 1991b), we showed that D-NOMINATE correctly classified 85 to 90 percent of all individual voting decisions on the minimum wage since the first bill was passed in 1938.

More importantly, minimum wage votes tended to split both parties. Some liberal Republicans joined northern Democrats, but southern Democrats historically voted with the Republicans. In the political science literature on Congress, the alliance of the southern Democrats and the Republicans is known as the "conservative coalition." Minimum wage was, until roughly 1980, a conservative-coalition issue. Although a three-party (northern Democrats, southern Democrats, and Republicans) model will classify much better than a two-party model, Figure 6.4 shows that a three party model is still inferior to a spatial model. The figure shows the two votes used in the Silberman and Durden (1976) study. The votes divide both southern Democrats and Republicans. Thus, the three-party model fails to tell us which southern Democrats are likely to oppose the minimum wage bill and which Republicans are likely to break party ranks and support minimum wage. In contrast, the spatial model can capture the diversity within party and regional blocs.

Models that use economic variables are far less successful than D-NOMINATE in accounting for roll call voting on minimum wages, as illustrated by the Krehbiel and Rivers (1988) essay.[18] These authors studied Senate votes on the Bartlett and Tower amendments to the minimum wage bill in 1977.

The Bartlett amendment was for a sharp reduction in the increase in the minimum wage contained in the bill proposed by the Democrats. The Tower amendment was for a more moderate reduction. Staunch conservatives could be expected to vote Yea on both amendments; moderates, Yea on Tower, but Nay on Bartlett; and liberals, Nay on both. No one, as was the case in fact, should vote Nay on Tower but Yea on Bartlett. Thus, the three categories of voting patterns could be ordered as to the degree they favored high minimum wages.

Krehbiel and Rivers estimated an ordered probit model of the probability a senator would fall into the three categories. They used the following independent variables: party, union membership, wages, unemployment, South, and the percentage of the population that is black. These variables include two, party and South, that are arguably more ideological than economic, particularly when union membership, wages, and percentage black are also present in the equation. Even so, Krehbiel and Rivers succeed in classifying only 74 percent to 76 percent of the observations, depending upon the specification chosen. The

Table 6.6
Classification Accuracy on the Bartlett
and Tower Amendments in 1977

Model	Percent Correctly Classified
D-NOMINATE, two-dimensional	85.7
Krehbiel-Rivers (1988), various specifications	73.9–76.1
Marginals (percent that voted no on both amendments)	68.1

Note: N = 91, the number of senators voting or announced on both the Bartlett and Tower roll calls.

relevant benchmark prediction for their study is the modal category, Nay on both amendments, which included 68 percent of the senators. The improvement afforded by use of economic variables is slight. In contrast, the D-NOMINATE two-dimensional predictions (no senator is predicted as Nay-Yea) for these three categories results in an 86 percent classification accuracy. Only thirteen of the ninety-one senators are misclassified. The results are summarized in Table 6.6.[19]

Although we did not conduct the complete horse race that we ran for railroads and food stamps, our thirteen classification errors seem unlikely to be residuals that can be reconciled by appeal to standard economic-interest considerations. To illustrate this point, we ask whether union membership — an independent variable used by Krehbiel and Rivers — or the presence of a right-to-work law might account for the thirteen errors.[20] Our two most serious errors were those for Danforth (R-MO) who voted Yea-Yea when predicted to vote Nay-Nay and Garn (R-Utah) who voted Nay-Nay when predicted Yea-Yea. Neither deviation would seem consistent with an economic interpretation. Missouri in 1977 was above the national average in union membership and did not have a right-to-work law, while Utah had a low degree of unionization and a right-to-work law.[21] The other Republican senator from Utah, Hatch, voted Yea-Yea as predicted. Any economic considerations that would explain Garn's vote would not explain Hatch's. A similar inspection of the eleven less serious errors (Nay-Yea predictions that fell into the other two categories or vice-versa) also failed to disclose any consistent pattern in terms of either unionization or right-to-work laws. The errors of the spatial model are likely to be linked as much to internal logrolling within Congress as they are to constituencies' economic interests that are specific to minimum wages.

We also looked at the two Senate roll calls, one from 1966 and the other from 1974, studied by Bloch (1978). We achieved classification success of 90 percent and 86 percent, respectively, for these two roll calls. Bloch does not report classification success, but it is unlikely his models would better D-NOMINATE since his independent variables are a subset of those used by Krehbiel and Rivers.

The final previous study we compare to the "ideological" model represented by D-NOMINATE is Silberman and Durden (1976). Like Krehbiel and Rivers, these authors used an ordered probit approach. They studied two 1973 roll calls: the Erlenborn amendment and final passage by the House.[22]

Silberman and Durden used five independent variables: South, labor's campaign contributions to 1972 Congressional winners, contributions by small business organizations, and measures of low wage workers and of teenage workers. It is difficult to compare this study to the spatial model, as the authors report only the estimated coefficients. Two points can be made. First, the most statistically significant coefficients are the region dummy and the two campaign contribution coefficients. In this respect, we note that campaign contributions and region cannot be specifically linked to minimum wages but are relevant to a whole set of interests that are captured by our spatial coordinates. Indeed, as shown by Poole and Romer (1985), Poole, Romer, and Rosenthal (1987), McCarty and Poole (1995), and McCarty, Poole, and Rosenthal (2006), campaign contributions, particularly by labor, are highly related to spatial position. In other words, there is an identification problem. Region and campaign contributions have a logical relationship to minimum wage interests. On the other hand, they relate to a whole set of other interests as well. Since southerners, for example, tend to vote as a bloc on a whole set of issues, it is difficult to distinguish the economic impact specific to minimum wage from general regional interests.

Second, campaign contributions do not measure within-constituency interests. Since the contribution variables are contributions to the winning candidate, variable values for individual districts will be highly sensitive to the outcomes of House races. For example, labor contributions are likely to be far higher if the winner is a Democrat rather than a Republican. In a swing district, a small shift in district preferences, expressed in a small shift in the congressional vote, can make a large difference to the labor-contribution variable. Moreover, many contributors, such as the United Auto Workers or the National Association of Manufacturers, are not local groups.[23] So if the Silberman-Durden probit equation is to be believed (as against a Bloch or Krehbiel-Rivers equation), we will have to believe that while economic interests may matter, they are not median voter interests.

In Figure 6.4, we have plotted the cutting lines and shown the cross-tabulation of the two roll calls. Table 6.7 contains the classification analysis. Excluding (therefore mimicking Silberman and Durden) legislators voting against the amendment and against passage, and legislators voting on only one of the roll calls, we correctly classify 81 percent of the joint decisions. The most seri-

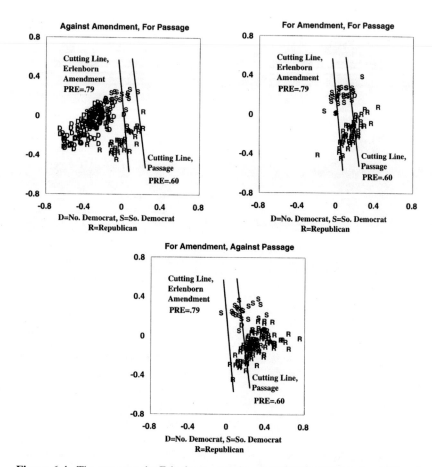

Figure 6.4. The votes on the Erlenborn amendment (VOTEVIEW number 119) and on passage of the minimum wage bill (VOTEVIEW number 129) in the House of Representatives, June 6, 1973. Members against the amendment and for passage are overwhelmingly to the left of the amendment cutting line. Members for the amendment and against passage are preponderantly to the right of the passage cutting line. Members in favor of the amendment and passage are concentrated between the two cutting lines, which are close to parallel. (The figure excludes Nay-Nay votes and members who voted on only one of the two roll calls.)

ous errors occur in the upper-right and lower-left corners of the table — these represent only 1 percent of the representatives. (Classification of the two roll calls separately shows 89 percent for Erlenborn and 87 percent for passage.)

More research would need to be done to ask if the Silberman-Durden variables would account for the errors of the spatial model. One of them clearly

Table 6.7
Comparison of D-NOMINATE—Predicted and Actual Votes
for the 1973 House Minimum-Wage Roll Calls

	ACTUAL VOTE		
Vote Predicted by D-NOMINATE	Against Erlenborn, for Passage	For Erlenborn, for Passage	For Erlenborn, against Passage
Against Erlenborn, for passage	188	16	3
For Erlenborn, for passage	11	35	27
For Erlenborn, against passage	2	17	102

will not, at least on its own. An inspection of Figure 6.4 shows that southern Democrats are spread out over the three categories. There is not a strong pattern to the classification errors for southern Democrats.

Bankruptcy[24]

In running horse races between NOMINATE scores and constituency variables for railroad legislation in the late nineteenth century, food stamps legislation in the 1960s, and minimum wage legislation since the 1930s, we have looked at economic policies for relatively narrow spans of history. In contrast, a set of papers by Berglöf and Rosenthal (2005, 2006) and Nunez and Rosenthal (2004) have examined votes on bankruptcy policy from the eighteenth century into the twenty-first.

The results on bankruptcy have the flavor of those we have just discussed for railroads, food stamps, and minimum wages. There is a marginal explanatory role for economic or regional variables. At the end of the eighteenth century into the early nineteenth, coastal or frontier districts vote somewhat differently. On the other hand, distance to the new federal courts does not appear to be related to opposition to a national bankruptcy law with federal jurisdiction. In the late nineteenth century, interest rates and trade associations are not important to votes on the 1898 Bankruptcy Act but the presence of a banking sector is. In the push for bankruptcy "reform" at the beginning of the twenty-first century, campaign contributions from the National Consumer Bankruptcy Coalition, put together by nine creditor organizations, such as Visa International, correlate with House roll call voting, after controlling for ideology. So does membership on the Judiciary Committee. On the other hand, the level of bankruptcy filings in the congressional district's judicial district has at best a very marginal influence.

In the 1898 Bankruptcy Act, nonetheless, DW-NOMINATE scores do the heavy lifting. The banking variable has a significant but secondary effect. In fact, the cutting lines on bankruptcy are very similar to those on the Interstate Commerce Act, with agrarian Republicans voting with the Democrats and "Wall Street" Democrats voting with the Republicans. Similarly, the DW-DOMINATE first dimension is by far the most important influence in contemporary voting on bankruptcy, especially when, as in our analysis of the minimum wage votes from the Silberman and Durden study, two roll calls can be used that permits DW-NOMINATE to capture splits in both of the two major parties.

There is a twist, however, to our usual story that NOMINATE scores capture party effects. The twist appears when we study the House passage vote for the 1800 bankruptcy vote. On this vote, the Jeffersonian Republicans were unanimously opposed to a national bankruptcy law and the Federalists were split. DW-NOMINATE has its greatest effect when it is used only to discriminate among Federalist supporters and opponents of a national bankruptcy law. This is seen in Table 6.8, results that were omitted from Berglöf and Rosenthal (2006) when the piece was abridged for publication. The first column of the table suggests that party, region, and spatial position all have effects on being favorable to a bankruptcy law, with Federalists, northerners, and the political right being the most favorable. The second and third columns indicate that, as single regressors, party and spatial position have roughly equal effects. Comparison of the fourth column to the first suggests that most of the effect of region is captured by its correlation with party and ideology. The fifth column, in contrast, shows that ideology has a much stronger effect among Federalists than among all legislators. The interaction of ideology and party reduces the effect of party as a separate regressor. The last column shows that coastal, that is, trading, areas were favorable to a bankruptcy law after controlling for ideology and party.

For the several economic policies we have considered, there appears to be just marginal interest in using economic models once the spatial nature of voting has been recognized. Perhaps the failure of economic models of roll call voting on minimum wages lies with the problem of measuring economic interests. Ideally one would like to calculate the general equilibrium implications of a change in the law. The change would leave some individuals better off — for example, those at the old minimum who saw their real wage increased and maintained the same number of hours of employment — and others worse off — for example, individuals who became unemployed as a result of the change or certain holders of capital. In any constituency, there is likely to be a mixture of winners and losers. After one had calculated the winners and losers, one would have to model whose preferences were decisive for the member of Congress. Given the complexity involved in constructing a realistic economic and

Table 6.8
House Voting on Passage of the 1800 Bankruptcy Bill

Variable	(1)	(2)	(3)	(4)	(5)	(6)
				MODEL		
Intercept	0.051	(0.778)ᵃ	0.231	0.047	0.304	0.047
	(0.778)ᵃ	(6.766)	(1.171)	(3.841)	(1.177)	(1.207)
REGION	0.126			0.331		
	(1.825)			(3.169)		
PARTY	0.439		0.821		0.291	0.209
	(3.339)		(13.734))		(2.322)	(1.650)
DW-NOMINATE 1	0.464	0.943				
	(3.039)	(14.503)				
DW-NOMINATE 2	−0.074	0.000				
	(−1.231)	(0.005)				
DW-NOMINATE -1×PARTY					0.846	0.809
					(4.796)	(4.683)
DW-NOMINATE -2×PARTY					−0.172	−0.213
					(−2.240)	(−2.768)
COASTAL						0.196
						(2.415)
Adjusted R²	0.718	0.688	0.667	0.087	0.734	0.747
Number of observations	96	96	96	96	96	96

Note: Ordinary least squares estimates. Dependent variable is vote on passage of the bankruptcy bill (VOTEVIEW # 19), February 21, 1800. Votes in favor coded 1, against 0. Sample is all House members voting except for Sedgwick-MA, who as Speaker, voted too few times to have a DW-NOMINATE score. REGION = 0.5 for Maryland, Delaware, 1 for states north of these, 0 for states south; Party = 1 for Federalists, 0 for Jefferson Republicans; COASTAL = 1 for congressional district fronting on the Atlantic Ocean or the Chesapeake Bay.
ᵃ t-statistics in parentheses.

political model of minimum wage voting, it is not surprising that naive attempts are inferior to the spatial model based on persistent patterns of voting.

Strip Mining

Even the most careful attempts at measurement are, however, unlikely to meet with success. We illustrate this point with another example, Kalt and Zupan's (1984) study of the Surface Mining Control and Reclamation Act.[25] This act both regulated strip mining and clarified property rights in strip mining areas.

Votes on the act would appear to be strong candidates for finding evidence of economic influences. At the same time, broader "ideological" views about the role of government in economic and environmental regulation might also play a role.

Kalt and Zupan's dependent variable was an index of opposition to strip mining, ANTISTRIP, which they constructed from twenty-one Senate roll call votes in 1977. The formula for the index for each senator i was:

$$ANTISTRIP = \ln\left[\frac{U_i + 0.5}{F_i + 0.5}\right]$$

where U_i is the number of votes cast by the senator that were unfavorable to strip mining, and F_i is the number favorable to strip mining. Only recorded Yea and Nay votes were used to construct this index.

Kalt and Zupan also carefully constructed six economic variables to measure the direct economic costs and benefits that would relate to the interests of both underground and surface coal producers, electric utilities and other coal consumers, non-coal land users, and environmentalists. These variables and their variants are:[26]

MC	The regulation-induced increase in the long-run average cost of surface mining in each coal-producing state
SURFRES	The state's surface reserves of coal
UNDERRES	The state's underground reserves of coal
SPLITR	The agricultural- and timber-revenue yield of surface acreage underlain by potentially strippable coal
ENVIROS	Fraction of voters who are active environmentalists
UNREC	Prospective value to noncoal interest of strip-mined unrestored acreage.
CONSUME	Fraction of state's electricity generated from coal
HSURF	The Herfindahl index for surface coal producers in each state
HUNDER	The Herfindahl index for underground coal producers in each state
HENVIROS	The Herfindahl index for active environmentalists in each state
HCONSUME	The Herfindahl index for coal consumers in each state

The measure of "ideological" positions was a PROLCV (for pro-League of Conservation Voters) index based on twenty-seven votes selected by the League of Conservation Voters.[27] These votes all dealt with environmental issues *other than* strip mining. The index used a formula similar to that for *ANTISTRIP*.

The horse-race results for the *ANTISTRIP* regressions are quite similar to those for railroads and food stamps. The level of fit of the economic variables is relatively low, but most of the estimated coefficients have the anticipated signs, as shown in the first data column of Table 6.9.

When *PROLCV* is included, as seen in column 2 of Table 6.9, explanatory power increases dramatically. (R^2, adjusted for degrees of freedom, rises from 0.21 to 0.53.) The estimated coefficient of *PROLCV* is of the correct sign and is more than ten times its standard error. Even a specification that includes only *PROLCV* (see column 3 of Table 6.9) outperforms the model of column 1.

When we compare the results of the first three columns with those in the last two, where the D-NOMINATE first dimension is substituted for *PROLCV* as a measure of ideology, we obtain a striking result. As a single independent variable, our dimension outperforms *PROLCV* (compare columns 3 and 5) and does as well when ideology and economics are combined (compare columns 2 and 4). The reason for this is disclosed in chapter 8, where we examine the ideological stance of the LCV and other interest groups. There we find that, in the main, the only distinction between interest groups is where they stand on a single liberal-conservative axis. There is nothing specific that distinguishes the evaluations of environmental groups from labor groups, business groups, civil liberties groups, etc. What counts is where the group stands in the basic space discussed in chapter 2.

Our discussion of strip mining reinforces, in an important way, our previous analysis of railroads, food stamps, bankruptcy, and minimum wages. Even the most serious attempts to find economic influences on roll call voting will tend to find that the representative's general liberal-conservative orientation is the primary influence on roll call voting behavior.[28]

A "Fishing" Expedition

Partly to check whether strip mining roll calls were just an odd set of roll calls fit badly by constituency models, we conducted a Peltzman (1984) "fishing expedition" (his apt term) using broad economic and demographic variables for 568 Senate roll calls in 1977.[29] Eight of these were made available to us by Kalt and Zupan from their study. These were party, income, growth, education, urbanization, union membership, age, and manufacturing. To these we added percentage of nonwhites. Party is, of course, a dubious choice as an "economic" variable but we deliberately included it to load the dice in favor of the constituency-interests hypothesis. This set of variables closely follows those used by Peltzman (1984).

Table 6.9
Regression Estimates for Kalt and Zupan's Anti-Strip Index (N = 100)

	MODEL				
Variable[a]	Economic	Economic and PROLCV	PROLCV	Economic and D-NOMINATE	D-NOMINATE
Constant	−0.154	1.414*	0.712*	0.704	0.659*
	(0.468)[b]	(0.494)	(0.058)	(0.476)	(0.058)
MC	−0.513*	−0.375*		−0.350*	
	(0.107)	(0.108)		(0.108)	
SURFRES	−16.765	−17.196		−14.865	
	(10.073)	(10.073)		(10.075)	
UNDERRES	12.512*	14.132*		11.330	
	(5.972)	(5.974)		(5.973)	
SPLITR	−26.548	68.478		29.323	
	(48.083)	(49.004)		(48.385)	
ENVIROS	83.373*	0.497		31.115	
	(18.602)	(20.349)		(19.275)	
UNREC	0.019*	0.015*		0.011*	
	(0.005)	(0.005)		(0.005)	
CONSUME	−0.0035	−0.0044		−0.0023	
	(0.0024)	(0.0024)		(0.0024)	
HSURF	−0.294	0.018		−0.297	
	(0.237)	(0.239)		(0.237)	
HUNDER	0.305	0.150		0.417	
	(0.277)	(0.277)		(0.277)	
HENVIROS	1.935	−1.287		−0.119	
	(1.085)	(1.132)		(1.103)	
HCONSUME	−0.486*	−0.261		−0.203	
	(0.201)	(0.202)		(0.203)	
PROLCV		0.466*	0.471*		
		(0.046)	(0.040)		
D-NOMINATE				−1.211*	−1.334*
(1st Dimension)				(0.117)	(0.106)
Adjusted R²	0.210	0.531	0.451	0.553	0.490

Source: Poole and Romer (1993).
[a] See text for variable definitions.
[b] Estimated standard errors are in parentheses.
* Denotes coefficient > 2 standard errors.

Peltzman estimated a logit equation for each roll call. Such a procedure can be interpreted as stating that individuals' ideal points vary across roll calls, so an individual i has an ideal point x_{ij} on roll call $j, j = 1, \ldots, 568$. The ideal point takes the form:

$$x_{ij} = \gamma_{0j} + \gamma_{1j}\nu_{i1} + \gamma_{2j}\nu_{i2} + \ldots + \gamma_{9j}\nu_{i9}$$

where the ν_i's are the nine constituency-interest variables for the senator's state and the γ's are coefficients estimated. Such a fishing expedition lacks parsimony since it estimates $10 \times 568 = 5,680$ parameters. We refer to the fishing expedition as the LINEAR model.

A more parsimonious constituency-interest model would hold that voting is one dimensional and that the ideal point is the same linear function for all roll calls:

$$x_{ij} = \gamma_0 + \gamma_1\nu_{i1} + \gamma_2\nu_{i2} + \ldots + \gamma_9\nu_{i9}$$

This model is equivalent to W-NOMINATE except that the ideal point is constrained to be a linear function of the constituency variables. When it is estimated, one estimates a signal-to-noise ratio and the two outcome coordinates for each roll call (see chapter 2) in addition to the 10 γ coefficients. Thus, there are $1 + 2 \times 568 + 10 = 1,147$ parameters for this CONSTITUENCY model. The basic W-NOMINATE model has only slightly more parameters. Since there are 100 senators in the estimation, one estimates the 100 ideal points directly rather than the 10 γ coefficients. This leads to a total of 1,237 parameters.

Although one can compare the fit of the W-NOMINATE model to that of the two constituency-interest models, there is no direct way to combine the models. To evaluate the marginal contribution of ideological models over constituency-interest models, we use a measure of ideology that is independent of the 1977 roll call data. These are the 1976 Poole and Daniels (1985) coordinates for senators serving in 1976 and the 1978 coordinates for senators entering in 1977. The Poole-Daniels coordinates correlate very highly with those from NOMINATE, as we explain later in chapter 8. We define a new independent variable as the residual from the regression of the Poole-Daniels coordinates on the constituency variables. That is, the residual is only that part of ideology that is not picked up by constituency factors. Thus, in the estimations, the effect of constituency will be exaggerated, since some purely ideological effects will be counted as constituency effects. The LINEAR model with the residual added as an independent variable is termed LINRES; the CONSTITUENCY model, CONRES.

Table 6.10
Logit Estimation for All Senate Roll Calls (1977)

Model[a]	Number of Estimated Parameters	Percentage Correctly Classified	Geometric Mean Probability
CONSTITUENCY, without party	1,146	73.2	0.585
CONSTITUENCY, with party	1,147	78.2	0.633
CONRES	1,148	81.0	0.668
NOMINATE	1,237	82.3	0.680
LINEAR	5,680	82.8	0.690
LINRES	6,248	86.2	0.740

Note: 568 roll calls, with more than 2.5 percent of votes on the minority side.
[a] CONSTITUENCY and LINEAR independent variables were income, growth, education, union membership, age, manufacturing, nonwhite population, and party. CONSTITUENCY constrains coefficients on independent variables to be identical across roll calls. In LINEAR, coefficients are unconstrained. LINRES and CONRES add an ideological residual as an independent variable to LINEAR and CONSTITUENCY. NOMINATE constrains ideal points to be identical across roll calls and estimates ideal points and roll call outcome locations

The performance of the various models is compared in Table 6.10. The constrained CONSTITUENCY model performs very poorly without party. Even with party included, it is inferior to W-NOMINATE, providing further evidence that the W-NOMINATE coordinates contain far more information than political party and constituency characteristics.[30] Moreover, the very unparsimonious LINEAR model betters NOMINATE only by one-half of 1 percent in classification and by 0.01 in geometric mean probability. Clearly, a parameter-expensive fishing expedition is not more productive than a simple spatial model of voting. Finally, the ideological residual substantially increases the performance of both CONSTITUENCY and LINEAR. Indeed, the residual is statistically significant at the 0.001 level or better, in 239 of the 568 roll calls for CONSTITUENCY and 286 for LINEAR, whereas it would, under the standard null hypothesis, be expected to be significant in less than one roll call.[31]

These findings suggest that Peltzman (1984) overinterpreted his results in support of the constituency story. Clearly, ideology plays an important independent role even when the constituency variables are allowed to do as much work as possible. Moreover, the simple spatial model, by itself, does very nearly as well as the atheoretical fishing expedition represented by the LINEAR model. One would expect even stronger results in favor of ideological voting in periods of history that were not in the 1960s and 1970s "textbook" Congresses, where local interests have been said to predominate.

The Projection of Economic Issues into the Basic Space

Projection and Parallel Cutting Lines

The results discussed above, supporting ideological over constituency models, are consistent with the primary argument of this book: Complicated issues, including those with economic conflict, can be represented as simple projections into a one- or two-dimensional space. If a quantitative variable, such as the minimum wage level, is a projected issue, the cutting lines for votes between alternative values of the variable should be parallel. We just, in Figure 6.4, provided a graphical illustration of parallel cutting lines for the Erlenborn amendment vote and the bill-passage vote in the House in 1973. Cutting lines are also roughly parallel for the Bartlett- and Tower-amendment votes that were analyzed by Krehbiel and Rivers. Another example, used in the theoretical discussion in chapter 2, were votes on the minimum number of employees that subject a firm to inspection by the Occupational Safety and Health Administration. The OSHA votes are discussed in greater detail later in this section.[32]

Parallel cutting lines can also occur on amendment voting to a bill when several different economic dimensions are active. For example, in regard to railroads, in the 48th Congress the Reagan version of the Interstate Commerce Act was debated, section by section, under a relatively open rule that allowed minority amendments. (The bill was passed in the House but not acted upon by the Senate.) Five votes were taken on rebates, on the short-haul-pricing constraint, and on whether the regulations should be enforced by the courts or an independent commission. These issues, while distinct, were anticipated, and the cutting lines on these votes, as well as two economic votes in the 49th House, had angles all of which fell in the narrow range from 34° to 58° (see Poole and Rosenthal, 1994a, for further details). In contrast, the amendments dealing with racial discrimination, which were not anticipated when the logroll was constructed, had sharply different angles, being vertical cutting lines (see chapter 7 for further discussion). Railroad regulation, OSHA, and minimum wage illustrate the point that economic issues, even if complex packages, appear, in the short run, as projections in our basic space.

But our spatial model is not a model of how these projections occur. A dramatic example is the contentious rejection in 1987 of Robert Bork as a nominee for the Supreme Court that was preceded by the 98–0 confirmation vote for the arguably equally conservative Antonin Scalia. But Scalia is only arguably as conservative as Bork. An even more compelling example is OSHA inspection levels, which the Senate voted on twice within a five-month period in 1972.

The OSHA bill considered by the Senate had no provision concerning the size of firm that could be inspected; therefore, if one presumed some bill would

Table 6.11
Minimum Number of Employees That Allow OSHA
to Inspect a Firm (1972 Votes)

VOTEVIEW Number	Date	Senator Making Motion	Number of Employees	FOR/AGAINST INSPECTION		Errors	PRE2[a]
				Actual Vote	With Pairs and Announced		
653	June 27	Curtis	25	44–41	46–42	10	0.76
654	June 27	Curtis	15	41–45	43–46	7	0.84
895	Oct. 13	Case	15	47–33	51–38	9	0.76
896	Oct. 13	Curtis	7	45–41	43–38	13	0.68
898	Oct. 13	Curtis	4	39–39	42–42	13	0.81
900	Oct. 13	Curtis	3	28–50	31–53	13	0.58

[a] PRE2 is the proportional reduction in error for the two-dimensional, linear-trend D-NOMINATE model (see chapter 3).

pass, the status quo was that all firms with employees were subject to inspection. The 1972 votes on inspection levels are summarized in Table 6.11. Senator Carl Curtis (R-NE) attempted to exempt smaller firms by attaching an amendment that would bar expenditure on inspection of any firm with twenty-five or fewer employees. Like all voting on the firm size issue, this vote was a "conservative coalition" vote with a cutting line of approximately −45°. The amendment failed, with 41 votes cast in favor of the amendment to 44 against it, on June 27, 1972. On the very next roll call, Curtis obtained a vote for barring inspections of firms with fifteen or fewer employees, again against the status quo of all firms subject to inspection. This time, Curtis received more votes, in line with the discussion in chapter 2. Lowering the level from twenty-five to fifteen should have produced and did produce more votes against the status quo. The level of fifteen employees passed, by a vote of 46 to 43.

The bill came up again in October. Senator Clifford Case (R-NJ), a liberal Republican, proposed to strike the Curtis amendment. That is, the status quo was now fifteen, and Case got a revote on fifteen against the old status quo of "all firms." Case's motion passed, by a vote of 47 to 33. Curtis then proposed a still lower limit of seven employees. This failed by a 38-to-43 vote, as did an attempt at four employees, which lost on a tied 39-to-39 vote. Finally, Curtis succeeded with a three-employee limit by a 50 to 28 margin.

In June, Curtis had been able to get a fifteen-employee limit passed; in October he had to settle for a limit of three. The angles of the cutting line were quite stable. Nonetheless, the projection of the issue into the basic space had changed. Senators' ideal points in the projection had shifted in a liberal direction. Undoubtedly, senators were responding to lobbying efforts by labor unions. Even though the votes can be accounted for by the basic space, economic interests played an important role in defining the projection of the issue.

A change in projection can also reflect longer-run forces. For example, persistent discussion in the 1970s and the 1980s of the negative employment effects of the minimum wage coupled with declining union membership may have reduced congressional preference for a high minimum wage. Making such an inference is difficult because each minimum wage bill is in fact a multi-attribute item. As a result, we will only work through some rough, back-of-the-envelope calculations.

We find that the cutting lines of the Tower Amendment vote in 1977 and the GOP substitute bill vote in 1989 both separated Senator Lugar, who took the conservative position, from Senators Hatfield, Packwood, and Heinz, who voted with the liberals. The four senators were reasonably close to both cutting lines. Therefore, if we can map a wage to a cutting line in both cases, we can get a rough estimate of how the preferences of moderate Republicans have changed over time.

As Krehbiel and Rivers (1988) point out, the 1977 vote on the amendment of John Tower (R-TX) was in fact a vote between the proposals of Tower and Harrison Williams (D-NJ). They differed most sharply in their proposed wages for 1980, $3.05 in Tower and $3.15 in Williams. Using these two alternative 1980 wages, we impute a value of $3.10 to the cutting line. In 1967 dollars, this amounts to $1.25.

The corresponding comparison for 1989 is between the 1991 wage of $4.55 in the Democratic bill and the wage of $4.25 in the GOP substitute. The imputed cutting line value is $4.40 or $1.07 in 1967 dollars. Comparing the $1.25 figure from 1977 to $1.07 for 1989 suggests an ebbing support for minimum wage. On the other hand, the differential would be less important if one argued that senators were conditioning their votes with a view to adopting a bill that would win presidential approval. Carter's acquiescence to labor demands and Bush's firmness may have influenced the spatial mapping in the legislative branch. Nonetheless, it is quite possible that the minimum wage ideal points of senators shifted downward.

In a nutshell, economic interests are important because they affect projections, as well as logrolls. Even when there is a stable angle of projection, economic interests can change the mapping of quantitative alternatives onto the basic space.

Evolution of the Angle of Projection

The angle of the projection into the basic space can evolve over time. In some cases this evolution will simply reflect changes induced by the overall evolution of the political system. This type of change in cutting-line angle is well illustrated by minimum wage legislation, where the angle of minimum wage votes was influenced by the changing ideological positions of southern Democrats. Another type of change is endogenous change where prior legislation creates an economic constituency that influences later voting behavior of the legislator. We illustrate this "hooking" effect with food stamps.

To begin our discussion of a change in the cutting line angle with minimum wages, we consider the entire set of minimum wage roll calls that occurred in the House of Representatives during the period spanned by the dynamic estimation reported in *Congress, 1997*. The first roll call occurred in the 75th House in 1937, the last in the 98th House in 1983.

The spatial model provides a better accounting of minimum wage voting after World War II than of votes before it. Voting on minimum wage occurred before the war in the 75th Congress, when the initial legislation was passed, and in the 76th, when revisions were considered. Subsequently, new legislation was made moot by the command economy of the war. Divided government occurred in 1947–48, with a Republican Congress and a Democratic president. In the labor area, the Republicans devoted their energies to overriding Truman's veto of the Taft-Hartley Act. Minimum wages did not get considered until the 81st Congress.

Consequently, we can divide the roll calls neatly into pre-World War II and post-World II samples. Classification of minimum wage roll calls using only the one-dimensional dynamic model is very high post World War II, averaging 88.2 percent but is much lower, at 71.2 percent, before World War II.[33] Moving to a two-dimensional model improves matters considerably before World War II, classifications jumping to 82.0 percent, but still below the 88.6 percent obtained for the postwar period.[34]

The finding that the second dimension is the key to classification of minimum wage voting prior to World War II shows that initially minimum wage was an unusual, non-standard issue that was not part of the main line of liberal-conservative conflict. The finding that, even in two dimensions, minimum wage voting is significantly less structured before World War II is indicative of the potential multidimensionality of most economic legislation. Since, for example, the level of the wage can be traded off against what type of employment will be covered, a vote between two alternative bills may not fit readily into the preexisting spatial pattern of voting. The complex nature of such trade-offs should, we suggest, be most apparent in the initial legislative handling of an issue. Eventually, however, the multidimensionality is packaged and shoe-horned into the spatial structure.

The packaging indeed results, at any one point in time, in minimum wage voting being nearly unidimensional. In Figure 6.5, we plot the cutting-line

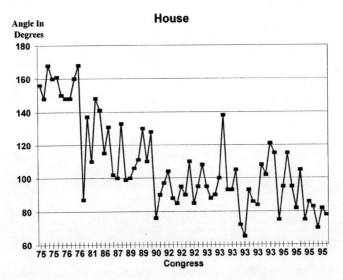

Figure 6.5. Cutting-line angles on minimum wage roll calls in the House of Representatives. Angles for all vote margins closer than 65 to 35. The minimum wage shifts from a second-dimension issue before World War II (angles are just under 180°) to a first-dimension issue (angles near 90°) as southern Democrats adopt conservative positions.

angles in chronological order. If the votes were unidimensional at a point in time, all the angles for a year would be identical. While there is some variation within years, it is quite small, particularly for roll calls with close (less than 65-to-35) margins.

In contrast, the angles vary strongly and linearly over time. In Table 6.12, we present the results of a regression of the angle against a constant, calendar time, and roll call margin. Angle declines sharply with time, especially for close roll calls.[35] The standard error of the estimate of 14.5° indicates the small variability in angle within a given year.

The results presented in chapter 4 help to understand why the angle has gradually shifted. At the beginning of the New Deal, positions of northern and southern Democrats did not have significant differences. The Roosevelt coalition represented a reasonably coherent voting bloc. The civil rights issues introduced significant and increasing polarization within the party. The passage of the Voting Rights Act in 1965, however, marked the beginning of a period in which southern Democrats have drifted back toward the party mainstream.

The changing position of southern Democrats is evidenced in Figures 3.4 and 5.15. By 1940, some of the separation of the southern delegation had

Table 6.12
Minimum Wage Votes: Cutting-Line Angles, Time, and Vote Margin

Variable	MODEL	
	(1)	(2)
Constant	3385.37	3291.22
	(268.11)[a]	(260.56)
Calendar year	−1.667	−1.622
	(0.136)	(0.132)
(Year X margin)/100[b]		0.8059
		(0.336)
Adjusted R^2	0.679	0.703
Standard error of estimate	15.037	14.467

Note: Dependent variable is the cutting-line angle in degrees.
[a] Standard errors are in parentheses.
[b] Margin = percent Yea − percent Nay.

occurred. They had moved above the northern Democrats on the vertical dimension but had not moved to the right on the horizontal dimension. By 1960, a time when civil rights began to dominate American domestic politics, southern Democrats had made the full transition. By 1977, there was less separation.

The spatial movement of Southern Democrats is tracked by the minimum wage cutting lines. The opposition of southern Democrats, and of Republicans, to the initial minimum wage legislation, led to a nearly horizontal cutting line before the war. As southern Democrats, flush with the manna of public works and military bases provided by the New Deal, switched from seeking to alleviate their economic situation vis-à-vis the North to seeking to protect the internal status quo vis-à-vis blacks, they became more conservative on the economic dimension. The cutting-line angle echoed this movement. The votes in the immediate postwar period gave, as was typical of conservative coalition votes, more emphasis to the first dimension. With more liberal southern Democrats, the cutting line became nearly vertical in the 1970s, as illustrated by Figure 6.4. In the 1980s, the cutting line had an angle smaller than 90°, showing that party-line voting was occurring on minimum wages, with the South's historical opposition to minimum wages now expressed by an increasing number of southern Republicans.

Although a standard economic explanation for the opposition of the South is that minimum wages cause low-wage regions to lose their comparative advantage in attracting investment, an alternative view is that enfranchised whites in the South sought to maintain disenfranchised blacks in a low-wage situation. When the first minimum wage roll calls took place in 1937, Congressman Martin Dies (D-TX) was unambiguous on this point: "There is a racial question involved here. Under this measure whatever is prescribed for one race must be prescribed for the others, and you cannot prescribe the same wages for the white man as the black man."[36]

Later developments support the view that the race issue was a central one. As southern Democrats acquired a black constituency in the 1970s, more of them began to favor minimum wages, even though southern states had low levels of unionization and nearly all had right-to-work laws. Only one southern Democrat voted against passage of the 1989 bill in the House, and only three supported the GOP substitute in the Senate.

The change in the angle for minimum wages is thus largely one of the projection adjusting to the perturbation of the space (see chapter 4) induced by the reappearance of race as a salient issue in American politics. The story is quite different for food stamps.

The change in the angle for food stamps is shown in the comparison of the top panel of Figure 6.6, which shows the 1964 vote, and the bottom panel, which shows the 1967 vote. The 1964 vote is nearly a party-line vote; this makes the cutting line nearly perpendicular to the conservative-coalition votes that occurred on minimum wage at this time. Northern Democrats supported food stamps nearly unanimously (141 to 2); over three-fourths of southern Democrats also voted for passage (75 to 24); the Republicans were nearly united (13 to 163) in opposition. By 1967, the food stamp program could be renewed because the northern Democrats (113 to 1) had enough Republican support (45 to 113) even though a majority of southern Democrats (38 to 41) were now against food stamps. The internal party logroll was no longer necessary, perhaps because of the "hooking" discussed previously. In 1967, food stamp programs were far more widespread in the North than in the South. State and local southern politicians, who were aware that blacks would be beneficiaries of food stamps, had frequently failed to implement a food stamp program. As a consequence, the effect of food stamp payments was smaller in the South than in the North, and southern Democrats and northern Republicans shifted votes in opposite directions on food stamps. The cutting-line angle changed to reflect the new coalition supporting the program.

Coalition Politics and the Angle

The need to build majority coalitions means that not only can the projection of an issue change in time but also can be different, at the same time, in the two Houses of Congress. The Interstate Commerce Act votes illustrate this possibility.

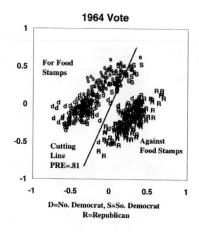

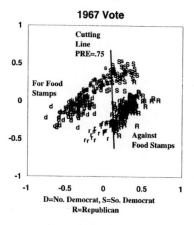

Figure 6.6. Votes on passage of the 1964 Food Stamp Act (VOTEVIEW number 149) and on the 967 conference report extending the food-stamp program (VOTE-VIEW number 134). The 1964 vote is nearly a party-line vote, while the 1967 vote is a conervative-coalition vote.

We have previously seen, in this chapter, that economic issue votes on railroad regulation in the 48th and 49th Houses had similar angles. The votes resembled the splits on bimetallism studied in chapter 5. Some Republicans from the current Middle West joined a core group of Democrats in supporting the various provisions of the Reagan bill while some northeastern Democrats joined Republican opponents of the bill. The Democratic majority in the House

Table 6.13
Senate Votes on Short-Haul Pricing, (1886)

		YEA-NAY VOTE								
		All		Democrats		Republicans				
Roll Call	Date	Y	N	Y	N	Y	N	PRE1	PRE2[a]	Topic
155	5 May	29	24	24	2	5	22	0.75	0.75	Camden (D-WV) amendment (committee of whole)
156	5 May	32	27	30	0	2	27	0.89	0.89	Cameron (R-PA) motion (committee of whole)
163	12 May	23	24	1	23	22	1	0.89	0.89	Edmunds (R-VT) amendment
164	12 May	26	24	23	1	3	23	0.75	0.82	Camden (D-WV) amendment
165	12 May	27	24	2	23	25	1	0.85	0.85	Edmunds (R-VT) amendment
166	12 May	20	29	2	21	18	8	0.55	0.50	Deletion of short-haul-pricing section

[a] *PRE*1 (*PRE*2) is the proportional reduction in error for the one-dimensional (and two-dimensional) linear trend D-NOMINATE model.

was large enough that Reagan's bill would pass; both parties could afford position-taking votes where regional economic interests went against the party line.

In contrast, in the Senate, especially when absences were taken into account, Cullom could count on only small Republican margins, particularly on critical votes concerning a strong-versus-weak short-haul-pricing constraint. These votes, all in 1886, can be seen in Table 6.13. The first four votes were won by the Democrats. On the first vote, the Democrats benefited from Republican defections. Subsequently, on the next four votes — critical ones — party ranks were closed and there were never more than four defections from the two parties. The first five votes turned around the question of whether short hauls should receive the relatively strict regulation proposed by Johnson Camden (D-WV) or the laxer regulation proposed by George Edmunds (R-VT). The Democrats were able to win votes 156, 163, and 164 — in large part because they had more actual voters than Republicans even though the Republicans had a majority in the Senate. The Edmunds amendment finally passed when the Republicans produced a majority on the floor. Following passage, Republican stalwarts opposed to any form of short-haul-pricing regulation were allowed a position-taking vote (vote 166).

In contrast to the short-haul votes in the House, which had angles of approximately 45°, the short-haul votes in the Senate all had angles in excess of 90°. But, because of the strong spatial separation between the legislators of the two parties at this time in the Senate, the votes would have been classified just as well by a vertical cutting line. Indeed, Table 6.13 shows that adding a second dimension provides no improvement for the Senate votes, consistent with Figure 3.3 showing that a second dimension does not improve the fit of party-line votes during this period. Thus, the cutting-line angles differ between the House and Senate, not because of differences of constituency interests on railroads but because of the differential exercise of party discipline in the two chambers.

Summary

The analysis in this chapter began by demonstrating that at no point in American history could a model of appropriately measured constituency interests outperform a simple spatial model of voting. This striking result holds even if the two major parties are viewed as representing distinct constituencies in each state. True, the work of Loomis (1995) disclosed that the party-constituency model might explain a part of what the spatial model does not explain. But the correlations between two senators from the same state and party were sufficiently modest that most of what is unexplained by ideology remains unexplained by the constituency-interest model. The results were confirmed by a direct confrontation of economic and ideological models in a variety of domestic policy areas.

On the other hand, the chapter provides some evidence that economic interests are important in the framing of the projection of issues into the space. Even when the angle of the mapping is relatively stable, as has been true for the minimum wage in the past two decades, the mapping may change as all legislators tend to shift their ideal points in a common direction. The angle itself may change as different coalitions are built, either via the impact of a major issue, such as civil rights, that influences voting on a wide variety of economic issues, or as a result of endogenous changes brought about by the effects of government spending, as seems to have been the case for food stamps. The angle is, however, not only influenced by economic interests but by the imposition of party discipline.

The finding that the spatial model, rather than constituency models, describes the data is an important regularity. While this and previous chapters have documented the regularity, it is important to understand how projection of issues occurs. Of the next three chapters, two rule out some potential possibilities. Chapter 7 shows that strategic behavior other than party discipline is not a major influence on issue projection. Chapter 9 shows that committees are unlikely to introduce major distortions in legislation. Chapter 8, in contrast, shows that interest groups have extreme preferences. These extreme preferences may be reflected in the extremity of winning outcome projections analyzed in chapter 4.

Notes

1. See Bloch (1980), Krehbiel and Rivers (1988), Silberman and Durden (1976).
2. Other important early work that finds that economic variables have modest explanatory power, in comparison to an ideological variable, is represented by several studies of Senate roll call voting: Kau and Rubin (1979), Kalt (1981), and Kau, Keenan, and Rubin (1982). Bernstein and Horn (1981) find that the ratings of the Americans for Democratic Action (ADA) have more explanatory power than measures of oil and gas interests in House voting on energy policy. For alternative analyses that mix ideological and economic measures, see Jackson and King (1989) and Jackson and Kingdon (1992).
3. Most of this chapter simply reproduces *Congress, 1997*, based on D-NOMINATE. The exceptions are Figures 6.1 and 6.2 and the new section on bankruptcy; these are based on DW-NOMINATE.
4. The measurement problem has two sources. First, the data to measure the underlying variables may be missing or very noisy. For example, in the case of strip mining, how does one measure the value constituents place on reclaimed land? Second, even if one has relevant variables, how does one relate the variables to the political process? (See Fiorina, 1974.) For example, did Jesse Helms respond to the median-income voter in North Carolina, the median-income voter among Republican primary voters, or the median-income campaign contributor? For an excellent, more technical discussion of measurement issues, see Jackson and Kingdon (1992).
5. See the various examples of killer amendments that are discussed in Riker (1982) and our analyses in chapter 7 of these same examples.
6. Levitt (1996) attempts to disentangle the influence of party ideology, voter preferences, and personal ideology of senators in the composite represented by one-dimensional ideological scores both by W-NOMINATE and by the ratings of the Americans for Democratic Action. He concludes that personal ideology is by far the greatest determinant of the score. See chapter 8 for the relationship of ADA ratings to W-NOMINATE scores.
7. In checking our results from *Congress, 1997* we discovered a computational error that caused us to exaggerate the error rate for this model and for the "100-party" model. Of the many results in the book that we checked, these were the only ones with errors.

8. We are indebted to Charles Brown for suggesting this test at a National Bureau of Economic Research conference in 1990. Krehbiel (1993) performs a similar test for the 101st Congress only. He calls this test a "match rate."

9. More precisely, Loomis estimated the correlation in the errors in the utility function (equation A2, Appendix A, *Congress, 1997*).

10. Margins cited in the text refer to those actually voting. The statistical analysis presented in the tables treats as voting actual voters plus pairs and announceds.

11. Although simple to interpret, the linear probability model has statistical problems, including producing estimated probabilities below 0 or above 1. For example, a representative with a 0 D-NOMINATE score on the first dimension and a +1 score on the second is seen as voting for Reagan with probability $0.502 + 0.980 = 1.482$. This problem vanishes with a logit model. Logit estimates can be found in Poole and Rosenthal (1993b). The substantive implications are similar to those developed on the basis of the linear-probability model.

12. Using the D-NOMINATE utilities for the two outcomes as regressors gives similar results.

13. For more detailed discussion of these variables, see Gilligan et al. (1989) and Poole and Rosenthal (1993b). For a much more detailed discussion of voting on railroad regulation see Poole and Rosenthal (1994a).

14. Although the second-dimension coefficient is slightly larger than the first's coefficient, the first dimension has more influence because variation in first-dimension scores is about twice that of the second dimension.

15. In the 49th Congress, 176 roll calls occurred before the Cullom bill was brought to the floor. Of these, we retained (for the estimation) 161 in which over 2.5 percent of those voting voted for the minority position. On these roll calls, 323 representatives voted twenty-five times or more and were retained for our analysis.

16. For other examples of party being insignificant after one controls for ideology, see Poole and Romer's (1993) discussion of Richardson and Munger's (1990) work on the Social Security Act and Poole and Rosenthal's (1993b) discussion of the Gilligan et al. (1989) study of the Interstate Commerce Act.

17. We used a standard modification to cope with the problem of state delegations that had 0 *PRO*s or 0 *CON*s. See Pindyck and Rubinfeld (1981, p. 252). In both 1964 and 1967, a Yea vote was in favor of food stamps

18. Krehbiel and Rivers were mainly interested in a method for estimating ideal points on minimum wages as a function of constituency characteristics. The usefulness of their technique depends, however, on the quality of the underlying model. This chapter argues that simple economic models are routinely of poor quality.

19. Again these results, mirroring our results above for railroads, are not sensitive to the sample used to construct the D-NOMINATE variables. Roll calls preceding all minimum wage voting in 1977 or roll calls from 1975–76 give similar results to the estimates taken from our two-dimensional dynamic model. We also do better than Krehbiel and Rivers with a one-dimensional model. In the case where the legislator coordinates have been estimated from prior votes, the one-dimensional model is just a model with one independent variable, whereas Krehbiel and Rivers used 6 to 8 independent variables. See Poole and Rosenthal (1991b, Table 7.2, p. 227) for details.

20. Our data are for 1975 and are from *Statistical Abstract of the United States, 1988*, p. 415.

21. Garn's votes in 1977 are even more puzzling when one observes that he was a stalwart opponent of minimum wage increases in 1988
22. The bill passed by the House went to the Senate and to conference. After the House accepted the conference report, the bill was vetoed by President Nixon.
23. See Snyder (1990) for a formal model and empirical analysis that differentiates local from national contributors in House races.
24. Unlike the other studies in this section, the bankruptcy results are from later work that uses DW-NOMINATE.
25. Our discussion of Kalt and Zupan draws heavily on Poole and Romer (1983, 1993). See also Poole and Rosenthal (1985a, pp. 52-56).
26. For more details on the variables, see Kalt and Zupan (1984). The Herfindahl indices are defined similarly to the definition for roll calls given in note 29, chapter 3.
27. Again, see Kalt and Zupan (1984) for details. See also chapter 8 where W-NOMINATE is used to estimate the position of the LCV.
28. Romano (1997) studied roll call votes on the regulation of futures markets. Like our discussion here, she compared D-NOMINATE scores to economic and demographic measures. Her results also show that, on the whole, ideology trumps measurements of economic interests.
29. This represents all roll calls with less than 2.5 percent on the minority side. Peltzman (1984) used a 25 percent cutoff.
30. The results are consistent with those obtained, using a different methodology, by Levitt (1994). (See note 6 above.)
31. Significance tests are based on chi-square probabilities from likelihood contribution for each roll call. See Poole and Rosenthal (1985a) for further details on the testing and model comparisons.
32. The OSHA votes were originally discussed by Romer and Rosenthal (1985).
33. The t statistic for the null hypothesis of equality is 8.6.
34. The t statistic for equality is 2.07. Since we hypothesize that classifications improve as new issues result in permanent legislation, a one-tailed test is appropriate, with $p = 0.02$.
35. This regression provides a better description than does the use of a pre-World War II dummy variable.
36. *New York Times*, December 14, 1937.

7

Sophisticated Voting and
Agenda Manipulation

In this chapter we examine the evidence that indicates whether there is strategic or sophisticated voting in Congress. A basic premise of this book is that on each roll call, legislators vote as if they were voting sincerely between a Yea outcome and a Nay outcome. That is, those who prefer the policies associated with the Yea outcome actually vote Yea while those who prefer the policies associated with the Nay outcome vote Nay. Preference is determined by the legislator's Euclidean distance to the alternatives and by random disturbances (see chapter 2).

The alternative to sincere voting is strategic or sophisticated voting. We need to consider two types of strategic behavior: vote trades and sophisticated voting on agendas. Vote trades occur when one actor says to another, "Let's make a deal." The deal might be a logroll, of the type explored in chapter 6, where votes on one issue (such as agricultural price supports) are traded for votes on another (food stamps). Another possible deal is represented by a White House phone call with an implicit promise that the legislator will acquire chips that can be cashed in the future. Still another would be trading a vote in response to campaign contributions, endorsements, or threats. A wide range of interest groups, from the National Rifle Association (NRA) to the American Israel Public Affairs Committee (AIPAC) are alleged to be particularly successful in manufacturing such trades. Nevertheless, the traders are likely to be legislators close to the "sincere" cutting line on an issue because the votes of these legislators, who are nearly indifferent on the issue, represent the cheapest votes. The most liberal members of Congress are unlikely to succumb to NRA threats to work against their reelection; the most conservative don't need to be pushed. Similarly, as we argued in chapter 2, logrolls are likely to take place between spatially adjacent actors. Vote trades involving actors close to sincere cutting lines largely preserve spatial voting. Such trades will not significantly influence the estimation of legislators' ideal points. Of course, the estimated cutting line and outcome locations can, depending on the extent of trading, differ substantially from those produced by sincere behavior.

Strategic behavior also arises when there is a series of votes on the agenda for a specific bill. Strategic voters look ahead to future votes. When future votes are considered, a self-interested voter may vote against his or her immediate preferences. The calculation is basically that a vote for one's first choice today may be wasted if it means an empty cupboard tomorrow. Instead, one votes for one's second choice, recognizing that half a loaf is better than none. Sophisticated behavior with respect to agendas, unlike logrolls, does not require implicit or explicit trades among legislators.

Strategic calculations make sense only if one anticipates a sequence of votes. In chapter 2, we indicated that the spatial model would still apply if there was a finite, binary agenda such that the agenda were known in advance and voter preferences were known in advance. Voters would simply replace the ostensible alternatives with sophisticated equivalents and continue to vote along spatial lines. Such sophisticated voting would not bias our estimation of the legislator coordinates. The outcome coordinates estimated would be those of the sophisticated equivalents rather than the true mappings of the alternatives.

In this chapter, we first look for sophisticated voting in the context of a one-dimensional model. We argue that truly sincere voting should almost always be observed, largely because the framers of bills should be able to anticipate how to draft their legislation to command a majority. Consistent with this hypothesis, our search of the literature on strategic voting found very few bothersome needles in our haystack of the 37,000 roll calls in the first 100 Congresses. In the few instances where the literature points to sophisticated voting, we find that the predictions of the complete–information model — with preferences and the agenda known in advance — are disconfirmed, indicating that some voters vote in a sophisticated fashion while others continue to vote sincerely.

The presence of a mixture of voting types suggests that the basic one-dimensional voting model with a single midpoint might be improved upon by a two-point model where extremists on both ends vote one way and moderates vote the other. This so called both-ends-against-the-middle voting might also arise because extremists are position-taking or expressing alienation. For example, Jesse Helms voted against a moderating, Republican amendment to the minimum wage bill in 1990, thereby expressing his opposition to minimum wages of any form. In this chapter we show, however, that a two-point model cannot improve classifications beyond the improvement expected from the random error process assumed by DW-NOMINATE.

When there is a mixture of sincere and sophisticated types, agenda manipulation is possible. There are in fact a few dramatic examples of successful killer amendments. These all involve race and are the final topic of this chapter.[1]

Saving Amendments, Killer Amendments, and One-Dimensional Voting

The basic framework for the analysis of strategic voting can be developed by the simple voting tree shown in Figure 7.1. In this tree, B stands for a bill, A stands for amendment, and Q stands for the status quo. The first vote involves the amendment and the bill with the winner being put against the status quo. Suppose that the unamended bill, B, would lose to the status quo, whereas the amended bill, A, would defeat it. That is, A > Q and Q > B, where the use of > in A > Q means A is preferred to Q by a majority. If A, B, and Q are one-dimensional — that is, they lie on a line through the basic space — A > Q and Q > B implies that A > B. Therefore, if everyone voted sincerely, the amendment would pass and then defeat the status quo. The amended bill would indeed be the winner.

To fix matters, let Q be a minimum wage of $3.35, B be a minimum wage of $4.75, and A be a minimum wage of $4.25. Sincere voting would have only liberals who preferred $4.75 to $4.25 voting against the amendment and only conservatives who preferred $3.35 to $4.25 voting against the amended bill. (To denote the preference of an *individual*, we use a simple > symbol.) As Figure 7.2 illustrates, we can have only four voter types with one dimension. Assume there were twenty voters with preferences B > A > Q (that is, B was preferred

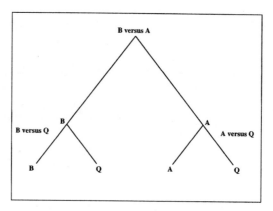

Figure 7.1. A simple agenda tree. An amendment (A) is voted against the bill (B). The winner of this vote then is voted on against the status quo (Q).

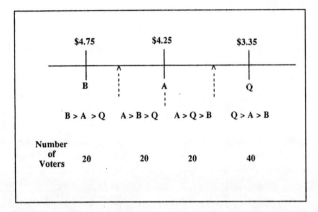

Figure 7.2. The minimum wage example. The bill (B) with a high wage of $4.75 is at the liberal end of the continuum. The amendment (A) is a more moderate proposal of $4.25. The status quo (Q) is $3.35. In one dimension, there are only four types of strict preferences. The number of voters of each type is shown under the type.

to A and A preferred to Q); twenty with A > B > Q; twenty with A > Q > B; and forty with Q > A > B. These are consistent with A > Q (by a vote of 60 to 40) and Q > B (also by a vote of 60 to 40). If the Q > A > B types, the most conservative members, saw all other types voting sincerely, they could vote for the $4.75 wage on the initial vote. This would win, combining twenty B > A > Q votes and forty Q > A > B votes. Then, on the final vote, Q would defeat B. Clearly, sophisticated behavior would pay for the conservatives.

Sophisticated behavior by conservatives poses a dilemma for liberal legislators with the preference ordering B > A > Q. If they vote for the bill on the first vote and they win, then they lose to the status quo. They are faced with a choice of either "compromising their principles" or "going down in flames." If they do choose to "compromise" and look ahead, they will realize, as explained in chapter 2, that the initial vote is really a vote between A and Q, the sophisticated equivalent of B. When all voters vote on the basis of the sophisticated equivalents, A wins the initial vote 60 to 40 and the final vote 60 to 40.

Three related observations are pertinent to this situation. First, A plays the role of a "saving" amendment, introduced when it is clear that the original bill would be defeated. Second, on the initial vote, liberals and conservatives flip-flop when they vote in a sophisticated fashion. Liberals vote for the lower wage, $4.25; conservatives vote for the higher wage, $4.75. Third, on a saving amendment agenda, the initial vote and the final vote should be identical. In our example, there should be two 60 to 40 votes with Q > A > B types forming the minority in both cases.

We argue that one should only rarely observe saving amendments, the reason being that the managers of bills should draft a bill that can win. One would expect few proposals with the property Q > B. Much more often one should see agendas where B > Q.

If B > Q, there might be amendments where A > B. Hence, in one dimension, A > Q. Such amendments would occur in cases where the bill managers report a bill that can defeat the status quo but opponents can come up with a measure that is more appealing to the median voter in the chamber. In this case, the sophisticated equivalents on the initial vote are simply the ostensible alternatives, A and B. Thus, the initial vote will be a sincere vote between A and B; and the second vote, a sincere vote between A and Q. Or, alternatively, one could see proposals where B > A > Q. In this case, the opposition is proposing amendments as a matter of position-taking. But again, the initial choice will be a sincere vote between A and B. A good illustration of this situation is provided by the Erlenborn amendment on the minimum wage shown in Figure 6.4.

An even more hopeless position-taking amendment would have the characteristic B > Q > A. In this case, the initial vote will be a sophisticated vote between B and Q and the second vote will be a sincere vote between B and Q. Consequently, if voters were sophisticated, the initial and final vote should have identical cutting lines. So if bill managers exercise care in making proposals, one should only find sincere voting, unless some legislators prefer to engage in position-taking and to "go down in flames."

Empirical tests do not reject the proposition that most voting is sincere. In chapter 6 we summarized the Romer and Rosenthal (1985) study of Senate voting on amendments to the minimum size that opened a firm to inspection by the Occupational Safety and Health Administration and the Poole and Rosenthal (1991b) study of amendment voting on minimum wages. Such amendments provide a direct test of sincere voting because the amendments are altering a quantitative parameter of a bill. With sincere voting, as the firm size is made smaller, the pro-OSHA vote should decrease, and as the minimum wage level is made higher, the pro-minimum wage vote should decrease. In both cases, the evidence was consistent with sincere voting. Ladha (1991, 1994), using a model derivative from NOMINATE, carefully studied all amendment voting in the 95th Congress through the 98th, for which, as with minimum wages or OSHA inspections, an a priori quantitative ordering could be given to the alternatives. Almost all cases he studied supported sincere voting.

Three important exceptions that illustrate sophisticated voting have been identified by Enelow and Koehler (1980) and Enelow (1981). How do these well-known examples — the Common Situs Picketing Bill in 1977; the Panama Canal Treaty ratification in 1978; and Title IV of the 1966 Civil Rights Act — appear in the DW-NOMINATE estimation?

Consider the Common Situs Picketing Bill, which was discussed in chapter 2. The situation was exactly that diagramed in Figure 7.1. The key vote was on the Sarasin amendment that was designed to weaken the original bill — which most members believed would be defeated. The Sarasin amendment passed by a vote of 246 to 177 but then the amended bill lost 205 to 217.[2] Figure 7.3 shows the two votes.

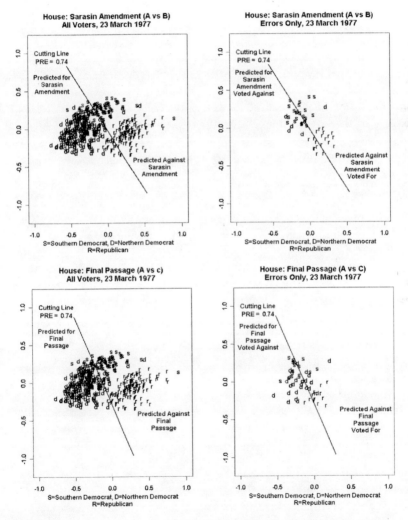

Figure 7.3. House voting on the Sarasin amendment and on passage of the Common Situs Picketing Bill (VOTEVIEW numbers 82 and 83, March 23, 1977).

The spatial model accounts very well for the two votes. The *PRE*s for the Sarasin amendment and for the final passage vote were both 0.74. Note that the two cutting lines are almost parallel, and that the representatives with voting errors tend to be clustered near the cutting lines. The Sarasin amendment was drafted to gain support among southern Democrats and Republicans. This objective was achieved — the cutting line passed through the southern Democrats and liberal Republicans. The party splits were: northern Democrats 184 to 10; southern Democrats 33 to 52; and Republicans 29 to 115. In contrast the splits on the final passage vote were: northern Democrats 171 to 23; southern Democrats 20 to 65; and Republicans 14 to 129.

The voting patterns shown in Figure 7.3 are consistent with sophisticated voting (on each vote) by both the extremes — the liberals and conservatives; and with sincere voting by the moderates — the group between the two cutting lines. For the moderates to be voting sincerely, their preferences would have to be the same as those of their more conservative brethren to the right of the Sarasin cutting line — namely, a preference ordering of $Q > A > B$. On the Sarasin amendment vote, the liberals and conservatives vote for the sophisticated equivalents (A versus Q), whereas the moderates vote sincerely on A versus B. On the final passage, the moderates now vote for Q. This behavior, echoed by the fact that the cutting lines are not identical, rejects the view that the Sarasin amendment was a saving amendment with $A > Q$.

Enelow and Koehler (1980, p. 406) note that the defeat of the amended bill "surprised both supporters and opponents of the bill alike." However, suppose, as Enelow and Koehler claim (p. 407), the amendment did not seriously weaken the bill — that is, A was almost as liberal as B. It is then possible that voters recognized that $Q > A$. In this case, since Q always wins in the final vote regardless of whether it faces A or B, voters can vote either way on the initial vote. Note, however, regardless of whether $Q > A$ or $A > Q$, if all parties are certain that $Q > B$, liberals cannot be worse off by voting for A on the initial vote and conservatives cannot be worse off by voting for B. Therefore, they can be expected to be sophisticated voters.

Among those representatives with preferences $Q > A > B$, those with relatively moderate DW-NOMINATE scores appear, as we argued earlier, not to have followed their more conservative brethren and instead to have voted sincerely. The end result is nonetheless a vote along spatial lines, although the cutting line on the initial vote neither has the interpretation of being generated by sincere voting nor the interpretation of being generated by sophisticated equivalents. Instead, the cutting line reflects both types of behavior. Ironically, the final outcome would have been exactly the same if all voters had voted sincerely.

An amendment whose purpose is exactly opposite to that of a saving amendment is known as a killer amendment. A killer amendment is designed to sink a bill (so that Q > A) that would defeat the status quo were it not amended (so that B > Q). Since B > Q and Q > A, in one dimension, B > A. Even with sincere voting, the killer amendment would fail. Sophisticated voters will treat the initial A-versus-B vote as a Q-versus-B vote, implying that B would defeat A on the first vote. Hence, in one-dimensional voting killer amendments must always fail!

Enelow and Koehler (1980) discuss several amendments offered by conservatives as killer amendments to the Panama Canal Treaties of 1978.[3] Although the intent of the conservatives was directly opposite to that of the saving Sarasin amendment to Common Situs favored by liberals, the voting patterns were similar. The amendments were of the motherhood and apple pie variety. For example, one concerned a cemetery in the Canal Zone where U.S. citizens were buried. The strategy of the conservatives was very simple: Propose something that it is embarrassing to vote against; then the amended bill also passes. But if any of the motherhood and apple pie amendments passed, the amended treaty would require renegotiation with Panama. Renegotiation would be preferred by the conservatives because, at a minimum, it would force a delay in implementation of the main treaty provisions.

Placing "motherhood and apple pie" in our basic ideological space is somewhat problematical because, when voted on sincerely, such proposals might attract unanimous support. Because voters voted strategically, however, the actual voting behavior on Panama Canal treaty amendments fits into a one-dimensional framework.

Figure 7.4 shows one of these amendments along with the final-passage vote on the Panama Canal Neutrality treaty. The amendment concerned the right of the United States to maintain military bases in the Canal Zone if the United States was at war. After it was offered by Senator James Allen (D-AL), Senator Frank Church (D-ID) made a motion to table. The motion to table passed by a vote of 57 to 38 on March 1, 1978, and the neutrality treaty was later passed by a vote of 68 to 32 on March 16, 1978.

Both votes fit the spatial model well. The *PRE* for the Church motion was .66 and the *PRE* on the final passage was .56. The two cutting lines are close to being parallel, indicating unidimensional voting on the issue, and the overall pattern is very similar to that shown in Figure 7.3 for the Common Situs Picketing Bill, but the interpretation of it is quite different.

Any vote for the Allen killer amendment can be interpreted as a sincere vote, since the amendment was of the "motherhood and apple pie" variety. But such a vote was also in accord with the strategic interests of conservatives who voted for the amendment (against the Church motion to table) but against the treaty. Liberals who voted against the amendment but for the treaty were, in voting against "motherhood and apple pie," being strategic, accepting an embarrassing vote in return for preserving the treaty.

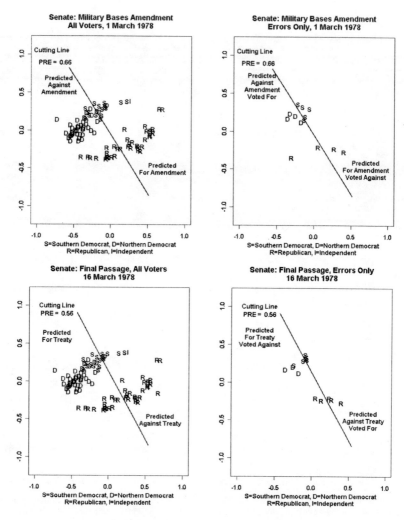

Figure 7.4. Senate voting on Church motion to table military bases amendment and on passage of the Panama Canal Neutrality treaty (VOTEVIEW numbers 673 and 702, March 1 and March 16, 1978).

The interesting case concerns the moderates in between the two cutting lines who voted both for the amendment and for the treaty. Although one could see them as being sincere voters, they may well also have been strategic. They wanted the treaty and may have been willing if necessary, "to take the fall" on the amendment, but they could presume that liberals wanted the treaty even more than they did. Moreover, there were enough liberals to defeat the amendment, leaving the moderates free to take the "patriotic" position on the amendment.

Enelow (1981) shows another interesting case where, unlike the Common Situs Picketing Bill, there was a successful saving amendment. The case is Title IV, the open-housing provision of the 1966 Civil Rights Bill. Title IV was aimed at prohibiting discrimination in the sale, rental, or financing of housing. Charles Mathias (R-MD)[4] — who supported Title IV — offered a saving amendment to weaken Title IV enough for it to survive an attempt to delete it from the bill. Figure 7.5 shows the three critical votes in the sequence: the Mathias amendment, which passed by a vote of 237 to 176; the motion by Moore (R-WV) to recommit with instructions to delete Title IV, which failed on a vote of 190 to 222; and the final passage vote of 259 to 157. The expectation of Mathias was that the original bill, B, would lose to recommit, R, but that the amended bill, A, would defeat both R and the status quo, Q.

Two things stand out in Figure 7.5. The three cutting lines are roughly parallel, again suggesting a single active dimension, but the fit of the spatial model is poor for the Mathias amendment. On the Moore motion and the final-passage vote the spatial model performs very well in that the errors are quite close to the cutting line. Not so for the Mathias amendment. The *PRE*s were 0.58, 0.81, and 0.72 respectively.[5]

The expected-utility theory of sophisticated voting developed by Enelow (1981) predicts that the only groups that may split their votes on a saving amendment are the extreme liberals and/or conservatives. Even if it means eventual defeat for the bill, some of the extremist legislators may not be able to bring themselves to compromise their principles. In short, the two-outcome spatial model we fit to the roll calls may not work well for this type of roll call.

The Mathias amendment is an example of this. Note that a number of liberal Democrats quite distant from the cutting line voted against the amendment (the topmost voting error plot in Figure 7.5). In distinction to the Sarasin and Allen amendments, where strategic voting led to a spatial, cutting-line pattern of voting, voting of the Mathias-amendment-type would, if pervasive, be counter to the basic premise of this book. Consequently, it is important to check whether "both ends against the middle" voting is prevalent.

Both-Ends-against-the-Middle Voting

The both-ends-against-the-middle type of voting on the Mathias amendment does not appear to occur very often. Among the examples of sophisticated voting we found in the literature — more of which we discuss below — it is the only one that shows this pattern. In addition, in chapter 3 we showed that the voting error from DW-NOMINATE closely matches the theoretical error distribution — especially on roll calls with at least 20 percent on the minority side.

To get a better measure of how frequently both-ends-against-the-middle voting occurs, we performed a simple experiment using a version of the optimal-classification method we described in chapter 2. Recall that the first step is

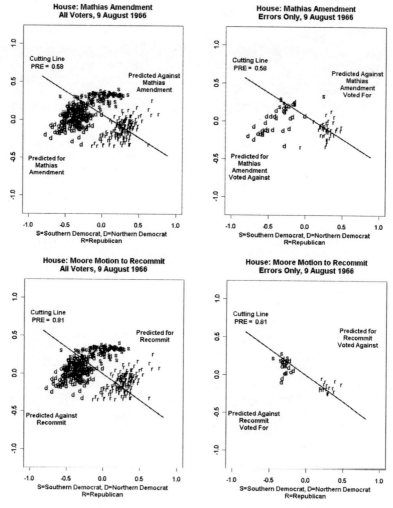

Figure 7.5. House voting on the Mathias amendment to Title IV, open-housing provision of 1966 Civil Rights Bill, the Moore motion to recommit, and passage (VOTEVIEW numbers 289, 292, and 293 respectively; August 9, 1966).

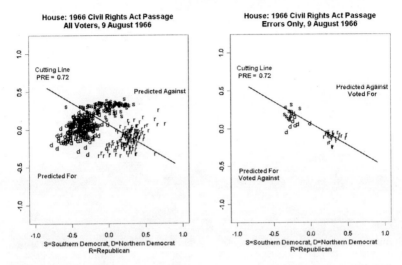

Figure 7.5. (*continued*)

to begin with an arbitrary ordering of the legislators. The optimal cutting point is found by a simple search of the midpoints between adjacent legislators. These roll call midpoints are then fixed, the optimal point for each legislator is found, and so on.

Here, we perform the same experiment, only now each roll call is represented by *two* cutting points. We now search *all pairs* of cutting points to find the optimal classifying pair. This allows for the both-ends-against-the-middle Y-N-Y (Yea-Nay-Yea) and N-Y-N patterns as well as the simple Y-N and N-Y patterns, where the two cutting points are the same. These roll call midpoint pairs are then fixed, the optimal point for each legislator is found, and so on.

Because the one-point model is a subset of the two-point model, the latter is guaranteed to do better. Accordingly, we show the gain in classification of the sophisticated two-point model over the one-point model for the House of Representatives in Figure 7.6.

Given our results in chapter 3, it is not surprising that the two-point model does not have much punch — for seventy-three of the 108 Houses we analyze, it added 1 percent or less to the classifications; and for ninety-four Houses it added 1.5 percent or less. Note, moreover, that since Reconstruction, the Houses with the largest gains all fall in the period of the civil rights perturbation (chapter 5) where a second dimension was important. Both-ends-against-the-middle in one dimension is largely a proxy for a two-dimensional world. Indeed, both-ends-against-the-middle has its least bite in the polarized, unidi-

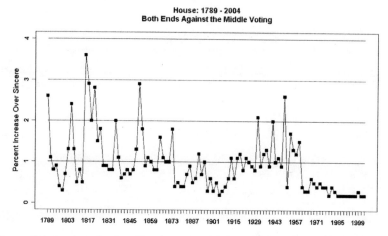

Figure 7.6. Increase in classification when both-ends-against-the-middle voting is allowed, 1789–2004. Optimal classifications with two cutting points on each roll call compared to standard optimal classification with one cutting point. Allowing for both-ends-against-the-middle voting does very little to improve classification, particularly after the late 1950s.

mensional Congress that has characterized the House since the election of Ronald Reagan in 1980. Indeed, for the eight Houses added since *Congress, 1997*, less than 0.3% was added to classification by allowing for a second cut-point.

To see whether an increase of 1 percent is a meaningful result, we performed a Monte Carlo analysis by applying the two-point classification procedure to artificial data created from legislator and roll call coordinates from D-NOMINATE.[6] We introduced error into the individual utility functions at roughly the level encountered in the actual roll call data. The two-point model always showed an increase of about 1 percent over the one-point model. In short, both-ends-against-the-middle voting is undeniably occurring but it clearly has only a very low level effect.

Killer Amendments in Two Dimensions

Until this point, we have considered strategic voting in the context of unidimensional issues. In the unidimensional case, the distinction between sincere and sophisticated voting has limited policy relevance. With a truly saving amendment, a majority should prefer the amendment to the bill, and a majority should prefer the amended bill to the status quo; so the amended bill should win even with sincere voting. If there were a truly unidimensional killer amendment (in distinction to the "motherhood and apple pie amendment"), the amendment should never pass in one dimension. If the original bill is liberal relative to the status quo, for example, the killer amendment needs to be even more liberal. In this case, a sincere majority would prefer the original bill.

Possibilities are quite different in two dimensions. Reconsider Figure 2.6. There are now, in contrast to the four types in one dimension, six possible types of strict preferences. If there were 32 A > B > Q types, 2 A > Q > B, 2 B > A > Q, 31 B > Q > A, 31 Q > A > B, and 2 Q > B > A, we would have Q > A by a 64 to 36 vote; B > Q by 65 to 35; and A > B 65 to 35. That is, we would have a voting cycle in which no one alternative defeats all others under majority voting. In particular, B > Q and A > B but Q > A. Sincere voting would lead to the amendment's killing the bill. In contrast, voting over sophisticated equivalents would lead to the recognition that the initial vote is truly one between B and Q; so B would win. Therefore, if voters vote strategically, killer amendments won't work in either one or two dimensions. If voters are sincere, the amendments might well succeed, but only in two or more dimensions. Not surprisingly, therefore, the interesting cases of killer amendments in the literature all involve two dimensions. Given that (in chapter 3) we identified race as the second dimension in those periods of American history where a second dimension was most important, it is also not surprising that the examples all involve race.

A killer amendment discussed by both Enelow (1981) and Riker (1982) is the Powell amendment. The amendment was offered by Adam Clayton Powell, Jr. (D-NY) to the 1956 School Aid Bill. The amendment "barred federal funds from going to states that had failed to comply with the decisions of the Supreme Court" (Enelow, 1981, p. 1080) and therefore would have denied aid to segregated schools. The amendment passed by a vote of 225 to 192 (northern Democrats voted 77 to 42; southern Democrats 0 to 104; and Republicans 148 to 46) on July 5, 1956, and the amended bill then failed by a vote of 194 to 224 (ND 116–3; SD 3–102; R 75–119) on that same day.[7] Note that, as an African American, Powell himself may have been more interested in position-taking than in strategic legislative activity. Presumably, Powell wanted both school aid and desegregation. His actions suggested that he preferred position-taking on desegregation to the half-loaf consisting of school aid.

The Powell amendment transformed the debate from one over the level of school aid to one over both school aid and school desegregation. The status quo, Q — no school aid and segregated schools in the South (in spite of the 1954 *Brown v. Board of Education* ruling) — would appear to be near the conservative pole on both dimensions. The unamended bill, B, was a combination of school aid and (implicitly) the status quo on segregation. That is, the bill was relatively liberal on one dimension and conservative on the other. The amended bill, A, was liberal on both dimensions. So if the Powell amendment were attached to the School Aid Bill, then southern Democrats would clearly vote for segregation, the status quo, while many Republicans would vote for the status quo of no school aid. According to our analyses in chapters 4 and 5, segregation, the status quo, would be near the top of the second dimension with the southern Democrats, and the status quo of no school aid would be on the right side of the first dimension with the conservative Republicans. The status quo was thus a conservative position on both dimensions.

Figure 7.7 shows the two votes. The *PRE*s were 0.55 and 0.71 respectively. The southern Democrats voted almost unanimously against both motions and were clearly sincere voters on both. The southern Democrats were probably a mix of the orderings $B > Q > A$ and $Q > B > A$ because no doubt some southern representatives would have liked the school aid if there were no strings attached (Riker, 1982, p. 154). The Powell amendment split the northern Democrats with the liberals voting for the amendment and the moderates voting along with the southern Democrats, against the amendment. The ordering of northern Democratic liberals was clearly $A > B > Q$ and the northern Democratic moderates were probably $B > A > Q$ so that both groups were voting sincerely on both motions. In addition, the Democratic Party fits the spatial model very well.

Not so for the Republicans — the cutting line for the Powell amendment produces the prediction that almost all the Republicans will vote for the amendment. This occurs because ninety-six Republicans voted for the Powell amendment but against final passage — indeed, they were Y-N voters. These Y-N voters were clearly voting in a sophisticated fashion if their preference ordering was $Q > B > A$ and sincerely if their ordering was $Q > A > B$ (Riker, 1982, p. 155). Most of these Y-N voters were moderates and conservatives. Of the ninety-six Y-N voters, seventy-nine were above the cutting line on the final-passage vote and seventeen were below the cutting line. These seventeen below the cutting line are errors according to the spatial model but they are quite close to the cutting line and they are adjacent to the Y-Y voters, all of whom were liberals. These seventeen Y-N voters could have had the ordering $Q > A > B$ because the liberal Republican Y-Y voters they were next to were undoubtedly sincere voters with the ordering $A > B > Q$ or $A > Q > B$. This would be consistent with the liberal Republicans still believing in the nineteenth-century civil rights tradition of their party. If some were more fiscally conservative than the others, then it is plausible that they would have had the ordering $A > Q > B$. Nevertheless, the bulk of the seventy-nine Y-N Republicans above the cutting line were clearly sophisticated voters.

In summary, the preference orderings from top to bottom for the Republicans were in all likelihood: $Q > B > A$, $Q > A > B$, $A > Q > B$, $A > B > Q$; and

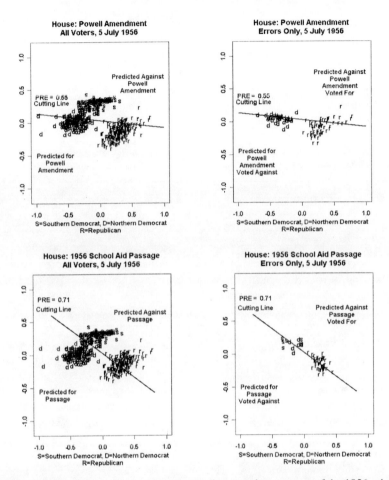

Figure 7.7. House votes on the Powell amendment and on passage of the 1956 school aid bill (VOTEVIEW numbers 122 and 124, July 5, 1956). The Powell amendment operated as a killer amendment since ninety-six Republicans voted for the desegregation provisions of the amendment but voted against passage.

for the Democrats, $Q > B > A$, $B > Q > A$, $B > A > Q$, and $A > B > Q$. Overall, everyone voted sincerely except the conservative Republicans who were split — most voted sophisticatedly while a minority voted sincerely. Note that the above preference orderings *require* the presence of two dimensions; no one-dimensional ordering can produce them.

Riker (1982) cites the Powell amendment as an example of a voting cycle produced by sophisticated voting. The bill was killed because northern Democrats voted sincerely while Republicans were sophisticated. Even though the status quo, Q, prevailed, as Riker shows, it was probably the case that B > Q. For Figure 7.7, without the Powell amendment the cutting line on passage would have probably been higher on the second dimension. Only fifteen of the more moderate southern Democrats near the cutting line would have been needed to pass the School Aid Bill.

Riker (1982) cites two other examples of cycles: the Wilmot Proviso, and the Depew amendment to the constitutional amendment for the popular election of senators. In 1846 President Polk, a Democrat, wanted a quick victory in the war with Mexico. Intending to bribe the Mexican military commanders, he asked Congress to appropriate $2 million for that purpose. Polk should have gotten his $2 million without much difficulty, because the Democrats had firm control of the 29th Congress. In the House the division was 142 Democrats, seventy-nine Whigs, six American Party members, and one vacancy. In the Senate the division was thirty-four Democrats, twenty-two Whigs, and two vacancies. Unfortunately for Polk, David Wilmot (D-PA) offered an amendment — which became known as the "Wilmot Proviso" — that prohibited slavery in any territories taken from Mexico. This amendment was passed by the House on a series of votes on August 8, 1846. The amended bill later died in the Senate.

As we discussed in detail in chapter 5, slavery had, by this time, emerged as a second dimension that divided both the Whigs and the Democrats. Consequently, just as was the case for the Powell amendment 110 years later, the status quo had two aspects. One involved providing no appropriation for the bribe; and the other meant, at a minimum, leaving the slavery question in the territories taken from Mexico as an open issue to be decided at a later date. Given the unified control of the government by the Democrats, the bill to provide funds for bribery would undoubtedly have passed in the absence of the Wilmot Proviso (Riker, 1982, p. 225).

The critical vote analyzed by Riker was on a procedural motion that would have killed the Proviso, so a Nay vote is for the Proviso. In the vote, shown in Figure 7.8, the procedural motion failed by a vote of 79 to 93 (northern Democrats 13 to 51; southern Democrats 47 to 0; northern Whigs 5 to 35; southern Whigs 14 to 2; American Party 0 to 5). The vote was almost purely a sectional one. It was very representative of literally hundreds of other roll calls that were taken, through this period, on a variety of slavery-related issues. (Compare Figures 7.8 and 5.6.) The *PRE* on this roll call was 0.86.

Because the House was rushing to adjournment and a filibuster in the Senate prevented a final vote, the only pairing observed was A versus B and A > B by 93 to 79. As we noted above, clearly B > Q because of unified control by the Democrats. Riker (1982, p. 227) argues that the southern Democrats and southern Whigs would certainly have voted for Q over A and, because most

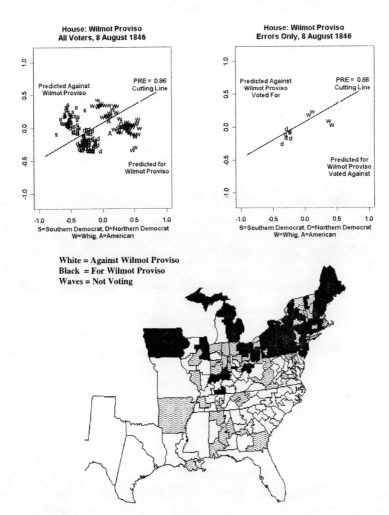

Figure 7.8. House voting on the Wilmot Proviso (VOTEVIEW number 456, August 8, 1846). The sectional nature of the vote is shown on the map. Only two slave state representatives, from the border state of Kentucky, supported the proviso.

of the northern Whigs opposed the war, they would also have probably voted for Q. Hence, Q probably would have gotten the forty-seven southern Democrats and fourteen southern Whigs who voted against the Wilmot Proviso along with the thirty-five northern Whigs who voted for the Proviso. This yields a total of ninety-six votes so that Q > A.

In effect, a unified Whig party, plus the southern Democrats, would have defeated the bribery bill as amended by the Wilmot Proviso. This would be consistent with a cutting line in Figure 7.8 that passed through the Democrats as it does for the Wilmot Proviso vote but at a sharper downward angle so as to include all or most of the northern Whigs. Sincere position-taking on slavery by northern Democrats would have led to defeat of Polk's proposal.

The other example of a voting cycle discussed by Riker involves the Depew amendment to the constitutional amendment to permit the direct election of senators (what became the Seventeenth Amendment). The Depew amendment is yet another example of the power of race in American politics — once again, the introduction of race, via an amendment to a bill, created a voting situation with a two-dimensional status quo. In this situation it had the interesting effect of derailing a bill that, unamended, had more than two-thirds backing in the Senate. Depew's clever maneuver had the effect of creating a voting cycle.

Riker (1982, p. 195) estimates that at least sixty-four of eighty-six (or eighty-eight, after Oklahoma was admitted to the Union in November of 1907) senators supported the constitutional amendment. Even with the two-thirds requirement for constitutional amendments, clearly B > Q. The Depew amendment was offered by Senator Chauncey Depew (R-NY) as a device to derail the constitutional amendment. The southerners interpreted the Depew amendment as giving the federal government the authority "to send the army into the South to register blacks and enforce their voting rights" (Riker, 1982, p. 194). During the lame-duck session of the 61st Congress in early 1911, the constitutional amendment reached the floor of the Senate. Opponents offered the Sutherland amendment, the negative equivalent to the Depew amendment, to strike language from the constitutional amendment that guaranteed white supremacy in the South.[8] Hence, a vote for the Sutherland amendment was equivalent to voting for the Depew amendment. The Sutherland amendment passed by a vote of 50 to 37 on February 24, 1911 (NDs, 0 to 7; SDs, 1 to 22; Rs, 49 to 8) and the constitutional amendment, as changed by the Sutherland amendment, failed by a vote of 54 to 33 on February 28, 1911, because a two-thirds vote was required (NDs, 7 to 0; SDs, 14 to 9; Rs, 33 to 24).[9]

Figure 7.9 shows the Depew-Sutherland amendment along with the final passage vote. The PREs were 0.92 and 0.50 respectively. The Depew-Sutherland amendment was opposed by all the Democrats plus a few progressive Republicans and supported by most of the Republican Party. The constitutional amendment was then opposed by many (but not all) southern Democrats and northeastern Republicans.

The recorded votes tell us that A > B and, because of the two-thirds requirement, Q > A. But the unaltered constitutional amendment clearly had two-thirds support in the Senate so that B > Q. Depew's clever maneuver was first

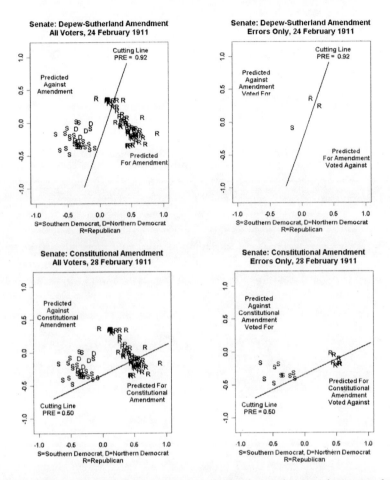

Figure 7.9. Senate voting on the Depew-Sutherland amendment and passage of the constitutional amendment for popular election of senators (VOTEVIEW number 244 and 28, respectively; February 24 and February 28, 1911). Republicans voted for the amendment, which concerned black voting rights in the South, and against passage. Southern Democrats voted overwhelmingly against passage.

used in 1902 during a committee's consideration of the amendment and had the effect of preventing the amendment from reaching the floor for a vote (Riker, 1982, p. 193). Since it was clear that Depew (or someone else) would offer his amendment from then on, it had the effect of delaying the passage of the Seventeenth amendment for nine years because Republicans were united in their support of voting rights for blacks. It was finally passed by the 62nd Senate on

June 12, 1911 after the Democrats made enough gains in the 1910 elections to defeat the Sutherland amendment. The amendment was sent to the states in 1912 and ratified by thirty-six of the forty-eight states on May 31, 1913.

The three successful killer amendments found by Riker were, until recently (see chapter 11), the only ones mentioned in the literature. We suspect the reason they are not more common is that potentially successful killer amendments are derailed either by strategic voting or by the introduction of subsequent saving amendments by bill managers.

An example of a saving amendment by a bill manager occurred in voting on the Reagan Interstate Commerce Bill in the 48th Congress. The Reagan bill eventually passed the House but the Senate did not act.[10] During the debate on interstate commerce, James O'Hara, an African American member from North Carolina, moved to eliminate racial segregation in passenger rail service. As with the Powell amendment in the twentieth century (discussed earlier), the O'Hara amendment passed with support of northern Democrats and Republicans. The O'Hara amendment was modified, however, by a saving amendment that prevented discrimination but held that "separate but equal" was nondiscriminatory. The language allowed just enough northern Democrats to switch from position-taking to strategic voting, so that the amendment to the amendment passed by a bare eight-vote majority. As a consequence, the Interstate Commerce Bill was not killed, as it would have been if it had been turned into a race issue for southern representatives.

This example shows that the supporters of killer amendments try to take advantage of the unwillingness of some of a bill's supporters to compromise their principles and vote strategically. At the same time, supporters can be clever in finding alternative language that circumvents the strategy of their opponents. In any event, there are relatively few observations of voting cycles in Congress.

Summary

Our analysis suggests that sophisticated voting is not pervasive in Congress. We found some saving and killer amendments that could be analyzed as essentially one-dimensional. Our analysis of these amendments disclosed only one example, the Mathias amendment, where voting strayed from a one-dimensional spatial pattern and became both ends against the middle. Such voting is rare, however, as disclosed by our analysis of the two-point model.

Voting is sophisticated in another fashion, illustrated by William Riker's examples of the Wilmot Proviso, the Depew amendment, and the Powell amendment. Each example is separated by approximately sixty years in time but each involves the same maneuver: the introduction of an amendment that taps into the second great organizing dimension of American politics — race — and the destabilization of the winning coalition along the primary dimension of voting. The Wilmot Proviso split the Democratic Party, which was a winning coalition and controlled the entire government in 1846. The Depew amendment caused a split between the Democratic Party and progressive Republicans, thereby reducing the winning coalition below two-thirds size. Finally, the Powell amendment split the Democratic Party internally in a rerun of 1846 and defeated the School Aid Bill, which had majority support. These three examples suggest that strategic manipulation of the agenda can have important effects when some legislators feel bound to engage in position-taking, sincere voting. But, as the interstate commerce example showed, additional manipulation can short-circuit manipulative strategies. On balance, strategic behavior appears to be destabilizing only very rarely. We thus continue to find that the spatial model is a reasonable summary of roll call voting behavior.

Notes

1. Mackie (2003) contains a more detailed analysis of both the theory and the empirical examples that are the topic of this chapter. His analysis has conclusions similar to ours.
2. With pairs and announced voters, the two votes were 249 to 179 and 207 to 220 respectively. The pairs and announced are shown with the actual voters in Figure 7.3. There were forty-seven errors on the Sarasin amendment and fifty-two errors on the final passage vote.
3. There were two Panama Canal treaties: one provided for the permanent neutrality of the canal, after its transfer to Panama, and the other covered the actual transfer.
4. Mathias was elected to the Senate in 1968.
5. The splits for those actually voting on the Mathias amendment: NDs, 150 to 33; SDs, 19 to 74; Rs, 68 to 69. On the Moore motion to recommit: NDs, 24 to 160; SDs, 80 to 12; Rs, 86 to 50. On final passage: NDs, 169 to 17; SDs, 14 to 79; Rs, 76 to 61. With pairs and announced, the votes were 241 to 180, 198 to 231, and 265 to 162 respectively.
6. Note that these tests were conducted in the early 1990s, using D- rather than DW-NOMINATE.
7. There were five pairs on both votes.
8. Indeed, the Sutherland amendment struck the following sentence: "The times, places, and manner of holding elections for Senators shall be prescribed by the legislatures thereof." Clearly, if the southerners controlled who could vote for senators, blacks would not be permitted to vote. See the discussion in Riker (1982, pp. 193–194).
9. With pairs, the vote totals were 51 to 39 for the Sutherland amendment, and 55 to 34 for final passage. There were three errors on the Sutherland amendment and seventeen errors on the final-passage vote.
10. Voting on interstate commerce regulation was covered in chapter 6. See Poole and Rosenthal (1994a) for a lengthier development of the voting on racial discrimination.

8

Roll Call Voting and
Interest Group Ratings

We now extend our analysis of legislative behavior to incorporate the role of
interest groups. We have previously established that there is a polarized distribution of legislator preferences. This polarization has been increasing since the
1960s. Polarization, when coupled with party discipline and majority rule,
results in relatively extreme swings in policy outcomes. Policy outcomes are
rarely close to the ideal point of the median legislator in one dimension or close
to the center of the space in two dimensions. And in chapter 6, we presented
very strong evidence that legislators could not be viewed as representing middle-of-the-road interests in their constituencies. It is interest groups that may
well play a key role in the polarization process.

The potentially polarizing role of interest groups is evident in the research
of Kirkpatrick (1976) and McClosky et al. (1960). They found that convention
delegates and political activists had extreme opinions relative to those of the
mass public. The result is quite consistent with the theory of rational participation. Active political participation in the form of time and money is far more
costly than voting. Theoretically, of course, moderates should be the ones who
do not participate, since they have less to lose from a disliked extreme outcome
than do extremists.[1] If activism, of which interest groups are one form, implies
extremism and if politicians are responsive to activists, polarization will result.
Since the beginning of the Clinton administration, there has been substantial
anecdotal evidence to support this view. The president, by responding to elements of his support coalition, drew substantial flak over his policies concerning
gays in the military, healthcare, and Haiti. Senator Bob Dole, in his quest for the
Republican nomination in 1996, initially ran toward the Right, not the center.
The post-1994 Republican majorities in Congress have kowtowed to the NRA.

Attempts by politicians to take a moderate position often come under attack from interest groups at both ends of the spectrum on an issue. Consider the problems of California governor Pete Wilson, a former senator, in dealing with the abortion issue:

> Press aide Dan Schnur said . . . Wilson had long opposed federal funding for abortion . . . [but] Wilson does support state tax spending on abortion because a 1981 California Supreme Court ruling guaranteed poor women access to abortion through Medi-Cal. . . . Wilson's comments sparked a negative reaction from both sides of the abortion debate. Proponents of abortion rights and their foes characterized the governor's remarks as waffling. . . . Susan Culman, national chairwoman of the Republican Coalition for Choice, said she was surprised to learn that "the only reason [Wilson] has supported state funding was because it's the law." . . . But the most vociferous criticisms came from anti-abortion advocates. . . . "Our concern would be that he's posturing himself for the presidential race," said Kenda Bartlett of Concerned Women for America. If those are truly his deeply felt feelings . . . . he would be actively pursuing some way to change [state law].[2]

In this chapter, we present systematic evidence that a large set of visible interest groups have extreme policy positions. We accomplish this by integrating their ratings with the roll call data.

Many interest groups rate members of Congress on a 0 to 100 scale. The raters include groups with a broad ideological orientation, such as the Americans for Democratic Action (ADA); groups with a special public interest mission, such as the League of Conservation Voters; labor unions, such as the United Auto Workers; business and industry associations, such as the Chamber of Commerce of the United States; and farm organizations, such as the National Farmers Union. In this chapter, we integrate the evaluations of the interest groups into the spatial model of legislative choice that underlies this book. In a nutshell, interest groups are treated as roll call voters. The combined analysis of the "votes" of interest groups, and of the choices of representatives and senators, leads to an important substantive conclusion: Interest groups, particularly labor unions and ideological groups of the Left and Right, are more extreme than members of Congress. If interest groups succeed in pulling legislators away from middle-of-the-road or moderate positions, they may be an important factor in the increasing polarization of American politics that we cited in chapter 4.

The chapter also provides three important methodological results. First, we validate the earlier D-NOMINATE estimates of spatial positions. Second, we are able to make direct comparisons of the House and Senate results since the interest groups effectively "vote" in both houses. In contrast, if just roll call voting data is employed, one must perform separate scalings of the House and

Senate with the consequence that the estimated locations of representatives and senators are not comparable. With the interest group data, we obtain a common scaling of the House and Senate. Third, we use the results to discuss whether interest group ratings, which are widely used in professional journals in economics and political science, fulfill their intended purpose of being reasonable measures of "liberalism/conservatism" or "ideology."

Interest Group Ratings

Interest groups, as part of their efforts to influence the political process, regularly publish ratings of members of Congress.[3] To construct its ratings, a typical interest group selects a set of roll calls. These typically number between ten to forty roll calls in each house. If a member of Congress supports the interest group's position on all the selected roll calls, the member receives a score of 100. Members who always oppose receive a score of 0. More generally, a legislator's rating equals the percentage of the selected roll calls where the legislator took the interest group's position.[4]

In this chapter, we study the 96th Congress (1979–80).[5] In Table 8.1, we list twenty-eight interest groups that issued ratings during the 96th Congress along with the number of roll calls each group used in its ratings. (Also included in the table is CARTER, which refers to the *Congressional Quarterly* rating of support for President Carter's legislative program.)

Does the information provided by the interest groups accord with the story laid out in the previous chapters? The answer is quite positive; in particular, the main liberal/conservative dimension found by D-NOMINATE is closely matched by the ratings. The commonly used interest group ratings correlate very highly with our first dimension.

Table 8.2 shows the Pearson correlations between the ratings of the groups and both dimensions of D-NOMINATE.[6] Correlations are provided for all members, for Democrats only, and for Republicans only. The correlations for all members between the first dimension and the ratings most commonly used by researchers — the ADA, COPE, the ACA, and the ACU — are all above 0.9. No first-dimension correlation is below 0.59 in magnitude. Liberal groups have a negative correlation; conservative groups a positive one. Note further that, on the first dimension, the House correlation is positive if and only if the Senate correlation is also positive. This finding demonstrates that the interest groups are consistent in evaluating the two houses.

The correlations with the second dimension for all members are much smaller; none exceed 0.65 in magnitude. For all interest groups and for both houses, the magnitude of the first-dimension correlation always exceeds the

Table 8.1
Interest Groups that Evaluated Congressional Votes in 1979–1980

Group	Abbreviation	NUMBER OF VOTES SELECTED[a]	
		Senate	House
American Civil Liberties Union	ACLU	15	15
American Conservative Union	ACU	44	47
Americans for Constitutional Action	ACA	53	50
Americans for Democratic Action	ADA	38	38
American Farm Bureau Federation	AFBF	_[b]	9
American Federation of State, County and Municipal Employees	AFSCME	13	14
American Federation of Teachers	AFT	11	15
American Security Council	ASC	10	10
Bread for the World	BFW	10	10
Building and Construction Trades Department (AFL-CIO)	BCTD	12	13
Congressional Quarterly presidential support votes	CARTER	276	235
Chamber of Commerce of the United States	CCUS	58	52
Child Welfare League of America	CWLA	16	16
Christian Voice	CV	14	14
Coalition for a New Foreign and Military Policy	CFNFMP	14	17
Committee on Political Education (AFL-CIO)	COPE	38	39
Congress Watch	CW	65	70
Consumer Federation of America	CFA	21	24
Friends' Committee on National Legislation	FCNL	21	28
League of Conservation Voters	LCV	30	50
League of Women Voters	LWV	20	20
National Alliance of Senior Citizens	NASC	20	20
National Council of Senior Citizens	NCSC	20	20
National Farmers Organization	NFO	16	19
National Farmers Union	NFU	23	18
National Federation of Independent Business	NFIB	18	15
National Women's Political Caucus	NWPC	_[b]	13
United Auto Workers	UAW	35	31
United Mine Workers	UMW	11	10

[a] All votes used by the interest group in either 1979 or 1980.

[b] This group did not evaluate the 96th Senate.

Table 8.2
Correlations of Interest Group Ratings
with D-NOMINATE Dimensions

| | SENATE | | | | | | HOUSE | | | | | |
| | All | | Democrats | | Republicans | | All | | Democrats | | Republicans | |
Group	1[a]	2[b]	1	2	1	2	1	2	1	2	1	2
ACLU	−.74	−.58	−.88	−.84	−.81	−.82	−.80	−.49	−.83	−.74	−.68	−.68
ACU	.95	.22	.88	.79	.94	.87	.96	.17	.91	.63	.87	.58
ACA	.96	.14	.84	.76	.95	.82	.96	.09	.91	.56	.87	.53
ADA	−.93	−.30	−.91	−.84	−.90	−.87	−.93	−.39	−.93	−.81	−.76	−.65
AFBF[c]							.77	.24	.64	.56	.60	.43
AFSCME	−.70	−.33	−.59	−.55	−.70	−.73	−.81	−.32	−.79	−.62	−.70	−.32
AFT	−.75	−.26	−.63	−.56	−.74	−.69	−.87	−.35	−.85	−.71	−.64	−.56
ASC	.89	.21	.84	.83	.77	.76	.88	.35	.88	.76	.60	.57
BFW	−.85	−.45	−.83	−.82	−.87	−.91	−.91	−.22	−.86	−.61	−.75	−.60
BCTD	−.74	.19	−.14	−.01	−.65	−.43	−.75	−.02	−.56	−.33	−.51	−.14
CCUS	.94	.08	.84	.73	.88	.76	.84	.33	.82	.74	.40	.44
CWLA	−.85	−.42	−.81	−.80	−.89	−.84	−.94	−.19	−.90	−.62	−.78	−.49
CV	.91	.30	.84	.78	.92	.85	.89	.23	.83	.60	.73	.60
CFNFMP	−.79	−.45	−.84	−.82	−.78	−.77	−.84	−.50	−.87	−.83	−.62	−.71
COPE	−.94	−.22	−.86	−.83	−.92	−.82	−.92	−.18	−.87	−.66	−.74	−.41
CW	−.82	−.41	−.81	−.81	−.80	−.80	−.88	−.43	−.87	−.87	−.62	−.65
CFA	−.88	−.37	−.91	−.86	−.83	−.81	−.89	−.39	−.87	−.83	−.63	−.56
FCNL	−.88	−.45	−.88	−.88	−.90	−.90	−.91	−.43	−.92	−.83	−.75	−.70
LCV	−.65	−.63	−.84	−.84	−.72	−.81	−.85	−.55	−.86	−.89	−.74	−.70
LWV	−.78	−.58	−.88	−.88	−.81	−.92	−.87	−.45	−.89	−.79	−.72	−.62
NASC	.94	.16	.85	.79	.90	.80	.94	.21	.92	.70	.72	.51
NCSC	−.88	−.33	−.81	−.74	−.88	−.84	−.93	−.22	−.90	−.69	−.75	−.48
NFO	−.78	−.08	−.30	−.38	−.80	−.65	−.59	.06	−.33	−.11	−.61	−.06
NFU	−.89	−.11	−.69	−.53	−.86	−.71	−.68	.17	−.32	−.01	−.62	.00
NFIB	.88	.13	.71	.60	.86	.76	.87	.18	.84	.63	.43	.11
NWPC[c]							−.89	−.20	−.82	−.59	−.71	−.54
UAW	−.95	−.24	−.88	−.83	−.92	−.88	−.94	−.27	−.92	−.72	−.79	−.54
UMW	−.77	−.19	−.56	−.49	−.79	−.68	−.88	−.35	−.85	−.80	−.68	−.43

Note: Our data are for 101 individual senators, including fifty-nine Democrats, forty-one Republicans, and one Independent. The corresponding figures for the House are 438 Representatives —278 Democrats and 160 Republicans. Senators total more than 100 and representatives total more than 435 because of within-Congress replacements.

[a] Correlations are with the first-dimension D-NOMINATE coordinates.

[b] Correlations are with the second dimension.

[c] The group did not publish ratings for the 96th Senate.

magnitude of the second-dimension correlation. No group issues ratings that primarily tap the second dimension. This supports our view (expressed in chapter 3) that American politics, particularly in the contemporary period, is largely unidimensional. We explore this finding in more detail later in this chapter.

When separate correlations are computed for each party, the first-dimension correlations remain high but the second dimension results change dramatically. This is no surprise. As first discussed in chapter 3, in the modern period, liberal Democrats lie at one end of the first dimension and conservative Republicans at the opposite end (see also Figures 8.5 and 8.6). Moderates from both parties are in the middle. Thus, the first dimension and the liberal/moderate/conservative positioning of the ratings correlate highly, overall. In contrast, moderate Democrats tend to be at one end of the second dimension, moderate Republicans at the other, extremists from either party tending to the middle. This alignment produces a low *overall* correlation between the D-NOMINATE second dimension and the interest-group ratings. In contrast to the overall pattern, *within* each party, the second dimension — as well as the first — discriminates along liberal/conservative lines, distinguishing liberal from moderate Democrats and moderate from conservative Republicans. Within each party, there are relatively high correlations on both dimensions.

The pattern of the correlations is echoed directly in the NOMINATE scores. Even though the overall correlations between the first and second dimensions were virtually zero, the correlations between the NOMINATE first and second dimensions for 1979–90 were 0.90 for the Senate Democrats, 0.88 for the Senate Republicans, and 0.71 and 0.43 for the respective party contingents in the House of Representatives.

As noted above, ratings of individual interest groups appear very frequently in professional journals in economics and political science as measures of the liberalism/conservatism or ideology of legislators.[7] Whether these ratings are being used as measures of preferences in a particular policy area or as general measures of ideology, the implicit assumption being made is that the group that issues the ratings *is at the periphery of the space spanned by the legislators*. That is, if the ADA rating measures liberalism with a score of 100 being the most liberal and a score of 0 being the least liberal, all members with less than perfect scores must be more conservative than the ADA. In short, the ADA has to anchor one end of the scale.

To see the effect of this assumption suppose that some interest group is truly centrist — for example, its ideal legislator is someone like Senator David Boren of Oklahoma. What would the ratings of such a group look like? Clearly, centrist legislators like Boren would receive scores near 100. If the centrist interest group were to evenly balance its ratings by including a number of roll calls with midpoints to its left and an equal number with midpoints to its right, both the very liberal Ted Kennedy types and the very conservative Jesse Helms types would receive scores near 50. This interest group's ratings would range from moderates to extremists. (Recall that, in one dimension, the roll call midpoint is the point equidistant between the Yea and Nay outcomes.)

If an interest group is instead exterior to the legislators, its ratings act much like a thermometer. Just as a thermometer tells us that 60° is hotter than 50° but cooler than 70°, an ADA rating of 60 is less liberal than an ADA rating of 70 but more liberal than an ADA rating of 50. Hence the legislators can be ordered by their "thermometer reading."

The upshot of the above is that the way researchers have used interest-group ratings implies a simple one-dimensional spatial model in which the interest group and the legislators can be represented as points on a line where the point representing the interest group is the furthest left or right point. Figure 8.1

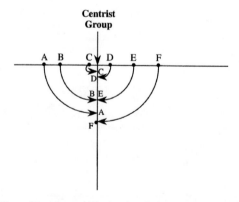

Figure 8.1. The folding of legislators' ideal points in interest-group ratings. A, B, C, D, E, and F denote the ideal points of legislators. An extremely liberal interest group like ADA (in the top part) rates legislators in a way that preserves the liberal/conservative order of the legislators. In contrast, the centrist interest group (in the bottom part) is about equally distant from the extreme liberal A and the extreme conservative F. The centrist group gives A and F similar ratings. These ratings "fold" the ideal points.

shows a hypothetical situation in which the ADA is to the left of six legislators—A, B, C, D, E, and F. In this situation, legislator A would receive the highest score and F would receive the lowest score. Now suppose our hypothetical centrist interest group were positioned between legislators C and D as shown in Figure 8.1. Then C would get the highest rating followed by D with F getting the lowest rating. As the panel shows, this is akin to defining a new dimension by *folding* the original dimension back onto itself at the location of the centrist interest group. Notice that if the centrist group's ratings could be *unfolded*, then they would be equivalent to the ADA ratings.

The folding problem is one reason why, even if the interest group ratings were based solely on votes that have cutting lines perpendicular to the first dimension, the correlations in Table 8.2 would not be 1.0. (Recall that the cutting line is the two-dimensional analog of the midpoint; it is the locus of points equidistant from the Yea and Nay outcomes.) A folded group in the center of the space would have a correlation near zero. Conservative groups that were near the end of the space would have a correlation that was positive but less than one. Another reason that the ratings would not produce perfect correlations is that, because they are based on a fairly small number of roll calls, the ratings are not very fine-grained (Kiewiet and McCubbins, 1991).

Looking at Figure 8.1, if legislator A receives a 100 rating based on ten roll call votes, then A votes with the ADA position ten out of ten times. By assumption the ADA is to the left of A. Hence, if there is perfect spatial voting (no errors), legislator A must be to the left of the midpoint of all ten roll calls. Suppose that not only A but also B was rated 100 and that legislators E and F were both rated 0. These ratings imply that, among the roll calls selected by the ADA, the furthest left midpoint is to the right of B and the furthest right midpoint is to the left of E. This situation is shown in Figure 8.2.

Figure 8.2 demonstrates that the implicit assumption that the interest group is exterior to the legislators can be more accurately phrased as: In a perfect voting world, if an interest group is exterior to the midpoints of its chosen roll calls, then the ordering of the legislators is weakly monotone with the true

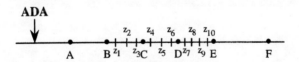

Figure 8.2. Ratings are biased by the roll calls selected by the interest group. If the ADA uses only the ten roll calls with midpoints z_1, z_2, ..., z_{10}, legislators A and B and legislators E and F will vote (errors aside) identically on all ten roll calls. The ratings for A and B and for E and F will then be identical, even though A is more liberal than B and F is more conservative than E.

ordering. Stated simply, the orderings are identical except that the coarseness of the ratings leads to ties. And the presence of ties will reduce correlations. More generally, the ratings are influenced by the distribution of the roll calls selected (Snyder, 1992a). For example, as in Figure 8.2, if the midpoints are concentrated in the center of the distribution of legislators, then the ratings will be bimodally distributed even if the legislator distribution is unimodal. Even if the interest group uses many roll calls, if the midpoints of the selected roll calls are all close to one point in the space, there will be a relatively low correlation of the ratings and the true legislator positions.

To illustrate the effect of an interest group's selecting a relatively small number of roll calls, with cutting lines that are heavily clustered in the space, we examine the ratings of the highly liberal ADA and highly conservative

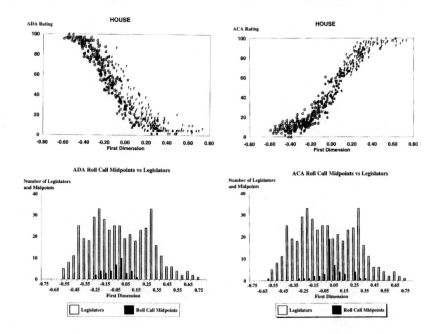

Figure 8.3. The D-NOMINATE scores for the 96th House of Representatives (1979–80) and the ratings of the Americans for Democratic Action (ADA) and the Americans for Constitutional Action (ACA). The top panels plot the ratings against the scores, with the letter d indicating northern Democrats, s southern Democrats, and r Republicans. The S shape of both curves shows how the ratings fail to differentiate among extreme liberals and among extreme conservatives. This failure results, as the bottom portions shows, from the interest groups' constructing their ratings from roll calls with midpoints near the center of the space.

ACA, two interest groups unlikely to be affected by the folding problem. The top portions of Figure 8.3 show the distribution of their ratings for the 96th House against the first dimension of D-NOMINATE. In both cases, a large number of 0 and 100 ratings lead to S-shaped curves. Distinctions that D-NOMINATE makes among both the most liberal and the most conservative representatives are lost in the ratings, leading to the flat portions of the S shapes. The bottom portion of the figure shows the distribution of the midpoints for the roll calls selected by the two groups vis-à-vis the distribution of the representatives. In both instances the midpoints are disproportionately drawn from the center of the legislator distribution. Concerns about bias in interest-group ratings (Snyder, 1992a) are well founded.

Figures 8.1, 8.2, and 8.3 raise two related issues. First, can we test the assumption that the interest group is to the exterior of the legislators; and second, can ratings be unfolded to recover a common ordering of interest groups? We deal with these issues in the next two sections.

Are Interest Groups Exterior to the Legislators?

Using W-NOMINATE we can test whether the interest groups are exterior to the legislators by treating the interest groups as legislators. For the 96th Congress, we identified every roll call vote used to compute the ratings of the twenty-eight interest groups shown in Table 8.1.[8] If an interest group uses a roll call in its rating, it has stated its position and has thus "voted." These "votes" allow us to treat the interest groups as legislators and include them in a W-NOMINATE scaling of the 96th Congress that combines the actual votes of the member of Congress and the "votes" of interest groups. (Given that the maximum number of roll calls selected by an interest group was seventy [see Table 8.1], most of the "votes" by the interest groups are abstentions.) In the first scaling we present, we used the eight interest groups that selected at least twenty-five votes during the 96th Senate. Figure 8.4 shows the results in one dimension.[9]

As Figure 8.4 shows, seven of the eight groups are estimated at or near the ends of the dimension (-1 and $+1$ respectively). The CCUS is the interesting exception. Its estimated first-dimension position of 0.86 is the most interior among the eight interest groups. It appears to be a genuine case of folding of the sort shown in Figure 8.1. Of the fifty-eight roll calls the CCUS used in its Senate ratings, three had less than 2.5 percent in the minority and were unscalable.[10] For the remaining fifty-five roll calls, eight had midpoints to the right and forty-seven had midpoints to the left of the CCUS's position. On fifty-four of the fifty-five roll calls, the CCUS "voted correctly" — that is, its actual position corresponded with the prediction of the spatial model fifty-four of fifty-five times. The selection of roll calls by CCUS fits the spatial model quite

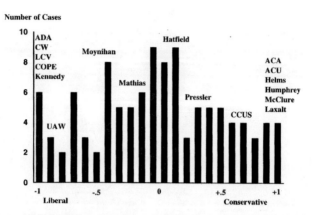

Figure 8.4. Interest groups and senators in a common one-dimensional space: W-NOMINATE scaling for 1979–80. The histogram shows the distribution of both senators and interest groups. All interest groups used in the scaling are named on the plot. Some senators are also named.

well. Because the CCUS has an interior position, however, its ratings are folded. In fact, the seven senators to the right of the CCUS received an average rating of 87 while the five senators equidistant to the left of the CCUS (between 0.72 and 0.86) received an average rating of 88.

As to the seven interest groups at the periphery of the space, the ACA and the ACU, the two groups at the right end, are *perfect* — that is, they are exterior to the midpoints of all their chosen roll calls. At the left end, COPE, the ADA, and the UAW fit the dimension very well. While they are not perfect, they have no more than two voting "errors." There are poorer fits for the LCV and for Ralph Nader's Congress Watch (CW). As we now demonstrate, a second dimension is required to account for their voting patterns.

We noted above that a one-dimensional spatial model with the interest group at the end of the dimension is the implicit model behind the use of interest-group ratings as measures of ideology. If the voting space of the legislators is in fact two-dimensional, and if all the interest groups are using the same dimension through the space to construct their ratings, then the interest groups should lie on a line through the two-dimensional space.

Figure 8.5 shows the W-NOMINATE results for the 96th Senate in two dimensions.[11] (As explained in Poole [2005], the space is constrained to be the unit circle.) Once again seven of the eight groups are on the rim of the unit circle exterior to the senators with the CCUS to the interior among the Republican senators. The second dimension dramatically improves the fit of the LCV — it now votes "correctly" on all roll calls, and its geometric mean probabil-

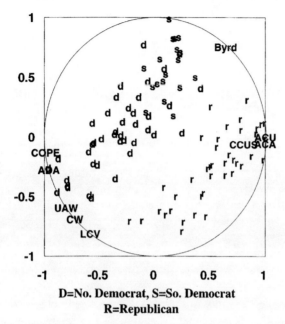

D=No. Democrat, S=So. Democrat
R=Republican

Figure 8.5. Interest groups and senators in a common two-dimensional space: W-NOMINATE scaling for 1979–80. The interest groups and Harry F. Byrd, Jr. are named on the plot. See Table 8.1 for identification of the interest groups. The circle shows that W-NOMINATE constrains the estimation to a circle of unit radius. All interest groups are at or near the periphery of the space. They are concentrated along an axis that runs roughly from the UAW to the ACU.

ity rises from 0.70 to 0.95. Ralph Nader's CW also fits better in two dimensions — its geometric mean probability rises from 0.59 to 0.67 and the number of voting errors drops from 14 to 10.

Note that a line running at a slight angle through the two-space — from the location of the UAW to the location of the ACU in Figure 8.5 — provides an axis that comes close to capturing the positions of the eight interest groups. This finding lends rough support to the implicit one-dimensional spatial model that underlies the use of interest group ratings as measures of liberalism/conservatism. Projection onto the axis would give results very close to those shown in Figure 8.4, including the folded position of CCUS. The locations of the interest groups are also consistent with the correlations reported in Table 8.2.

We also need to make two methodological observations about Figure 8.5. First, compared to the senators, the interest groups are imprecisely estimated because the number of votes they cast is so small. The estimated standard errors for the interest group locations are on average more than ten times larger than those for the senators.[12] Nevertheless, the extreme positions of the interest groups are not a consequence of the imprecise estimates.[13] Second, adding the interest groups to the roll call data does not affect the recovery of the legislators. The R^2 (squared Pearson correlation) between the first dimension with and without the interest groups was 0.99 for the Senate and 0.96 for the House. For the second dimension, the R^2s were 0.99 and 0.98 respectively.

Unfolding the Interest-Group Ratings

In our analysis in the previous section the only information about the interest groups that we used were those roll calls for which they had announced their positions. This is not identical to the information contained in the ratings. Some groups weight some roll calls when they calculate their ratings (for example, the ACU), other groups count absences as "no" votes (for example, the ADA), and still others do not take pairs into account (for example, the LCV). Consequently, in this section we analyze the ratings directly as a check upon our results.

Figure 8.1 was deliberately designed to be identical to Figure 5.1 in Clyde Coombs' classic book *A Theory of Data* (1964). Coombs labeled the common dimension of legislators and midpoints (individuals and stimuli in his discussion) as a "J" Scale and the interest group ratings (the observed individual preference orderings) as an "I" Scale. Coombs stated the problem: "The data consist of a set of I scales from a number of individuals, and the analytical problem is how to unfold these I scales to recover the J scale."

In our earlier work (Poole, 1981, 1984, 1990; Poole and Daniels, 1985; Poole and Rosenthal, 1998) we developed a method of unfolding and applied it to a large collection of interest-group ratings from 1959 through 1981. In this model the ratings are treated as inverse distances — the higher the rating, the closer the legislator is to the interest group. The aim of the analysis is to estimate points representing the legislators and points representing the interest groups in such a way that the Euclidean distances between the two sets of points reproduce the ratings as closely as possible.[14]

Table 8.3 shows the R^2 between the corresponding legislator coordinates from D-NOMINATE and the interest group unfolding. Two sets of estimations were analyzed: dynamic estimations for the 1959–1981 period and estimations for the 96th Congress only.[15] Like D-NOMINATE, the dynamic unfolding model of the ratings treats the spatial positions of legislators as linear functions of time. The procedure is detailed in Poole and Rosenthal (1998) and Poole (1990).

The unfolding procedure recovers the same first dimension from the interest-group ratings that D-NOMINATE recovers from the whole set of roll calls. The second dimension recovered from the interest-group ratings appears to dif-

Table 8.3
R Squares between D-NOMINATE Dimensions
and Interest-Group Unfoldings

	SENATE			HOUSE		
		Dimension			Dimension	
Legislators	n	1	2	n	1	2
		Dynamic Coordinates: 1959–81				
All	331	.82	.35	1,352	.90	.61
Democrats	167	.78	.39	772	.82	.61
Republicans	142	.58	.21	580	.74	.42
		Static Coordinates: 96th Congress				
All	101	.94	.38	438	.91	.37
Democrats	59	.90	.35	278	.86	.30
Republicans	41	.92	.13	160	.70	.17

Note: The dynamic coordinates are from an analysis of all interest-group ratings issued from 1959 through 1981, reported in Poole and Rosenthal (1998). The static coordinates are from a separate scaling of the 96th Congress.

fer somewhat from that estimated by D-NOMINATE although the dynamic interest-group analysis for the House—which is based on the largest number of ratings—is closer to the corresponding D-NOMINATE second dimension than the other estimations.

Why do the D-NOMINATE and the interest-group-unfolding results from the second dimension differ? The pattern of correlations between individual interest-group ratings and the D-NOMINATE dimensions (presented in the previous section) suggests an explanation. The interest groups are picking roll calls primarily from the first dimension, so that the ratings contain very little information about the second dimension. To test this hypothesis, we separated the roll calls into two subsets—those chosen by the interest groups, and those not chosen—and applied W-NOMINATE to both subsets of roll calls and to all the roll calls. Table 8.4 shows the distribution of all percentage of votes, on the majority side, for all the roll calls, for the chosen subset, and for the non-chosen subset. It also shows the R^2s between the estimated legislator coordinates from the three applications of W-NOMINATE.

The distribution of the roll calls chosen by the interest groups is not representative of the overall distribution—it is skewed towards the closer roll calls. More than 70 percent of the roll calls selected by the interest groups have winning margins of 70–30 or less with over 40 percent at 60–40 or less. Even

Table 8.4
Difference between Roll Calls Chosen and Those Not Chosen, by Interest Groups in 1979–1980

| | DISTRIBUTION OF ROLL CALLS (PERCENT) | | | | | |
| | SENATE | | | HOUSE | | |
Majority Percentage	All	Chosen	Not Chosen	All	Chosen	Not Chosen
50-60	32	43	27	27	45	22
61-70	22	30	18	19	26	16
71-80	15	15	14	12	13	12
81-90	11	7	13	11	9	12
91-97.5	9	4	11	14	6	17
97.6-100	12	1	17	16	2	21
All	101[a]	100	100	99	101	100
n (roll calls)	1,054	334	720	1,276	312	964
n (scalable)	928	331	597	1,067	306	761

| | R-SQUARES OF W-NOMINATE SCALINGS | | | | | |
| | SENATE | | | HOUSE | | |
Legislators	All	Chosen	Not Chosen	All	Chosen	Not Chosen
All	—	—	—	—	—	—
Chosen	.99/.92[b]	—	—	.98/.92	—	—
Not chosen	1.00/.95	.98/.79	—	.99/.96	.94/.82	—
n (legislators)	101			438		

[a] Columns do not total 100 due to rounding.
[b] The first number is the R^2 between the estimated first dimensions; the second number is for the corresponding second dimensions.

though the sample of interest-group roll calls is skewed, W-NOMINATE recovers essentially the same legislator configuration from both samples. The correspondence of the estimated second dimensions for the two samples is weaker than the first, but the R^2 is still quite high (0.79 for the Senate and 0.82 for the House), and the correspondences of the estimated second dimensions with those estimated from the total set are all above 0.92. In addition, the increase in geometric mean probability and the increase in classification from adding the second dimension is about the same in both sets of roll calls.

In sum, the roll calls chosen by the interest groups contain essentially the same amount of information about the second dimension as do the roll calls they do not select. Given this fact, why isn't the second dimension accurately estimated by the group-unfolding analysis?

For one thing, the second dimension is not very important relative to the first dimension. During this time period the first dimension typically classifies about 80–82 percent of the roll call votes correctly. The second dimension typically adds about 2–3 percent to the correct classifications and the geometric mean probability climbs about 0.02–.04. All in all, the second dimension, while important, is minor compared to the first dimension. Consequently, the variation across legislators of the ratings—which are based on relatively small samples of roll calls—due to the second dimension will be quite small and will be sensitive to voting errors by legislators. The NOMINATE method is less sensitive to errors, even when applied only to those roll calls chosen by the interest groups, because it pools *all* the roll calls chosen by *all* the interest groups in estimating the positions of legislators.

To demonstrate the sensitivity of ratings to the errors of legislators, we performed an experiment in which we constructed ratings based upon perfect voting by senators and interest groups on the roll calls the groups chose for the 96th Senate. We used both the roll call coordinates and the legislator coordinates (shown in Figure 8.5) estimated by W-NOMINATE. But rather than use the actual votes on each roll call, we used the votes predicted by W-NOMINATE. This generated perfect spatial voting. When the ratings are constructed—using the roll calls actually selected by the interest groups—from perfect voting, the second dimension is recovered almost as accurately as the first (R^2's of 0.88 and 0.85 respectively).

Thus, an unfolding analysis of the ratings in one dimension produces essentially the same results as W-NOMINATE. Beyond the first dimension, the ratings contain very little information because the ratings are noisy evaluations of legislator locations on a second (or higher) dimension. Better results can be obtained by pooling all the information about the "voting" records of the legislators and the interest groups. This pooling occurs when one treats the interest groups as legislators and analyzes the augmented roll call data with NOMINATE.

Using the Interest Groups to Estimate a Joint House-Senate Scaling

The fact that the interest groups are regarded here as "legislators" who are, so to speak, members of both chambers, makes it possible to apply NOMINATE to the House and Senate simultaneously by assuming that the interest groups occupy the same spatial position within both chambers. Ideally, those roll calls for which the substance was identical in both the House and Senate should be treated as a single roll call with 535 voters. Examples include veto-override and conference-report votes.

In the 96th Congress there were only two veto override votes: One overrode President Carter's attempt to impose an oil import fee, and the other was on special pay bonuses for Veterans Administration doctors. Only the oil import vote was scalable and we treated it as a single roll call in both chambers. The VA-doctor-pay veto was overridden unanimously in the Senate and by a 401–5 margin in the House. These margins were too lopsided for the vote to be scaled by W-NOMINATE for either chamber. However, the oil-import vote was scalable, and we treated it as a single roll call in both chambers.

With respect to conference-report votes, we found only seven roll calls for which it was clear that identical bills were being voted upon. Most conference report votes were very lopsided and many were passed by voice vote in the Senate, leaving very few votes for analysis.

Even when the *text* of the bill is identical in both houses, the political interpretation of the vote within the two chambers may differ. For example, the Panama Canal Treaty was ratified in 1978 by the Senate, but the House felt its prerogatives were being trampled on because the treaty disposed of government property. The 1979 vote on the conference report on implementation of the treaty failed by a close margin of 192 to 203 in the House on September 20. This first vote appeared to exhibit a great deal of position-taking on the "turf war" between the two houses. A vote more directed at the substance of the treaty occurred five days later when the report was approved by a vote of 232 to 188. On the same day, the twenty-fifth, the Senate, too, passed the report, by a vote of 59–29. We combined the House and Senate votes that occurred on the twenty-fifth into one roll call.

Table 8.5 shows the eight roll calls (one veto override and seven conference reports) that were combined. In the estimation, we used all the groups shown in Table 8.1.[16] The two-dimensional results are displayed in Figure 8.6. Not surprisingly, the estimated legislator coordinates from the combined scaling are virtually identical to those estimated in separate scalings without the interest groups. The R^2 between the two sets of coordinates for the first dimension of the House of Representatives was 0.99 and for the second dimension 0.98. The R^2s for the Senate were both 0.99. The distribution of the senators and representatives over both dimensions is approximately the same.[17]

In the combined one-dimensional scaling, twelve of the twenty-eight interest groups are exterior to the members of Congress, and another six groups are near the ends. The CCUS is once again in the interior and it is joined by several other labor, business, and farmer's interest groups. Adding the second dimension dramatically increases the number of groups exterior to the legislators — twenty of twenty-eight are now on the rim of the space, and the UMW, though not on the rim, is also clearly to the exterior.

The recovery of the interest groups in the combined scaling is almost the same as that from separate scalings of the House and Senate. A comparison of Figure 8.5 with Figure 8.6 shows that the interest groups common to the two scalings are recovered in nearly the same positions.

With respect to the eight identical votes, the fit was quite good. Table 8.5 shows the classification results for two dimensions. As expected, constraining the cutting lines to be the same increases the classification error vis-à-vis the separate scalings. However, the respective *PRE*s (recall that the *PRE* controls for the margin of the roll call) are fairly close in magnitude.[18]

Figure 8.6 shows the estimated cutting line for the veto-override vote as well as the conference-report vote on the bill to implement the Panama Canal Treaty. The cutting line for the veto override forecasts nearly a unanimous vote because President Carter's veto was overridden by a margin of 335 to 34 in the House and 68 to 10 in the Senate. Of more interest is the Panama Canal Treaty implementation vote. As we noted above, the vote was 232 to 198 in the House and 59 to 29 in the Senate. In the separate scalings, counting pairs and announced as voting, 362 of 428 representatives were correctly classified, as were 80 of 97 senators, for a total of 83 errors. In the combined scaling the total number of errors is 91 — or an 82.7 percent classification rate.

We estimated President Carter's position by assuming he "voted" on the roll calls chosen by *Congressional Quarterly* to construct its presidential-support score. President Carter's "votes" were a good fit to the spatial model. In one dimension the geometric mean was 0.71, with 83.4 percent of 463 roll calls correctly classified. In two dimensions the geometric mean was 0.72, with 85.1 percent correctly classified.

In two dimensions, President Carter is positioned almost exactly midway between the northern and southern wings of his party. On the first dimension, Carter is considerably to the left of his party median — eighteen Democratic senators are to his left and forty-one to his right. The numbers for the House are fifty-two and 226 respectively. In fact only two southern Democrats, Mickey Leland and Bob Eckhardt, both representatives from Texas, were to Carter's left. On the second dimension Carter is much closer to his party median — twenty-four senators and 125 representatives are above him, and thirty-five senators and 153 representatives are below. Of the 105 Southern Democrats in both Houses, eighty-six were higher than Carter on the second dimension. Although one might expect a president with a legislative agenda to adopt, for strategic reasons, positions of moderation, Carter's positions appeared to be

Table 8.5
Identical Roll Calls in the 96th Congress

Roll Call Number and House of Congress	Yeas	Nays	ERRORS NOMINATE	ERRORS Combined	PRE[a] NOMINATE	PRE[a] Combined	Subject Matter
House	463[b]	236[c]	192	66[d]	72[e]			Panama Canal implementation
Senate	310	64	33	17	20			
Total		300	225	83	92	0.63	0.59	
House	468	219	205	109	99			Establishment of Department of Education
Senate	309	71	23	16	18			
Total		290	228	125	117	0.45	0.49	
House	527	301	112	78	78			Emergency program of energy conservation
Senate	363	79	18	15	23			
Total		380	130	93	101	0.28	0.22	
House	672	254	138	87	85			Chrysler loan guarantees
Senate	506	43	37	21	24			
Total		297	175	108	109	0.38	0.38	
House	800	305	109	79	77			Windfall-profits tax on crude oil
Senate	575	66	34	12	15			
Total		371	143	91	92	0.36	0.36	

Table 8.5 *(continued)*

Roll Call Number and House of Congress	Yeas	Nays	ERRORS		PRE[a]		Subject Matter
			NOMINATE	Combined	NOMINATE	Combined	
House	885	326	82	31	29			Food stamp authorization
Senate	644	65	25	14	13			
Total		391	107	45	42	0.58	0.61	
House	945	340	37	37	38			Veto override on oil-import fee
Senate	683	68	12	9	10			
Total		408	49	46	48	0.06	0.02	
House	1,237	213	201	48	65			Budget resolution
Senate	986	50	38	32	34			
Total		263	239	80	99	0.67	0.59	

[a] Proportional reduction in errors (see chapter 3 for definition).

[b] VOTEVIEW number of roll call.

[c] Includes pairs and announced.

[d] Total number of classification errors from separate NOMINATE two-dimensional scalings.

[e] Total number of classification errors from combined scaling, with roll calls in this table being constrained to a common cutting line in both houses.

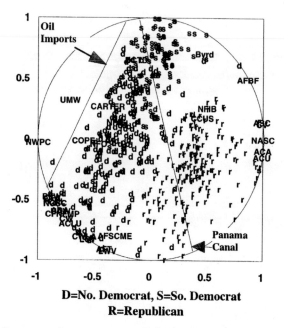

Figure 8.6. Representatives, senators, and twenty-eight interest groups in a common two-dimensional space: W-NOMINATE scaling for 1979–80. The interest groups and Harry F. Byrd, Jr. are named on the plot. Results are very similar to those in Figure 8.5, although a few interest groups have interior positions. The Figure also shows the cutting line for roll call votes on oil imports and the Panama Canal.

more those of a representative agent of his party and certainly not those of a typical southern Democrat.

Summary

We have shown that interest group ratings confirm this book's basic message that roll call voting is largely accounted for by a low-dimensional spatial model. A major new finding is that most interest groups issuing ratings are exterior to the legislators. This is good news for the interpretation of previous studies of Congress that have used ratings as measures of ideology. Although these measures are coarse, they correlate highly with the W-NOMINATE estimates.

The exterior nature of interest groups is important because, to the extent the interest groups influence legislators, they will be polarizing, moving the legislators away from middle-of-the-road positions. On the other hand, the interest groups that issue ratings are a select group of all interest groups. They are overwhelmingly either labor unions, public interest organizations, or ideological groups like Americans for Constitutional Action.

Our methods could be applied, however, to a wider array of evaluating groups since the key to using the methodology is not having quantitative ratings from a group but to having positions on a reasonable number of roll calls. For example, newspapers frequently take positions on legislation before Congress. They, too, are effectively voting on roll calls. Consequently, newspapers could be integrated with the roll call voting base just as we have integrated interest groups. This approach would be particularly attractive in dealing with American history before World War II, when interest group ratings are hard to come by but when American cities had several newspapers.

A variant of the NOMINATE methodology, called PAC-NOMINATE, provides information about interest groups—including those that do not issue ratings — from the contributions of their Political Action Committees. In PAC-NOMINATE, the interest groups are treated as legislators who vote on incumbents and challengers, both playing the role of roll calls. (For a detailed discussion, see McCarty and Poole, 1998.) Labor PACs are, consistent with their ratings, concentrating their money overwhelmingly on liberal Democrats. But the bulk of PAC money is from corporations and trade and industry associations. With the exception of oil firms, which are ideologically focused, business PACS seem as concerned with buying access as with policy. (Or to put it differently, they are more concerned with policies that affect their immediate interests than with national policy.) Their contributions tend to be spread widely across the spectrum and only moderately conservative, since they usually exclude only the most liberal Democrats.

The data analysis of the interest groups in this chapter and the analysis of PAC-NOMINATE were both conducted on data from Congresses that preceded the shift to Republican control that followed the election of 1994. We have more recently, with our colleague Nolan McCarty, analyzed campaign contribution data from both before and after this watershed election. An advantage of this later analysis is that it uses the amounts of the contributions to estimate the ideological position of the contributors, both individuals and PACs. The position of the contributor is just the money-weighted average of the liberal/conservative positions of those representatives and senators receiving contributions. This analysis shows that, once the Republicans controlled Congress, business contributions became more concentrated. Contributions to PACs became more polarized.[19]

Ideological groups issuing ratings appear to have polarized much earlier than business PACs. The core of this chapter was the analysis of the 1979-80 data for the 95th Congress. The raters, as we showed, have long been forces of extremism.

Notes

1. See chapter 10 for a fuller discussion of the rational theory of abstention.
2. Ken Chavez, "Wilson Backs State Abortion Funding," San Francisco *Examiner*, August 8, 1995, p. A-7.
3. Fowler (1982), in her interviews with staff members of the interest groups, found that the staffers were skeptical of the way academics used their ratings. In the view of the staffers, the ratings had "their greatest impact on the distribution of campaign funds, because they provide a simple test of support or opposition" (p. 403).
4. Some groups count absences as "incorrect" votes, and other groups weight votes in their ratings.
5. We used the 96th Congress because it was the latest Congress in the dataset used by Poole and Daniels (1985).
6. The correlations were computed between the D-NOMINATE estimates for the 96th House and Senate and the corresponding ratings. We recalculated the ratings using all the votes chosen by each group for the entire 96th Congress. The correlation would be lower if we, like many authors of applied papers, had used annual ratings rather than two-year ratings. Thus, this chapter conservatively understates the problem of using interest-group evaluations as direct measures of ideology.
7. See Peltzman (1984), who uses the Americans for Democratic Action rating in a broad-based analysis of roll call voting; Kalt and Zupan (1984), who use the League of Conservation Voters ratings in an analysis of strip mine legislation; or Weingast and Moran (1983) who use ADA ratings in a study of legislation affecting the Federal Trade Commission. See also the various papers we discuss in chapter 9 that use interest-group ratings to measure preferences of members of committees.
8. These data were originally compiled by Keith Poole and have been used by Poole and Daniels (1985) and by Snyder (1992a).
9. The geometric mean probability for the scaling was 0.66 with 80.3 percent of the votes classified correctly. For the roll calls, 928 of 1,054 had margins of at least 2.5 percent in the minority and were scalable.
10. The 2.5 percent criterion is discussed in chapter 2.
11. The geometric mean probability for two dimensions was 0.69, with 82.7 percent of the votes classified correctly.
12. Standard errors used in this book are discussed in Poole and Rosenthal (1997, Appendix A). Better estimators of standard errors are provided in Lewis and Poole (2004).
13. We conducted a simulation study in which we created eight additional "interest groups" by duplicating the records of Senators Lloyd Bentsen (D-TX), Quentin Burdick (D-ND), Robert Byrd (D-WV), Howard Cannon (D-NV), Frank Church (D-ID), Barry Goldwater (R-AZ), Daniel Inouye (D-HI), and Henry Jackson (D-WA) (the first eight senators in the VOTEVIEW data). We then randomly drew fifty roll calls from the total of 1,054 to simulate the effect of adding the eight interest groups to the 101-senator roll call matrix. (The total number of scalable roll calls for each of the eight simulated interest groups varies from forty to fifty because the random draw will include varying numbers of nonscalable roll calls.) This approach allows us to compare the recovery of the simulated interest group with the senator from which it was created.

We performed ten experiments and found that the average absolute difference between the eight senators and their clones was 0.065 on the first dimension and

0.063 on the second dimension. On average, the positions of the simulated interest groups that had only a small number of votes were more towards the periphery of the space than their corresponding senators were. Thus, small sample sizes lead to some bias toward peripheral positions. But the small absolute average deviations show that the bias is quite small, certainly much too small to account for the systematically extreme positions of the real interest groups. The standard errors for the simulated groups were four to five times the size of those for their corresponding senators. But the standard errors for the simulated interest groups are smaller than those for the actual groups because the actual groups are near the rim of the space and, as a consequence, will have larger standard errors.

14. Technically the ratings are converted to distances by the linear transformation $d_{ij}^* = (100 - \delta_{ij})/50 = d_{ij} + e_{ij}$, where, δ_{ij} is the rating issued by the jth interest group of the ith legislator and d_{ij} is the corresponding Euclidean distance. (The division by 50 is an arbitrary normalization that has no effect on the analysis.) The following loss function is minimized:

$$\sum_i \sum_j e_{ij}^2 = \sum_i \sum_j \left\{ d_{ij}^* - \left[\sum_{k=1}^s (x_{ik} - z_{jk})^2 \right]^{1/2} \right\}^2$$

where s is the number of dimensions and x_{ij} and z_{jk} are the legislator and interest-group coordinates on the kth dimension.

In one dimension, the loss function reduces to a combinatorial problem; in more than one dimension standard gradient techniques can be used. Unfortunately, the statistical properties of this loss function are not known. Rivers (1987) has shown that, under certain conditions in one dimension, the estimates are not consistent. Brady (1989), using the generalized method of moments (GMM) approach, argues that the loss function above is inappropriate. However, Monte Carlo work reported by Poole (1984, 1990) shows that the estimation method is highly accurate. Finally, Poole and Spear (1991) show that, for the unidimensional problem under restricted conditions, the correct ordering of the points will be estimated.

The fact that the methods are indeed accurate vitiates the criticisms. Indeed the accuracy of the methods is consistent with more than forty years of experience with multidimensional scaling techniques pioneered by Shepard (1962) and Kruskal (1964a, b). A close variant of the loss function shown above is used in one form or another in all these techniques.

15. The interest-group ratings were computed from the roll calls each interest group chose for 1979 and 1980.

16. There were 101 senators, 439 representatives, twenty-eight interest-groups, and President Carter, for a total of 569 "legislators." (Senators total more than 100 and representatives total more than 435 because of within-Congress replacements.) We used all twenty-eight groups rather than the eight used in the Senate analysis because combining the House and Senate ratings typically doubled the number of roll calls per interest group, leading to sample sizes generally sufficient for analysis. Of the 1,276 roll calls cast in the House, 1,067 had at least 2.5 percent in the minority and were scalable. The corresponding figures for the Senate were 1,054 and 928, respectively. In the combined scaling there were a total of 1987 roll calls (1,067 + 928 − 8). In one dimension, the geometric mean probability was 0.696 with 83.6 percent correctly classified. The corresponding numbers for two dimensions were 0.717 and 83.9 respectively.

17. We performed simple difference-of-means tests between the House and Senate on the coordinates of northern Democrats, southern Democrats, and Republicans, and none was significant. In fact, the largest t value in the six comparisons was less than 0.2.
18. The increase in classification and *PRE* for two of the eight roll calls is not unexpected for two reasons: First, maximizing likelihood is not the same as maximizing classification; second, W-NOMINATE is maximizing likelihood across all roll calls. Repositioning the legislators can improve overall classification even if classification falls on a few roll calls.
19. In resonance with the results of this chapter, it was, moreover, largely extremist contributors who supplemented their hard money contributions to candidates with soft money contributions to the political parties.

9

Committees and Roll Calls

Congressional committees are critical in the framing of the roll call vote choices that we analyzed in previous chapters. A committee system by its very nature carves up the policy universe into jurisdictions. Members should gravitate towards those committees with jurisdictions closest to their interests. These interests are predominantly ones that further the members' chances of reelection (Fenno, 1973, 1978; Mayhew, 1974; Fiorina, 1989).

Shepsle (1978), in his study of the committee assignment process in the House, found that members do self-select. The assignment process generally respects seniority, somewhat overrepresents the majority party, and is constrained by the limited size of the most desirable committees; but the preferences of individual members are important. If, indeed, members do self-select, then the committee system should produce systematically biased policy. That is, in comparison to the House as a whole, the Agriculture Committee will be more pro-agriculture; the Veterans' Affairs Committee will be more pro-veteran; the Armed Services Committee more pro-defense contractor or pro-military; and so on. Thus, the committees will tend to be "preference outliers" with respect to the chamber as a whole.

The basic logic of Shepsle's approach is that committees are opportunities to reward special interests that are highly important to certain members. As a result, policy is distorted from that which would be produced by a majority rule legislature without a committee system (Niskanen, 1971). A quite opposite view of the committee system is found in the work of Gilligan and Krehbiel (1990).[1] These authors recognize that the chamber is sovereign. A chamber would not delegate policy formation to a committee that systematically distorted policy from the chamber's wishes unless such distortions were in the chamber's interests. Indeed, their view of the raison d'être of committees is not that committees arise for the selective allocation of benefits but that committees arise as a result of a classical division of labor. Policy formation requires information; committees are specialized information-gathering bodies. Because committees composed of preference outliers with private information have an incentive to distort their reports to the full chamber, the chamber prefers committees that are not outliers. Committee preferences should closely mirror chamber preferences. As noted by Gilligan and Krehbiel (1990, p. 558): "Organization of informative committees by a rational legislature is *not* a process culminating in committees that are composed of preference outliers."

Cox and McCubbins (1993) take a position somewhat similar to Gilligan and Krehbiel, except that they argue that the focus should be on the match between party contingents on the committees and the party as a whole. In particular, they argue that parties will allow self-selection but will also pay very close attention to committees whose jurisdictions impact large numbers of voters and, hence, bear heavily on the electoral prospects of all party members, not just those on these important committees. For example, decisions of the Appropriations Committee affect everyone. This committee, and others like it,[2] should have party contingents reflective of the whole party.

These diverse theoretical views have sparked a series of empirical studies of whether committees are preference outliers (Krehbiel, 1990, 1992; Hall and Grofman, 1990; Londregan and Snyder, 1994; Groseclose, 1994b; Maltzman, 1994; Maltzman and Smith, 1994). And the empirical literature has given rise to a lively debate.

The outlier debate has usually been conducted on the assumption — either explicit or implicit — of a one-dimensional model of policy preferences. The outlier question is then decided by evaluating whether there is a significant difference between the committee medians and the chamber median on the dimension.[3] To measure positions on the dimension, Krehbiel (1990) and Groseclose (1994b) use jurisdiction-specific interest-group ratings, Hall and Grofman (1990) use corrected interest-group ratings, Cox and McCubbins (1993) use D–NOMINATE scores, Londregan and Snyder (1994) use a variety of interest-group ratings and W-NOMINATE scores.[4]

The results of these efforts are mixed. Londregan and Snyder (1994) claim that about one-third of committees in the 82nd House through the 98th are preference outliers. Cox and McCubbins (1993) find strong support for their party support model with only the Veterans' Affairs Committee being an outlier. Krehbiel (1990) and Groseclose (1994) find few committee outliers, Hall and Grofman (1990, p. 1154) argue that "roll call data will understate committee-chamber differences" (p. 1154) and that the diversity of most committee jurisdictions raises formidable measurement problems, and Maltzman (1994) finds that "party committee contingents are frequently more extreme and rarely more moderate than their caucus."

We join this debate using the D-NOMINATE scores. Our methodology is presented below. Readers interested only in the substantive punch line may choose to skip ahead to the subhead "Are Committees Preference Outliers?"

All the literature cited above is concerned only with the period since the Legislative Reform Act of 1946, which greatly reduced the number of committees in both chambers. With respect to the debate over this period, we find that there are a moderate number of committees that are outliers, largely because the Democratic contingents on four committees (Agriculture, Armed Services, Education and Labor, and Veterans' Affairs) are outliers with respect to the median member of their party.

Our major finding, however, arises from extending the period of analysis to include all of the first 100 Congresses. Before the 80th Congress, outlier committees are rare. We define an outlier committee as one where the median member's position is sufficiently far to the left or the right that it would have been produced by a random assignment process less than one time in twenty. In other words, the committee median has a p value (see Technical Terms box) less than 0.05. In no House of Representatives before the 80th Congress (1947–48) are these significant outliers more than 15 percent of all the committees (Figure 9.1). In thirty–five of the first seventy-nine Houses and twenty–two of the first seventy–nine Senates, fewer than one–twentieth of the committees — the fraction expected by pure chance — are significant outliers.

There are even fewer outliers prior to the 80th Congress under a more stringent and substantively relevant test. This test looks at party contingents on a committee. If a party contingent median had a significant extreme position in one Congress, we required that it have a significant extreme position in the same direction in the preceding Congress to be counted as an outlier. This is because the self-selection hypothesis on committee formation predicts persistence in the types of legislators who join committees. This persistence would be absent, for example, if the Republican contingent on the Armed Services committee went from being unusually conservative in one Congress to being unusually liberal in the next. Under our measure of consistent outliers, only once in each chamber (the 71st House and 74th Senate) does the proportion of outliers exceed 5 percent before the 80th Congress (Figure 9.3).

In contrast, after 1946 we find that a small but important minority of House committees are either exceptionally liberal or exceptionally conservative. As a result of a few committees not being representative of the House, for most Houses after the 80th, we overwhelmingly reject the null hypothesis that the entire committee structure is representative. The pattern for the postwar House is not echoed in the Senate. Most importantly, when we look for "consistent" outliers (Figure 9.3), we find no evidence, with the exception of the 98th Senate, supporting the self-selection hypothesis.

The whole debate, however, might be framed differently. Legislators who especially value military bases in their constituency might, quite aside from their general liberal-conservative preferences, be prone to join the Armed Services Committee in the hope of influencing the geographic allocation of defense spending as well as the global level of spending. We agree with Krehbiel (1990), Hall and Grofman (1990), and Shepsle and Weingast (1994) that such interests are difficult to discern in terms of overall voting patterns. Consequently, we analyze whether committee members vote differently on bills in their committee's jurisdiction than on other legislation. We find that common interests are evident in that committee members are, ceteris paribus, more likely to support committee bills than are noncommittee members. However, the comparison of the roll call voting of committee members and noncommittee members also provides support for the informational theory of committees. We thus conclude the chapter with the suggestion that committees advance self-selected interests of members with specialized information.

Measuring the Representativeness of Committees

To perform a statistical test of whether Congressional committees are representative of the chamber from which they are chosen, the measure that is used as a basis of evaluation, the statistic, and the sample space all must be specified.

Measuring Preference

A member's one-dimensional D-NOMINATE score is the measure of preference we use to assess whether committees consist of preference outliers.[5] Although using a one-dimensional measure has limitations that we address below, it is, as indicated earlier, standard in the literature. Moreover, even a one-dimensional measure has the potential for disclosing important differences across committees. For example, conservative guns seekers could choose to join the Armed Services Committee, while liberal butter seekers could choose the Public Works and Transportation Committee.

Any measure of preference will contain some error. The real question is how serious a problem the measurement error is. Kiewiet and McCubbins (1991) and Londregan and Snyder (1994) point out that most of the measures used in the literature, such as ADA (Americans for Democratic Action) ratings, are inappropriate since they contain significant selection bias and measurement error. (See chapter 8.) Londregan and Snyder (1994, p. 235) assess the measurement error by averaging the Congress-by-Congress W-NOMINATE scores across a large number of Congresses and by then treating the year-to-year variation in the scores as the measurement error. They find that the measurement error is very small relative to the span of the space. Their technique overestimates measurement error because some of the intertemporal variation in scores is the result of genuine change in liberal/conservative preferences. To allow for some intertemporal change while retaining the benefits of averaging, we use the D-NOMINATE scores from the estimation in which legislator positions change linearly over a career (see chapter 2). We can safely treat these scores as having no measurement error given not only the results of Londregan and Snyder (1994) but also our own bootstrap estimates of the standard errors of the estimated scores (Poole and Rosenthal, 1991a; Lewis and Poole 2004). Since the D-NOMINATE scores are, unlike the ratings, based on the entire set of roll calls,[6] the selection bias problem also disappears.

The Statistic of Evaluation

In assessing whether a specific committee is a preference outlier, we compute the magnitude of the difference between the committee median and the median of the whole chamber.[7] We also assess whether major party contingents are outliers. Here, we compute the magnitude of the difference between the median of the party contingent on the committee and the party median in the whole chamber. This comparison of medians is standard. An outlier committee, or an outlier party contingent on a committee, is one for which the discrepancy between the committee and the chamber is so large as to be statistically significant. When we examine whether the *entire committee structure* of a chamber reflects preference outliers, we use the sum of squared differences between committee medians and the chamber median.

The Sample Space

The critical issue in assessing outliers is specifying the sample space. The concept of statistical significance presupposes a sample space from which a random sample is drawn. Londregan and Snyder (1994) do not deal with this problem. If there is no *measurement error*, they treat any difference between the committee median and the chamber median as significant. Such an approach is clearly inappropriate and is guaranteed to find that most committees are outliers. To see why, consider the 100th House. There were twenty-two standing committees, but no member had more than four committee assignments. Since a member of at most four of the twenty-two committees could thus represent the chamber median, at least eighteen must, in the Londregan-Snyder approach, be outliers. Such a conclusion is, to say the least, not very helpful.

Congressional scholars know, even without resorting to elaborate methodologies, that individual committee assignments are limited and that committee medians must invariably differ from chamber medians. The relevant question is whether the actual distribution of committee medians — or the median on a given committee — could have just arisen as the outcome of a purely random assignment process or if, alternatively, the assignment was likely to have arisen only if there was a deliberate tilt to producing outlier committees. Specification of a random process defines a sample space. In order to test the a priori alternative hypothesis that the median of, for example, the Armed Services Committee was significantly different from the floor median, standard two-tailed p values can be used (see the Technical Terms box). The key issue is: What is the appropriate random assignment process?

Defining the sample space is somewhat tricky. As indicated above, the random assignment process must reflect the fact that a given individual receives very few committee assignments. Consequently, there is interdependence in committee assignments. For example, once a member is assigned to the Armed Services Committee, the chances of this member's being assigned to any other committee are reduced. In addition, party imbalances on committees must also be accounted for. The majority party is typically somewhat overrepresented on a committee. Finding that committee medians differ from chamber medians because of this overrepresentation would not be very interesting. Therefore, letting the random assignment process reflect overrepresentation is appropriate.

There are two related aspects of committee formation that we do not deal with directly. The first is that some committee assignments, such as the Appropriations Committee, are almost universally more valued than others, such as the Post Office Committee. Obtaining one plum, such as Appropriations, may affect the likelihood that a second or third assignment is another plum, such as Rules. Since our interest pertains to the *effects* of committee formation on the preference makeup of committees, we eschew any attempt to model the details of committee formation.[8] However, since the *FULL* model below reproduces the actual distribution of individuals across committees, tradeoffs between plums and lemons are captured indirectly. The second aspect is seniority. Since seniority is only weakly related to D-NOMINATE scores (see chapter 4), not stratifying on seniority is not of major consequence to the analysis. Therefore, we have restricted our sampling methods to controlling for party overrepresentation and limited committee assignments per individual member.

The relevance of these controls is nicely illustrated by considering the simpler question of whether committee *chairs* are representative. Because chairs must be from the majority party, even if chairs were randomly chosen from the majority, they obviously would not be representative of the floor. Chairs would be distributed about the party median, not the floor median. For this reason, we would want to define the sample space with respect to the majority party, not the whole chamber.

How should we sample the majority party? Suppose the majority party has D members and there are, as in the 100th House, twenty-two committees. We could draw the twenty-two committee chairs from an urn of D balls — each ball labeled with a D-NOMINATE score — with *replacement*. If we did this thousands of times, we would obtain, for each committee, a distribution of chair D-NOMINATE scores that could be used to test whether the position of an actual committee chair was "significantly" distinct from the party median.[9] But sampling with replacement ignores the constraint that no individual can head more than one committee. This constraint has an effect on any test of whether the set of twenty-two committee chairs constitutes a set of preference outliers. Consequently, we must sample without replacement.

Technical Terms

p value: When committee medians are compared to chamber medians, the *p* value measures the probability that a random assignment of legislators to committees would produce a difference between the chamber median and the floor median that is greater than, or equal to, the observed difference. The magnitude of the difference is used in calculating the *p* value because the randomly assigned committee could be either a liberal outlier or a conservative outlier. That is, in the jargon of statistics, the *p* values are "two-tailed." Similar *p* values are calculated for the differences between the median of a party's committee contingent and the party's floor median.

Standard Error: The standard error is a measure of the precision of the estimate of a parameter (for example, the D-NOMINATE estimate of a legislator ideal point); the larger the standard error, the less precise the estimate.

Combinations $\binom{D}{d}$: This notation denotes the number of distinct ways of forming a group of d individuals from a larger group of D individuals.

It is well known that $\binom{D}{d} = \dfrac{D!}{d!(D-d)!}$ where $D! = D(D-1)(D-2)...(2)(1)$.

Multiplication with an Index $\displaystyle\prod_{j=1}^{n} x_j = x_1 x_2 x_3 ... x_n$

Summation with an Index $\displaystyle\sum_{j=1}^{n} = x_1 + x_2 + x_3 + ... + x_n$

To illustrate the difference, assume a very, very small legislature with D = 3 and 2 committees. Suppose the 3 legislators had D-NOMINATE scores of -0.5, 0, and +0.5. Our null hypothesis is random assignment; the alternative hypothesis is that the extremists get the chairs. We then observe that the 2 extremists are the committee chairs. If we sampled with replacement, there are $3 \times 3 = 9$ possible ways of assigning the chairs, 4 of which have 2 extremists heading the committees. So the p value would be 4/9. If we sample without replacement, there are only $3 \times 2 = 6$ ways of assigning the chairs, with 2 ways having extremists heading both committees. In this case, the p-value would be 2/6 or 3/9, which is less than the "with replacement" value of 4/9.

We now extend these ideas, developed for the simple case of chairs, to the analysis of committee medians. After we define the appropriate sample spaces, we report the results of Monte Carlo experiments designed to test the representativeness of committees. As with chairs, we need to incorporate real-world structure into the experiment. Because we focus not on an individual characteristic (chairing) but on a distributional characteristic (the committee median) our sampling scheme must reflect the actual number of representatives on each committee. Moreover, we must use the actual number of Republicans and Democrats on the committee. The reason is directly analogous to our only sampling from among the majority party when we consider chairs. The party percentages on committees are skewed from those in the full House. For example, in the 100th Congress, the Rules Committee was 69 percent (9 of 13) Democratic whereas Democrats had only 59 percent (258 of 435) of the seats in the House.

To define the sample space in a way that incorporates the party allocations to committees, let j be an index for committees, let D be the total number of Democrats, D_j be the number of Democrats on the jth committee, R_j be the number of Republicans on the jth committee, and R be the total number of Republicans. Therefore, the number of ways to form the jth committee with D_j and R_j unique members is:

$$\binom{D}{D_j}\binom{R}{R_j}$$

Now, if each committee is formed the same way, then the number of ways to construct n committees — that is, the number of elements in the sample space — is:

$$\prod_{j=1}^{n}\binom{D}{D_j}\binom{R}{R_j} \tag{1}$$

The sample space implied by model (1) would be appropriate to tests of whether *individual* committees are made up of preference outliers. But it is not a realistic model with which to test hypotheses about the *overall structure of the committee system.* After one committee is formed, members of the next committee are drawn with replacement. Thus, each member has some chance of serving on all the committees. In practice all members have a limited number of committee assignments. We therefore introduce constraints that reproduce the observed distribution of committee assignments. For example, across the twenty-two standing committees in the 100th House, sixty-six Democrats and fifty-one Republicans had only one committee assignment; 155 Democrats and 113 Republicans had two committee assignments; and thirty-four Democrats and twelve Republicans had three committee assignments. One Democrat, Chester Atkins of Massachusetts, had four committee assignments: Budget, Education and Labor, Foreign Affairs, and Standards of Official Conduct. In addition, the mix of the assignment types varies across the committees. For example, there were twenty-six Democrats and seventeen Republicans on the Agriculture Committee. Of the twenty-six Democrats, one had only one assignment, nineteen had two assignments, and six had three assignments; of the seventeen Republicans, three had one assignment, thirteen had two assignments, and one had three.

Let $D^{(T)}$ be the total number of Democrat seats on all committees, $D^{(1)}$ be the number of Democratic Party members with one assignment, $D^{(2)}$ be the number of members with two assignments, and so on. Now, to choose a committee contingent randomly, we increase the number of Democrats from D to $D^{(T)}$ by cloning those individuals with multiple committee assignments. That is,

$$D^{(T)} = \sum_{t=1}^{T} t D^{(t)} = \sum_{j=1}^{n} D_j > D = \sum_{t=1}^{T} D^{(t)}$$

In the 100th House, for example, $D^{(T)} = 66 + 2 \cdot 155 + 3 \cdot 34 + 4 \cdot 1 = 482$ and $R^{(T)} = 313$.

Because the number of Democratic committee seats and the number of Democratic "members" are now the same, the committee contingents can be drawn without replacement. The first step is to randomly assign the D and R D-NOMINATE scores to the types corresponding to $D^{(1)}$, $D^{(2)}$, $R^{(1)}$, $R^{(2)}$, and so on. That is, an actual D-NOMINATE score is drawn at random from the scores for Democrats and assigned as a one-committee-assignment type. Then, without replacement, another D-NOMINATE score is drawn at random and also assigned as a one-committee-assignment type. The process continues until the number of assigned scores equals $D^{(1)}$. Continuing without replacement, one next allocates the two-committee-assignment types, and so on. A similar process takes place with Republican scores. The number of ways of assigning all the scores can be written as the product of two multinomial coefficients:

$$\frac{D!}{\prod\limits_{t=1}^{T} D^{(t)}!} \frac{R!}{\prod\limits_{t=1}^{T} R^{(t)}!} \tag{2}$$

The next step is to allocate the randomly assigned individuals to seats that correspond to their types. That is, a randomly selected person with one committee assignment is assigned to one of the committee seats actually held by a real member with only one committee assignment. Assignments continue, *without* replacement, until all the seats are filled for one-assignment types. Next, a randomly selected individual with two assignments is allocated to one of the committee seats actually held by real members with two committee assignments and also randomly assigned to a similar seat on another committee. The process continues until all committee seats are filled.

The possible committee assignments for the randomly drawn one-assignment members are easy to calculate. There are $D^{(1)}!$ and $R^{(1)}!$ ways that they can be assigned to the $D^{(1)}$ and $R^{(1)}$ committee seats held by one-assignment types. Note that this cancels a term in the denominator of expression (2). Hence, the number of possible assignments that satisfy the constraint of assigning an individual with t committee memberships to seats held by actual members with t memberships is given by:

$$\frac{D!}{\prod\limits_{t=2}^{T} D^{(t)}!} \frac{R!}{\prod\limits_{t=2}^{T} R^{(t)}!} N_{d2} N_{d3} ... N_{dT} N_{r2} N_{r3} ... N_{rT} \tag{3}$$

where N_{d2} is the number of ways the $D^{(2)}$ Democrats can be assigned to 2 $D^{(2)}$ seats, N_{d3} is the number of ways the $D^{(3)}$ Democrats can be assigned to $3D^{(3)}$ seats, and so on.

To illustrate how the assignments are made, consider the case of Democrats with three assignments in the 93rd House. In the actual House, eight Democrats, whom we label $a, b, \ldots, f$ had three assignments on a total of sixteen committees, which we label $A, B, \ldots, P$. The assignment problem can be specified as one of constructing an 8-by-16 matrix of zeros and ones where the rows sum to 3 and each column sums to the number of three assignment individuals on the committee. One solution for this assignment problem is shown as:

Total Number of Assignments ↓

			A	*B*	*C*	*D*	*E*	*F*	*G*	*H*	*I*	*J*	*K*	*L*	*M*	*N*	*O*	*P*	
	a	3	0	0	0	0	0	0	1	1	0	0	0	0	0	1	0	0	
	b	3	0	0	0	0	0	0	0	0	1	0	0	0	0	0	1	1	
	c	3	1	0	1	1	0	0	0	0	0	0	0	0	0	0	0	0	
Representative	d	3	0	0	0	0	0	0	0	0	0	1	0	1	1	0	0	0	
	e	3	0	0	0	1	0	0	0	0	0	1	1	0	0	0	0	0	
	f	3	0	0	0	1	0	0	0	0	0	1	0	0	0	0	1	0	
	g	3	0	1	0	1	0	1	0	0	0	0	0	0	0	0	0	0	
	h	3	0	0	0	1	1	0	0	0	0	0	0	1	0	0	0	0	
		24	1	1	1	5	1	1	1	1	1	3	1	2	1	1	2	1	← Total Number of Committee Members with Three Assignments

Given a solution, clearly any permutation of the $D^{(3)}$ rows is also a solution. Hence, $D^{(3)}!$ is one of the terms in N_{d3}. This reasoning holds for any assignment type with two assignments or more. Note that this will cancel the denominator factorials in equation (3), which allows us to write (3) in a simpler form:

$$D!\,R!\,M_{d2}M_{d3}\ldots M_{dT}M_{r2}M_{r3}\ldots M_{rT} \tag{4}$$

where, with reference to the example above, M_{d3} is the number of ways of filling the matrix with 0's and 1's such that the row and column marginals are satisfied. Although the complexity of the assignment process prevents us from giving formulas for the *M*'s, it is straightforward enough to generate elements of the sample space by a random-assignment process.[10] We refer to this process, which preserves the structure of committee assignments, as the *STRU* model.

As an alternative to equation (4), we impose some additional structure by fully replicating the observed pattern of committee assignments, simply replacing each member's actual D-NOMINATE score with a randomly assigned one. This *FULL* model is just a simple "people and chairs" permutation. For example, some Democrat may be assigned to both the Agriculture and Armed Services committees. We replace the member's true score with a randomly drawn one (from the set of Democrat D-NOMINATE scores for that House). Do this, without replacement, for each member and the total number of combinations is simply:

$$D!R! \tag{5}$$

Before we turn to a historical summary of our results, we illustrate the tests we have conducted with a discussion of the 100th House. Results for both the *STRU* and *FULL* models are shown in Table 9.1. The table was

Table 9.1
100th House: Committee-Outlier Two-Tailed *p* Values

Committee	STRU Model	FULL Model	p Value Is for:	Dispersion
	SAMPLE SPACE			
All	.004	.004	All	.257
	.007	.009	Dem.	.436
	.155	.137	Rep.	.400
Agriculture	.511	.484	All	.110
	+.021	+.015	Dem.	.701
	.513	.500	Rep.	−.215
Appropriations	−.020	−.028	All	−.382
	.940	.951	Dem.	−.017
	.167	.197	Rep.	−.403
Armed Services	+.008	+.010	All	.437
	+.000	+.000	Dem.	1.284
	.674	.696	Rep.	−.118
Banking, Finance,	.991	.985	All	−.002
and Urban Affairs	.718	.750	Dem.	.085
	.361	.366	Rep.	−.270
Budget	.629	.622	All	.028
	.286	.286	Dem.	−.403
	.713	.700	Rep.	.126
District of Columbia	−.004	−.007	All	−1.001
	.186	.180	Dem.	−.810
	.655	.683	Rep.	−.270
Education and Labor	.062	.086	All	−.366
	−.023	−.019	Dem.	−.816
	−.038	−.040	Rep.	−.821
Energy and Commerce	.532	.546	All	−.091
	.972	.966	Dem.	.010
	.380	.380	Rep.	.318
Foreign Affairs	−.051	−.047	All	−.354
	.059	.056	Dem.	−.556
	.420	.413	Rep.	−.252
Government Operations	.337	.339	All	−.165
(Expenditures in the	.526	.522	Dem.	−.193
Executive Branch)	+.001	+.001	Rep.	1.162
House Administration	.181	.193	All	−.375
	.657	.649	Dem.	−.200
	.267	.253	Rep.	.570
Interior and Insular	.248	.248	All	−.210
Affairs (public lands)	.177	.162	Dem.	−.471
	.073	.058	Rep.	.662
Judiciary	.265	.282	All	−.203
	.525	.507	Dem.	−.220
	.186	.174	Rep.	.511

Table 9.1 (*continued*)

| | SAMPLE SPACE | | | |
Committee	*STRU* Model	*FULL* Model	*p* Value Is for:	Dispersion
Merchant Marine and	.256	.264	All	.182
Fisheries	.061	.062	Dem.	.566
	.404	.427	Rep.	−.289
Post Office	−.040	−.041	All	−.506
	.341	.384	Dem.	−.417
	.088	.069	Rep.	−.858
Public Works and Transportation	.828	.806	All	.034
	.392	.356	Dem.	−.257
	.306	.314	Rep.	.318
Rules	.144	.155	All	−.535
	.811	.809	Dem.	−.136
	.803	.788	Rep.	.170
Science, Space, and Technology	.815	.795	All	.033
	.605	.629	Dem.	.125
	.242	.252	Rep.	.348
Small Business	.608	.596	All	−.079
	.071	.082	Dem.	.532
	.206	.202	Rep.	.466
Standards of Official Conduct	.471	.509	All	.392
	.212	.207	Dem.	−.745
	.923	.910	Rep.	−.052
Veterans' Affairs	.378	.391	All	.160
	.061	+.043	Dem.	.654
	.181	.210	Rep.	.533
Ways and Means	.912	.937	All	.019
	.267	.252	Dem.	−.403
	.855	.830	Rep.	.067

Number of Committees That Are Preference Outliers

Significance Level	*STRU* Model	*FULL* Model	Results Are for
5%	4	4	All
	3	5	Dem.
	2	1	Rep.
10%	6	7	All
	7	8	Dem
	4	2	Rep.

Note: The p values at or below 0.055 receive a + sign if the committee is a conservative outlier, a − sign if the committee is a liberal outlier. See the text for an explanation of the computation of p values and the dispersion measures.

generated, for each sample space, by 1,000 Monte Carlo random assignments of committees.

At the top of the table we present overall results for the test of the joint null hypothesis that the observed committee medians are produced randomly. The entries are p values. The first entry is for the full committees, the second is for the Democrat contingents, and the third is for the Republican contingents. Because this is a test of whether the committee structure as a whole is non-representative, the test statistic does not use the magnitude of the difference between a single committee median and a floor median. Instead, for each experiment, we calculated the sum of squares of the artificial committee medians around the grand median and compared it with the actual sum of squares. The p value is the proportion of the 1,000 experiments for which the artificial sum of squares exceeded the actual sum of squares. For example, 155 of the 1,000 experiments using *STRU* model produced a set of artificial contingents more dispersed about the Republican median than the actual medians; thus we would not reject the null hypothesis that Republican assignments are representative at the traditional 5 percent level. In contrast, the House as a whole and the Democratic contingent appear to have been assigned in a nonrepresentative fashion.

Even if committee medians are significantly different from the true median in a statistical sense, the difference may not have important policy consequences if the difference is small relative to the dispersion of legislators' ideal points. Consequently, we report "Dispersion" in the final column of Table 9.1. "Dispersion" is a statistic that normalizes the dispersion of committee medians about the true median by the dispersion of all legislators about the true median. More precisely, "Dispersion" is the ratio of the average absolute difference between the overall median and true medians of the twenty-two committees to the average absolute difference between the overall median and the legislators. For example, for the Democrats, this is the ratio of the average absolute difference between the twenty-two Democratic Party-contingent medians and the Democratic Party median to the average absolute difference between each Democrat and the Democratic Party median. The closer this number is to zero, the more representative the twenty-two committee medians are of the chamber/party contingent.

Individual committee results also appear in the table. Each committee entry shows the proportion of the 1,000 experiments that produced a median that was further away from the grand median than the true committee median was. Each committee for each House also has three entries: one for the entire committee, one for the Democrats, and one for the Republicans. For example, for the Agriculture Committee in the 100th House in Table 9.1, 484 of the 1,000 experiments using the *FULL* model produced committee medians further from the grand median than the actual median of the committee was. For the Democrats, only fifteen random-contingent medians were farther from the overall committee median than the actual contingent median, and for the Republicans the corresponding number was 500.

The numbers for the committees in the table are quite literally two-tailed p values for the null hypothesis that the corresponding committee is *not* an outlier. Those values that are at or below .055 are signed according to whether or not the actual median is above or below the grand median. If the sign is negative, this means that the committee is significantly (at the traditional 5 percent level) to the left of the House median; vice versa if the sign is positive.

Under the "Dispersion" column for individual committees we report the ratio of the difference between the committee median and the floor median to the average absolute difference between the legislators and the overall median. For example, for the Agriculture Committee Democrats, this is $(-0.154 - -0.257)/0.147 = 0.701$, where -0.154 is the median of the twenty–six committee Democrats, -0.257 is the overall Democratic Party median, and .0147 is the average of the absolute differences between all Democrats and -0.257.

The results for the *STRU* and *FULL* models in Table 9.1 are different for two reasons. First, the Monte Carlo draws are different. Second, with reference to "All Committees," the different sample spaces have an impact on results. With reference to individual committees, results should be identical except for variation introduced by the Monte Carlo draws.[11] Thus, comparison of the *STRU* and *FULL* results for individual committees indicates how much sampling variability remains after 1,000 experiments.

Because the results for the *STRU* and *FULL* model are very similar, we present results for Houses 80 to 100 only for the *FULL* model in Table 9.2. As we will see in the next section, these Houses contain most of the outliers in American history. Note that it is possible that a full committee can appear as an outlier even when both party contingents have medians very close to the overall medians of their parties — the reason is that the committee median is typically determined by the moderate tail of the distribution of the majority party in the committee. Even if the median Democrat on the committee is close to the party median, a conservative Democrat could represent the committee median. Consequently, the committee as a whole could be an outlier, but the two party medians could be representative of the respective parties. An example of this is the Agriculture Committee in the 80th and 89th Houses.

Similarly, a party contingent can be an outlier relative to the overall party median and the overall committee median can still be quite close to the chamber median. Again the Agriculture Committee provides the example — in fourteen of the twenty-one Congresses shown in Table 9.2, the Democrat contingent was a conservative outlier but the overall committee was not.

Table 9.2
Committee Outliers Using Medians: Sample Space Defined by Full Model

Committee		HOUSE									
	100	99	98	97	96	95	94	93	92	91	90
All	.004	.000	.000	.000	.049	.002	.004	.000	.005	.007	.000
	.009	.001	.000	.000	.000	.000	.001	.005	.040	.009	.001
	.137	.350	.650	.377	.038	.009	.002	.046	.003	.036	.104
Agriculture	.484	.955	.809	.761	.364	.310	.584	.267	.099	+.041	.061
	+.015	+.010	+.028	+.055	+.030	+.014	+.042	+.010	+.003	+.002	+.000
	.500	.398	.930	.802	.762	.671	.455	.743	.067	.279	.218
Appropriations–	-.028	-.046	.123	.109	.353	.736	.623	.842	.582	.927	.967
	.951	.492	.324	.916	.803	.245	+.035	.070	.211	+.032	+.038
	.197	-.043	.271	.967	.308	.832	.864	.770	.558	.578	.229
Armed Services	+.010	+.002	+.015	+.031	+.002	+.001	+.000	+.018	.107	.222	.844
	+.000	+.000	+.000	+.000	+.000	+.003	+.001	+.000	+.003	+.003	+.053
	.696	.629	.405	.960	.911	+.054	.308	+.016	.158	.487	.754
Banking, Finance, and Urban Affairs	.985	.534	.486	.356	.136	-.054	.198	-.001	.194	.637	.345
	.750	.877	.892	.351	.638	.622	.445	.372	.318	.565	.352
	.366	.392	.803	.223	.740	-.043	.789	.120	.260	.484	.911
Budget[a]	.622	.473	-.007	.549	.113	.115	.971	-.028			
	.286	.100	.306	.749	.237	.226	.622	.387			
	.700	.156	.787	.519	.577	.338	.623	.384			
District of Columbia	-.007	-.000	-.001	-.000	.460	.531	.157	.065	.483	.566	.691
	.180	-.054	-.022	-.007	-.017	.264	.545	-.048	.076	.060	.119
	.683	.747	.906	.643	-.011	-.000	-.001	.802	.468	.672	.391

[a]Blank entries occur when a committee did not exist.

254

Table 9.2 (continued)

HOUSE

Committee	100	99	98	97	96	95	94	93	92	91	90
Education and Labor	.086	-.053	-.005	-.039	-.047	.069	.080	-.004	-.002	-.001	-.000
	-.019	-.022	-.022	-.045	.069	.174	.056	-.054	-.037	-.025	-.054
	-.040	-.011	.085	.191	.514	.058	-.030	-.037	-.052	.139	.193
Energy and Commerce	.546	.913	.256	.084	.278	.213	.777	.467	.607	.710	.677
	.966	.861	.565	.360	.298	.374	.671	.507	.304	.486	.649
	.380	.505	.402	.968	.631	.563	.794	.623	.681	.996	.986
Foreign Affairs	-.047	-.009	-.039	.321	.381	-.002	-.052	-.003	-.025	-.003	-.014
	-.056	-.011	-.046	.339	.200	-.052	.173	.638	.646	.227	.162
	.413	.394	.411	-.002	.159	.431	.157	-.035	.168	.967	.938
Government Operations	.339	.771	.647	.703	.734	.587	.139	.079	-.014	-.017	-.023
	.522	.199	.655	.433	.099	-.026	.096	.331	.306	.371	.812
	+.001	.186	.901	.601	.692	.738	.176	.076	.122	-.030	.416
House Administration	.193	.108	.092	.112	.286	.422	.570	.914	.857	.844	.302
	.649	.765	.750	.869	.398	.647	.225	.675	.971	.776	.228
	.253	.439	.832	.632	.510	.561	.189	.777	.295	.909	.389
Interior	.248	.516	.164	.695	.867	.181	.130	.421	.822	.975	.180
	.162	.149	.159	.332	.211	.397	.815	.572	.951	.768	.659
	.058	.160	.118	.271	.820	.359	.521	.788	.802	.586	.533
Internal Security								.423	.057	.682	+.035
								.298	.821	.181	.063
								.398	+.012	+.030	+.033

255

Table 9.2 (*continued*)

Committee	HOUSE										
	100	99	98	97	96	95	94	93	92	91	90
Judiciary	.282	.285	.301	.571	.501	.395	.375	.316	.172	.267	.358
	.507	.278	-.021	.464	-.012	.136	-.033	-.004	-.019	.106	.593
	.174	.134	.120	.312	.371	.665	.753	.333	.158	-.025	.138
Merchant Marine And Fisheries	.264	.199	.797	.859	.744	.947	.757	.479	.889	.699	.777
	.062	.122	.127	.078	.861	.947	.665	.935	.539	.664	.369
	.427	.227	-.015	-.016	.097	-.055	-.007	-.001	-.001	-.010	.123
Post Office	-.041	-.052	-.042	-.024	.371	-.025	.164	.810	.476	.121	.075
	.384	.115	.169	-.050	.463	.193	.143	.217	.973	.411	.282
	.069	.504	.268	.535	.828	.249	+.027	.356	.123	.819	.717
Public Works and Transportation	.806	.925	.745	.445	.076	.080	.101	.584	.160	.451	.802
	.356	.615	.899	.477	+.020	.072	.739	.904	.972	.566	.533
	.314	.480	.608	.435	.371	.280	.343	.200	.493	.519	.480
Rules	.155	.066	.120	.101	.170	.319	.532	.135	.123	.154	.129
	.809	.380	.410	.354	.296	.306	.394	.561	.684	.705	.499
	.788	.553	.288	.160	.142	.072	.108	.099	.121	.146	.114
Science, Space And Technology	.795	.979	.794	.389	.941	.269	.671	.956	.943	.777	.833
	.629	.241	.350	.524	.179	.094	.806	+.012	.727	.626	.725
	.252	.749	.907	.704	.950	.617	.161	.656	.115	.169	.404
Small Business	.596	.859	.536	.996	.730	.572	.603				
	.082	.147	.088	.891	.536	.357	.995				
	.202	.338	.496	.153	-.009	-.015	-.022				

256

Table 9.2 *(continued)*

HOUSE

Committee	100	99	98	97	96	95	94	93	92	91	90
Standards of	.509	.448	.304	.712	.775	.351	+.017	+.029	.181	.176	.290
Official Conduct	.207	.211	.101	.734	.354	+.013	+.001	.082	+.053	.072	.318
	.910	.349	.969	.697	.193	.476	.383	.168	.197	.235	.418
Veterans' Affairs	.391	.331	.433	+.020	+.000	+.007	.243	.320	.278	.252	.760
	+.043	+.047	.131	+.000	+.003	+.002	.829	.095	.442	+.032	+.008
	.210	.182	.340	.924	.784	.900	.562	.175	.755	.648	.135
Ways and Means	.937	.806	.804	.554	.458	.862	.838	.587	.780	.495	.282
	.252	.486	.200	.394	.679	.568	.785	.703	.966	.969	.695
	.830	.732	.951	.972	.646	.468	.137	.490	.618	.513	.326
Number of Committees That Are Preference Outliers											
5% All	5	6	6	5	3	5	3	6	3	4	4
5% Dem.	4	6	6	6	6	6	5	6	5	6	5
5% Rep.	2	2	1	2	2	5	5	4	3	4	1
10% All	6	7	7	7	4	7	5	8	5	4	6
10% Dem.	7	7	8	7	8	8	7	9	6	7	6
10% Rep.	4	2	2	2	3	7	5	6	4	4	1

257

Table 9.2 *(continued)*

Committee	HOUSE									
	89	88	87	86	85	84	83	82	81	80
All	.000	.000	.000	.001	.098	.164	.089	.378	.079	.026
	.015	.000	.018	.044	.031	.009	.009	.154	.249	.004
	.073	.001	.001	.006	.400	.536	.032	.168	.487	.159
Agriculture	+.006	.090	.087	.065	.232	.492	+.013	.870	.718	+.008
	.117	.074	+.036	+.019	.075	.135	+.038	+.031	+.022	.333
	.233	.222	.286	.973	.194	.283	.329	.669	.922	.710
Appropriations	.838	.717	.813	.117	.725	.366	.062	.181	.962	.154
	+.052	.332	.151	+.050	.145	.849	.176	.714	.412	.899
	+.027	+.055	+.031	+.026	.284	.912	+.010	.276	.775	.548
Armed Services	.133	.602	.561	.292	.690	.424	.777	.680	.663	.851
	+.030	+.041	.094	.169	.182	.303	.128	.327	.117	.174
	.729	.549	.266	.421	.348	.182	.739	.950	.911	.981
Banking, Finance. and Urban Affairs	.169	-.004	-.001	-.009	-.002	-.049	.108	-.009	-.006	.073
	.172	.182	-.032	.059	.058	-.014	-.016	.289	.264	.305
	.301	.633	.862	.237	.534	.461	.564	.580	.734	.683
Budget										
District of Columbia	+.032	.221	.270	+.045	.205	.173	.785	.645	.112	.210
	.905	+.000	-.001	+.048	+.006	+.001	.260	.138	.124	.074
	.564	.187	.251	.274	.169	.117	.124	.141	.767	.836

Table 9.2 (continued)

Committee		HOUSE								
	89	88	87	86	85	84	83	82	81	80
Education and Labor	-.029	-.000	-.001	-.001	-.017	-.001	.535	.634	.287	.260
	-.020	-.019	-.036	-.017	.088	.058	.146	.787	.161	-.019
	.533	.729	.492	.952	.673	.365	.699	.057	.520	.259
Energy and Commerce	+.039	.636	.553	.168	.893	.652	.548	.902	.626	.278
	.950	.195	.178	.084	.623	.861	.792	.919	.231	.964
	.774	.206	.239	.837	.856	.355	.573	.421	-.025	.225
Foreign Affairs	.204	.546	.076	.062	.085	.338	.357	-.041	.495	-.009
	.134	.279	.196	.056	.707	.757	.372	.113	.272	-.006
	.561	.516	-.026	.440	.882	.621	.275	.074	.087	.203
Government Operations	.383	-.040	.134	.407	.677	.190	.515	.121	-.035	.394
	.944	.862	.625	.599	.187	-.027	-.001	.108	.072	.306
	.539	-.040	.514	.622	.086	.317	.955	.687	.638	.715
House Administration	.237	.422	.761	.227	.963	.899	.571	.840	.357	+.030
	.607	.392	.638	.399	.643	.971	.515	.535	.983	+.010
	.941	.655	.270	.915	.972	.527	.988	.936	.831	.598
Interior	.893	.133	.226	.766	.918	.834	.136	.517	.793	.913
	.369	.589	.983	.785	.476	.244	.405	.901	.288	.644
	.758	.351	.950	.765	.313	.551	.564	+.036	.578	.845
Internal Security	+.005	+.000	+.028	+.007	.253	.240	.158	.156	.134	.740
	+.044	+.007	.359	.392	.621	.640	.980	.841	.590	.168
	.060	+.001	+.002	+.010	.435	.161	.107	.569	.791	.488

Table 9.2 (continued)

Committee	HOUSE									
	89	88	87	86	85	84	83	82	81	80
Judiciary	.296	.638	.973	.696	.666	.870	.159	.637	.969	.798
	.987	.994	.703	.540	.813	.858	.743	.699	.313	.388
	.412	.909	.773	.922	.547	.193	.320	.404	.191	.300
Merchant Marine And Fisheries	.933	.829	.944	.506	.518	.146	.306	.343	.801	.449
	.818	.923	.705	.938	.453	.071	.207	.057	.367	.076
	.093	-.020	-.055	-.024	-.023	.625	.076	.748	.235	.224
Post Office	.296	.464	.435	.987	.677	.295	.706	.638	.198	.539
	.313	.746	.214	.918	.994	.776	.538	.445	.609	.995
	.969	.944	.758	.722	.476	.282	.209	.418	.087	.216
Public Works and Transportation	.703	.139	.059	.276	.318	.095	.126	.293	.560	.538
	.459	.707	.882	.686	.208	.180	.639	.767	.977	.341
	.964	.302	.653	.430	.762	.512	.535	.601	.323	.403
Rules	.736	.096	.082	.788	.354	.621	.221	.999	.319	.136
	.527	.699	.644	.819	.644	.552	+.047	.818	.495	.270
	.100	.096	+.039	.102	.297	.432	.794	.457	.444	+.032
Science, Space, and Technology	.331	.755	.551	.962						
	.790	.368	.424	.406						
	-.045	-.029	.097	.107						

260

Table 9.2 *(continued)*

Committee	HOUSE									
	89	88	87	86	85	84	83	82	81	80
Small Business										
Standards of Official Conduct										
Veterans' Affairs	.082	.676	.923	.971	.692	.582	.982	.625	.743	.263
	+.004	+.004	+.045	.347	.212	.984	.176	+.006	.629	.903
	.082	.068	-.044	-.033	.248	.697	-.000	.090	.411	.111
Ways and Means	.761	.226	.165	.540	.107	.236	.656	.077	.252	+.054
	.923	.334	.672	-.019	-.014	-.007	.258	.209	.507	.721
	.161	.122	.092	.048	.260	.430	.155	+.032	+.023	+.020
Number of Committees That Are Preference Outliers										
5% All	5	4	3	4	2	2	1	2	2	4
5% Dem.	5	5	5	4	2	4	4	2	1	3
5% Rep.	2	5	6	5	1	0	2	2	2	2
10% All	6	6	7	6	3	3	2	3	2	5
10% Dem.	5	6	6	8	5	6	4	3	2	5
10% Rep.	5	7	8	6	2	0	3	5	4	2

Are Committees Preference Outliers?

Having set forth our methodology, we now proceed to address the central question of this chapter. Are committees preference outliers? We define an outlier committee as one where the median member's position is sufficiently far to the left or the right that it would have been produced by a random-assignment process less than 1 time in 20. In other words, the committee median has a p value of less than 0.05

Figure 9.1 shows the proportion of outlier committees for the House and Senate for Congresses 1 to 100.[12] In the House there is a clear change in the proportion of outlier *committees* after the passage of the Legislative Reform Act in 1946. Before the 80th House (1947–48), the proportion of outliers oscillates around 5 percent, rarely exceeds 10 percent of the committees, and never goes over 15 percent. In thirty-five of the first seventy-nine Houses and in twenty-two of the first seventy-nine Senates, fewer than one-twentieth of the committees — the fraction expected by pure chance — are significant outliers.

After the reforms of 1946, which cut the number of committees from forty-seven to nineteen in the House, the proportion of outliers begins to rise to around 20 percent. In the Senate, the proportion of outlier committees appears to increase after the passage of the Seventeenth Amendment in 1913 mandating the popular election of senators (the 64th Senate was the first to be affected by the amendment); nevertheless, the increase is not very large and there is no coherent pattern after the 80th Congress in contrast to the rise in the House. (The reforms of 1946 cut the number of Senate committees from thirty-three to fifteen.)

Figure 9.2 shows the proportion of outlier party *contingents* for the twentieth-century Houses. The change (after 1946) in the proportion of outlier committees shown in Figure 9.1 appears to be a result of a dramatic shift towards less representative committee contingents on the part of the Democrats after the 83rd House. Table 9.2 shows that the Democrat outliers to be concentrated primarily in four committees: Agriculture, Armed Services, and Veterans' Affairs are conservative outliers, while Education and Labor is a liberal outlier. In addition, the District of Columbia contingent tends to be a liberal outlier after the 93rd House.

If self-selection along the lines suggested by Shepsle (1978) is taking place, then this implies that the party contingents should be biased in the same direction over time. Table 9.2 suggests this is the case. Note, for example, that the Agriculture Committee's Democratic contingent has a significant conservative bias in sixteen of the twenty-one Congresses and never has a significant liberal bias. To better measure this form of bias, we count the number of com-

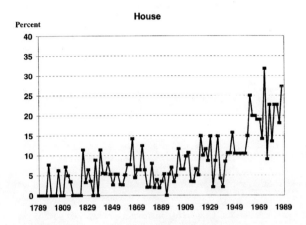

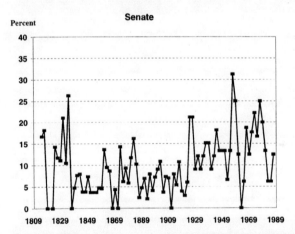

Figure 9.1. Percentage of committees with p values less than 0.05 for testing the null hypothesis that the committee is randomly assigned from the floor membership (1789–1988). By chance, 5 percent of the committees should have p values less than 0.05. The Senate has never witnessed a prolonged period where committees were systematically not representative of the floor. About 20 percent of the committees in the House were not representative in the period beginning with the 85th House (1957–58).

mittee party contingents that are same-direction outliers in the current and previous Houses and Senates.[13] Figure 9.3 shows the proportion of these consistent-bias committees over time. The difference between the House and Senate is striking. The Senate shows no pattern, but the House clearly changed in the 1950s. What is interesting about these results for the House is that they run

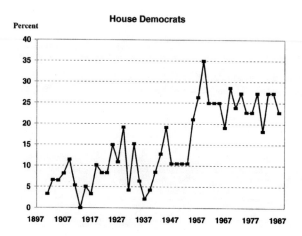

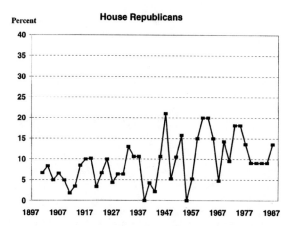

Figure 9.2. Percentage of party contingents on House committees with p values below 0.05 for testing the null hypothesis that the delegation is randomly assigned from party members on the floor (1901–1988). By chance, 5 percent of the delegations should have p values below 0.05. The figure shows that the outlier committees in the House, after 1956, resulted from the Democrats' delegations being non-representative. Republican delegations were always largely representative of the party.

counter to what would be the expected consequence of reducing the number of committees after 1946. The larger the number of committees, the greater the opportunity for self-selection. With fewer committees, the committees must be larger and therefore should be more representative of the chamber. Therefore, the proportion of consistently biased committees should be higher before the 80th House than after if self-selection were taking place in both periods. It is not higher.

As a check on these results, we compared p values controlling for committee size over time by performing simple linear regressions of committee size on the corresponding p value. We tried a variety of specifications using committee size, the square of committee size, and time as independent variables, and

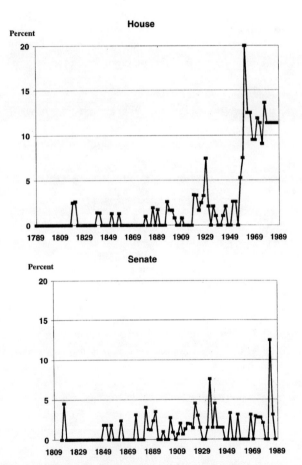

Figure 9.3. Consistent bias in committees. This shows the percentage of committees that had p values less than 0.05 in a particular Congress and the preceding Congress, and that were biased in the same direction (conservative in both or liberal in both). The Senate shows no periods where bias persists. About 12 percent of House committees are consistently biased, but again, only starting in 1957–58.

found nothing of consequence. Separate regressions for the first seventy-nine Houses, Houses 80–100, and all Houses were performed for the entire committee and majority and minority party contingents. In no specification were the coefficients on size of committee statistically significant.

To check whether the dramatic change in our overall p values for the entire committee system that occurred after the 80th Congress was affected by the majority- and minority-party ratios, we formed random committees in the same way as we did for the *FULL* model, only we randomized the D-NOMINATE coordinates across all members first. In effect we used (D+R)! as a sample space. This experiment produced results very similar to those produced by the FULL model for the overall committee medians. The reason is that the average majority- and minority-party ratios on committees have tracked the actual party ratio fairly closely throughout the twentieth century.

In sum, the changes shown in Figures 9.1, 9.2, and 9.3 are not due to changes in the size of committees or party ratios. Other explanations have to be found.

Do Committee Members Have Common Interests?

Self-selection implies that committee members have a greater stake in their committee's success on the floor than do legislators not on the committee. Presumably, if self-selection is at work, then the members of a committee have a set of common interests that, at times, may overpower their party affiliation. This implies that when a committee bill is on the floor, the minority-party contingent will vote with the majority-party contingent more often than they would if they were not members of the committee.

We tested this proposition with data collected by Cox and McCubbins (1993) on the committee origin of bills in the even-numbered Houses 82 through 98. For each committee we computed an agreement score — much like the *Congressional Quarterly* party-support or conservative-coalition-support scores — with the committee majority using all committee-related roll calls. We then aggregated the scores across committees for committee and non-committee members. Figure 9.4 shows the difference between these aggregated agreement scores for the Republicans (always the minority party in the House) over the eight even-numbered Congresses.

The agreement score results provide striking evidence supporting the hypothesis that individuals with common interests self-select on committees. Republicans on a committee vote with a majority of committee Democrats on 8 percent more of the roll calls than do non-committee Republicans. As a benchmark, this 8 percent figure can be compared to the fact that Democratic committee members vote with a majority of committee Democrats on 10 percent more of the roll calls than do Democrats who are not committee members. This percent discrepancy is not surprising since the committee majority shapes bills in the commit-

Percent Difference

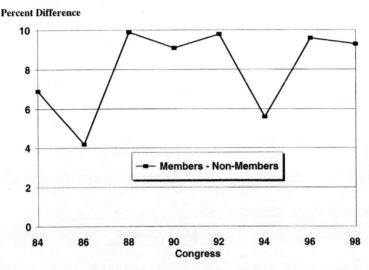

Figure 9.4. Republican committee members support committee bills more than do Republican nonmembers. The figure shows the difference between the percentage of committee members who support committee bills and the percentage of nonmembers who support. The data is aggregated across all committees and bills coded by Cox and McCubbins (1993). They coded roll calls for committee origin only for even–numbered Congresses from the 84th through the 98th. For these Congresses, the Republicans were the minority party.

tee's jurisdiction. What is surprising is that the pull on minority members, relative to other members of their party, is nearly as great.

An alternative test of committee behavior comes from looking at the D-NOMINATE classification errors. In terms of the spatial model, if self-selection is at work, then the Republicans should be making more voting "errors" because of their defections — that is, the Republican committee members are occasionally voting contrary to their basic beliefs but in favor of their constituents' interests. Put somewhat differently, the cutting line on roll calls will tend to divide Democrats and Republicans. If Republican committee members support the committee position, they will be making errors in the spatial model. On the other hand, if Democratic committee members support the committee position, they will typically be voting correctly. Figure 9.5 shows the difference between the correct classifications of the committee and non-committee members, by party, for the committee related roll calls.[14]

On average the committee Republicans are making about 2 percent more voting "errors" than the noncommittee Republicans. For the Democrats, the situation is reversed. The committee Democrats make about one percent fewer errors than the noncommittee Democrats on committee-related roll calls. This is most

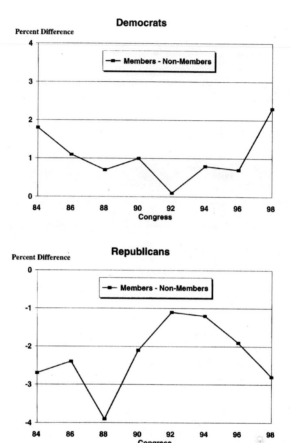

Figure 9.5. Difference in classification success for committee members and nonmembers on committee bills. Classifications are from the D–NOMINATE two–dimensional model with a linear trend. Democrats on committees always vote more in accord with the spatial model on their own bills than do nonmembers. The reverse is true for Republican committee members, who tend to become classification errors by supporting the committee position. The data is aggregated across all committees and bills coded by Cox and McCubbins (1993). They coded roll calls for committee origin only for even–numbered Congresses from the 84th through the 98th. For these Congresses, the Democrats were the majority party, and the Republicans were the minority party.

likely an information effect. Committee members have more information than noncommittee members and, therefore, can more accurately map the outcome of the committee related roll call into their basic beliefs. Checking these findings for earlier periods of history where we do not have information on the committee origin of bills can be done indirectly because if there was a change in behavior after the 80th House, then it should be detectable in the classification results over all roll calls controlling for majority versus minority party.

The upper panel of Figure 9.6 shows the difference between the majority-party and minority-party classification successes for the House for all Congresses. The period after the 80th House stands out clearly. In the constituency-service era

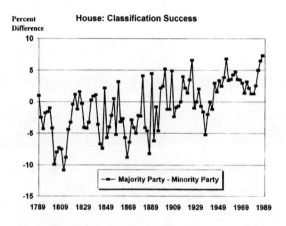

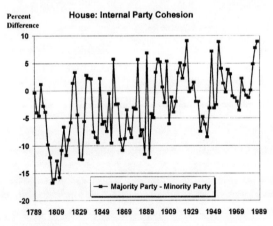

Figure 9.6. Majority and minority parties compared on classification success and cohesion. The top panel shows the difference between the percentage of decisions correctly classified by D–NOMINATE for the majority party and the minority party. The minority party is typically better classified before 1946, but subsequently the majority party is better classified. The bottom panel shows differences in cohesion — the percentage of party membership that votes with the party majority on a roll call. In the first fifty Congresses, the minority party was frequently far more cohesive than the majority. In the second fifty Congresses, the minority was relatively less cohesive, particularly since 1946.

(Cain, Ferejohn, and Fiorina, 1987; Fiorina, 1989; Alford and Brady, 1993), all twenty-one of the Houses from 80 to 100 show a positive difference between the majority-party and the minority-party classification results. The minority party exhibits more spatial voting errors, arguably because constituency interests force defections to support majority-sponsored bills. Before the 80th, sixty of the seventy-nine Houses showed either no differences or, in most cases, negative differences, due to the fact that the minority-party members were more cohesive — they voted together more often as a bloc ("we either hang together or hang separately") than did the majority party. This fact is displayed in the lower panel of Figure 9.6, which shows the difference between the majority- and minority-cohesion scores.[15] Until approximately the 80th Congress, the cohesion graph shows the minority party is typically more cohesive than the majority. In the modern period, this distinction is muted. Correspondingly, the correlation between the classification difference and the cohesion difference for Houses 1 to 79 is 0.89 while the correlation for Houses 80 to 100 is only 0.63.

Summary

Something changed fundamentally in House committees after the Legislative Reform Act of 1946. It is not clear that the change is due to the Reform Act — indeed, as we noted above, if self-selection existed before the reforms there should have been more outliers as a proportion before the 80th than after it. The Republicans controlled the House in the 80th and 83rd Congresses and Figures 9.1 to 9.3 show that the change occurred approximately between the 85th and 86th Houses (during Eisenhower's second term) very early in the forty-year period of uninterrupted Democratic Party control of the House. The timing of the change closely coincides with the increases in constituency-service representation in the House of Representatives (Fiorina, 1989; Cain, Ferejohn and Fiorina, 1987; Alford and Brady, 1993) and the emergence of seemingly permanently divided government in the United States (Fiorina, 1992; Alesina and Rosenthal, 1995).

The committee-outlier debate has been concerned only with the committee system in the House during and after the 80th Congress. Our findings for this period are generally supportive of the view that the committee system is representative of the chamber. This is certainly the case for the Senate; in the House, the proportion of outlier committees is small. If a reasonably stringent definition of outlier is used — namely, looking at the proportion of committee party contingents that are biased in the same direction between Congresses — then the proportion of outlier committees is further reduced.

In the post–World War II period, our evidence is consistent with the party-support model of Cox and McCubbins (1993). With the notable exception of the House Veterans' Affairs Committee Democrats, all of the committees that they define as "uniform externality committees" reflect the whole party. Since committees as well as party contingents are largely representative, the evidence is also consistent with Gilligan and Krehbiel's (1990) informational theory. However, Shepsle and Weingast (1994, p. 175) criticize the work of Gilligan and Krehbiel and Cox and McCubbins by arguing that their theoretical and empirical work rests upon the assumption of unidimensionality. They attempt to salvage the Structure Induced Equilibrium view of congressional committees by arguing for the need of "a comprehensive, spatially organized theory in many dimensions."

The many-dimensions view of the world fails, as we have shown in earlier chapters, to be at all helpful in understanding roll call voting decisions. If preference outliers are of great importance, they should be present among those dimensions that organize roll call voting. That they are not is bad news for the view that committees exist to solve equilibrium problems with majority voting. The many-dimensions view can, however, lay claim to some role given our findings that minority-party committee members tend to support the committee's position and to make spatial voting "errors" in doing so. But since this finding pertains only to the post-1946 period, the findings provide more evidence of strengthened "electoral connections" (Mayhew, 1974) than of the fundamentals of legislative committees. The fundamentals seem to be that committees are tools of the majority party (Cox and McCubbins, 1993) and that the tools are used to develop information (Gilligan and Krehbiel, 1990).

Notes

1. See also Krehbiel (1992).
2. Cox and McCubbins (1993, p. 200) define committees with widespread impact as "uniform externality committees." The committees of this type are Science, Post Office, Veterans, Public Works, Appropriations, Rules, Ways and Means, Commerce, Government Operations, and House Administration.
3. Some authors have compared means rather than medians.
4. Maltzman (1994) takes a somewhat different approach. He uses issue dimensions defined by a cluster analysis of Yule's Q's, computed between jurisdiction-specific roll calls.
5. The results we develop below concern party contingents on a committee and the committee as a whole. As we discuss in chapter 8, within a party, positions on the first and second dimensions in the two-dimensional model, after World War II, are highly correlated because the Democrats and Republicans lie in ellipses roughly at 45-degree angles (see Figure 3.3, for example). Consequently, the results for the second dimension for the party contingents will be almost the same as for the first dimension. We checked the overall committee results — that is, when both parties are included — on the second dimension, and there were no substantial differences from those we found using the first dimension.

6. See chapter 8 for further discussion of this point.
7. When the relevant number of legislators is even, we compute the median as the average of the two D-NOMINATE scores in the center of the distribution.
8. This topic is the focus of Shepsle (1978).
9. The twenty-two committee distributions for *chairs* should be identical, except for sampling variations. Indeed, the empirical distribution of D-NOMINATE scores could be directly used for a test. If for example, 4 percent of the actual Democrats had a D-NOMINATE score further from the party median than the actual chair, the p value would be 0.04. Nevertheless, it should be recognized that the twenty-two tests are not independent. If, for example, an archconservative heads one committee, that person cannot head another committee.
10. There is no formula for the M's because of the dependency imposed by the row and column sums. In the example in the text, there are $\binom{16}{3}$ ways to assign seats to the member represented by the first row. If the first member draws all three of her assignments from committees, with only one three-assignment member, then 0's have to be in these three committees' columns to satisfy the marginals. Consequently, there would be $\binom{13}{3}$ ways to assign the member represented by the second row. Note that, at a minimum, the last row of the matrix will always be determined by the assignments above it.
11. To see why, consider the following. Divide the committees into two sets: the Agriculture Committee and all other committees. Because sampling without replacement is being used, if the Agriculture Committee members are drawn first, then the results for the Agriculture Committee, based on either the *STRU* model or the *FULL* model, will be identical except for sampling variations. This is so because in both instances the constraints embedded in the two models get invoked in the set of all other committees — *not* for the Agriculture Committee.
12. The Senate did not have many committees until the 14th Senate (Nelson, 1994). The plots for Figures 9.1 to 9.4 are based on Monte Carlo analyses with sample sizes of 100 rather than 1,000. We found that a sample size of 100 gave essentially the same results so we used the smaller sample sizes for these large analyses.
13. Note that the overall committee comparison would not be informative because changes in party control would result in the level of consistent bias being underestimated.
14. These classification results are from our two-dimensional dynamic scaling.
15. The party cohesion score is simply a pooled party support score. For each roll call we determine which way a majority of the party voted and then calculate the proportion supporting the party position across all roll calls. In symbols, let $C_{ij}=1$ if the ith party member voted with the party majority on the j_{th} roll call; let $\delta_{ij}=1$ if the ith party member voted on the j_{th} roll call; then

$$\text{Party cohesion} = \frac{\sum_i \sum_j C_{ij}}{\sum_i \sum_j \delta_{ij}}$$

10

Abstention from Roll Call Voting

In previous chapters, we have shown that, throughout nearly all of the history of the United States, the bulk of individual congressional roll call voting decisions can be accounted for by a low-dimensional spatial model. In this chapter, we analyze the decision to *abstain* rather than to choose between Yea and Nay — that is, equivalently, we study turnout in congressional roll call voting.

A framework for our analysis is provided by the theory of "rational abstention." The theory suggests several hypotheses:

- Turnout should be inversely related to the degree of indifference, as measured by spatial utilities (see chapter 2 and Poole, 2005) computed from NOMINATE coordinates.

- Turnout should be higher when preferences on a roll call are evenly divided rather than lopsided.

- Turnout should decrease as the cost of voting increases.

- Turnout should be higher on the minority side of an issue than on the "silent" majority side.

- Turnout should decrease as the number of members of the legislative body increases.[1]

Even though we were aware that the abstention data had the potential to enrich our analysis substantially, we ignored information on abstentions in the development of NOMINATE. We did this in part as a way of simplifying the construction of the scaling algorithm and in part because, particularly in the modern period when abstention is quite low (see Figure 10.1), considering abstention would have little impact on our estimates of the ideal points of the legislators or the locations of the roll call alternatives.[2] Since abstention has continued to be quite low from 1989 through 2004, we have elected to simply incorporate our earlier analysis, based on D-NOMINATE, into this book without modification. If we have with D-NOMINATE indeed succeeded in capturing the preferences of the legislators on each roll call vote, we can use the D-NOMINATE results to test the hypotheses mentioned above.

In this chapter, we summarize the predictions of abstention theory we seek to test and discuss the variables we use to measure indifference, cost, and closeness. We then specify a logit model that is used for hypothesis testing; and, finally, we present the empirical results.

Tests of the Theory of Abstention

Congressional roll calls are similar to two-candidate elections in that they are choices among two alternatives. For this case, the decision-theoretic model is expressed in the well-known equation (Downs, 1957; Riker and Ordeshook, 1968):

$$R = PB - C + D$$

In this equation, R is the net reward from voting. It equals the *instrumental* benefit of voting, PB, less fixed costs, C (such as the opportunity cost of the time spent in voting), plus fixed benefits, D (such as a sense of a citizen's duty). The instrumental benefit is simply the voter's utility gain if the side he or she favors wins, B, multiplied by the subjective probability, P, the individual assigns to his or her chances of casting the decisive vote.

If, without loss of generality, the utility of abstention is set at zero, then voting takes place if and only if the reward is positive or $R > 0$. It is common to focus only on the net fixed cost, $c = C - D$. We thus obtain:

Vote if and only if $R = PB - c > 0$

Testing the decision-theoretic model requires measuring P, B, and c. The easiest part is the B term, since the maintained hypothesis of the D-NOMINATE model is that the expected value of B, $E(B)$, is the absolute value of the difference in the utility of the Yea and Nay outcomes:

$$E(B) = |\Delta U|$$
$$\text{where } \Delta U = U(\text{Yea}) - U(\text{Nay})$$

We will, therefore, estimate B by using the spatial utilities calculated from the D-NOMINATE model.[3] The term P is difficult to measure especially since subjective probabilities may depart sharply from objective probabilities (Tversky and Khaneman, 1974). There are at least three ways to compute P empirically. First, we could view P as a decreasing function of the actual margin on the roll call.[4] Second, we could view P as being a decreasing function of the margin if everyone had voted as predicted by the D-NOMINATE estimates. Third, we could view P as being a decreasing function of the expected margin implied by the probability of a "Yea" vote the model assigns to each legislator. In the latter two approaches, one could or could not include abstainers in the computation. We have chosen the first method for simplicity. We suspect that all alternative measures would be strongly correlated with the actual margin.

The cost variable, c, is also difficult to measure. Maintaining a good overall voting record may be a benefit in terms of one's reputation with constituents but the value of the benefit may vary across individuals and over time. Similarly, the cost of being present in Washington may vary over time and cross-sectionally, particularly because different members have different travel times from Washington to their constituencies.

The direct cost of travel should be closely approximated by using the distance to the constituency. As an independent variable in our analysis of the House, we used $LNDIS$, the natural logarithm of the distance from the congressional district to Washington.[5] The relationship of $LNDIS$ to both turnout and travel time is an ambiguous one. If each member were to spend the same number of days in the district, more distant members would miss more votes since they, particularly in the era prior to air travel, would spend more time in transit. However, for the more distant districts, the travel times might be prohibitive, in which case the more distant members would miss fewer votes. Consequently, we use $LNDIS$ only to explore whether $LNDIS$ influences the level of turnout.

The theoretical ambiguity of a distance measure illustrates how difficult it is to measure cost. Nonetheless, it is important to control for its variations in cost in order to assess the effect of the P and B terms in the voting calculus. A good indicator of the value of c is provided by the legislator's prior turnout record. We use two proxies. The variable $ABSPREV$ equals 1 if the legislator abstained on the previous roll call and equals 0 if the legislator voted. $ABSAVG$ is the fraction of times the legislator abstained on the second through twenty-sixth preceding roll calls.[6] (When these variables are used, our analysis will be confined to the twenty-seventh and later roll calls of each Congress.)

The two ABS variables will pick up costs induced by illness or trips back to the constituency. They are also a potential way of proxying for the effects of other roll calls. As throughout most of this book, we make the simplifying assumption that decisions on successive roll calls are independent ones.[7] If, in contrast, a legislator decided to be present for a critical vote on a trade treaty, the legislator would find it cheaper to be present for other roll calls on the same day. This type of interdependence would be picked up by our two *ABS* variables. However, in a detailed examination of the context surrounding each roll call vote on railroad regulation in the 49th Congress (Poole and Rosenthal, 1994), we did not find any evidence of important effects on turnout and choice that could be traced to the types and substance of other roll calls that preceded each roll call. This result leads us to conjecture that *ABSAVG* and *ABSPREV* are mainly picking up long-term costs that are not strongly related to the roll call agenda. Nonetheless, the impact of the agenda merits further investigation since railroad regulation in the 49th Congress is but a small slice of the historical record.

In addition to the costs that are proxied for by the legislator's prior absenteeism, other costs may be present for legislators who know they will not be present in the next Congress. Some of those who will not return to the next Congress may be abstaining because they have decided to retire or to pursue another career or higher office. These legislators, particularly those leaving politics, find voting relatively costly, as they no longer have an incentive to present their electorate with a good attendance record. They can thus "shirk" by not voting.[8] Of course, causality can run the other way. A poor voting record may result in involuntary exit by electoral defeat. We can control for the direction of causality by considering only roll calls that occurred after elections for the next Congress. Post-election roll calls always took place in Congresses before the 74th. The traditional lame duck sessions generally ran in the first three months of years following elections. With the passage of the Twentieth Amendment in 1933, lame-duck sessions were rare, occurring in only eight special sessions in Congresses 74–100 the end point for the analysis in this chapter.[9] In all post-election sessions, costs should be similar for those who had been defeated and those who had retired.

From the basic decision-theoretic equation for the reward for voting, we can make the following predictions, other things being equal:

1. As net fixed costs decrease, turnout should increase. Abstentions should be positively related to both *ABSAVG* and *ABSPREV*.
2. As the perceived probability of being decisive increases, turnout should increase. Abstentions should be negatively related to the variables measuring *P*.
3. As benefits increase, turnout should increase. Abstentions should be negatively related to B.

4. As the expected instrumental benefit from voting increases, turnout should increase. Abstentions should be negatively related to *PB*.

Additional predictions result from considering the game-theoretic approach to abstention. In this approach, the decision-theoretic model is embedded in a voting game where the legislators interact strategically. The level of turnout in an equilibrium of the game reflects two forces. One force arises because legislators with Yea preferences compete for victory with those with Nay preferences. This competitive force, which is increasing in B but decreasing in c, results in positive turnout. The second force is free riding. Legislators with, say, a Yea preference have an incentive to abstain, as they can free ride on the votes of others with a Yea preference. The interplay between the forces of competition and free riding leads to the endogenous determination of P. That is, in the game-theoretic approach, actual probabilities and subjective probabilities of casting the decisive vote must be equal.

The actual probability that a given voter is decisive depends on the distribution of benefits, B, and costs, c, across the set of legislators. If a substantial number of legislators with negative net costs prefer one roll call outcome and a smaller number prefer the other, the outcome will be lopsided if only individuals with negative net costs vote. Thus, there can be an equilibrium where no one with positive costs votes, with $P = 0$.

There can also be equilibria where those with positive as well as negative net fixed costs vote. But in this case, the expected outcome must be close to a tie. If it were not, one of the positive-cost voters would want to abstain. For the outcome to be close to a tie, expected turnout among those who represent the majority preference must be less than the expected turnout among those who represent the minority. That is, there must be a relatively silent majority (Palfrey and Rosenthal, 1983). This leads to an additional prediction:

5. Turnout among those representing the majority's preferred position on a roll call should be less than among those representing the minority's preferred position.[10]

This prediction needs to be modified because of the constitutional quorum requirement that legislation can be passed only if a majority of the membership is present.[11] The strategic aspects of the quorum requirement have been largely ignored in formal models of rational turnout. If the minority side expects that less than 50 percent of the membership will be present to vote for the majority position, the minority has an incentive to be absent if the minority supports the status quo.[12] That is, when turnout is very low, abstentions may be disproportionately drawn from those on the minority side. This quorum effect is likely to have been most pronounced in the late nineteenth century when over-all turnout levels were low. For example, in the 52nd House, there was no quorum present for thirty-four of the 304 recorded roll calls. Most of these had lop-sided majorities, suggesting strategic abstention by the minority. (We will take this strategic element into account in our empirical work below.)

The game-theoretic model also predicts (Palfrey and Rosenthal, 1985) that, other things being equal, turnout (as a percentage of the membership) will decline as the size of the legislature increases. This is because P tends to zero as size increases. Thus, there are two further predictions:

6. At any given point in time, abstention will be greater in the House than in the Senate.
7. As the size of either the House or Senate increases, other things being equal, abstention increases.

Strictly speaking, the game-theoretic model does not account for the data. Since the average majority throughout American history is around 63 percent of the vote cast, it is hard to believe that a tie is expected on all votes. On most roll calls only those with negative net costs should be voting. Nonetheless, the game theory prediction that majorities will be silent is worth investigating.

An alternative theory of abstention has recently been developed by Cohen and Noll (1991). They observe that "on virtually all roll call votes, the outcome is virtually certain and winning margins are very large . . . High rates of voting combined with virtually certain outcomes are at odds with a naive instrumental theory of voting."[13] In their model, the behavior of legislators is driven by the reelection motive rather than by a consideration of being pivotal on any one roll call. Legislators view voting as costly because the time spent voting could be used in providing constituency services, raising campaign money, and so on.

The predictions of the Cohen and Noll model differ from those of the rational turnout model for several important reasons: (1) roll calls vary in salience to constituents; (2) some constituencies have conflicts in that some constituents are pro, others anti, on an issue; and (3) constituents weigh legislative losses more heavily than legislative victories. This last feature of their model demands voter behavior that is not always consistent with other literature (such as Wilson, 1980) that argues that constituents are more concerned with *utility* losses than with utility gains. If the loss/gain view were true, for example, we might find constituents weighing a victory on a motion that protected them from losses (for example, on a motion blocking the closing of a military base) more heavily than a defeat on a motion that promised gains (a new military base). In any event, since we are unable to measure constituency conflict and salience for all issues in American history, we will confine our analysis to predictions from the rational-abstention model.

In the next section, we proceed to test the seven predictions stated above. In doing so, we must exercise great caution because a number of institutional factors are at odds with the underlying assumption that each roll call outcome depends on simple majority rule. First, supermajorities are important on some roll calls, including those that involve veto overrides, constitutional amendments, discharge petitions in the House, and filibuster clotures in the Senate. Since votes of this type are a relatively small proportion of the total, we chose, in view of the effort required to screen such votes, to ignore the problem of supermajorities.[14] Second, on occasion abstention was used strategically, for example, to block the necessary quorum for the majority vote to be valid. (We address this problem later.) Third, ICPSR data records announced votes for recent Congresses but not for earlier ones. The issue of announced votes poses a comparability problem in defining the dependent variable, abstention. Although we used announced votes in the scaling, including them as votes in this chapter would distort intertemporal comparisons. Consequently, we define votes as actual votes and pairs. Those absent, present but not voting, and announced are treated as abstaining.

A Framework for Empirical Tests

Our first and third predictions (stated earlier) are that turnout should increase as net fixed costs, represented by *ABSAVG* and *ABSPREV* decrease; and that turnout should increase as the estimated utility difference $E(B) = |\Delta U|$ increases. To test these two predictions in a single framework, for each roll call, we estimated a trichotomous logit model — the three probabilities were Yea (a Yea vote or a paired Yea); Nay (a Nay vote or a paired Nay); or an abstention (absent, present but not voting, or announced).[15] These probabilities can be viewed as reflecting the comparison of three utilities. Without loss of generality, one can express the utility of abstention as just zero plus an error term:

$$UA = \text{utility of abstaining} = 0 + \text{error}_{\text{ABSTAIN}}$$

For Yea votes to become more likely as the utility difference increases, and less likely when the cost variables increase, we specify the Yea *differential* utility (relative to abstentions and Nay) as:

$$UY = \beta_{0y} + \beta_{1y}\Delta U + \beta_{2y}ABSPREV + \beta_{3y}ABSAVG + \text{error}_{\text{YEA}}$$

Our predictions tell us that we expect $\beta_{1y} > 0$; $\beta_{2y} < 0$; $\beta_{3y} < 0$. The expression for the Nay choice is directly parallel to that for the Yea choice.

$$UN = \beta_{0n} + \beta_{1n}\Delta U + \beta_{2n}ABSPREV + \beta_{3n}ABSAVG + \text{error}_{NAY}.$$

Here, our predictions tell us that we expect $\beta_{1n} < 0$; $\beta_{2n} < 0$; $\beta_{3n} < 0$. Moreover, ignoring, for the time being, the strategic aspects of silent majorities, the symmetry of the spatial model implies $\beta_{1y} = -\beta_{1n}$; $\beta_{2y} = \beta_{2n}$; $\beta_{3y} = \beta_{3n}$.

Under the standard assumptions about the errors in a logit model, it is well-known that the probabilities are given by:

$$\Pr(\text{Yea}) = \frac{\exp(UY)}{1+\exp(UY)+\exp(UN)}, \ \Pr(\text{Nay}) = \frac{\exp(UN)}{1+\exp(UY)+\exp(UN)}$$

$$\Pr(\text{Abstain}) = \frac{1}{1+\exp(UY)+\exp(UN)} = 1 - \Pr(\text{Yea}) - \Pr(\text{Nay})$$

The bottom line is that once we have estimated the β coefficients, we can calculate the (estimated) probabilities. To illustrate, Table 10.1 shows the estimates for one of the thousands of roll calls in our analysis. This is the vote

Table 10.1
Trinomial Logit Estimates for the
Reagan-versus-Cullom Vote

	Coefficient	Estimate
β_{0y}	Constant	3.268
	Yea/abstain	(0.545)[a]
β_{0n}	Constant	3.068
	Nay/abstain	(0.531)
β_{1y}	D-NOMINATE	9.672
	Yea/abstain	(2.116)
β_{1n}	D-NOMINATE	−9.845
	Nay/abstain	(2.107)
β_{2y}	ABSPREV	−3.430
	Yea/abstain	(0.550)
β_{2n}	ABSPREV	−3.174
	Nay/abstain	(0.530)
β_{3y}	ABSAVG	−5.289
	Yea/abstain	(1.058)
B_{3n}	ABSAVG	−4.465
	Nay/abstain	(0.937)
	Log-Likelihood	−134.917

Note: VOTEVIEW number 191, 49th House; n = 322.

[a] Standard errors in parentheses. All coefficients are statistically significant with *p* values less than 0.01.

(which we discussed in chapter 6) on the Reagan bill (a House version of the interstate commerce bill) vs. the Cullom bill (a Senate version) that preceded passage of the Interstate Commerce Act of 1887. For a legislator who had always voted on the past twenty-six roll calls and who was completely indifferent ($ABSAVG = ABSPREV = \Delta U = 0$), the estimated probability of abstention was $1/(1 + \exp(3.286) + \exp(3.080)) = 0.02$. Voters with $\Delta U > 0$ were even less likely to abstain, whereas those who had failed to turn out on previous roll calls were more likely to abstain. We developed estimates like those shown in Table 10.1 for every roll call included in the D-NOMINATE scaling.[16]

Empirical Analysis of Abstention in Congress

The overall abstention rates for the first 100 Congresses are plotted in Figure 10.1. The patterns for the House and Senate are quite similar and belie any simple predictions about size and turnout. Although initially abstentions increase in time, as the memberships of the House and Senate are also increasing, abstention in the Senate begins to fall after, roughly, the 50th Senate, even though the Senate grew in spurts until the 63rd Senate (when Arizona and New Mexico were admitted) and grew slightly in the 88th Senate (with the addition

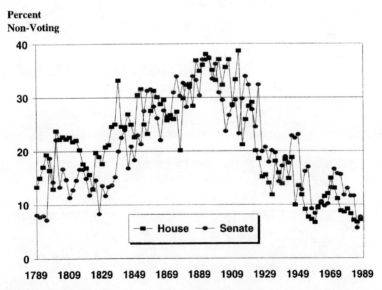

Figure 10.1. Nonvoting in Congress, 1789–1988. The percentage abstaining is the percentage of members absent, present but not voting, and announced, on all roll calls with over 2.5 percent in the minority.

of Alaska and Hawaii). Similarly, abstention in the House falls, dramatically, after roughly the 60th House even though membership in the House plateaued at 435 (with the 63rd House).

Further, these data suggest that the trends are mainly the interaction of improvements in passenger transportation technology and the representative's need to maintain contact with the constituency. Note that in the first twenty Congresses, abstentions are relatively low, around 15 percent in the Senate and 20 percent in the House. In this pre-railroad period, a journey to Washington was sufficiently arduous that once a member arrived for a session, a brief trip back home was out of the question. In 1800, a trip from Washington to New York took three days; to Boston, six days; and to Savannah nearly two weeks. By 1830 travel times in the east had improved but the nation had expanded. Although New York could be reached from Washington in a little more than one day, it was still nearly a week to Savannah and to Cincinnati. As the rail network developed, a trip back home was feasible but would lead to an absence of several days, particularly for representatives of the newer, more distant states. By 1857, one could reach Savannah, St. Louis, or Des Moines in less than three days. Perhaps as a result, abstention rose. Further developments in transportation made it possible for representatives to both visit the constituency and get back in Washington for votes.[17]

That technological change, rather than institutions, is the primary force driving intertemporal variation in turnout is confirmed by the strong correlation ($R^2 = 0.71$) between the Senate and House series in Figure 10.1. (See the first column of Table 10.2.)

A further indication of the role of better technology and of better health is provided by Figure 10.2. The figure is based on the computation of the maximum nonvoting string, that is, consecutive abstentions, for each legislator in a Congress. Votes with an under–55-percent turnout were excluded from the

Table 10.2
Descriptive Regression for Senate Abstention

Variable	MODEL	
	(1)	(2)
Constant	3.300	−0.782
House abstention	0.805	0.932
	(0.052)	(0.052)
Senate directly elected		3.440
		(1.245)
R^2	0.71	0.73

Note: The dependent variable is Senate abstention; n =100.

**Percent of all
Roll Calls**

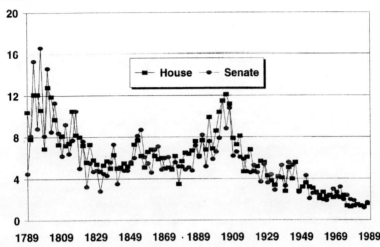

Figure 10.2. Average of the maximum percentage of consecutive abstentions, as a percentage of all roll calls in the Congress, 1789–1988. For each member, the percentage is 100 × (the maximum number of consecutive roll calls missed in the Congress) divided by (the total number of roll calls in the Congress). The plot shows the average of these percentages. Large blocks of votes were missed in the early Congresses and at the turn of the twentieth century. (Members must have had an overall turnout rate of 50 percent to be included in computation.)

computation in order to eliminate strategic abstentions with respect to the quorum. The strings were computed as a proportion of the total roll calls in a Congress — the figure shows the mean string for each house in each Congress. To eliminate those with very prolonged illnesses, legislators voting on less than 50 percent of all roll calls were eliminated from computation of the mean.

In the first fifteen Congresses, legislators were typically absent for large chunks, about 10 percent of the roll calls in a Congress. As turnout averaged about 85 percent in this period, almost all abstention was indeed the result of prolonged absence. From the 15th to the 45th Congress, there were fewer prolonged absences; typically legislators missed only about 5 percent of the roll calls. Nonetheless, nonvoting began a steady increase, exacerbated by the increase in prolonged absences from the 45th Congress to the 60th. By the 60th Congress, representatives were missing chunks of votes as large as those missed a century earlier. But as modern transportation improved, legislators rarely had prolonged absences. By the 1980s, the average longest consecutive string of roll calls missed was just over 1 percent of the total.

How Turnout Responds to Costs

Our first test of how turnout responds to cost is to look at the signs of the abstention terms in the trichotomous logit model developed in the previous section. All four of these coefficients should be negative. Indeed, this is overwhelmingly the case — the evidence is summarized in Figure 10.3. The figure plots the percentage of roll calls in each Congress for which all four coefficients were negative. The same percentage is plotted for votes that were close, that is, votes having less than a 60–40 split. All four signs are correct on over 75 percent of the close votes in the eighty-five Houses since the 15th and on over 90 percent of the close votes in fifty-nine of the eighty-five Houses. Missing a recent vote systematically increases the chances of not casting a vote or being paired. The curve for all votes is not very different from that for close votes. In fact, the average proportion of four correct signs for close votes is only 0.004 greater than for all votes. This similarity suggests that *ABSPREV* and *ABSAVG* variables are picking up absences that are largely the result of "prohibitive"

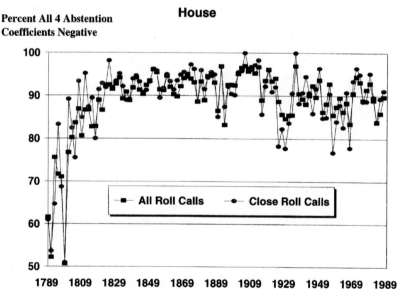

Figure 10.3. Percentage of roll calls for which all four coefficients on ABSAVG and ABSPREV variables are negative. By chance, only 25 percent of all roll calls should have all coefficients negative, but, with the exception of the eighteenth century, about 90 percent are as theoretically predicted. Because the pattern for close roll calls is the same as for all roll calls, the ABSAVG and ABSPREV variables should be accounting for illnesses, trips home, and other non-strategic, non-issue-specific sources of abstention.

costs — those of illness and trips home — that prevent attendance regardless of the individual's chance of playing a pivotal role.

Our second look at the effects of cost on turnout involves a comparison of the turnout rates of members who continued service into the next Congress versus those who did not. When we look at roll calls that occurred prior to congressional elections, in the House, we find, in Figure 10.4, overwhelming evidence that non-continuing members vote less. The difference between these and continuing members is relatively small, however, typically between 5 percent and 10 percent in recent Congresses. Moreover, in six Houses (all before the twentieth century), the relationship is reversed. And the difference may indeed be small if marginal members seeking reelection vote frequently to curry favor with constituents. That this is the case is suggested by the data on post-election roll calls also shown in Figure 10.4. Here the difference is in the expected direction in all but two early Houses and the difference is substantial, around 15 percent in the twentieth century. (The absence of a point in the figure indicates the absence of a lame-duck session.) Most of the increase in lame-duck shirking has occurred in the past 100 years. In the first fifty Congresses, the difference between continuing and non-continuing members was only 1.4 percent but it averaged 8.9 percent in the thirty-two of the last fifty Congresses that had lame-duck sessions.

The story for continuing versus non-continuing members in the Senate is basically the same as for the House, except there is more variability, no doubt a reflection of the smaller size of the Senate (see Figure 10.4). Thus, there are, for pre-election roll calls, eleven Congresses in which continuing members turned out less than non-continuing members prior to elections versus only six such Congresses for the House. Similarly, continuing members turn out less for post-election votes than non-continuing members in six of the first twenty-two Senates. There is also less of an increase in lame-duck "shirking" in the last fifty Congresses. Whereas the difference of 1.6 percent in the first fifty Senates is similar to the 1.4 percent for the first fifty Houses, the 3.0 percent in the last fifty Senates is substantially below the 8.9 percent for the last fifty Houses. In both chambers, however, the bulk of the evidence points to considerable shirking of duty by non-returning members, particularly when their electoral fates are known.

Closeness Counts in Congressional Voting

Our second prediction is that turnout should increase as P, the probability of casting a decisive vote, increases. A legislator's subjective estimate of P for a roll call should be a decreasing function of the legislator's forecast of the margin of the roll call. To the extent that actual margins are, on average, indica-

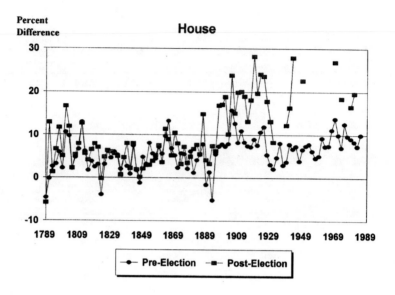

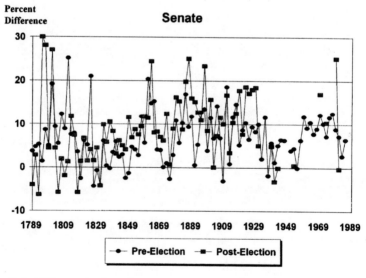

Figure 10.4. Difference in abstention between non-continuing and continuing members (1789–1989). Non-continuing members have almost always "shirked" by voting less. The difference is particularly large for roll calls that took place in lame-duck sessions in the twentieth century.

**Difference in Percent
Non-Voting, Lopsided
Versus Close Roll Calls**

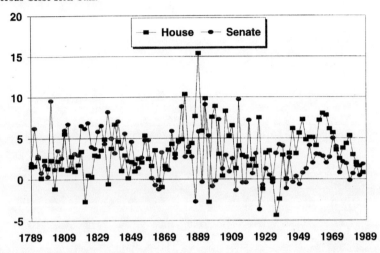

Figure 10.5. Difference between abstention on lopsided roll calls (majorities greater than 60 percent to 40 percent) and close roll calls (1789–1988). There are more abstentions on lopsided votes.

tive of forecast margins, we should find that abstention increases when the actual margin proves to be lopsided. To show that this is the case, we have, for both houses, computed the abstention rate for close roll calls (with margins equal to or less than 60 to 40) and those for lopsided margins (greater than 60 to 40). As expected, the lopsided roll calls have more abstention. The result holds for ninety-one of 100 Houses and eighty-four of 100 Senates. The results are shown in Figure 10.5. For the first 100 Congresses, turnout has been 3.3 percent higher on close votes than on lopsided votes in the House and 2.8 percent higher in the Senate.

Abstention Due to Indifference

Our third prediction is that voters who are indifferent — as measured by a low B term from the D-NOMINATE model — should abstain. If this hypothesis holds, we should obtain a positive coefficient on ΔU in the estimated Yea equation in the logit model and a negative coefficient in the estimated Nay equation. In Figure 10.6, we show, for all roll calls, the proportion of roll calls for which

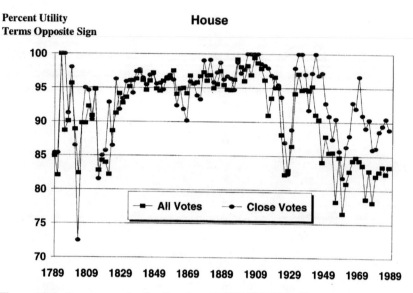

Figure 10.6. Percentage of roll calls where D-NOMINATE utility terms have oppo-site signs (1789–1988). Most roll calls have the theoretically expected pattern of opposite signs. The pattern is especially true on close roll calls (majorities of no more than 60 percent to 40 percent).

the expected pattern of coefficient signs holds. The evidence is most impressive for the period between the 25th and the 60th Congress when almost always over 95 percent of all the roll calls were as expected. Although always over 80 percent, the percentage of roll calls as expected was more erratic in the first twenty-five Congresses, and even more so in modern times when the percent-age of correct coefficients falls as low as 76 percent. Thus, the poorer results occur in periods when the general turnout level is very high.

With very low abstention levels, the effective sample sizes that distinguish abstainers from voters are small, making coefficient estimates more variable. In addition, the few nonvoters may be "alienated" legislators at the periphery of the space (Hinich and Ordeshook, 1969; Rosenthal and Sen, 1973). The expected pattern of opposite signs on the coefficients arises more frequently on close roll calls, as also shown in the figure. The failure to find the expected pat-tern on lopsided votes is indeed suggestive of abstention due to alienation. The fact that, for nearly all Congresses, the expected pattern is more prevalent on close votes also supports the fourth hypothesis: that the B term is important only when the perceived value of P is high.

Regarding the results on indifference, then, we found that the attractiveness of abstention relative to voting either Yea or Nay is inversely related to the
B term. And the effect is heightened for close roll calls.

Silent Majorities

To test our fifth prediction — that abstentions are more prevalent on the majority side of an issue — we compared the percentage of legislators, among
abstainers, that had been predicted to vote on the winning side (if they had
voted) with the percentage that actually voted on the winning side. The difference between these two percentages, plotted in Figure 10.7, should be positive.
Because the minority has an interest in abstaining to block a quorum when
turnout is close to 50 percent, we considered only votes with turnout in excess
of 55 percent. Beginning with the 65th House, the difference is always in the
expected direction. But results are erratic for the first sixty-four Houses. The
general pattern for the Senate is similar to, but weaker than, the House. The
results are as expected only for lopsided roll calls and, for these, only after the
80th Senate. Thus, the silent-majority hypothesis receives support only in the
modern era. It is an open question as to why the hypothesis was not supported
in the earlier Congresses.

Does Size Matter in Turnout?

Our earlier examination of Figure 10.1 indicated that it would be difficult, without controls, to find any simple relationship between the size of either legislative body and turnout. Clearly, changes in nonvoting patterns are driven by
changes in transportation technology; changes in the relationship between legislators, constituents, partisan support groups, campaign contributors, and party
leaders; and, undoubtedly, other factors. Nevertheless, many of the influences
on nonvoting can be controlled for by comparing House and Senate turnout
within a given Congress. Clearly, transportation technology, communications
technology, the size of government, the influence of PACs, and many other factors have similar effects on both chambers at any one point in time.

Within given Congresses, there are systematic, if relatively small differences in turnout between the House and Senate, that are not apparent in Figure 10.1. Over the first 100 Congresses, nonvoting patterns were in line with
our sixth prediction, 1.09 percent greater in the House than in the Senate.[18]
But this overall difference masks an important variation in time. Before popular election of the Senate, as shown by Figure 10.8, the House, indeed, typically
had more nonvoting than the Senate — the difference was 2.85 percent over the
first sixty-four Congresses. But after the 65th Congress, the Senate had more

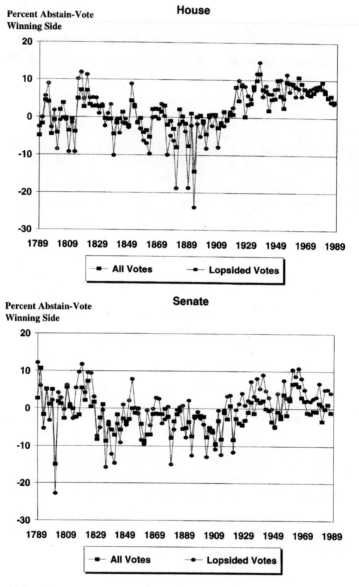

Figure 10.7. Difference between the percentage of legislators, among abstainers, that had been predicted to vote on the winning side and the actual percentage of voters on winning side (1789–1988). The "silent majority" hypothesis predicts the difference to be positive. The result is as expected only for the House of Representatives since the 65th Congress.

Difference House and Senate Percent Non-Voting

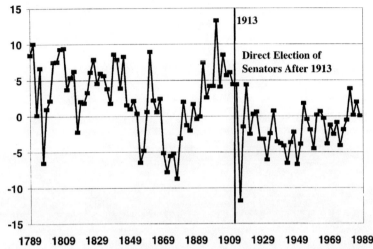

Figure 10.8. Difference in the percentage of legislators abstaining in the House and the Senate. Since the House is larger than the Senate, this difference is expected to be positive. The actual difference is typically positive until the Senate is directly elected. Subsequently, the difference is typically negative.

nonvoting than the House — the difference was −1.93 percent. Some of this difference reflects the largest negative difference in the series, −11 percent in the 65th Congress, when many indirectly elected senators were likely to have been shirking. But the difference is still significantly negative, at −1.66 percent when computed only for the 66th Congress forward.

The same point is made in Table 10.2. We regressed Senate abstention on House abstention, a constant, and a dummy variable that equals one for the directly elected Senates, and zero otherwise. As seen in the table, abstention, after controlling for the level of abstentions in the House, is 3.4 percent greater in directly elected Senates than in indirectly elected Senates.

We can only conjecture why direct election of the Senate sharply lowered turnout in the Senate relative to the House. The data suggest that when voters, rather than a state's legislators, are one's constituents, one spends more time at home and less in Washington. If Senate races are generally more competitive than those for the House, senators could well wind up voting less than representatives, even if the Senate is a smaller body than the House. On the other hand, Table 4.4 showed that House abstention is very weakly increasing in safeness of the seat. This observation does not provide an explanation for the shift brought about by direct election.

Summary

Our comparison of the House and Senate indicates some difficulties in testing theories of turnout. Although abstentions appear related to cost, closeness of the vote, and indifference throughout the history of Congress, the predictions concerning silent majorities and size effects are supported only for some historical periods. Explaining the anomalies is obviously a topic for future research, where more effort can be placed on finding controls — such as electoral margins and campaign contributions — that would create better natural experiments.

Notes

1. The theory of rational abstention was initially developed in a decision-theoretic framework by Downs (1957) and formalized by Riker and Ordeshook (1968). Ledyard (1981, 1984) integrated the decision-theoretic model into an equilibrium game-theoretic, incomplete-information model that encompassed both choice, in two-alternative votes, and abstention. Palfrey and Rosenthal (1983, 1985) developed the game-theoretic model for complete information and characterized the incomplete-information equilibrium for large voting populations. This chapter's focus comes from these theoretical developments.

2. Note that the spatial utilities themselves are unlikely to contain a substantial level of bias even though we have ignored abstention in D-NOMINATE. As long as members on opposite sides of the true cutting line are, if they vote at all, more likely to vote Yea than to vote Nay, we will — conditional on the legislator coordinates — obtain *accurate* estimates of the roll call cutting lines. Similarly, conditional on the roll call coordinates, we will obtain accurate estimates of the legislator coordinates. The estimates could be improved by using abstentions. If, for example, abstentions tended to be from legislators close to the cutting line, the pattern of abstentions on a roll call would provide additional information about the cutting line. The gain from this information would not be substantial given the large number of observations available to us for estimating both the roll call coordinates and the legislator positions.

3. In applying the model to elections, one is often concerned with what happens if the election ends in a tie. In the case of Congress, tied votes are broken in the House by the speaker and in the Senate by the vice president. We assume that the speaker and the vice president always vote in such cases and that their preferences are common knowledge. This assumption implies that a decisive voter will always change the outcome completely rather than, in the standard electoral model, creating or breaking a tie. Thus, B is appropriately defined. In measuring B, we ignore the measurement error induced by the fact that our values of the legislator ideal points and outcome coordinates are estimates. We also ignore the measurement error introduced by our excluding the stochastic portion of utility.

4. This approach was followed by Cohen and Noll (1991).

5. We approximated distance to Washington using the software we had developed for VOTEVIEW. The U.S. maps of congressional districts prepared by Martis

(1989) were digitized into a Euclidean coordinate system. For each congressional district, we had, for display purposes, placed a center-dot coordinate at roughly the geographical center of the district. LNDIS was based on the Euclidean distance between the center dot and the coordinates representing Washington, D.C. The usual problems with the curvature of the earth and rail lines not following the minimum distance apply. These should be minor inaccuracies relative to the disparities in distance between, say, Virginia and Montana.

6. Cohen and Noll (1991) analyzed abstention on eight roll calls on the Clinch River Breeder Reactor project that took place between 1975 and 1982. They used the members' participation rate (one minus the abstention rate) for the year as an independent variable. The smallest t-statistic on this variable, in any of their three specifications, was −11.0. The largest t-statistic (in magnitude) of any of fifteen other variables in any specification was 3.57. These results attest to the importance of controlling for the legislator's overall propensity. As against using the participation rate for an entire year, our ABSAVG and ABSPREV variables have the slight advantage of being predetermined.

7. We note that the problem we have of applying the classical decision-theoretic model to roll calls also pertains to mass elections where voters have more than one choice, as in simultaneously voting for president and representative. Typically, the problem is handled in empirical work by adding independent variables. For example, equations for turnout in the races for Senate seats might include a dummy variable for presidential years and another dummy for the presence of a gubernatorial race. The joint turnout decision is rarely modeled explicitly.

8. Shirking was first discussed, and the literature referenced, in chapter 4.

9. Lame-duck sessions are once again the rule, perhaps a symptom of the gridlock brought about by polarization. They have occurred in the 103rd, 105th, 106th, 107th, and 108th Congresses.

10. Cohen and Noll (1991) also make this prediction but with a different motivation. They hypothesize that legislators are more likely to abstain on bills that are less salient to constituents. They also hypothesize that constituents are more sensitive to being on the losing side of an issue than to being on the winning side. As a result, a vote for the winning side is less salient than a vote for the losing side. Hence it is less costly for a legislator to abstain if the legislator's constituents support the winning side.

11. United States Constitution, Art. 1, sec. 5, par. 1.

12. Note that being present but abstaining does not prevent a quorum from being reached.

13. Cohen and Noll (1991, p. 99). Of course, virtually certain outcomes would be consistent with instrumental voting if most legislators have negative net voting costs, c.

14. We did exclude the votes that were plurality votes among multiple candidates for congressional offices.

15. Recall that, throughout this book, legislators voting fewer than twenty-five times in a given Congress are excluded for that Congress.

16. Of course, the logit technique does not permit computation of estimates for roll calls for which perfect classification is possible. We exclude such votes from the computations of all figures in this chapter. As these roll calls typically fit our models of turnout and voting excellently, omitting these roll calls only introduces a conservative bias.

17. The discussion of travel times is based on maps presented by Chandler (1977, pp. 84–5).
18. The percentage, like others in this section, was computed by averaging the turnout rates for the 100 Congresses. All mean differences are significantly different from 0, at the 0.05 level or better, by conventional t tests.

11

The NOMINATE Literature

After the appearance of "Patterns of Congressional Voting" (Poole and Rosenthal, 1991a) and *Congress, 1997*, the research frontier built outward from our initial work. First, researchers began making extensive use of NOMINATE scores in the analysis of American politics. Second, researchers began to use NOMINATE and related techniques to analyze many legislatures other than Congress. Third, there have been many methodological advances. For much more on this last topic, see Poole's *Spatial Models of Parliamentary Voting* (2005). We comment briefly on the second development and then concentrate our attention on the topic most central to this volume, the substance of American politics.

The Globalization of NOMINATE

Applications of roll call scaling to other voting bodies have spread over the globe almost as much as that can of Sherwin-Williams paint. We have studies of the United Nations General Assembly (Voeten, 2000, 2001), the European Parliament (Hix, Noury, and Roland, 2005, 2006; Hix, 1999, 2001, 2002, 2004; Hix, Kreppel, and Noury, 2003; Noury, 2002), the Czech Parliament (Noury and Mielcova, 2005), the Russian Duma (Myagakov and Kiewiet 1996), the British House of Commons (Schonhardt-Bailey, 2003, 2006), Brazil (Desposato, 2001, 2006a, 2006b), a variety of National Assemblies in Latin America (Morgenstern, 2004), the Korean National Assembly (Jun and Hix, 2006) and the French Fourth Republic (Rosenthal and Voeten, 2004). A relevant characteristic of the large majority of these studies is that, echoing chapter 3, they show low dimensionality, at most two.[1] This low dimensionality occurs even when there are no formal parties (the UN) or many parties (Czech Republic and France). These findings suggest that the need to form parliamentary majorities limits dimensionality.

NOMINATE and the Study of American Politics

Scores of articles have made serious use of NOMINATE coordinates in the study of American politics. The NOMINATE estimation procedures have also been applied independently to state legislatures and other voting bodies. We here comment on some of the developments. The literature is too vast for our coverage to be comprehensive and systematic. We have almost certainly failed to capture important contributions to the literature. Books and book chapters have been given much less attention than articles in refereed journals. Our efforts in the remainder of this chapter are directed to giving readers a taste of the research rather than a full and generous serving.

Sophisticated versus Sincere Voting

Sophisticated voting was the topic of chapter 7. As indicated there, Gerry Mackie (2003) conducted a more systematic analysis of the votes we looked at in that chapter. Additional important work has been carried out by Jeffery A. Jenkins and colleagues.

In work with Brian Sala (Jenkins and Sala, 1998), Jenkins contested the traditional notion that the House broke the deadlocked election of 1824 by awarding the presidency to John Quincy Adams after a "corrupt bargain" that had short-changed Andrew Jackson. Jenkins and Sala used Poole's (2000) common space technique to combine House and Senate scores for members of the House and the three candidates, Adams, Crawford, and Jackson. When the Electoral College fails to deliver a winner, the House votes by state delegations, with each state having one vote. Jenkins and Sala find that the state delegations acted as if they voted sincerely; that is, the states that voted for Adams were "closer" to Adams than to the other two candidates.[2, 3]

In methodologically similar work with Timothy Nokken, Jenkins studied how the Republican Party in the House was forged in the speakership election that proceeded over several ballots in the winter of 1855-56. Because there were more than two candidates receiving votes, these votes were not included in the D-NOMINATE estimation. Jenkins and Nokken found that sincere spatial models accounted for the voting. For example, there was over 90 percent correct classification on a ballot with votes for Richardson, Banks, and Fuller (Jenkins and Nokken, 2000, pp. 111–112). The findings in this paper and those in Jenkins and Sala (1998) buttress our argument, in chapter 7, that voting in Congress is far more ideological than strategic.

In two very important papers with coauthors, Jenkins continued his work on strategic behavior by providing a far more systematic treatment to the study of killer amendments than we were able to develop in chapter 7. The first, by

Michael C. Munger and Jenkins, presents a formal theory that can be used to test for the presence of killer amendments. For a killer amendment to be observed, a bill has to be defeated after an amendment has passed. For the amendment to be a true killer, Jenkins and Munger (2003) show that a requirement is that the two votes have different cleavages—the cutting lines should not be parallel, that is, on different dimensions, and substantial numbers of voters (see the figures of chapter 7) should fall in each of the four pie slices demarcated by the cutting lines. From this perspective, it is not surprising that killer amendments generally involve *race* issues, which arise whenever a strong second dimension is present in American history. Jenkins and Munger discovered two Reconstruction-era killer amendments, both of which involved race. The second paper, by Charles J. Finnochairo and Jenkins, studied all House roll calls from 1953 through 2004. These authors catalogued all final passage votes that were defeated but had been preceded by an amendment that had passed. Over the thirty-two-year period covered in their analysis, Finnochairo and Jenkins (2005) found that only the Powell amendment, discussed in chapter 7, was a "likely" killer amendment and that only four additional bills had "possible" killer amendments. This is compelling evidence on the prevalence of sincere voting in the House.[4] One would, of course, like to extend this study to the Senate, where amendments are more freely introduced. One would also like to investigate the possibility that amendments passed in one house kill a bill by making the conference report unacceptable to the other house (Nunez and Rosenthal, 2004).

The work of Jenkins and his coauthors and our own work in chapter 7 assesses strategic voting on the basis of NOMINATE coordinates estimated from an entire legislature (W-NOMINATE) or set of legislatures (DW-NOMINATE). This methodology has been subject to an important critique by Joshua Clinton and Adam Meirowitz (2001, 2003, 2004). One problem is that some forms of strategic behavior may contaminate the estimation of ideal points using the assumption of sincere voting (or voting over sophisticated equivalents) with common perceptions of outcome locations. We are not inclined to view this problem as a major one, since, when ideal points are estimated from hundreds of roll call votes over a large set of issues, the biases are likely to wash out. A second problem is that a given agenda tree may contain important, issue-specific dimensions that are ignored by the broad brush of NOMINATE. It thus may be useful to impose dimensionality a priori in terms of the substantive issues. Clinton and Meirowitz use the example of the Compromise of 1790 with one dimension for the location of the federal capitol and another for assumption of state debt. A third problem is that the study of an agenda can clearly show how it should constrain the estimation of legislators and roll calls. Scaling methods should take this into account as much as possible. For example, with reference to the Powell amendment covered in chapter 7, the Yea location for when the Powell amendment was voted against the una-mended bill should be the same Yea location as when the amended bill was voted against the status quo. Finally, with reference to the fact that killer amendments will succeed when there is a mixture of "sincere" vs. "sophisti-cated" voting, one can alter the estimation to allow different groups to perceive different bill locations on a given vote. For example, when the House voted on the conference report on the bankruptcy bill in 2002 (Nunez and Rosen-thal, 2004), the report incorporated Senator Schumer's amendments on abor-tion clinics. Many Democrats saw the bill as a conservative, anti-consumer bill while many Republicans saw the bill as a liberal, pro-choice bill. Both-ends-against-the-middle voting killed the bill.

Clinton and Meirowitz (2001, 2003, 2004), in perhaps the most important methodological innovation since the original NOMINATE model in Poole and Rosenthal (1985), have developed estimation techniques that allow for broad testing of different hypotheses about both agenda constraints and perceptual differences. Not only does specifying the models for these techniques require a lot more attention to detail than does NOMINATE, applications suffer from the results not being embedded in the larger historical context of roll call vot-ing. Intensive use of these methods should, nonetheless, permit a deeper under-standing of legislative behavior.

Institutional Analysis: Rules versus Elections

Eric Schickler (2000) made extensive use of DW-NOMINATE scores to study changes in the rules of the House of Representatives in the period 1865–1997. He computed the median score in each Congress and the standard deviations of scores as measures of party homogeneity. He used the data to test several the-ories of when rules were likely to be changed. He found most support for the hypothesis that rules change as the ideological balance in the House changes. Specifically, "Rules changes that advantage the majority party and its leaders are more likely when the floor median moves in the direction favoring the majority party. Rules changes that reduce majority party advantages are more likely when the floor median moves in the direction favoring the minority party" (Schickler, 2000, p. 275).

A similar study for 1789–1844 was carried out by Evelyn C. Fink (2000). She used D-NOMINATE scores to develop measures of party conflict. She found that conflict was related to the adoption of more restrictive rules but was unrelated to the easing of the rules.

Gary Cox and Mathew McCubbins (2005) use DW-NOMINATE exten-sively in their study of the rules changes in the House of Representatives in the 1880s and 1890s. The "Reed Rules" were an historic watershed because they ensured that a majority of the majority party was able to block legislation that it did not like. Cox and McCubbins develop the Procedural Cartel Model (PCM) to account for the behavior of the majority party *after* the adoption of the Reed rules and compare it to alternative models using various measures of House activity during the post-Reconstruction era. Because there are enough Houses *before* the Reed rules were permanently adopted, they are able to perform statistical tests using indicators such as "roll rates" that show the clear superiority of the PCM.

Sarah A. Binder and Steven S. Smith (1998) use first- and second-dimension D-NOMINATE scores in their study of twelve Senate votes on cloture reform between 1919 and 1979. These two scores are nearly always the only or the most significant variables in their multivariate analysis. They use these results to conclude that preferences on cloture rules are driven by political interests rather than a concern for freedom of speech and minority rights.

Jeffery A. Jenkins (1998) analyzed a specific change in House institutions, the shift from select committees to standing committees that occurred in the House between 1810 and 1825. Jenkins studies both demand- and supply-side forces in the process of institutional change. On the demand side, he argues that increased heterogeneity in the majority, Jeffersonian coalition would lead to a demand for a change in the system of bill referral. He uses D-NOMINATE scores to document increasing heterogeneity within the Jeffersonians.

The work we have covered in this section argues for the importance of the distribution of ideology for internal changes in rules. On the other hand, in this book we have argued that internal rules are not all that important, at least from the perspective of changes in the distribution of ideology being quite similar across the two chambers. In chapter 5, we showed that the two chambers differed the most in the influence of farm state progressive Republican senators in the 1920s. This difference, however, appears to reflect differences in apportionment, with the thinly populated farm states being over-represented in the Senate, rather than in internal rules. Similarly, Sean Gailmard and Jenkins (2006) show that "rolls," where a minority party picks off enough majority party members to defeat a majority of the majority party, are very infrequent in the Senate as well as in the House, with the interaction of ideology and the institutional feature of the filibuster, computed from NOMINATE scores, having very little effect.

The importance of electoral (as against institutional rules) is pursued further in Gailmard and Jenkins (2005). Recall that in chapter 10 we showed that the passage of the Seventeenth Amendment, providing for direct election of senators, made a significant change in the turnout of senators, with turnout falling after the amendment as, we conjectured, senators spent more time at home min-

istering to constituents. Gailmard and Jenkins support this conjecture by showing that the average NOMINATE score of a state's Senate delegation became
more sensitive to constituency preferences, as measured by the presidential
vote, after passage of the Seventeenth Amendment. At the same time, after controlling for split-delegation effects, senators exhibited more diversity in voting behavior; as they were freed from the monitoring of state legislatures, they
were freer to pursue the objectives of either personal ideology or personal-
support coalition. Direct election also made a small, but significant, decrease in
polarization, after controlling for House polarization.

William Bernhard and Brian R. Sala (2006) ran W-NOMINATE for individual years to study the effect of the Seventeenth Amendment on how senators
adjusted their ideological position when up for reelection. They concluded
that senators polarized before the Seventeenth Amendment and moderated
afterwards. This result and the corresponding one in Gailmard and Jenkins
(2005) seems to run counter to our claim, in chapter 4, that there is little movement in spatial position throughout the careers of twentieth-century legislators.
Methodological caveats aside, we note that the estimated movement is reasonably small in magnitude. The House, as well as the Senate, was polarizing
for much of their sample period before the Seventeenth Amendment and moderating afterwards (see Figure 4.11). We continue to believe that the issues that
confront American society—slavery, civil rights, the rise of conservatism as a
response to the New Deal and its aftermath, technological change that pro-
moted large corporations—drive polarization. Indeed, the Seventeenth Amendment itself may have reflected a "progressive" response to the polarization of
the late nineteenth century.

Another indication of sensitivity to constituency preferences is contained
in the study of James Fowler (2005). He looked at the case where a party had
two different candidates for election to the Senate in successive elections.
Where possible, he compared the common space scores of these candidates.
His major conclusion was that the later candidate was likely to be more conservative if the Republicans had obtained a large vote share in the previous
election. The result is an interesting variant to our theme that replacement is the
driving force of change in Congress.

Rules themselves, we add, appear to make little difference to NOMINATE
scores. In an important paper, Jason M. Roberts and Steven S. Smith (2003)
observe that there was a dramatic increase in roll call votes taken in the Committee of the Whole beginning in 1971. They then ran DW-NOMINATE separately for Committee of the Whole votes and for full House votes. The DW-
NOMINATE scores correlate at 0.97 for the two procedures although the
distribution of cutpoints differs sharply. This work, therefore, confirms the

robustness of DW-NOMINATE as long as there are "enough" cutpoints everywhere to pin down the legislator locations (see McCarty, Poole, and Rosenthal, 2001). In chapter 3 we showed that estimates are robust to sorting by type of issue and in Poole (2005) and McCarty, Poole, and Rosenthal (2006) that they are robust to controlling for the distribution of cutpoints and to computing separate estimates excluding southern representatives.

On the other hand, institutional structure may make a great deal of difference to the interaction of Congress and a regulatory agency. Charles R. Shipan (2004) uses actions by the Food and Drug Administration to test a formal model of pivotal politics (Krehbiel, 1998). Common space NOMINATE stores and the assumption that the FDA is largely the agent of the president are used to classify each year from 1947 to 1995 into three decision-making regimes: floor, committee-floor, and gate-keeping. The temporal variation of monitoring activities nicely follows the theoretical predictions of the model.

Party Discipline

There is an active debate as to the extent to which parties discipline their members' voting beyond the discipline that is reflected in the overall ideological position or NOMINATE score. To attack this issue, Hager and Talbert (2000) used NOMINATE scores directly. Snyder and Groseclose (2000) used an alternative scaling technique. Cox and Poole (2002) used a technique closely related to NOMINATE. McCarty, Poole, and Rosenthal (2001) used a variant of Poole's one-dimensional optimal classification procedure. As we, in the last two cited publications, have had an ample say on both sides of this debate, we here refer readers to the literature.

Polarization

Political polarization, which we first identified over twenty years ago (Poole and Rosenthal, 1984), has become an important research topic. One avenue of research concerns how polarization in Congress relates to preferences in the mass electorate. Polarization influences the ability of the mass electorate to distinguish between the parties. This is shown in a study by Marc J. Hetherington (2001), who used a polarization measure similar to ours. David W. Brady and Hahrie Han (2004) present evidence that preferences on issues polarized in terms of partisan identification and presidential voting before the recent period of polarization in Congress. They then show how polarization in Congress changes as the result of replacement (see chapter 4) of members whose congressional voting was not in accord with constituent preferences.

Two earlier studies anticipate the results of Brady and Han. D. Roderick Kiewiet and Langche Zeng (1993) used NOMINATE scores in a study of congressional career decisions for the period 1947–1986. Although ideology had no significant effect on Republican representatives, more conservative Democrats were more likely than liberal ones to retire than to run for reelection while more liberal Democrats were more likely to run for higher office. Kiewiet and Zeng note that these decisions can contribute to the polarization we discussed in chapter 4. Kevin S. Price (2002) looked at House cohorts that entered and exited during the Eisenhower presidency. His findings support our idea that change in Congress is largely a matter of replacement and our claim that Republicans became more moderate in the 1950s.

Recent, sophisticated work by Jamie L. Carson (2005) adds to our knowledge of replacement and its effect on polarization. In a model of challenger entry and incumbent retirement decisions, Carson finds that extremists were less likely to retire than moderates between 1975 and 2000, although the effect is statistically significant only for the Senate. In the period from 1874 to 1914, also polarizing for most of the period, Carson and Jason M. Roberts (2005) find that quality challengers were more likely to emerge against moderates and extremist incumbents were more likely to win reelection.

Jeffery A. Jenkins, Erik Schickler and Jamie L. Carson (2004) obtain a result similar to that of Brady and Han for a much earlier period, 1879–1913. They show that our polarization measure is tracked, for 1879–1913, by polarization of congressional districts both in terms of presidential voting and the value added in manufacturing.

Another body of research focuses on the policy effects of polarization. Nolan McCarty and Rose Razaghian (1999) use a polarization measure similar to those shown in chapter 4 to model the length of time required for the Senate to confirm appointees. They looked at over 3,000 appointments from 1885 to the present. Polarization creates delay (a form of gridlock); the delay is exacerbated by the interaction of polarization and divided government. Tajuana D. Massie, Thomas G. Hansford, and Donald R. Songer (2002) focused on nominations to lower federal courts. These authors looked at delay as being influenced not only by divided government but also by the W-NOMINATE distance between the president and the home state senator. David E. Lewis (2002) investigated agency terminations. Charles R. Shipan and Megan L. Shannon (2003) studied Supreme Court confirmations, using a measure of the distance between the president and the majority party in the Senate in periods of divided government. John J. Coleman (1999) uses the within-party distance measures we developed in chapter 4 to address the debate over whether divided government impedes the passage of legislation.

The Economics of Constituency Politics

Jeffery Jenkins and Marc Weidenmier (1999) present a refinement to our analysis in chapter 6 on the comparison of economic and ideological models. Their paper compares voting on the first bank of the United States, in 1811, under the Federalist-Jeffersonian party system to voting on the second bank, in 1816, during the one-party Era of Good Feelings. While the first vote was ideological, the second was much less so. (For a similar result on bankruptcy, see Berglöf and Rosenthal, 2006.) Economic measures of state taxation on banks and of population growth were highly significant in the second period. Indeed, the data presented in Figure 6.3 suggest that economic models will outperform ideological ones in the absence of a party system. These results suggest that, while economic interests are undoubtedly always present, they are filtered and deflected when they must be expressed through party politics.

Similar results occur in other studies. Robert Fleck and Christopher Kilby (2001) found that the level of USAID spending in a congressional district was unrelated to voting for foreign aid expenditures once one controlled for W-NOMINATE scores. Republicans representing Beltway districts were, however, more likely to be supportive of foreign aid. Richard Sicotte (1999) found that D-NOMINATE scores were the most important determinant of voting on the Shipping Act of 1916, a bill that established a large government-owned merchant marine and shipbuilding operation. Colleen M. Callahan, Judith A. McDonald, and Anthony Patrick O'Brien (1994) find that, of several economic variables, only unemployment remains significant once NOMINATE scores are introduced in the analysis of voting on the Smoot-Hawley tariff bill in 1929 and 1930. Roberta Romano (1997) finds little evidence that variables related to future markets improve upon ideology in roll calls on future markets.

Douglas A. Irwin and Randall S. Kroszner (1999) show that D-NOMINATE scores are related to Senate voting for trade liberalization in passing the Reciprocal Trade Agreement Act of 1934 while, controlling for ideology, neither party nor export and import interests are significant. On the other hand, the interaction of economic interests and party, not ideology, is what drove voting on renewal of the Act in 1945. The analysis of Irwin and Kroszner resonates with our analysis of food stamps in chapter 6. The mapping of an issue to ideology can change as legislated policies change the economic interests influencing the legislator. From an analysis of 219 trade liberalization votes in the House from 1963 to 1992, Jeffrey W. Ladewig (2005) concludes that the non-ideological period of voting on trade policy ended by 1979 and that votes have once again become polarized. More specifically, scaled ideal points on trade policy votes become increasingly consistent with the overall liberal-conservative lineup measured by NOMINATE.

Vincent G. Moscardelli, Moshe Haspel, and Richard S. Wike (1998) present a variant of the ideology versus economic interest horse race that is informative as to when both-ends-against-the middle is likely to occur. These authors studied the failure of the Republican House leadership to pass a campaign finance "reform" bill in 1996. They looked at the votes of Republicans. By far the most significant variable was D-NOMINATE distance to the left of Speaker Newt Gingrich, but, at the same time those more to the right of Gingrich were also less supportive. Contributions from Labor PACs were related to opposing the bill but constituency contributions were not.

Another study that ran a horse race within parties is Richard S. Conley's (1999) analysis of support for fast-track legislation in 1991 and 1997. This is an issue where economic interests, represented by blue-collar workers, appear to be as or more important than ideology, particularly for Republicans.

Our analysis in chapter 6 and those of the authors just reviewed argue that complex economic interests in the constituencies are largely expressed through simple liberal-conservative voting in Congress. To be sure, the studies just surveyed often find important effects for economic variables. On the other hand, ideology typically remains an important predictor. Moreover, we conjecture there is selection bias in the publication process. Studies that look for economic effects and fail to find them also fail to get published.

Roll call voting leads to policy. An innovative study by Matthew Potoski and Jeffrey Talbert (2000) argues that the policy outputs of the votes result in complex multidimensional allocations to congressional districts. They used NOMINATE to scale over 1,000 distributive awards programs for each of the three years 1994, 1995, and 1996.[5] If a district has received an award from a program, it has "voted" Yea on the program. The programs exhibit relatively high dimensionality with a second dimension that is far more important than a second dimension is in Congress.

The presence of federal awards suggests that not only do economic interests in constituencies have a potential influence on roll call voting behavior but also that electoral interests in Washington may affect the allocation of resources to constituencies. Fleck (1999) used NOMINATE scores to study how the distribution of federal funds across the states was shifted by the Roosevelt administration from 1933 to 1938 so that states that were moderately conservative tended to do better than states that were more extreme. That is, as Roosevelt sought to expand his base, funds flowed to states that, unlike the South, had not traditionally supported the Democrats. After electoral losses in the midterm elections of 1938, the administration abandoned its goal of expansion and directed its funds to maintaining support in moderately liberal states.

Policy is also the focus of work by Brandace Canes-Wrone and Kenneth W. Shotts (2004). These authors were interested in how presidential budgetary policies reflected public opinion. They used Poole's common space scores (derived from NOMINATE) to measure the congruence of policies with presidential and congressional preferences. The president's position was measured by Poole through the *Congressional Quarterly* presidential support scores, using the methods we developed in chapter 8.

Michele L. Swers (1998) found that the DW-NOMINATE score was generally the most significant predictor on women's issue votes in the 103rd House but that, after controlling for ideology and constituency characteristics, Republican women representatives were very likely to vote for the "female" alternative. This study is another nail in the coffin of a simple median voter story since the sex ratio is close to 50–50 in all constituencies. It offers support for the view that personal ideology or support coalitions are important determinants of roll call voting.

Historical Analysis: Race and Other Topics

Cobb and Jenkins (2001) add to our knowledge of mid-nineteenth-century politics by studying the roll call voting behavior of black representatives during Reconstruction (1869–75). They used the "Ratings" option in VOTEVIEW to construct a RACESCORE variable that indexed voting on measures, such as voting rights, of particular concern to blacks. They found important distinctions between black and white representatives on the index and on W-NOMINATE scores after controlling for constituency characteristics. This echoes recent findings of McCarty, Poole, and Rosenthal (2006) who show that personal characteristics, such as race and gender, affect NOMINATE scores even with controls for party and constituency characteristics.

Race is also a concern in Jenkins and Charles Stewart (2005). These authors studied votes on the "gag rule" on antislavery petitions, an antebellum device intended to shield the Democratic Party from becoming divided over slavery. They show, complementing our work on realignment in chapter 3, that the first gag rule enactments in 1836 were first-dimension votes, along party lines. As slavery intensified as an issue—in part, from popular resentment of the gag rule—voting shifted to include the second, regional or race, dimension, until the gag rule was repealed in 1845.

David Lublin (1997) explores race and politics in the late twentieth century. He uses D-NOMINATE to study minority representation in the House of Representatives. He finds, using D-NOMINATE to measure the ideology of representatives, that the practice of concentrating minorities in a handful of majority-minority districts allows conservative Republicans to maximize their influence. He argues for districting that would slightly dilute minority concentration and argues that this would maximize minority representation in the House. In contrast, Kenneth W. Shotts (2003) argues that racial redistricting has increased the number of southern representatives to the left of the House median (as calculated from DW-NOMINATE) scores.

Some other work can be covered more briefly:

1. Jenkins and Stewart (1998) provide substantial insight into important House votes that occurred between 1817 and 1823. In particular, this piece provides an in-depth use of NOMINATE to study the Missouri Compromise—and how the Compromise related to the committee structure of Congress—that amplifies the discussion in McCarty, Poole, and Rosenthal (2002); the piece also provides insights into the Panic of 1819 that complements Bolton and Rosenthal (2002) and Berglöf and Rosenthal (2006).

2. Jenkins and Stewart (2003) use NOMINATE scores to show that the switch from secret to open voting for the speakership in the 25th, 26th, and 27th Congresses was largely a matter of first-dimension voting with the D-NOMINATE scores effectively separating those moderate Whigs who sided with the highly unified Democrats. The same authors show, in contrast, that internal party ideological divisions were generally unimportant to internal party splits on voting for the clerk of the House in the 25th to the 37th House.

3. Jenkins (2004, 2005) has studied 732 contested elections (who gets seated) votes in the House and Senate. He finds that, in terms of aggregate classification, the NOMINATE scores somewhat outperform party-line voting although the party model outperforms NOMINATE on a greater number of individual roll calls in the House. These contested elections would appear to be an ideal context for a partisan model to outperform an ideological model. The fact that ideology does well on contested election votes supports our claim that ideology is a better, more fine-grained measure than party.

4. Jenkins, Crespin, and Carson (2005) studied how the positions of exiting members who retired or sought higher office may have changed in their last six months of service and whether the change was greater on procedural votes or on final-passage votes. The analysis was based on W-NOMINATE run separately for final-passage votes and for procedural votes in the last six months of Congresses beginning with the 94th. While there were some significant effects expected from different incentives that face exiting members, these effects were small compared to the range

of W-NOMINATE scores. The only substantial effect, in line with our discussion in chapter 4, came from party-switchers.

5. John Carey (1994) also finds significant but small effects in movement in the last session of terms for representatives who leave Congress to run for statewide offices. They have more movement and movement in the direction of their state delegations.[6]

6. Alana Jeydel and Andrew J. Taylor (2003) used NOMINATE scores as a control variable in a study of gender differences in the ability of representatives to enact legislation. Ideology does not appear to be related to effectiveness.

7. Susan W. Johnson and Donald R. Songer (2002) relate the liberalism of the decisions of district court judges to the W-NOMINATE scores of the appointing presidents and the difference between the W-NOMINATE scores of home state senators and the average score of the Senate delegation of the party. Presidential appointments of district court judges are generally subject to approval of senators from the state of the judicial district. While the effects are small, more liberal presidents and more liberal home state senators lead to more liberal judicial decisions. Similarly, Songer and Martha Humphries Ginn (2002) investigated if decisions by appeals court judges were related to the ideological preferences of the appointing president and the senatorial delegation of the appointee's state. They found a strong effect for presidential preferences but a weaker one for senatorial preferences.

8. Another study using president-chamber differences in NOMINATE scores is the analysis of the issuing of executive orders by Christopher J. Deering and Forrest Maltzman (1999). They also measure differences in NOMINATE scores between the presidents and the veto pivots. As the differences grow, they find fewer executive orders, in accord with the theoretical view that the president will not issue orders likely to be overturned.

9. David Auerswald and Maltzman (2003) look at veto pivots in the Senate relative to the president in a study of when reservations were attached to Senate ratification of treaties. Using NOMINATE to estimate pivot positions is also found in a study of the Supreme Court confirmation process by Timothy R. Johnson and Jason M. Roberts (2004).

10. Andrew J. Taylor (2003) used DW-NOMINATE scores in studying campaign contributions from the tobacco and alcoholic beverage industries.

11. Two innovative studies made use of the DW-NOMINATE bill coordinates as well as the legislator coordinates. Alan E. Wiseman (2004) mea-

sured "Veto Threat" as the distance between President Clinton's ideal point and the bill coordinate. He found that the size of the Yea vote for the bill bore a significant negative relationship to the threat of a veto. Brian R. Sala and James F. Spriggs, II (2004) used legislator and bill coordinates in a study of the interaction between Congress and the Supreme Court.

12. Eric D. Lawrence, Forrest Maltzman, and Paul J. Wahlbeck (2001) used D-NOMINATE scores in a study of "The Politics of Speaker Cannon's Committee Assignments."

13. William G. Howell and David E. Lewis (2002) studied the conditions under which federal agencies are created by executive action as compared to legislated statute. They use NOMINATE scores to construct measures of congressional weakness. They find that executive action becomes more likely as Congress becomes weaker.

14. Glen S. Krutz (2005) studied which bills introduced in Congress managed to get as far as receiving committee action. As a control, he used the NOMINATE distance between the bill sponsor's ideal point and that of the committee chair. The expected negative effect was found in both chambers but was statistically significant only for the House.

15. William T. Bianco and Itai Sened (2005) estimate the uncovered set in two dimensions. (The uncovered set is a region in the center of the space that is precisely defined in voting theory.) They do this for the state legislature NOMINATE estimates of Aldrich and Battista (2002) and for the 106th House of Representatives using not only W-NOMINATE but the Heckman and Snyder (1996) and Clinton, Jackman, and Rivers (2004) methods. There are differences between the three scaling methods but these are largely questions of the second dimension. We have shown that the 106th Congress is really unidimensional. It is not surprising that the methods give different and noisy results when imposing a second dimension on the errors from unidimensional voting. On the first dimension, the uncovered set is on the left edge of the Republican Party for all three scaling methods. That is, the uncovered set is essentially the median voter.

Other American Legislatures

NOMINATE has been used to scale a number of state legislatures. Gerald C. Wright and Brian F. Schaffner (2002) compared the Kansas Senate to Nebraska's unicameral legislature. (They also used W-NOMINATE to scale candidate positions measured by the National Political Awareness Test.) In Kansas, roll call voting was strongly unidimensional. In contrast, there was little spatial structure to voting in the Nebraska legislature. Fits there were as poor as those observed in the periods of political instability in the antebellum Congress.

John H. Aldrich and James S. Coleman Battista (2002) used NOMINATE to scale not only Nebraska but also 100–175 votes for ten other states, all in years spanning 1997–1999. They do not report the fit of the spatial model but do report that six of their eleven states have polarization of first-dimension scores similar to that observed for Congress in chapter 4. They find that polarization is more likely when electoral politics are more competitive.

Like Congress, the California legislature is highly unidimensional. This result appears in Elisabeth R. Gerber and Jeffrey B. Lewis (2004). They used the interest-group technique we developed in chapter 8 to tie together the California Assembly, the California Senate, and the United States House for 1993 and 1994. They were then able to compare the NOMINATE scores of Los Angeles County legislators in all three legislative bodies to the preferences of constituents as estimated from 2.8 million individual ballots cast in the election of 1992. They found that the NOMINATE scores reflect not only partisan effects but also median voter preferences. The effect of median voter preferences, however, is attenuated as district heterogeneity increases. This last finding is consistent with our finding, in chapter 6, that aggregate measures of constituency interests do not perform well as predictors of roll call voting.

Thad Kousser, Jeffrey B. Lewis, and Seth Masket (2006) perform an innovative experiment provided by California's 2003 recall election of Governor Gray Davis—held at the midpoint of the state's legislative session—to test theories about the strategic entry of candidates and the ideological mobility of legislators. They show that electorally vulnerable members of the legislature moderated their positions somewhat between Governor Schwarzenegger's election and the 2004 elections. This runs counter to our basic findings of stable positions in Congress. However, the situation in California, with term-limited legislators, makes the comparison to Congress somewhat problematic.

Jeffery A. Jenkins obtained an interesting counterpoint to our analysis of Congress by studying the House of the Confederate States of America (Jenkins, 1999, 2000). He used W-NOMINATE to scale the Confederate House. He found that the U.S. and Confederate Houses in the Civil War were both unidimensional with splits on issues that concerned "central-state authority" with regard to conscription, habeas corpus, slavery, impressment, and war finance (Jenkins, 1999, p. 153). The finding of unidimensionality echoes our own finding, in Table 3.2, that there were no important second-dimension issues in the Civil War Houses, the 37th and 38th. Jenkins calls our attention to the point that the issues that map onto the main dimension of conflict will be quite different in wartime as against peacetime. It is interesting that there was no realignment after the Civil War since both types of issues mapped onto the same underlying dimension.

On the other hand, Jenkins attributes the sharply lower fit for the Confederate House, in comparison to the United States House, to the absence of a party system in the Confederate House. The low fits were comparable to those we observed in the Era of Good Feelings and the spatial collapse in the 32nd House following the Compromise of 1850. The work of Voeten (2000), who scaled the United Nations General Assembly using W-NOMINATE, however, shows that good fits can occur in the absence of a party system. More basically, it seems to us, poor fits will occur in periods of political instability.[7]

Jenkins (2000) also studied the stability of the positions of individual members by computing correlations similar to those we report in Table 4.2. Some members of the U.S. House later served in the Confederate House. Jenkins reports that their positions in the two chambers were virtually uncorrelated. This result echoes both our Table 4.2 findings of lower correlations in period of political instability and our finding and that of Rosenthal and Voeten (2004), Hager and Talbert (2000), Nokken (2000), McCarty, Poole, and Rosenthal (2001), and Nokken and Poole (2004) that members who change political parties undergo substantial change in position. Those individuals who switched from the Union to the Confederacy switched from a stable party system to an unstable legislature without a strong party system. On the other hand, Jenkins found more stability of position within the Confederate House, especially as time progressed and more stable coalitions formed.

In addition to Congress and the fifty state legislatures, there are probably many other institutions within the United States that have fairly large memberships and use roll call voting. Voting patterns in these institutions can be analyzed with NOMINATE methods. For the National Collegiate Athletic Association (NCAA), Lawrence DeBrock and Wallace Hendricks (1996) have scaled 248 roll calls voted on by 284 Division I schools between 1984 and 1996. They use the results to contrast economic and non-economic theories of the objectives of NCAA member schools. Although voting in the NCAA appears somewhat noisier than in Congress, it is still largely unidimensional, even though the NCAA does not have a party system.

Summary: When Are Legislatures Low-Dimensional?

When does the spatial model capture roll call voting in legislatures? When is voting low, even one-dimensional? These basic questions tie together much of the literature we have reviewed. Some degree of political stability appears to be necessary for the spatial model to fit. Instability was present in the two periods of congressional history where the spatial model failed to account for the data. It also appears to be a factor in the failed legislature of the Confederacy. On the other hand, stability does not appear to be sufficient for a good fit. The evidence comes from the unicameral legislature of Nebraska, a state better known for Warren Buffet and national championships in college football than for political unrest.

The poor scaling of Nebraksa might suggest that parties are necessary. However, the results for the NCAA and for the United Nations show that a formal party system in the legislature is not necessary for a good fit. Furthermore, a *two*-party system is not necessary for a largely unidimensional fit. The Czech Republic is unidimensional with multiple parties. These results show that the conditions that produce low-dimensional spatial voting are as yet not fully understood. Given the power of the spatial model of voting in legislatures and the findings of psychologists that show low dimensionality in the perceptions of similarities and preferential choice data (Poole, 2005), this is an important open area for research.

Notes

1. For a more detailed discussion of some of these studies, see Poole and Rosenthal (2001).
2. Jenkins and Morris (2006) use a similar technique to investigate the "what if" the presidential election of 1860 had been decided by the House of Representatives.
3. In another paper dealing with the 1824 election, Carson and Engstrom (2005) used DW-NOMINATE as a control in studying whether representatives who had voted for Adams were punished by voters in districts that had voted heavily for Jackson.
4. Conversely, Wawro and Schickler (2004) use NOMINATE results to establish that tariff votes from 1827 to 1930 were unidimensional, thus appropriate to a test of the pivotal politics model of Krehbiel (1998).
5. Another use of NOMINATE to scale non-roll call data is found in Ichniowski, Shaw, and Prennushi (1997).
6. This and many other studies have a number of methodological problems that result from incomparability of NOMINATE scores across independent scalings, and the imprecise estimation of the positions of more extreme members, a problem that is aggravated by carrying out separate estimations for subsamples of the data.
7. We note that we strongly disagree with Jenkins on his use of the Snyder and Groseclose (2000) method to assess party effects. See McCarty, Poole, and Rosenthal (2001).

12

The Unidimensional Congress

The United States of America, and its Congress, is now remarkably entering its third century with its original institutions modified but largely intact. Such stability is indeed remarkable in the larger agony of human history.

Stability did not come easily. The Civil War suggests that the Constitution of 1787 was a failure, or at least far from the glorified success story that we ingested in high school. The watershed marked by the Civil War is echoed in our analysis of roll call voting. Prior to the war, as two-party systems arose and then collapsed, there were periods when a spatial model of voting failed to fit the data. In other words, the form of coalitions on each roll call varied greatly. Another indication of instability is the far greater changes in the individual positions of legislators prior to the Civil War than in subsequent times.

After the Civil War, the modern party system arose, legislators slowed down in their movement, and the spatial model fit well. Legislators moved a little more than usual during the mass voting realignments in the 1890s and 1930s, but on the whole the changes in mass voting behavior were reflected in Congress by changes in the location of new members in the space, not by a realignment of the space. A second dimension (as had been the case a century earlier) was needed to handle the perturbation introduced by the race issue from the late 1930s to the 1970s, but the basic liberal/conservative configuration was maintained.

Because the low-dimensional spatial model fails to account for roll call voting only in the two periods when the two-party system collapsed, political parties might appear to be the critical element in promoting stable voting alignments. Stable patterns of roll call voting are, however, more than just party-related. The many scatter diagrams and histograms of legislators' ideal points that are presented in this book demonstrate that there are important distinctions within parties. The differences between an Arlen Specter or a Mark Hatfield, on the one hand, and a Phil Gramm or a Jesse Helms on the other, are visibly important to even casual observers of Washington politics. They often, as in the vote to confirm Robert Bork to the Supreme Court or, as in the 1995 vote on a balanced-budget amendment, have a real impact on policy. Our scaling technique makes internal party distinctions in a rigorous manner and does so for all of American history.

Except for those periods of American history when race was prominent on the agenda, whenever voting can be captured by the spatial model, a one-dimensional model does almost all the work. In large part, this is, as our examination of realignment suggests, because policy objectives must largely be accomplished through the party system. While a balanced-budget amendment may fail when a Mark Hatfield defects, it would never have had a ghost of a chance without solid support from Republican senators. And feminist groups, in moving to align themselves with the Democratic Party, have shown their understanding of the game.

After documenting, in chapters 3 to 5, the low-dimensional spatial character of congressional voting and, in particular, the move toward stability of voting patterns after the Civil War, we sought to confront the spatial model with alternative models of roll call voting. Chapter 6 pursued pocket-book voting on constituency interests. We gave constituency-interest models their best possible shot and found them inferior to the spatial model. In addition, we found only a marginal role for economic variables as explanations for voting on minimum wages, strip mining, food stamps, railroad regulation, and bankruptcy; the major effects were from the NOMINATE spatial utilities. Moreover, as chapter 8 showed, the evaluation of senators and representatives by some major groups with economic interests — namely labor unions and business and farm organizations — could also be accounted for by our spatial model. We did find a supplementary role for economic interests apparent both in the correlations between the voting "errors" of two senators from the same state and, in chapter 9, the tendency of minority-party committee members to support the position of the committee majority. We also showed how economic interests, even if they do not distort spatial patterns of voting, influence the mapping of economic issues onto the space.

In chapter 7, we looked at strategic voting as an alternative to the sincere or naïve spatial voting that is assumed in our estimations. One manifestation of strategic behavior, within the context of a one-dimensional model, might be both-ends-against-the-middle voting. We gave the both-ends-against-the-middle concept its best shot, and the spatial model easily withstood the challenge. As illustrated by Jesse Helms' position on minimum wages in 1990, a cantankerous conservative will, on occasion, vote with the liberals, but such out-of-character voting is too rare to be of concern. Moreover, one form of strategic voting — voting on binary-amendment agendas under complete information — is, as argued in chapter 2, fully consistent with spatial voting. The strategic votes will not bias our estimates of legislator ideal points, but interpretation of roll call outcomes coordinates will be affected. We examined the needles of strategic voting the literature has identified in the roll call haystack. Most of these well-known examples produced roll calls that fit the spatial model quite well.

The finding that the spatial model describes the pattern of roll call voting does not pin down the nature of policy produced by Congress. In chapter 4, we found that the average locations of winning outcomes were far more volatile than the average location of legislators' ideal points. Winning outcomes are consistently pulled away from the congressional center and toward the mean location of the majority party. Parties, rather than committees, appear to be the source of this policy distortion. In chapter 9, we found that throughout American history, committees had been representative of views of the floor of Congress, with the exception of the Democrat contingent on a few committees since the late 1950s. The distinction between the period since the late 1950s and earlier times attests to the value of pursuing a long-term, historical study. Much of the current political economy approach to legislatures has been based on scholars' experience with the textbook Congresses of the 1960s and 1970s. Such a time span is too short for accumulating the stylized facts that need to be explained by a theory of legislatures in general or of Congress in particular. The usefulness of the historical approach was also manifest in our discovery of chaos in a few Congresses, such as the 32nd, where we found convincing examples that there is nothing that guarantees that a one- or two-dimensional model will fit the data. Similarly, while our analysis of abstention in chapter 10 largely verified most predictions developed on the basis of the rational-choice theory of participation, the prediction that the majority side votes less was supported for only the most recent Congresses. Such an anomaly is indicative of the future research agenda that is opened by this book.

There are at least three further directions to follow. First, now that we have the capacity to extract the date of each roll call, we have the opportunity to improve, vastly, the study of dynamics. One important topic in dynamics is learning: Do legislators learn their place in the space, in which case behavior will be more variable on early votes, or do they arrive with pre-wired ideology? Another is the dynamics of spatial collapse: When and how do stable patterns of voting fall apart? When and how does a new alignment emerge? A second important direction is to incorporate nonvoting into the spatial estimation. A third is to widen the spatial study of Congress to the study of the larger society. This can be done, not only (as we show in our study of interest groups in chapter 8) with newspapers and other sources taking positions, but with mass voting data: Citizens have the opportunity to "rate" their representatives every two years.

Epilogue 1997: Congress in its Third Century

Our study of Congress was restricted to the first 100 Congresses, or two centuries of roll call voting. From the turn of the century until the mid 1970s, we have, with some interruptions, seen a decline in party polarization and a shrinking of the space. Toward the end of the period of decline in polarization, a sociologist told us of *The End of Ideology* (Bell, 1960) and political scientists became focused on constituency-service models (Cain, Ferejohn, and Fiorina, 1987).

In contrast, since we started our research collaboration, we have been convinced that contemporary American politics are ideological and polarizing. Our very first publication related to Congressional voting was entitled "The Polarization of American Politics" (1984); the work therein was based on scaling of interest group ratings (see chapter 8 of this book) rather than on NOMI-NATE. It was restricted to data that covered only the period from 1958 to 1980. Nonetheless, we were able to discern the increase in polarization in the 1970s and 1980s that we documented in chapter 4 — we wrote that "support [coalition] interests . . . are more polarized than ever" (Poole and Rosenthal, 1984, p. 1073). Shortly afterward, we began the work discussed in this book. In an unpublished work (Poole and Rosenthal, 1987b), which was titled "The Unidimensional Congress," our conclusion was based on data that covered the period from 1919 to 1984. Since 1984, the polarized, unidimensional character of Congress has become even more accentuated. The most recent Congresses are highly unidimensional, very polarized, and fit the spatial model extremely well. Figure 12.1 shows the classification percentages in one and two dimensions for the House of Representatives from W-NOMINATE that was applied separately to each House over the 1887 to 2004 period (50th to 108th Houses).[1]

Since the mid 1970s, voting has become increasingly unidimensional and the percentage of the roll call choices accounted for by the first dimension has climbed steadily. In the 102nd House the first dimension accounts for about 86 percent of the choices; in the 103rd House 88 percent of the choices; and for the first session of the 104th House (1995) 90 percent of the choices. In addition, the importance of the second dimension is in free-fall. It peaked during Eisenhower's second term when it accounted for an additional 6 percent of the choices then fell to around 3 percent during the mid 1960s and then fell

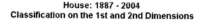

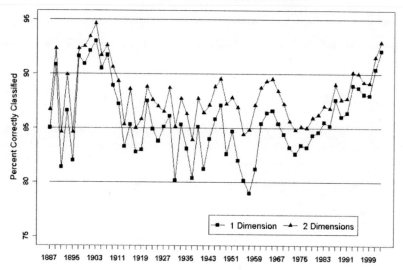

Figure 12.1. Percentage correctly classified by W-NOMINATE in one and two dimensions for the House (1885–2004). The second dimension is increasingly less important after the mid-1970s and accounts only for an additional 1 percent or less beginning in 1991.

again to around 1.5 percent in the late 1970s and early 1980s. It now accounts for only an additional 1 percent.

In chapter 5 we discussed at length the fact that the second dimension, from the late-New Deal period until the early 1970s, was related to voting on race and picked up the division of the Democratic Party into northern and southern blocs. What happened to the second dimension? The short answer is that the southern Democratic bloc has splintered into black and white sub-blocs. The black Democrats, both northern and southern, are at the far Left of the Democratic Party, and the white male southern Democrats are at the far Right of the Democratic Party. Voting on race-related issues has been absorbed by the first dimension.

Figure 12.2 shows a histogram of the W-NOMINATE one-dimensional scaling of the first session of the 104th House in 1995. The polarization of the two political parties is obvious. The bars for Democrats and Republicans, indeed, show a high degree of polarization of the two parties; only three Democrats are to the right of the leftmost Republican, and two of these Democrats have switched to the Republican Party. Nonetheless, the parties, particularly the Democrats, have important internal distinctions.

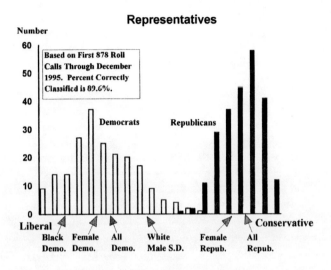

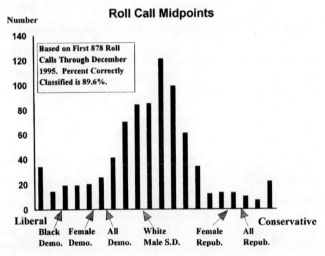

Figure 12.2. Histogram of the W-NOMINATE one-dimensional scaling of the first 878 roll calls in 1995 (the 104th House). The Democrats and Republicans are very polarized; only three Democrats are to the right of the leftmost Republican. The roll call midpoints are concentrated among the conservative Democrats.

The congressional black caucus (there were only two black Republicans in the 104th House) anchors the far left, with female Democrats close by. Reflecting a finding documented in Poole and Zeigler (1985, chapter 5) and McCarty, Poole, and Rosenthal (2006), women in both parties are to the left of their respective party means. The Republicans are far more tightly clustered, reflecting the fact that a large number of conservative freshmen — men and women — were elected in 1994 and the high degree of Republican Party unity during the voting on the Republican Contract With America. The distribution of the cutpoints is concentrated in the right wing of the Democratic Party near the mean position of the white male southern Democrats. Although the 1994 elections shifted the House Republican Party to the right, the positions of the various subgroups of the Democratic Party hardly changed from their locations in the 102nd and 103rd Houses — all that changed was the number of Democrats.

Much has been written since the historic victory of the Republican Party in the 1994 congressional elections about the changes taking place in the South. Many local and state politicians and several members of Congress have switched to the Republican Party since the elections. Almost all these switchers have been white males. The switching is not surprising in light of Figure 12.2, which shows that the Democrats are far more spread out ideologically than the Republicans. Moreover, even though there was a working majority in the House, consisting only of Republicans to the right of all the Democrats, most roll call votes in 1995 were structured to gain the support of the more conservative Democrats. Figures 12.1 and 12.2, taken together, make it more evident that the long-awaited realignment of the South is now finally happening.

Race was drawn into the first dimension in Congress because race-related issues became, increasingly, redistributional ones — welfare, affirmative action, food stamps, and so on. In response, it was only a matter of time before white southerners, who began voting Republican in presidential elections in 1964, switched to the Republican Party at the congressional level. Indeed, this change was going on before the 1994 election, which was simply the straw that broke the donkey's back.

The degree of polarization in Congress is approaching levels not seen since the 1890s. Race and redistribution have merged into one voting dimension in Congress and the polarization on both has sharply increased. This heightened level of conflict will not end, even after the hard-fought 1996 elections. This is a beginning, not an end. The collapse of the old southern Democratic Party has produced, for the first time in nearly sixty years, two sharply distinct political parties. Intense conflict between these two "new" parties will continue.

Postscript 2006

This book documents that the polarized, unidimensional world stressed in the Epilogue above, written in 1996, has continued unabated over the past decade. Polarization has in fact worsened. Political cheap talk abounds with words of moderation, famous expressions such as "kinder, gentler" and "compassionate conservative." The reality of congressional roll call voting and many other markers of the political process is, on the contrary, one of polarization.

The ethnic/racial polarization of Congress is now also as complete as it can be. Despite the efforts of George W. Bush to attract African American and Hispanic voters, all African American, Hispanic, and Asian members of the 108th Congress are Democrats, with the exception of two Cuban Americans from Florida. There is also a congressional gender gap. Although the Republicans are a majority in both houses, Democratic women outnumber Republican women by about two-to-one in both the House and the Senate.[2] Hispanics, women, and, especially, African American members are significantly more liberal than non-Hispanic, non-African American males, even after controlling for their partisan affiliation and the socioeconomic characteristics of their districts (McCarty, Poole, and Rosenthal, 2006, p. 237).

At one time moderate white males were prominent in Congress. Pete McCloskey (R-CA, entering DW-NOMINATE score, +0.032) recently came out of retirement only to be trounced by incumbent Richard Pombo (R-CA) in a Republican primary. McCloskey was quoted as describing Pombo as "Tom DeLay's handmaiden."[3] Indeed, Pombo's DW-NOMINATE score for the 108th House is +0.543, slightly more conservative than DeLay's +0.539. "[McCloskey] said he no longer recognized the Republican Party in which he served alongside such moderate and liberal luminaries as Mark O. Hatfield [entering DW-NOMINATE -0.003], Charles H. Percy [-0.038] and John V. Lindsay [-0.031]. He remembers with a nostalgic sigh being befriended by the moderate Republican rookie congressman from Houston, George [H. W.] Bush."[4] Bush (R-TX) was more conservative than Percy, Hatfield, and Lindsay but his DW-NOMINATE score of +0.244 was very similar to the scores of New York and New Jersey Republicans in the 108th House and distant from current Texas Republicans like DeLay. In response to McCloskey's candidacy, a spokesman for Pombo rejoined, "[McCloskey's not only out of the mainstream of the Republican Party, he's outside the mainstream of American society . . . He's like Austin Powers, trapped in the 1970's."[5]

The level of polarization is now the highest that it has been in 100 years. The last time that the political elites were this polarized was just before World War I at the peak of industrial capitalism, which was a period of tremendous wealth inequality. Political violence was not uncommon, as eloquently told by Anthony Lukas in *Big Trouble* about the assassination of the former governor of Idaho in 1905. We hope and pray that our country does not see a repeat of the level of conflict of 100 years ago.

Our politics suffers from the disappearance of moderate leaders of the past. Men like Dan Rostenkowski, Sam Rayburn, Chuck Percy, Mark Hatfield, and Howard Baker were able to reach across party lines and craft compromises.

With ideology substituted for cryogenics, the country, like Austin Powers, has been frozen for thirty years. It's time that it woke up.

Notes

1. We have added Congresses 105 to 108 to the figure that appeared in *Congress, 1997*. While we have retained, in the main text, our original discussion of the 102nd and 103rd Congresses, the discussion applies *a fortiori* to the more recent Congresses.
2. Source for the demographics: www.senate.gov/reference/resources/pdf/RS21379.pdf; downloaded February 15, 2006.
3. John M. Broder, "Seeing a Jungle in Congress, a Lion of the Nixon Era Runs Again," *New York Times*, February 12, 2006.
4. Ibid.
5. Ibid.

References

Aldrich, John H. (1983). "A Spatial Model with Party Activists: Implications for Electoral Dynamics." *Public Choice*, 41:63–100.

Aldrich, John H. and James S. Coleman Battista (2002). "Conditional Party Government in the States." *American Journal of Political Science*, 46:164–172.

Alesina, Alberto and Howard Rosenthal (1995). *Partisan Politics, Divided Government, and the Economy*. New York: Cambridge University Press.

Alford, John R. and David W. Brady (1993). "Personal and Partisan Advantage in U.S. Congressional Elections, 1846–1990." In Lawrence C. Dodd and Bruce Oppenheimer, editors, *Congress Reconsidered*. Washington: CQ Press.

Ansolebehere, Stephen, David W. Brady, and Morris Fiorina (1992). "The Marginals Never Vanished?" *British Journal of Political Science*, 22:21–38.

Asher, Herbert B. and Herbert F. Weisberg (1978). "Voting Change in Congress: Some Dynamic Perspectives on an Evolutionary Process." *American Journal of Political Science*, 22:391–425.

Auerswald, David and Forrest Maltzman (2003). "Policymaking through Advice and Consent: Treaty Consideration by the United States Senate." *Journal of Politics*, 65:1097–1110.

Bailey, Stephen K. (1950). *Congress Makes a Law*. New York: Columbia University Press.

Bell, Daniel (1960). *The End of Ideology*. New York: Collier.

Berglöf, Erik and Howard Rosenthal (2005). "The Political Origin of Finance: The Case of U.S. Bankruptcy Law." Manuscript, Princeton University.

Berglöf, Erik and Howard Rosenthal (2006). "Power Rejected: Congress and Bankruptcy in the Early Republic." In David W. Brady and Mathew D. McCubbins, editors, *Process, Party and Policy Making: New Advances in the Study of the History of Congress*. Stanford: Stanford University Press.

Bernhard, William and Brian R. Sala (2006). "The Remaking of an American Senate: The 17th Amendment and Ideological Responsiveness." *Journal of Politics*, 68:345–357.

Bernhardt, M. Daniel and Daniel Ingberman (1985). "Candidate Reputations and the 'Incumbency Effect.'" *Journal of Public Economics*, 27:47–67.

Bernstein, Robert A. and Stephen R. Horn (1981). "Explaining House Voting on Energy Policy: Ideology and the Conditional Effects of Party and District Economic Interests." *Western Political Quarterly*, 34: 235–245.

Bianco, William T. and Itai Sened (2005). "Uncovering Evidence of Conditional Party Government: Reassessing Majority Party Influence in Congress and State Legislatures." *American Political Science Review*, 99:361–371.

Binder, Sarah A. and Steven Smith (1998). "Political Goals and Procedural Choice in the Senate." *Journal of Politics*, 60:398–416.

Black, Duncan (1958). *The Theory of Committees and Elections*. Cambridge, England: Cambridge University Press.

Bloch, Farrell (1980). "Political Support for Minimum Wage Legislation." *Journal of Labor Research*, 1:245–53.

Bolton, Patrick and Howard Rosenthal (2002). "Political Intervention in Debt Contracts: Moratoria and Bailouts." *Journal of Political Economy*, 110:1103–34.

Brady, David W. (1979). "Critical Elections, Congressional Parties and Clusters of Policy Changes." *British Journal of Political Science*, 8:79–99.

Brady, David W. (1982). "Congressional Party Realignment and Transformations of Public Policy." *American Journal of Political Science*, 26:333–60.

Brady, David W. and Charles S. Bullock III (1980). "Is There a Conservative Coalition in the House?" *Journal of Politics*, 42:549–559.

Brady, David W. and Hahrie Han (2004). "An Extended Historical View of Congressional Party Polarization." Working Paper. Stanford University.

Brady, Henry (1989). "Multidimensional Scaling in Political Science." Working Paper. Department of Political Science, University of Chicago.

Bullock, Charles S. III (1981). "Congressional Voting and the 1982 Congressional Elections." *Journal of Politics*, 45:767–70.

Burnham, Walter D. (1970). *Critical Elections and the Mainsprings of American Politics*. New York: Norton.

Cain, Bruce, John Ferejohn, and Morris P. Fiorina (1987). *The Personal Vote: Constituency Service and Electoral Independence*. Cambridge, MA: Harvard University Press.

Callahan, Colleen M., Judith A. McDonald, and Anthony Patrick O'Brien (1994). "Who Voted for Smoot-Hawley?" *Journal of Economic History*, 54:683–690.

Canes-Wrone, Brandice and Kenneth W. Shotts (2004). "The Conditional Nature of Presidential Responsiveness to Public Opinion." *American Journal of Political Science*, 48:690–706.

Carey, John (1994). "Political Shirking and the Last Term Problem: Evidence for a Party-Administered Pension System." *Public Choice*, 81:1–22.

Carson, Jamie L. (2003). "Strategic Interaction and Candidate Competition in U.S. House Elections: Empirical Applications of Probit and Strategic Probit Models." *Political Analysis*, 11:368–80.

Carson, Jamie L. (2005). "Strategy, Selection, and Candidate Competition in U.S. House and Senate Elections." *Journal of Politics*, 67:1–28.

Carson, Jamie L., Michael H. Crespin, Charles J. Finocchiaro, and David Rohde (2003). "Linking Congressional Districts across Time: Redistricting and Party Polarization in Congress." Paper presented at the 2003 Midwest Political Science Association Meetings, Chicago: Ill.

Carson, Jamie L. and Erik J. Engstrom (2005). "Assessing the Electoral Connection: Evidence from the Early United States." *American Journal of Political Science*, 49:746–757.

Carson, Jamie L. and Jason M. Roberts (2005). "Strategic Politicians and U.S. House Elections, 1874–1914." *Journal of Politics*, 67:474–496.

Chandler, Alfred D., Jr. (1977). *The Visible Hand*. Cambridge, MA: Harvard University Press.

Clausen, Aage (1973). *How Congressmen Decide: A Policy Focus*. New York: St. Martin's Press.

Clausen, Aage and C. Van Horn (1977). "The Congressional Response to a Decade of Change: 1963–1972." *Journal of Politics*, 39:624–66.

Clinton, Joshua D., Simon Jackman, and Douglas Rivers (2004). "The Statistical Analysis of Roll Call Data." *American Political Science Review*, 98:355–370.

Clinton, Joshua D. and Adam H. Meirowitz (2001). "Agenda Constrained Legislator Ideal Points and the Spatial Voting Model." *Political Analysis*, 9:242–59.

Clinton, Joshua D. and Adam H. Meirowitz (2003). "Integrating Voting Theory and Roll-Call Analysis: A Framework." *Political Analysis*, 11:381–396.

Clinton, Joshua D., and Adam H. Meirowitz (2004). "Testing Explanations of Strategic Voting in Legislatures: A Reexamination of the Compromise of 1790." *American Journal of Political Science*, 48:675–689.

Cobb, Michael D. and Jeffrey A. Jenkins (2001). "Race and the Representation of Blacks' Interests during Reconstruction." *Political Research Quarterly*, 54:181–204.

Cohen, Linda and Roger Noll (1991). "How to Vote, Whether to Vote: Decisions about Voting and Abstaining on Congressional Roll Calls." *Political Behavior*, 13:97–127.

Coleman, John J. (1999). "Unified Government, Divided Government, and Party Responsiveness." *American Political Science Review*, 93:821–835.

Conley, Richard S. (1999). "Derailing Presidential Fast-Track Authority: The Impact of Constituency Pressures and Political Ideology on Trade Policy in Congress." *Political Research Quarterly*, 52:785–799.

Converse, Philip E. (1964). "The Nature of Belief Systems in Mass Publics." In David E. Apter, editor, *Ideology and Discontent*. New York: Free Press.

Coombs, Clyde (1964). *A Theory of Data*. New York: John Wiley & Sons.

Cooper, Joseph, and David W. Brady (1981). "Institutional Context and Leadership Style: The House from Cannon to Rayburn." *American Political Science Review*, 75:411–25.

Costner, Herbert L. (1965). "Criteria for Measures of Association." *American Sociological Review*, 30:341–53.

Cox, Gary W. and Mathew D. McCubbins (1993). *Legislative Leviathan*. Berkeley: University of California Press.

Cox, Gary W. and Mathew D. McCubbins (2005). *Setting the Agenda: Responsible Party Government in the U.S. House of Representatives*. New York: Cambridge University Press.

Cox, Gary W. and Keith T. Poole (2002). "On Measuring Partisanship in Roll Call Voting: The U.S. House of Representatives, 1877–1999." *American Journal of Political Science*, 46:477–489.

Davis, Otto A., Melvin Hinich, and Peter C. Ordeshook (1970). "An Expository Development of a Mathematical Model of the Electoral Process." *American Political Science Review*, 65:426–48.

DeBrock, Lawrence and Wallace Hendricks (1996). "Roll Call Voting in the NCAA." *Journal of Law, Economics, & Organization*, 12:497–516.

Deering, Christopher J. and Forrest Maltzman (1999). "The Politics of Executive Orders: Legislative Constraints on Presidential Power." *Political Research Quarterly*, 52:767–783.

Denzau, Arthur and Robert Mackay (1981). "Structure-Induced Equilibria and Perfect Foresight Expectations." *American Journal of Political Science*, 25:762–79.

Denzau, Arthur and Robert Mackay (1983). "Gatekeeping and Monopoly Power of Committees." *American Journal of Political Science*, 27:740–61.

Desposato, Scott W. (2001). "Legislative Politics in Authoritarian Brazil." *Legislative Studies Quarterly*, 26:287–317.

Desposato, Scott W. (2006a). "Parties for Rent? Ambition, Ideology, and Party Switching in Brazil's Chamber of Deputies." *American Journal of Political Science*, 50:62–80.

Desposato, Scott W. (2006b). "The Impact of Party-Switching on Legislative Behavior in Brazil." Manuscript, University of California, San Diego.

Donald, David Herbert (1960). *Charles Sumner and the Coming of the Civil War*. New York: Fawcett Columbine.

Downs, Anthony (1957). *An Economic Theory of Democracy*. New York: Harper.

Eckart, Carl and Gale Young (1936). "The Approximation of One Matrix by Another of Lower Rank." *Psychometrika*, 1:211–18.

Enelow, James (1981). "Saving Amendments, Killer Amendments, and an Expected Utility Theory of Sophisticated Voting." *Journal of Politics*, 43:1062–89.

Enelow, James, and Melvin Hinich (1984). *The Spatial Theory of Voting*. New York: Cambridge University Press.

Enelow, James, and David H. Koehler (1980). "The Amendment in Legislative Strategy: Sophisticated Voting in the U.S. Congress." *Journal of Politics*, 42:396–413.

Feddersen, Timothy (1992). "A Voting Model Implying Duverger's Law and Positive Turnout." *American Journal of Political Science*, 36:938–62.

Fenno, Richard F. Jr. (1973). *Congressmen in Committees*. Boston: Little, Brown and Company.

Fenno, Richard F., Jr. (1978). *Home Style: House Members in Their Districts*. Boston: Little, Brown and Company.

Ferejohn, John (1986). "Logrolling in an Institutional Context: The Case of Food Stamps." In Leroy Resielbach et al., editors, *Congress and Policy Change*. New York: Agathon Press.

Fink, Evelyn C. (2000). "Representation by Deliberation: Changes in the Rules of Deliberation in the U.S. House of Representatives, 1789–1844." *Journal of Politics*, 62:1109–1125.

Finocchiaro, Charles J. and Jenkins, Jeffrey A. (2005). "In Search of Killer Amendments in the Modern Congress." Manuscript, Northwestern University.

Fiorina, Morris P. (1974). *Representatives, Roll Calls, and Constituencies*. Lexington, MA: Heath.

Fiorina, Morris P. (1989). *Congress: Keystone of the Washington Establishment*, second edition. New Haven: Yale University Press.

Fiorina, Morris P. (1992). *Divided Government*. New York: MacMillan.

Fleck, Robert K. (1999). "Electoral Incentives, Public Policy, and the New Deal Realignment." *Southern Economic Journal*, 65:377–404.

Fleck, Robert K. and Christopher Kilby (2001). "Foreign Aid and Domestic Politics: Voting in Congress and the Allocation of USAID Contracts across Congressional Districts." *Southern Economic Journal*, 67:598–617.

Fogel, Robert W. (1989). *Without Consent or Contract: The Rise and Fall of American Slavery*. New York: W. W. Norton.

Fogel, Robert W. (1990). "Modeling Complex Dynamic Interactions: The Role of Intergenerational, Cohort, and Period Processes and of Conditional Events in the Political Realignment of the 1850s." National Bureau of Economic Research, Working Paper Series on Historical Factors in Long Run Growth. Working Paper No. 12.

Fogel, Robert W. and Stanley L. Engerman (1974). *Time on the Cross*. Boston: Little, Brown & Co.

Fort, Rodney, William Hallagan, Cyril Morong, and Tesa Stegner (1993). "The Ideological Component of Senate Voting: Different Principles or Different Principals?" *Public Choice*, 76:39–57.

Fowler, James (2005). "Dynamic Responsiveness in the U.S. Senate." *American Journal of Political Science*, 49:299–312.

Fowler, Linda L. (1982). "How Interest Groups Select Issues for Rating Voting Records of Members of the U.S. Congress." *Legislative Studies Quarterly*, 7:401–13.

Freehling, William W. (1990). *The Road to Disunion: Secessionists at Bay 1776–1854*. New York: Oxford University Press.

Friedman, Milton and Anna Schwartz (1971). *A Monetary History of the United States*. Princeton: Princeton University Press.

Gailmard, Sean and Jeffery A. Jenkins (2005). "Agency Problems and Electoral Institutions: The 17th Amendment and Representation in the Senate." Manuscript, Northwestern University.

Gailmard, Sean and Jeffery A. Jenkins (2006). "Negative Agenda Control in the Senate and House: Fingerprints of Majority Party Power." Paper presented at the Conference on Party Effects in the U.S. Senate, April 7–8, Northwestern University.

Gaines, Brian and Geoffrey Garrett (1993). "The Calculus of Dissent: Party Discipline in the British Labour Government 1974–79." *Political Behavior*, 15:113–135.

Gerber, Elisabeth R. and Jeffrey B. Lewis (2004). "Beyond the Median: Voter Preferences, District Heterogeneity, and Political Representation." *Journal of Political Economy*, 112:1364–1383.

Gienapp, William E. (1987). *The Origins of the Republican Party 1852–1856*. New York: Oxford University Press.

Gilligan, Thomas W. and Keith Krehbiel (1990). "Organization of Informative Committees by a Rational Legislature." *American Journal of Political Science*, 34:531–64.

Gilligan, Thomas W., William Marshall, and Barry R. Weingast (1989). "Regulation and the Theory of Legislative Choice: The Interstate Commerce Act of 1887." *Journal of Law and Economics*, 32:35–61.

Ginsberg, Benjamin (1972). "Critical Elections and the Substance of Party Conflict: 1844–1968." *Midwest Journal of Political Science*, 16:603–25.

Ginsberg, Benjamin (1976). "Elections and Public Policy." *American Political Science Review*, 70:41–49.

Groseclose, Tim (1994a). "A Model and Test of Blame-Game Politics." Mimeo, Carnegie-Mellon University.

Groseclose, Tim (1994b). "Testing Committee Composition Hypotheses for the U.S. Congress." *Journal of Politics*, 56:440–58.

Groseclose, Tim and James M. Snyder, Jr. (1996) "Buying Super Majorities." *American Political Science Review*, 90:303–315.

Hager, Gregory L. and Jeffrey C. Talbert (2000). "Look for the Party Label: Party Influences on Voting in the U.S. House." *Legislative Studies Quarterly*, 25:75–99.

Hall, Richard L. and Bernard Grofman (1990). "The Committee Assignment Process and the Conditional Nature of Committee Bias." *American Political Science Review*, 84:1149–66.

Heckman, James N. and James M. Snyder, Jr. (1996). "Linear Probability Models of the Demand for Attributes with an Empirical Application to Estimating the Preferences of Legislators." *RAND Journal of Economics*, 28:S142–S189.

Hetherington, Marc J. (2001). "Resurgent Mass Partisanship: The Role of Elite Polarization." *American Political Science Review*, 95:619–631.

Hibbing, John R. (1993). "Careerism in Congress: For Better or For Worse." In Lawrence C. Dodd and Bruce I. Oppenheimer, editors, *Congress Reconsidered*. Washington: CQ Press.

Hildebrand, David K., James D. Laing, and Howard Rosenthal (1977). *Prediction Analysis of Cross Classifications*. New York: Wiley.

Hinich, Melvin and Peter C. Ordeshook (1969). "Abstentions and Equilibrium in the Electoral Process." *Public Choice*, 7:81–106.

Hinich, Melvin and Walker Pollard (1981). "A New Approach to the Spatial Theory of Electoral Competition." *American Journal of Political Science*, 25:323–41.

Hix, Simon (1999). "Dimensions and Alignments in European Union Politics: Cognitive Constraints and Partisan Responses." *European Journal of Political Research*, 35:69–106.

Hix, Simon (2001). "Legislative Behaviour and Party Competition in European Parliament: An Application of Nominate to the EU." *Journal of Common Market Studies*, 39:663–688.

Hix, Simon (2002). "Parliamentary Behaviour with Two Principals: Preferences, Parties, and Voting in the European Parliament." *American Journal of Political Science*, 46:688–698.

Hix, Simon (2004). "Electoral Institutions and Legislative Behavior: Explaining Voting Defection in the European Parliament." *World Politics*, 56:194–223.

Hix, Simon, Amy Kreppel, and Abdul Noury (2003). "The Party System in the European Parliament: Collusive or Competitive?" *Journal of Common Market Studies*, 41:309–331.

Hix, Simon, Abdul Noury, and Gerard Roland (2005). "Power to the Parties: Cohesion and Competition in the European Parliament, 1979–2001." *British Journal of Political Science*, 35:209–234.

Hix, Simon, Abdul Noury, and Gerard Roland (2006). "Dimensions of Politics in the European Parliament." *American Journal of Political Science*, 50:494–511.

Hofstadter, Richard (1969). *The Idea of a Party System: The Rise of Legitimate Opposition in the United States, 1780–1840.* Berkeley, University of California Press.

Hofstadter, Richard, William Miller, and Daniel Aaron (1959). *The American Republic*, two volumes. Englewood Cliffs, New Jersey: Prentice Hall.

Howell, William G. and David E. Lewis (2002). "Agencies by Presidential Design." *Journal of Politics*, 64:1095–1114.

Ichniowski, Casey, Kathryn Shaw, and Giovanna Prennushi (1997). "The Effects of Human Resource Management Practices on Productivity: A Study of Steel Finishing Lines." *American Economic Review*, 87:291–313.

Irwin, Douglas A. and Randall S. Kroszner (1999). "Interests, Institutions, and Ideology in Securing Policy Change: The Republican Conversion to Trade Liberalization after Smoot Hawley." *Journal of Law and Economics*, 42:643–673.

Jackson, John E. and David C. King (1989). "Public Goods, Private Interests, and Representation." *American Political Science Review*, 83:1143–1164.

Jackson, John and John W. Kingdon (1992). "Ideology, Interest Group Scores and Legislative Votes." *American Journal of Political Science*, 36:805–23.

Jenkins, Jeffery A. (1998). "Property Rights and the Emergence of Standing Committee Dominance in the Nineteenth-Century House." *Legislative Studies Quarterly*, 23:493–519.

Jenkins, Jeffery A. (1999). "Examining the Bonding Effects of Party: A Comparative Analysis of Roll-Call Voting in the U.S. and Confederate Houses." *American Journal of Political Science*, 43:1144–65.

Jenkins, Jeffery A. (2000). "Examining the Robustness of Ideological Voting: Evidence from the Confederate House of Representatives." *American Journal of Political Science*, 44:811–22.

Jenkins, Jeffery A. (2004). "Partisanship and Contested Election Cases in the House of Representatives, 1789–2002." *Studies in American Political Development*, 18:112–135.

Jenkins, Jeffery A. (2005). "Partisanship and Contested Election Cases in the Senate." 1789–2002." *Studies in American Political Development*, 19:53–74.

Jenkins, Jeffery A., Michael H. Crespin, and Jamie L. Carson (2005). "Parties as Procedural Coalitions in Congress: An Examination of Differing Career Tracks." *Legislative Studies Quarterly*, 30:365–389.

Jenkins, Jeffery A. and Irwin L. Morris (2006). "Running to Lose? John C. Breckinridge and the Presidential Election of 1860." *Electoral Studies*, 25:306–28.

Jenkins, Jeffery A. and Michael C. Munger (2003). "Investigating the Incidence of Killer Amendments in Congress." *Journal of Politics*, 65:498–517.

Jenkins, Jeffery A. and Timothy P. Nokken (2000). "The Institutional Origins of the Republican Party: Spatial Voting and the House Speakership Election of 1855–56." *Legislative Studies Quarterly*, 25:101–30.

Jenkins, Jeffery A. and Brian R. Sala (1998). "The Spatial Theory of Voting and the Presidential Election of 1824." *American Journal of Political Science*, 42:1157–79.

Jenkins, Jeffery A., Eric Schickler, and Jamie L. Carson (2004). "Constituency Cleavages and Congressional Parties: Measuring Homogeneity and Polarization, 1857–1913." *Social Science History*, 28:537–573.

Jenkins, Jeffery A. and Charles Stewart, III (1998). "Committee Assignments as Side Payments: The Interplay of Leadership and Committee Development in the Era of Good Feelings." Manuscript, Michigan State University.

Jenkins, Jeffery A. and Charles Stewart, III (2003). "Out in the Open: The Emergence of Viva Voce Voting in House Speakership Elections." *Legislative Studies Quarterly*, 28:481–508.

Jenkins, Jeffery A. and Charles Stewart, III (2004). "More than Just a Mouthpiece: The House Clerk as Party Operative, 1789–1870." Manuscript, Northwestern University.

Jenkins, Jeffery A. and Charles Stewart, III (2005). "The Gag Rule, Congressional Politics, and the Growth of Anti-Slavery Popular Politics." Manuscript, Northwestern University.

Jenkins, Jeffery A. and Marc Weidenmeir (1999). "Ideology, Economic Interests, and Congressional Roll-Call Voting: Partisan Instability and Bank of the United States Legislation, 1811–1816." *Public Choice*, 100:225–43.

Jeydel, Alana and Andrew J. Taylor (2003). "Are Women Legislators Less Effective? Evidence from the U.S. House in the 103rd–105th Congress." *Political Research Quarterly*, 56:19–27.

Johnson, Susan W. and Donald R. Songer (2002). "The Influence of Presidential versus Home State Senatorial Preferences on the Policy Output of Judges on the United States District Courts." *Law and Society Review*, 36:657–676.

Johnson, Timothy R. and Jason M. Roberts (2004). "Presidential Capital and the Supreme Court Confirmation Process." *Journal of Politics*, 66:663–683.

Jun, Hae-Won and Simon Hix (2006). "A Spatial Analysis of Voting in the Korean National Assembly." Manuscript, Government Department, London School of Economics and Political Science.

Kalt, Joseph P. (1981). *The Economics and Politics of Oil Price Regulation*. Cambridge: M.I.T. Press.

Kalt, Joseph P. and Mark A. Zupan (1984). "Capture and Ideology in the Economic Theory of Politics." *American Economic Review*, 74:279–300.

Kau, James B., Donald Keenan, and Paul H. Rubin (1982). "A General Equilibrium Model of Congressional Voting." *Quarterly Journal of Economics*, 93:271–93.

Kau, James B. and Paul H. Rubin (1979). "Self-Interest, Ideology, and Logrolling in Congressional Voting." *Journal of Law and Economics*, 21:365–84.

Kennedy, John F. (1955). *Profiles in Courage*. New York: Harper & Row.

Kiewiet, D. Roderick and Mathew D. McCubbins (1991). *The Logic of Delegation*. Chicago: University of Chicago Press.

Kiewiet, D. Roderick and Langche Zeng (1993). "An Analysis of Congressional Career Decisions, 1947–1986." *American Political Science Review*, 87:928–941.

Kirkpatrick, Jeanne (1976). *The New Presidential Elite*. New York: Russell Sage Foundation.

Koford, Kenneth (1989). "Dimensions in Congressional Voting." *American Political Science Review*, 83:949–62.

Koford, Kenneth (1991). "On Dimensionalizing Roll Call Votes in the U.S. Congress (controversy with Keith T. Poole and Howard Rosenthal)." *American Political Science Review*, 85:955–75.

Koford, Kenneth (1994). "What Can We Learn about Congressional Politics from Dimensional Studies of Roll Call Voting?" *Economics and Politics*, 6:173–86.

Kousser, Thad, Jeffrey B. Lewis, and Seth Masket (2006). "Does the Electoral Connection Link the Branches? Legislative Responsiveness to Executive Elections." Manuscript, University of California, San Diego.

Krehbiel, Keith (1990). "Are Congressional Committees Composed of Preference Outliers?" *American Political Science Review*, 84:149–63.

Krehbiel, Keith (1992). *Information and Legislative Organization*. Ann Arbor: The University of Michigan Press.

Krehbiel, Keith (1993). "Constituency Characteristics and Legislative Preferences." *Public Choice*, 76:21–38.

Krehbiel, Keith (1998). *Pivotal Politics: A Theory of U.S. Lawmaking*. Chicago: University of Chicago Press.

Krehbiel, Keith and Douglas Rivers (1988). "The Analysis of Committee Power: An Application to Senate Voting on the Minimum Wage." *American Journal of Political Science*, 32:1151–74.

Krehbiel, Keith and Douglas Rivers (1990). "Sophisticated Voting in Congress: A Reconsideration." *Journal of Politics*, 52:548–78.

Kruskal, Joseph B. (1964a). "Multidimensional Scaling by Optimizing Goodness of Fit to a Nonmetric Hypothesis." *Psychometrika*, 29:1–28.

Kruskal, Joseph B. (1964b). "Nonmetric Multidimensional Scaling: A Numerical Method." *Psychometrika*, 29:115–30.

Kruskal, Joseph B. and Myron Wish (1978). *Multidimensional Scaling*. Beverly Hills, CA: Sage Publications.

Krutz, Glen S. (2005). "Issues and Institutions: 'Winnowing' in the U.S. Congress." *American Journal of Political Science*, 49:313–326.

Ladewig, Jeffrey W. (2005). "Conditional Party Government and the Homogeneity of Constituent Interests." *Journal of Politics*, 67:1006–1029.

Ladha, Krishna K. (1991). "A Spatial Model of Legislative Voting with Perceptual Error." *Public Choice*, 68:151–74.

Ladha, Krishna K. (1994). "Coalitions in Congressional Voting." *Public Choice*, 78:43–64.

Lawrence, Eric D., Forrest Maltzman, and Paul J. Wahlbeck (2001). "The Politics of Speaker Cannon's Committee Assignments." *American Journal of Political Science*, 45:551–562.

Ledyard, John O. (1981). "The Paradox of Voting and Candidate Competition: A General Equilibrium Analysis." In G. Horwich and J. Quirk, editors, *Essays in Contemporary Fields of Economics*. West Lafayette, Ind.: Purdue University Press.

Ledyard, John O. (1984). "The Pure Theory of Large Two-Candidate Elections." *Public Choice*, 44:7–41.

Levitt, Steven (1996). "How do Senators Vote? Disentangling the Role of Party Affiliations, Voter Preferences, and Senator Ideology." *American Economic Review*, 86:425–441.

Lewis, David E. (2002). "The Politics of Agency Termination: Confronting the Myth of Agency Immortality." *Journal of Politics*, 46:89–107.

Lewis, Jeffrey B. and Keith T. Poole (2004). "Measuring Bias and Uncertainty in Ideal Point Estimates via the Parametric Bootstrap." *Political Analysis*, 12:105–127.

Londregan, John and James M. Snyder, Jr. (1994). "Comparing Committee and Floor Preferences." *Legislative Studies Quarterly*, 19:233–66.

Loomis, Michael (1995). "Constituent Influences Outside the Spatial Structure of Legislative Voting." Unpublished doctoral dissertation, Carnegie Mellon University, Pittsburgh, PA.

Lott, John R., Jr. and Stephen G. Bronars (1993). "Time Series Evidence on Shirking in the U.S. House of Representatives." *Public Choice*, 76:125–50.

Lublin, David. (1997). *The Paradox of Representation: Racial Gerrymandering and Minority Interests in Congress*. Princeton, NJ: Princeton University Press.

Macdonald, Stuart E. and George Rabinowitz (1987). "The Dynamics of Structural Realignment." *American Political Science Review*, 81:775–96.

Mackie, Gerry (2003). *Democracy Defended*. Cambridge, UK: Cambridge University Press.

MacRae, Duncan, Jr. (1958). *Dimensions of Congressional Voting*. Berkeley: University of California Press.

MacRae, Duncan, Jr. (1970). *Issues and Parties in Legislative Voting*. New York: Harper & Row.

Maltzman, Forrest (1994). "Meeting Competing Demands: Committee Performance in the Post-Reform House." *American Journal of Political Science*, 39:653–82.

Maltzman, Forrest and Steven S. Smith (1994). "Principals, Goals, Dimensionality, and Congressional Committees." *Legislative Studies Quarterly*, 19:457–76

Martis, Kenneth (1989). *The Historical Atlas of Political Parties in the United States Congress: 1789–1989*. New York: Macmillan.

Massie, Tajuana D., Thomas G. Hansford, and Donald R. Songer (2004). "The Timing of Presidential Nominations to the Lower Federal Courts." *Political Research Quarterly*, 57:145–154.

Mayhew, David R. (1974). *Congress: The Electoral Connection*. New Haven: Yale University Press.

McCarty, Nolan and Keith T. Poole (1995). "An Empirical Spatial Model of Congressional Campaigns." *Political Analysis*, 7:1–30.

McCarty, Nolan, Keith T. Poole, and Howard Rosenthal (2001). "The Hunt for Party Discipline in Congress." *American Political Science Review*, 95:673–687.

McCarty, Nolan, Keith T. Poole, and Howard Rosenthal (2002). "Congress and the Territorial Expansion of the United States." In David Brady and Matthew McCubbins, editors, *Party, Process, and Political Change in Congress: New Perspectives on the History of Congress*. Palo Alto, CA: Stanford University Press.

McCarty, Nolan, Keith T. Poole, and Howard Rosenthal (2006). *Polarized America: The Dance of Ideology and Unequal Riches*. Cambridge, MA: MIT Press.

McCarty, Nolan and Rose Razaghian (1999). "Advice and Consent: Senate Responses to Executive Branch Nominations 1885–1996." *American Journal of Political Science*, 43:1122–1143.

McClosky, Herbert, P. J. Hoffman, and Rosemary O'Hara. (1960). "Issue Conflict and Consensus among Party Leaders and Followers." *American Political Science Review*, 54:406–427.

Mendenhall, William, Richard Scheaffer, and Dennis Wackersley (1986). *Mathematical Statistics with Applications*. Boston: Ducksbury.

Morgenstern, Scott (2004). *Patterns of Legislative Politics. Roll-Call Voting in Latin America and the United States*. New York: Cambridge University Press.

Morrison, Richard J. (1972). "A Statistical Model for Legislative Roll Call Analysis." *Journal of Mathematical Sociology*, 2:235–47.

Moscardelli, Vincent G., Moshe Haspel, and Richard S. Wike (1998). "Party Building through Campaign Finance Reform: Conditional Party Government in the 104th Congress." *Journal of Politics*, 60:691–704.

Myagkov, Mikhail and D. Roderick Kiewiet (1996). "Czar Rule in the Russian Congress of People's Deputies?" *Legislative Studies Quarterly*, 21:235–47.

Nelson, Garrison (1994). *Committees in the U.S. Congress*. Washington, D.C.: CQ Press.

Nevins, Allan (1947). *Ordeal of the Union: A House Dividing 1852–1857*. New York: Charles Scribner's Sons.

Niskanen, William A. (1971). *Bureaucracy and Representative Government*. Chicago: Aldine-Atherton.

Nokken, Timothy P. (2000). "Dynamics of Congressional Loyalty: Party Defection and Roll-Call Behavior, 1947–97." *Legislative Studies Quarterly*, 25:417–444.

Nokken, Timothy P. and Keith T. Poole (2004). "Congressional Party Defection in American History." *Legislative Studies Quarterly*, 29:545–568.

Noury, Abdul (2002) "Ideology, Nationality and Euro-Parliamentarians." *European Union Politics*, 3:33–58.

Noury, Abdul and Elena Mielcova (2005). "Electoral Performance and Voting Behavior in the Czech Republic." Institute of Governmental Studies, University of California, Berkeley, Paper WP, 2005–14.

Nunez, Stephen and Howard Rosenthal (2004). "Bankruptcy 'Reform' in Congress: Creditors, Committees, Ideology, and Floor Voting in the Legislative Process." *Journal of Law, Economics, and Organization*, 20:527–557.

Ordeshook, Peter C. (1976). "The Spatial Theory of Elections: A Review and a Critique." In Ian Budge, Ivor Crewe, and Dennis Farlie, editors, *Party Identification and Beyond*. New York: Wiley.

Ordeshook, Peter C. (1986). *Game Theory and Political Theory*. New York: Cambridge University Press.

Palfrey, Thomas R. and Howard Rosenthal (1983). "A Strategic Calculus of Voting." *Public Choice*, 41:7–53.

Palfrey, Thomas R. and Howard Rosenthal (1985). "Voter Participation and Strategic Uncertainty." *American Political Science Review*, 79:62–78.

Peltzman, Sam (1984). "Constituent Interest and Congressional Voting." *Journal of Law and Economics*, 27:181–210.

Peltzman, Sam (1985). "An Economic Interpretation of the History of Congressional Voting in the Twentieth Century." *American Economic Review*, 75:656–75.

Pindyck, R. and D. Rubinfeld (1981). *Econometric Models and Economic Forecasts.* New York: McGraw-Hill.

Polsby, Nelson (1968). "Institutionalization of the U.S. House of Representatives." *American Political Science Review*, 62:144–168.

Poole, Keith T. (1981). "Dimensions of Interest Group Evaluation of the U.S. Senate, 1969–1978." *American Journal of Political Science*, 25:49–67.

Poole, Keith T. (1984). "Least Squares Metric, Unidimensional Unfolding." *Psychometrika*, 49:311–23.

Poole, Keith T. (1990). "Least Squares Metric, Unidimensional Scaling of Multivariate Linear Models." *Psychometrika*, 55:123–49.

Poole, Keith T. (1998). "Recovering a Basic Space from a Set of Issue Scales." *American Journal of Political Science*, 42: 954–993.

Poole, Keith T. (2000). "Non-Parametric Unfolding of Binary Choice Data." *Political Analysis*, 8:211–237.

Poole, Keith T. (2005). *Spatial Models of Parliamentary Voting*. New York: Cambridge University Press.

Poole, Keith T. and R. Steven Daniels (1985). "Ideology, Party, and Voting in the U.S. Congress, 1959–80." *American Political Science Review*, 79:373–99.

Poole, Keith T. and Thomas Romer (1983). "Economic versus Ideological Factors in Congressional Voting." GSIA Working Paper. Carnegie-Mellon University.

Poole, Keith T. and Thomas Romer (1985). "Patterns of Political Action Committee Campaign Contributions to the 1980 Campaigns for the U.S. House of Representatives." *Public Choice*, 47:63–111.

Poole, Keith T. and Thomas Romer (1993). "Ideology, Shirking and Representation." *Public Choice*, 77:185–96.

Poole, Keith T., Thomas Romer, and Howard Rosenthal (1987). "The Revealed Preferences of Political Action Committees." *American Economic Review*, 77:298–302.

Poole, Keith T. and Howard Rosenthal (1983). "A Spatial Model for Legislative Roll Call Analysis." GSIA Working Paper No. 5–83–84.

Poole, Keith T. and Howard Rosenthal (1984). "The Polarization of American Politics." *Journal of Politics*, 46:1061–79.

Poole, Keith T. and Howard Rosenthal (1985a). "The Political Economy of Roll Call Voting in the 'Multi-Party' Congress of the United States." *European Journal of Political Economy*, 1:45–58.

Poole, Keith T. and Howard Rosenthal (1985b). "A Spatial Model for Legislative Roll Call Analysis." *American Journal of Political Science*, 29:357–84.

Poole, Keith T. and Howard Rosenthal (1987a). "Analysis of Congressional Coalition Patterns: A Unidimensional Spatial Model." *Legislative Studies Quarterly*, 12:55–75.

Poole, Keith T. and Howard Rosenthal (1987b). "The Unidimensional Congress, 1919–84." Working Paper #44–84–85, Graduate School of Industrial Administration, Carnegie Mellon University, Pittsburgh, PA. (Original working paper issued in 1985.)

Poole, Keith T. and Howard Rosenthal (1991a). "Patterns of Congressional Voting." *American Journal of Political Science*, 35:228–78.

Poole, Keith T. and Howard Rosenthal (1991b). "The Spatial Mapping of Minimum Wage Legislation." In Alberto Alesina and Geoffrey Carliner, editors, *Politics and Economics in the 1980s*. Chicago: University of Chicago Press.

Poole, Keith T. and Howard Rosenthal (1991c). "On Dimensionalizing Roll Call Votes in the U.S. Congress (controversy with Kenneth Koford)." *American Political Science Review*, 85:955–75.

Poole, Keith T. and Howard Rosenthal (1993a). "Spatial Realignment and the Mapping of Issues in American History: The Evidence from Roll Call Voting." In William H. Riker, editor, *Agenda Formation*. Ann Arbor: University of Michigan Press.

Poole, Keith T. and Howard Rosenthal (1993b). "The Enduring Nineteenth Century Battle for Economic Regulation: The Interstate Commerce Act Revisited." *Journal of Law and Economics*, 36:837–60.

Poole, Keith T. and Howard Rosenthal (1994a). "Congress and Railroad Regulation: 1874–1887." In Claudia Goldin and Gary Libecapp, editors, *The Regulated Economy*. Chicago: University of Chicago Press.

Poole, Keith T. and Howard Rosenthal (1994b). "Dimensional Simplification and Economic Theories of Legislative Behavior." *Economics and Politics*, 6:163–172.

Poole, Keith T. and Howard Rosenthal (1997). *Congress: A Political-Economic History of Roll Call Voting*. New York: Oxford University Press.

Poole, Keith T. and Howard Rosenthal (1998). "The Dynamics of Interest Group Evaluations of Congress." *Public Choice*, 97:323–61.

Poole, Keith T. and Howard Rosenthal. (2001). "D-NOMINATE After 10 Years: A Comparative Update to *Congress: A Political-Economic History of Roll Call Voting*." *Legislative Studies Quarterly*, 26:5–26.

Poole, Keith T. and Stephen Spear (1992). "Statistical Properties of Metric Multidimensional Scaling." Manuscript, Graduate School of Industrial Administration, Carnegie-Mellon University.

Poole, Keith T. and L. Harmon Zeigler (1985). *Women, Public Opinion and Politics*. New York: Longman.

Potoski, Matthew and Jeffrey Talbert (2000). "The Dimensional Structure of Policy Outputs: Distributive Policy and Roll Call Voting." *Political Research Quarterly*, 53:695–710.

Price, Kevin S. (2002). "The Partisan Legacies of Preemptive Leadership: Assessing the Eisenhower Cohorts in the U.S. House." *Political Research Quarterly*, 55:609–632.

Redman, Eric (1973). *The Dance of Legislation*. New York, NY: Simon and Schuster.

Richardson, L. E., Jr. and Michael Munger (1990). "Shirking, Representation, and Congressional Behavior: Voting on the 1983 Amendments to the Social Security Act." *Public Choice*, 67:11–33.

Riker, William H. (1962). *The Theory of Political Coalitions*. New Haven: Yale University Press.

Riker, William H. (1980). "Implications from the Disequilibrium of Majority Rule for the Study of Institutions." *American Political Science Review*, 74:432–46.

Riker, William H. (1982). *Liberalism Against Populism*. San Francisco: W. H. Freeman and Company.

Riker, William and Peter C. Ordeshook (1968). "A Theory of the Calculus of Voting." *American Political Science Review*, 52:25–42.

Rivers, Douglas (1987). "Inconsistency of Least Squares Unfolding." Paper presented at the Political Methodology Meetings, Durham, N.C.

Roberts, Jason M. and Steven S. Smith (2003). "Procedural Contexts, Party Strategy, and Conditional Party Voting in the U.S. House of Representatives, 1971–2000." *American Journal of Political Science*, 47:305–317.

Romano, Roberta (1997). "The Political Dynamics of Derivative Securities Regulation." *Yale Journal on Regulation*, 14:279–406.

Romer, Thomas and Howard Rosenthal (1978). "Political Resource Allocation, Controlled Agendas, and the Status Quo." *Public Choice*, 33:27–43.

Romer, Thomas and Howard Rosenthal (1979). "Bureaucrats vs. Voters: On the Political Economy of Resource Allocation by Direct Democracy." *Quarterly Journal of Economics*, 93:563–87.

Romer, Thomas and Howard Rosenthal (1985). "Modern Political Economy and the Study of Regulation." In Elizabeth E. Bailey, editor, *Public Regulation: New Perspectives on Institutions and Politics*. Cambridge, MA: M.I.T. Press.

Romer, Thomas and Barry R. Weingast (1991). "Political Foundations of the Thrift Debacle." In Alberto Alesina and Geoffrey Carliner, editors, *Politics and Economics in the 1980s*. Chicago: University of Chicago Press.

Rosenthal, Howard (1992). "The Unidimensional Congress is not the Result of Selective Gatekeeping." *American Journal of Political Science*, 36:31–35.

Rosenthal, Howard and Subrata Sen (1973). "Electoral Participation in the Fifth French Republic." *American Political Science Review*, 67:29–54.

Rosenthal, Howard and Erik Voeten (2004). "Analyzing Roll Calls with Perfect Spatial Voting: France 1946–1958." *American Journal of Political Science*, 48:620–32.

Sala, Brian R. and James F. Spriggs, II (2004). "Designing Tests of the Supreme Court and the Separation of Powers." *Political Research Quarterly*, 57:197–208.

Schattschneider, E. E. (1942). *Party Government*. New York: Holt, Rinehart and Winston.

Schickler, Eric (2000). "Institutional Change in the House of Representatives, 1867–1998: A Test of Partisan and Ideological Power Balance Models." *American Political Science Review*, 94:269–288.

Schonhardt-Bailey, Cheryl (2003). "Ideology, Party and Interests in the British Parliament of 1841–1847." *British Journal of Political Science*, 33:581–605.

Schonhardt-Bailey, Cheryl (2006). *From the Corn Laws to Free Trade: Interests, Ideas, and Institutions in Historical Perspective*. Cambridge: MIT Press.

Shepard, R. N. (1962). "The Analysis of Proximities: Multidimensional Scaling with an Unknown Distance Function." *Psychometrika*, 27:125–139, 219–246.

Shepsle, Kenneth A. (1978). *The Giant Jigsaw Puzzle*. Chicago: University of Chicago Press.

Shepsle, Kenneth A. and Barry R. Weingast (1994). "Positive Theories of Congressional Institutions." *Legislative Studies Quarterly*, 19:149–80.

Shipan, Charles R. (2004). "Regulatory Regimes, Agency Actions, and the Conditional Nature of Congressional Influence." *American Political Science Review*, 98:467.

Shipan, Charles R. and Megan L. Shannon (2003). "Delaying Justice(s): A Duration Analysis of Supreme Court Confirmations." *American Journal of Political Science*, 47:654–668.

Shotts, Kenneth W. (2003). "Does Racial Redistricting Cause Conservative Policy Outcomes? Policy Preferences of Southern Representatives in the 1980's and 1990's." *Journal of Politics*, 65:216–226.

Sicotte, Richard (1999). "Economic Crisis and Political Response: The Political Economy of the Shipping Act of 1916." *Journal of Economic History*, 59:861–884.

Silberman, Jonathon and Gary Durden (1976). "Determining Legislative Preferences on the Minimum Wage: An Econometric Approach." *Journal of Political Economy*, 84:317–29.

Silbey, Joel (1967). *The Shrine of Party*. Pittsburgh: University of Pittsburgh Press.

Sinclair, Barbara (1977). "Party Realignment and the Transformation of the Political Agenda: The House of Representatives, 1925–1938." *American Political Science Review*, 71:940–53.

Sinclair, Barbara (1981). "Agenda and Alignment Change: The House of Representatives, 1925–1978." In Lawrence C. Dodd and Bruce I. Oppenheimer, editors, *Congress Reconsidered*. Washington, D.C.: CQ Press.

Smith, Steven S. (1981). "The Consistency and Ideological Structure of U.S. Senate Voting Alignments, 1957–1976." *American Journal of Political Science*, 25:780–95.

Snyder, James M., Jr. (1990). "Campaign Contributions as Investments: The U.S. House of Representatives 1980–1986." *Journal of Political Economy*, 98:1195–1227.

Snyder, James M., Jr. (1992a). "Artificial Extremism in Interest Group Ratings." *Legislative Studies Quarterly*, 17:319–45.

Snyder, James M., Jr. (1992b). "Committee Power, Structure-Induced Equilibria, and Roll Call Votes." *American Journal of Political Science*, 36:1–30.

Snyder, James M., Jr. and Tim Groseclose (2000). "Estimating Party Influence in Congressional Roll-Call Voting." *American Journal of Political Science*, 44:193–211.

Snyder, James M., Jr. and Tim Groseclose (2001). "Estimating Party Influence on Roll Call Voting: Regression Coefficients versus Classification Success." *American Political Science Review*, 95:689–698.

Songer, Donald R. and Martha Humpries Ginn (2002). "Assessing the Impact of Presidential and Home State Influences on Judicial Decision-making in the United States Courts of Appeals." *American Political Science Review*, 55:299–328.

Stewart, Charles III and Barry R. Weingast (1992). "Stacking the Senate, Changing the Nation: Republican Rotten Boroughs, Statehood Politics, and American Political Development." *Studies in American Political Development*, 6:223–71.

Stone, Walter J. (1980). "The Dynamics of Constituency: Electoral Control of the House." *American Politics Quarterly*, 8:399–424.

Sundquist, James L. (1983). *Dynamics of the Party System*. Washington, D.C.: The Brookings Institution.

Swers, Michele L. (1998). "Are Women More Likely to Vote for Women's Issue Bills than Their Male Colleagues?" *Legislative Studies Quarterly*, 23:435–448.

Taylor, Andrew J. (2003). "Conditional Party Government and Campaign Contributions: Insights from the Tobacco and Alcoholic Beverage Industries." *American Journal of Political Science,* 47:293–304.

Torgerson, W. S. (1958). *Theory and Methods of Scaling.* New York: Wiley.

Tversky, A. and D. Kahneman (1974). "Judgment under Uncertainty: Heuristics and Biases." *Science,* 125:1124–1131.

Unger, Irwin (1964). *The Greenback Era.* Princeton, N.J.: Princeton University Press.

Van Doren, Peter (1990). "Can We Learn the Causes of Congressional Decisions from Roll Call Data?" *Legislative Studies Quarterly,* 15:311–40.

Voeten, Erik. (2000). "Clashes in the Assembly." *International Organization,* 54:185–215.

Voeten, Erik. (2001). "Outside Options and the Logic of Security Council Action." *American Political Science Review,* 95:845–858.

Wawro, Gregory J. and Eric Schickler (2004). "Where's the Pivot? Obstruction and Lawmaking in the Pre-cloture Senate." *American Journal of Political Science,* 48:758–774.

Weingast, Barry R. (1991). "Political Economy of Slavery: Credible Commitments and the Preservation of the Union, 1800–1860." Paper presented at the Seventh International Symposium in Economic Theory and Econometrics, St. Louis, Mo.

Weingast, Barry R. and Mark Moran (1983). "Bureaucratic Discretion or Congressional Control? Regulatory Policymaking by the Federal Trade Commission." *Journal of Political Economy,* 91:775–800.

Weisberg, Herbert F. (1968). *Dimensional Analysis of Legislative Roll Calls.* Ph.D. dissertation, University of Michigan.

Weiss, Roger (1970). "The Issue of Paper Money in the American Colonies, 1720–1774." *Journal of Economic History,* 30:770–84.

White, Halbert (1980). "A Heteroskedasticity-consistent Covariance Matrix Estimator and a Direct Test for Heteroskedasticity." *Econometrica,* 48:817–38.

Wilson, Woodrow (1885/1969). *Congressional Government.* New York: Meridian Books.

Wilson, James Q. (1980). *The Politics of Regulation.* New York: Basic Books.

Wiseman, Alan E. (2004). "Tests of Vote-Buyer Theories of Coalition Formation in Legislatures." *Political Research Quarterly,* 57:441–450.

Wright, B. D., and G. A. Douglas (1976). "Better Procedures for Sample-Free Item Analysis." Research Memorandum no. 20, Statistical Laboratory, Department of Education, University of Chicago.

Wright, Gerald C. and Brian F. Schaffner (2002). "The Influence of Party: Evidence from the State Legislatures." *American Political Science Review,* 96:367–379.

Young, Roland (1956). *Congressional Politics in the Second World War.* New York: Columbia University Press.

Index